Nothing is straightforward about Russian strategic culture, and the book examines rigorously its rich contradictions and distortions. Dr. Herd's conceptualizations are challengingly innovative, generalizations are convincing, and the attention to detail is impeccable – a rewarding read indeed.

—**Pavel Baev**, *Peace Research Institute Oslo (PRIO) Norway*

Is Putin's Russia something new and distinctive, or the inevitable product of Russia's history? As this densely-argued and conceptually-rich book argues, to understand tomorrow's decisions, we need to place them not just within the context of the operational code of today's leaders, but a strategic culture that has been forming for centuries.

—**Mark Galeotti**, *University College London, UK*

This fascinating book offers a timely and comprehensive scholarly investigation of the historical and cultural roots of contemporary Russian foreign policy. Prof. Herd provides the most detailed and informed analysis to date of the many strands and themes in Russian strategic culture, and demonstrates how these long-standing beliefs and norms continue to shape Russian foreign policy today.

—**David Lewis**, *University of Exeter, UK*

Understanding Russian Strategic Behavior: Imperial Strategic Culture and Putin's Operational Code is a masterstroke from Herd – it manages to "solve" Churchill's "Russia riddle." Blending various aspects of Putin's Russia into a wide ranging and clever text, Herd meticulously plots the drivers of Russian strategy and behavior under Vladimir Putin. Herd diligently incorporates contemporary strategic affairs into the text and in analyzing Kremlin responses, the book imparts on the reader a clear understanding of how and why Putin's Russia operates. Engaging and accessible, the book will be of interest to Russianists (new and old hand) across all stages of academia, various government agencies and even the private sector. Herd's book will no doubt assist those seeking to navigate the complex world of Russian strategic behavior. This book is a crucial guide understanding a key stakeholder in the international security environment and indeed, a significant shaper of strategic competition yet to come.

—**Elizabeth Buchanan**, *Australian War College,*
Canberra and Fellow of Modern War Institute, West Point, USA

An excellent examination of the reasons why North American, the EU and Britain are stuck in a strategic confrontation with Russia. Russian strategic culture, as Herd convincingly shows, has seen many changes from the Czarist times to the present. Under Putin, however, the ruling elite had defined Russia's strategic interests and values as incompatible with those of the West. This has created "a new normal" that has made it difficult to find a way out of what essentially is a dead end.

—**Hannes Adomeit**, *Senior Fellow, Institute for Security Studies*
at Kiel University (ISPK), Germany

UNDERSTANDING RUSSIAN STRATEGIC BEHAVIOR

This book examines the extent to which Russia's strategic behavior is the product of its imperial strategic culture and Putin's own operational code.

The work argues that by conflating personalistic regime survival with national security, Putin ensures that contemporary Russian national interest, as expressed through strategic behavior, is the synthesis of a peculiar *troika*: a long-standing imperial strategic culture, rooted in a partially imagined past; the operational code of a counter-intelligence president and decision-making elite and the realities of Russia as a hybrid state. The book first examines the role of structure and agency in shaping contemporary Russian strategic behavior. It then provides a conceptual understanding of strategic culture and applies this to *Tsarist* and Soviet historical developments. The book's analysis of the operational code, however, demonstrates that Putinism is more than the sum of the past. At the end, the book assesses Putin's statecraft and stress-tests our assumptions about the exercise of contemporary power in Russia and the structure of Putin's agency.

This book will be of interest to students of Russian politics and foreign policy, strategic studies and international relations.

Graeme P. Herd is Professor of Transnational Security Studies and Chair of the Research and Policy Analysis Department at the George C. Marshall European Center for Security Studies, Garmisch-Partenkirchen, Germany.

Contemporary Security Studies

Series Editors: James Gow and Rachel Kerr, King's College London

This series focuses on new research across the spectrum of international peace and security, in an era where each year throws up multiple examples of conflicts that present new security challenges in the world around them.

Transitional Justice in Peacebuilding
Actor-Contingent and Malleable Justice
Djeyhoun Ostowar

NATO and Transatlantic Relations in the 21st Century
Foreign and Security Policy Perspectives
Edited by Michele Testoni

Reconciliation After War
Historical Perspectives on Transitional Justice
Edited by Rachel Kerr, Henry Redwood and James Gow

Militia Order in Afghanistan
Guardians or Gangsters?
Matthew P. Dearing

Prosecutorial Discretion in the International Criminal Court
Legitimacy and the Politics of Justice
Farid Mohammed Rashid

Drones and Global Order
Implications of Remote Warfare for International Society
Edited by Paul Lushenko, Srinjoy Bose, and William Maley

For more information about this series, please visit: www.routledge.com/
Contemporary-Security-Studies/book-series/CSS

UNDERSTANDING RUSSIAN STRATEGIC BEHAVIOR

Imperial Strategic Culture and Putin's Operational Code

Graeme P. Herd

Routledge
Taylor & Francis Group

LONDON AND NEW YORK

Cover image: © Getty Images

First published 2022
by Routledge
2 Park Square, Milton Park, Abingdon, Oxon OX14 4RN

and by Routledge
605 Third Avenue, New York, NY 10158

Routledge is an imprint of the Taylor & Francis Group, an informa business

British Library Cataloguing-in-Publication Data
A catalogue record for this book is available from the British Library

Library of Congress Cataloging-in-Publication Data
Names: Herd, Graeme P. author.
Title: Understanding Russian strategic behavior : imperial strategic
    culture and Putin's operational code / Graeme P. Herd.
Description: London ; New York, NY : Routledge, Taylor & Francis
    Group, 2022. | Series: Contemporary security studies | Includes
    bibliographical references and index.
Identifiers: LCCN 2021040853 (print) | LCCN 2021040854 (ebook) |
    ISBN 9780367205218 (hardback) | ISBN 9780367205225 (paperback) |
    ISBN 9780429261985 (ebook)
Subjects: LCSH: National security—Russia (Federation) | Putin, Vladimir
    Vladimirovich, 1952—Political and social views. | Russia (Federation)-
    Russia (Federation) | Russia (Federation) | Russia (Federation)—
    Foreign relations.
Classification: LCC UA770 .H46 2022 (print) | LCC UA770 (ebook) |
    DDC 355/.033547—dc23
LC record available at https://lccn.loc.gov/2021040853
LC ebook record available at https://lccn.loc.gov/2021040854

ISBN: 978-0-367-20521-8 (hbk)
ISBN: 978-0-367-20522-5 (pbk)
ISBN: 978-0-429-26198-5 (ebk)

DOI: 10.4324/9780429261985

Typeset in Bembo
by Apex CoVantage, LLC

This book is dedicated to Lt. Gen. (ret) Keith W. Dayton, Director, George C. Marshall European Center for Security Studies (GCMC), December 2010 to May 2021. This dedication, in its small way, honors Gen Dayton's Foreign Area Office training, his commitment to defense diplomacy throughout his career and, especially, and more personally, marks my appreciation of his leadership at the GCMC, where he encouraged critical and reflective thinking toward Churchill's "riddle, wrapped in a mystery, inside an enigma."

CONTENTS

TABLES

ACKNOWLEDGMENTS

The birth of this book can be traced to a request sent to the George C. Marshall European Center for Security Studies (GCMC) in September 2015 to provide a 25-minute open-source scene-setter presentation to introduce a 2-day Senior Leaders Seminar (SLS). This seminar was to be held in February 2016 at "The Wargame Center" of U.S. Special Operations Command (SOCOM), MacDill Air Base, Tampa, Florida. I am grateful to Dr. Bob Brannon, the then Dean at the GCMC, and LTG (ret.) Keith W. Dayton, the GCMC's Director (to whom I dedicate this book) for encouraging me to participate in this SLS. This SLS highlighted to me the need to study further the relationship between structure and agency in Russia today and between Russian strategic culture and President Putin's operational code in order to understand contemporary Russian strategic behavior better.

Inspiration and institutional encouragement is one factor, putting pen to paper another. The GCMC's Alumni Programs Department invited me to present on aspects of this topic before GCMC alumni practitioner and policy audiences at events in partner countries. As GCMC alumni have first-hand experience of Russian malign activity and coercive practices, these presentations had a useful forcing function: I was able to clarify key arguments, refine and qualify the analysis, and identify and integrate competing perspectives. In particular, I would like to thank Alumni Programs Director Chris Burelli, who either personally hosted or entrusted me to his team (Donna Janca, Mark Johnson and Drew Beck) to enable presentations in Athens, Berlin, Bishkek, Bratislava, Budapest, Chisinau, Kyiv, Nur-Sultan, Prague, Pristina, Riga, Sofia, Tallinn, Tbilisi, Tirana, Vienna, Vilnius, Warsaw and Zagreb and some on more than one occasion.

I would also like to acknowledge the support of the Russia Strategic Initiative (RSI) and the U.S. Department of Defense's (DoD) effort to enhance the understanding of the Russian way of war in order to inform strategy and planning. RSI funded a GCMC-led research project titled "Understanding Russia's Strategic

Behavior" in 2018–2020. This project sought to investigate the proximate and contextual drivers of Russian decision-making in key military-strategic theaters, including the Arctic, Nordic–Baltic, Ukraine and Black Sea region. Thanks are due to Dr. Dima (Dmitry) Adamsky, Dr. Pavel Baev, Dr. Samuel Charap, Dr. Mark Galeotti, Dr. Dmitry Gorenburg and Dr. David Lewis, who as researchers on the project published a series of *MC Security Insights* and attended research workshops twice a year in Garmisch-Partenkirchen. RSI also kindly funded project conference panels at the Association for Slavic, East European and Eurasian Studies (ASEEES) in November 2019 (San Francisco) and International Studies Association (ISA) Annual Conference in 2019 (Toronto) and ISA in March 2020 (Hawaii) – the latter being cancelled due to COVID-19 restrictions.

Within RSI itself, my thanks in particular to COL. David "Woody" Woodward and COL. Philip Forbes, both of whom served as RSI's Chief of Research. In addition, I specially thank Jules Silberberg, RSI's superb former Senior Strategic Advisor, and RSI Director Ken Stolworthy for funding this project, the first on his watch, and supporting it throughout. I am also grateful to the Center for Naval Analysis (CNA) and RAND Corporation for agreeing to be project partners, enabling publication copyediting and contracting. I very much appreciate the professionalism and dedication of RAND's David Cozad.

As this theme of *Understanding Russian Strategic Behavior* remains a critical focus for the United States in this era of strategic competition, the GCMC has initiated a monthly "Hybrid Seminar Series" (RHSS), beginning January 2020. I gratefully acknowledge the superb insights from a number of subject matter experts and other participants and take this opportunity to thank Dr. Katrin Bastian as online moderator and Andrew Brinkman as event planner at the GCMC for supporting this endeavor so ably.

This books leans into some of my most recent research into Russian strategic behavior. In April 2021, the GCMC published an online edited book titled *Russia's Global Reach*, which helped shape the analysis in Chapter 7. Chapter 6 benefitted from two 2020 *MC Security Insights* examining Putin's constitutional change proposals and his responses to COVID-19 through the prism of his operational code, a focus I had first elaborated as a chapter in *The Routledge Handbook of Russian Security* in 2019, edited by Roger Kanet. In 2018, I published an article in the *RUSI Journal* that attempted to unpick the nature of Russia's "hybrid state," a concept first developed by Mark Galeotti, and this analysis informed Chapter 5. Chapter 3 reflects insights gleaned from my postgraduate archival studies into Scottish influences on early modern Russian historical development, undertaken between 1989 and 1993 in Moscow (*Rossiiskii Gosudarstvenyi Arkhiv Drevnikh Aktov* and especially *Rossiiskii Gosudarstvenyi Voenno-Istoricheskii Arkhiv*), Tallinn (*Tallinna Linnaarchiv*), London (*British Library* and the *Public Record Office*, Chancery Lane) and Edinburgh (*Scottish Record Office*).

My special thanks are due to Dr. Pál Dunay and Dr. Igor Zevelev for their very helpful comments on much earlier drafts of Chapters 1–5 of this book and Professor Hannes Adomeit for his close readings of Chapters 5 and 6, which greatly benefitted from his attention. I am also very grateful for all GCMC interns whom I have been lucky enough to work with and who kindly read chapters for sense and sensibility, particularly Matti Dimmick, Sean Boyle and then Martin Heli. The GCMC Research Library has been immensely helpful: I am delighted to acknowledge with real gratitude the work undertaken by Anthony Micchelli, Librarian, in ordering the chapter's selected bibliographies in Chicago style and providing 2021 literature updates around the themes "strategic culture" and "red lines."

Throughout the process, from contracting to delivery of the final manuscript, I acknowledge the patience, advice and help I have received from Andrew Humphrys, Senior Editor, and Bethany Lund-Yates, Editorial Assistant, Military, Strategic and Security Studies, Routledge. Professor James Gow, as Series Editor, kindly provided valuable feedback which helped contextualize Chapters 1 and 9.

At the end, I thank my family, my wife Birgit and my son Philip for their forbearance during the winter holidays of 2015 in Tenerife when I took time out to develop arguments and ideas for the February 2016 Tampa presentation. Their patience lasted through to the German Pentecost holiday of late May to early June 2021, when in Adriabella, Duna Verde, on the Italian Adriatic coast, I finalized the completed first draft of the book. What you are about to read is the fifth draft just submitted. Of course, responsibility for all errors of fact and weaknesses in interpretation remains mine alone.

Graeme P. Herd
Garmisch-Partenkirchen, November 2021

1

INTRODUCTION

Understanding Russian strategic behavior

Churchill's Russia challenge: late spring, early summer 2021

For Winston Churchill, the master key to understanding Russia was "national interest." Speaking to rally the British public in a BBC radio broadcast in October 1939 he noted:

> I cannot forecast to you the action of Russia. It is a riddle, wrapped in a mystery inside an enigma; but perhaps there is a key. That key is Russian national interest.
>
> *(Putin et al., 2000)*

Following the invasion of the Soviet Union by Germany on 22 June 1941, which violated the non-aggression Molotov–Ribbentrop Pact of 1939, the Union of Soviet Socialist Republics (USSR) abandoned its neutrality toward the Allied–Axis conflict. A Grand Alliance between the United Kingdom, United States and the Soviet Union was created, formalized by the declaration of the United Nations, on 1 January 1942. National interest (existential survival) dictated pragmatic Soviet strategic behavior.

Eighty years later, when analyzing contemporary "Russian action," that is strategic behavior, it is clear that relations between Russia and the United States have continuously deteriorated since 2014. Russia has become more insular and internally repressive. By 2021, Moscow reduced the U.S. diplomatic footprint in Russia and continued a military buildup around Donbas (100,000 Russian troop mobilization) and threatened to intervene to the line of demarcation or beyond. On 14 April 2021, Russian Security Council Secretary Nikolai Patrushev stated that Ukrainian special services and extremist organizations constantly arrange provocation on the state border: "At the suggestion of Western sponsors, training centers for sabotage and reconnaissance formations have been deployed on the territory of Ukraine" (Yegorov, 2021). The next day on 15 April, President Biden signed a new versatile U.S. Executive Order (EO), which, unlike the Countering America's Adversaries Through Sanctions Act (CAATSA), does not require congressional

DOI: 10.4324/9780429261985-1

review to terminate. The EO creates groundwork for a broad future framework of scalable sanctions to, for example, Russian sovereign debt and prevents U.S. financial institutions from trading in the secondary market for ruble-denominated bonds or exclude Russia from the SWIFT international financial system.

By 21 April 2021, Putin, in his annual state of the nation address, stated that U.S. sanctions were "unlawful, politically motivated" and part of a "crude attempt" of the United States "to enforce its will on others." Instead of compliance, Putin warned of an "asymmetrical, rapid and harsh" response, if the West crosses "red lines," that is undermined Russia's external security interests or interfered in Russian domestic affairs (Shagina, 2021). He referenced a joint Belarusian Committee for State Security (KGB) and Russian Federal Security Service (FSB) operation that had exposed an alleged U.S.-backed coup against President Lukashenka of Belarus earlier that month. Kremlin spokesman Dmitry Peskov noted the alarming growth of a "confrontational potential" between Russia and the West and that "[t]he president [Putin] has said that we will not cross the 'red lines' [of other countries] ourselves, and will not allow anybody to cross the 'red lines' that we define ourselves." He went on to criticize and reject European "schizophrenia," which he claimed had crept: "over the EU territory in the form of the so-called "European solidarity." It is unacceptable to us, it is outrageous." Vyacheslav Volodin, chairman of the Russian Federation State *Duma*, bluntly stated: "The United States will have to move and give way to Russia." For Russia, the United States uses Ukraine as a "convenient bridgehead" to pressurize Russia (Zapesotsky, 2021). Former Prime Minister Dmitry Medvedev penned an opinion editorial ("The Unlearned Lessons of History") warning of a return to the Cold War era, with Russia forced to respond to Western aggression.

On May 4, a Group of Seven (G-7) developed nations' (the United Kingdom, the United States, Canada, France, Germany, Italy and Japan) Foreign and Development Ministers' Meeting was held in London to discuss critical geopolitical challenges, not least Russia and China. Ahead of this meeting, the UK and U.S. foreign ministers reiterated a shared commitment to "maintaining transatlantic unity in defense of our common values and in response to direct threats." U.S. Secretary of State Antony Blinken noted:

> With regard to Russia, as Dominic said, we are focused very much on Russia's actions and what course it chooses to take. President Biden's been very clear for a long time, including before he was President, that if Russia chooses to act recklessly or aggressively, we'll respond.

On May 7, at an online meeting of the UN Security Council, Russian Foreign Minister Sergei Lavrov stated that Moscow views attempts by the United Sates and the EU to impose totalitarianism as unacceptable:

> Russia calls on all states to unconditionally follow the objectives and principles of the [UN] Charter when developing their foreign policy, ensuring

respect for the sovereign equality of states, non-interference in their internal affairs, settlement of disputes by political and diplomatic means, and refusal to threaten to use force or use force.

("Lavrov accused," 2021)

Lavrov argued that Western countries instrumentalize the notion of a "rules-based order" and sanctions as a substitute of the norms of international law to constrain Russia's capacity to take decisions and prevent the formation of a polycentric world. In late June 2021, Lavrov further elaborated on this belief, arguing that the "West wanted to send a clear message: it stands united like never before and will do what it believes to be right in international affairs, while forcing others, primarily Russia and China, to follow its lead." Lavrov purports to believe that the "rules-based world order concept" is a "counterweight to the universal principles of international law with the UN Charter as its primary source," with Russia supporting the latter. He argues that

> the West deliberately shies away from spelling out the rules it purports to follow, just as it refrains from explaining why they are needed. . . . The beauty of these Western "rules" lies precisely in the fact that they lack any specific content. When someone acts against the will of the West, it immediately responds with a groundless claim that "the rules have been broken" (without bothering to present any evidence) and declares its "right to hold the perpetrators accountable". The less specific they get, the freer their hand to carry on with the arbitrary practice of employing dirty tactics as a way to pressure competitors. During the so-called "wild 1990s" in Russia, we used to refer to such practices as laying down the law.

(Lavrov, 2021)

On 9 May, state-run *Rossiya* 1 and Gazprom-Media's *NTV* described NATO's ongoing Defender Europe exercise as not only the largest since the end of the Cold War and anti-Russian in nature but also designed to practice taking Russian territory. At the same time, DarkSide ransomware, a Russian cybercrime gang, was deemed responsible for the attack on Colonial Pipeline that shut down strategic energy infrastructure in the United States – a fuel pipeline, which provides nearly half of the gasoline and fuels used on the East Coast. The Main Directorate of the General Staff of the Armed Forces of the Russian Federation (the GU, commonly know by the abbreviation GRU) was also suspected of involvement in directed-energy attacks ("Havana syndrome") on American personnel: microwave pulse weapons, using a form of electromagnetic radiation, were able to target and damage U.S. government military and diplomatic targets from 500 to 1,000 yards away. A former U.S. national security official commented: "It looks, smells and feels like the GRU. When you are looking at the landscape, there are very few people who are willing, capable and have the technology. It's pretty simple forensics" (Seligman and Desiderio, 2021).

A G7 head of state Summit took place on 11–13 June, followed by a Summit with NATO and the EU in Belgium. Amid this confrontational rhetoric and escalatory sanctions, White House national security adviser Jake Sullivan and Russian Security Council Secretary Nikolay Patrushev met in Geneva for preparatory talks ahead of the Putin–Biden Summit, held on 16 June. Although there were no preconditions set before the meeting, expectations for breakthroughs were low, given the poor state of relations and lack of trust. President Biden stated: "This is not about trust. This is about self-interest, and verification of self-interest" (Albats, 2021). The following week on 23 June, Russia claimed that the Royal Navy destroyer HMS Defender violated Russian territorial waters off Crimea, and this "provocation" was subjected to warning shots by FSB Border Guard ships, and then Su-24 aircraft dropped bombs in its path, forcing the UK vessel to hastily leave "Russian waters." The UK Ministry of Defense denied shots had been fired or bombs dropped or that HMS Defender deviated from its transit route. Deputy Foreign Minister Sergei Ryabkov commented: "[W]e can appeal to common sense, demand respect for international law, and if this does not help, we can bomb" (Galeotti, 2021). On the same day, in remarks at the Moscow Conference on International Security, Russian Defence Minister Sergei Shoigu noted: "The world is rapidly descending into a new confrontation, a far more dangerous one than it used to be during the Cold War" adding that "some European countries are interested in escalating the conflict with Russia" (BBC Report, 2021).

The publication of Russia's latest National Security Strategy (NSS) on 2 July noted:

> Destructive forces abroad and at home are attempting to exploit objective social economic difficulties in the Russian Federation in order to stimulate negative social processes, exacerbate inter-ethnic and sectarian conflicts, and manipulate the information sphere. The activity of intelligence and other activities of special services and organizations of foreign states, including the use of Russian public associations and individuals controlled by them, continues to be intensified. The capabilities of global Internet companies are widely used to disseminate false information and organize illegal public actions.
>
> *(National Security Strategy, 2021)*

According to this NSS, "traditional Russian spiritual, moral, cultural, and historical values are being actively attacked by the U.S. and its allies, as well as by transnational corporations." These traditional Russian spiritual and moral values include life, dignity, human rights and freedoms; patriotism, citizenship, service to the Fatherland and responsibility for its fate; high moral ideals, a strong family; constructive work; priority of the spiritual over the material; humanism, mercy and justice and collectivism. The United States and its allies, along with transnational corporations, allegedly, "have an informational and psychological influence on individual, group, and public consciousness by spreading social and moral attitudes that contradict the traditions, convictions, and beliefs of the peoples of the

Russian Federation" ("What you need to know," 2021). Foreign Minister Lavrov was quick to support this assertion, accusing the West of preparing "to provoke protests, most likely violent ones, as the West likes doing" ahead of the September elections to the State *Duma*:

> It can be assumed that ahead of the upcoming elections to the State Duma new attempts to upset, destabilise the situation, provoke protests, most likely violent ones, will take place as the West likes doing. Then a campaign will probably be launched against recognising the results of our elections. They have such plans, we are aware of them. But we will focus primarily on the opinion, the position of our people, [the people] are able to assess the actions of the authorities and express their opinion on how their want to further develop their country.
>
> *(BBC Monitoring, 2021a)*

Cumulatively, this snapshot of events from April to July 2021 highlights the following: Russia's confrontation with the United States is now the current norm, relations with the EU have deteriorated to a record low and will continue to remain there for the foreseeable future and offensive cyber operations as well as "active measures" against the political West are ongoing and unremitting. The strategic interests and values of Russia and the West are incompatible and irreconcilable. It is notable that President Putin, Secretary of the Security Council Patrushev, Defense Minister Shiogu, Foreign Minister Lavrov and head of the Foreign Intelligence Service Naryshkin, for example, share the same escalatory rhetoric, threat assessment (unremitting Western containment and encirclement) and endorse Russian strategic responses as defensive and reactive. The intensity and rapidity of points of friction steadily increased. The HMS Defender incident is a case in point. Russia's defense minister accuses the West of escalation while its deputy foreign minister endorsed Russian state-controlled media reports that Russian military aircraft had indeed dropped bombs in the path of the British capital ship. How can we explain such Russian strategic behavior? Why have relations between Russia and the political West deteriorated so badly?

Threat assessments: risks of miscalculation, escalation and conflict?

After the Second World War, the Truman administration successfully created and led a rules-based liberal international order based on the values of freedom, the rule of law, human dignity, tolerance, pluralist institutions, and open and free trade. Excepting President Trump (2017–2021), all subsequent U.S. presidents, whether Republican or Democrat, have followed this broadly bipartisan liberal internationalist tradition. *Pax Americana* or the "American Century" was underpinned by U.S. global engagement through the exchange of ideas, peoples, trade and alliances. This Western-centered system was based on Wilsonian liberalism and multilateral institutions. It was supposed that in a predictable interdependent one-world system, shared strategic threats would create interest-based incentives and functional benefits that would drive global cooperation with the United States as a European power (institutionalized through NATO) and indispensable partner.

The end of the Cold War and collapse of the Soviet Union lifted structural restraints on the United States, which proceeded to push for the expansion of the U.S. liberal international order. As with China, post–Cold War engagement with Russia during the Clinton Presidency in the 1990s was underpinned by a theory of change based on the notion of convergence. President Clinton's "Enlargement and Engagement" doctrine suggested that were Russian companies to register on New York or London stock exchanges then this would entail adherence to corporate good governance rules and the creation of a business elite that would become a driving force for political and economic liberalization and change in Russia, facilitating further integration into the global system. President Putin's December 1999 Manifesto – "Russia at the Turn of the Millennium" – promoted the creation of a state capitalist model of development in Russia, allowing for economic growth protected by a strong stable state, a vision that resonated with the Russian people (Belton, 2020).

However, when President Putin came into office on 6 May 2000, though he appeared to attempt to integrate Russia into a "Greater West," he could not do so on his own terms and abandoned the strategy. Performance or legal-rational legitimation of his political authority had by 2011–12 given way to charismatic and historical legitimation. Dominant official Russian narratives toward Europe reflected emotions of rejection, resentment and disillusionment. Narratives include the notion of European Russo-phobia, unjustified prejudice and Western hypocrisy: Putin believes that in the West, commercial and financial imperatives outweigh any legal or moral concerns and democratic principles but that the West pretends otherwise, instrumentalizing the language of virtue to further their naked interests. Russia promotes itself as a bastion of "traditional" religious, societal and other values in contrast to the more liberal, "decadent" West. Russia, although the largest European country in terms of population and territory, no longer views market-democratic Europe as a model or institutional mentor. By 2021, Western liberalism was targeted as a source of insecurity, legitimizing outright anti-Westernism and ideological confrontation and creating an atmosphere of national emergency.

Russia views the world in terms of *realpolitik*, balance of power and zero-sum thinking, rejecting the rules-based order imposed by a "totalitarian West." If the strategic center of gravity in the political West is the belief of elites and societies in democratic ideals (checks and balances, transparency, free and independent media, vibrant civil societies) and functioning law-based institutions and diverse identities and shared norms and values, then its operational center of gravity is the transatlantic partnership between the United States and Germany – the Berlin–Washington, DC, axis. Russia views the United States as its primary adversary. At best, it appears that Moscow's strategy is to compel the West to recognize Russia's security interests and its status as a global great power and regional hegemon. At worst, Russia is determined to take part in asymmetric Great Power competition and, to that end, consciously integrates conventional and sub-conventional proxy tools to destabilize neighbors through hybrid interference (Wigell, 2021). In this structural context, cross-domain coercion and compellence, raiding and brigandage constitute a rational Russian strategy.

In 2019, General Nick Carter, former UK Chief of Defense Staff, suggested that while Russia does not want a war, it may unleash a war accidentally, as a consequence of reckless behavior and a lack of respect for international law. In May 2019, an unclassified "Strategic Multilayer Assessment" concluded that America is losing the race for global influence, in part because the United States "lacks a compelling 'story' to present as a counter to competing narratives" emerging from Russia (Arquilla and Peterson, 2019). Other assessments argue:

> Russia will not refrain from getting involved in any conflict that affects its interests. The U.S. military should expect Russian forces, even if only covertly or in low numbers, to be present in nearly any conflict zone in the Middle East, North Africa, and beyond. Planners should always be cognizant of Russian interests in each country in the region and expect competition both for basing and for influence in those states where Moscow has made diplomatic and political-military inroads.
>
> *(Charap et al., 2019)*

Russian officials look to NATO's existence and enlargement as evidence of a desire to encircle Russia. The integration of Georgia into NATO would lead to conflict between Russia and NATO as Russia considers Abkhazia and South Ossetia independent states, and not potential NATO territory. In his 1 March 2018 address to the Federal Assembly, President Putin referenced five new hypersonic weapons systems with the power to strike the United States undetected. Indeed, in graphics illustrating the speech, missiles could be seen targeting Tampa in Florida, home to U.S. Special Operations Command and Central Command. President Putin commented: "We've never ceased to be a major nuclear power but no one would listen to us. Listen to us now!" (Bershidsky, 2018). Since February 2014, a nuclear-armed Russia has annexed Crimea, destabilized eastern Ukraine, aggressively penetrated NATO Baltic airspace, undertaken submarine operations near vital undersea cables that carry internet communication in the Atlantic, launched *Kalibr* missiles from the Caspian flotilla against targets in Syria and almost came to blows with Turkey. President Putin calmly stated that Russian troops could reach not just Kyiv but Riga, Vilnius, Tallinn, Warsaw or Bucharest in 2 days, a conclusion broadly supported by a 2016 RAND Corporation Report:

> Across multiple games using a wide range of expert participants in and out of uniform playing both sides, the longest it has taken Russian forces to reach the outskirts of the Estonian and/or Latvian capitals of Tallinn and Riga, respec-

tively, is 60 hours. Such a rapid defeat would leave NATO with a limited number of options, all bad.

(Shlapak and Johnson, 2016)

In such a security context, where Russia mobilizes military and other conventional tools, alongside sub-conventional assets, and uses nuclear weapons to strategically signal, there are multiple sources of miscalculation. A large number of military forces operating in close proximity are one source of risk leading to miscalculation. Aggressive Russian posturing and the readiness of NATO to show resolve heighten the risk of potential incidents in the air and at sea. Accidental collisions and miscommunication could initiate a chain of events leading to conflict between Russian and U.S./NATO military forces. Cold War notions around "escalation ladders" and the "rungs" on those ladders and the nature of "escalation cycles" and "escalation dominance" theories are all being tested in practice.

The Biden administration attempts to create a transatlantic consensus over how best to respond to Russian strategic behavior in ways that both protect national interest and values while reducing the possibilities of escalation. After the annexation of Crimea in 2014, a Western policy mix toward Russia based on defense, dialogue and deterrence emerged. An influential RAND Corporation study identified two strategic options, a "punishment and separation" strategy based on meeting Russian force symmetrically with equal force and a "stability and involvement" strategy based on making NATO member states more resilient in the face of Russian challenge (Oliker et al., 2015). Steven Pfifer, a former U.S. ambassador to Ukraine and Strobe Talbott, who served as deputy U.S. secretary of state from 1994 to 2001, argued that in order to prevent the conflict in Ukraine from deteriorating further and to promote a "genuine negotiated settlement," President Putin's calculus would need to change. To that end, they advocated "pushback" in the shape of "giving the Ukrainian military sufficient means to make further aggression so costly that Putin and the Russian army are deterred from escalating the fight." Otherwise, they warned that the United States would face "challenges, even armed challenges, from Russia elsewhere that will require far more costly responses" (Pfifer and Talbott, 2015). Eight former U.S. national security practitioners issued a report with recommendations for immediate action, titled "Preserving Ukraine's Independence, Resisting Russian Aggression: What the United States and NATO Must Do." Following this logic, U.S. Army Major-General Robert Scales, former commandant of the U.S. Army War College, bluntly contended: "The only way (the U.S.) can turn the tide is start killing Russians, killing so many Russians that even Putin's media can't hide the fact that Russians are returning to their motherland in body bags." (Eleftheriou-Smith, 2015). General Sir Richard Shirreff, NATO's former Deputy Supreme Allied Commander Europe (DSACEUR), in a book titled *2017 War with Russia*, predicted that an "aggressive and opportunistic" President Putin will order a Russian invasion into Latvia backed by the threat of nuclear war if NATO responds militarily: "A hesitant NATO will face catastrophe; the day of reckoning for its failure to match strong political statements with strong military forces finally arrives" (Sengupta, 2016).

On the other side of the debate and in a response, Fiona Hill and Clifford Gaddy argued to an opposite conclusion. Their starting point was to note that President Putin has "escalation dominance" in Ukraine – "Whatever move we make, he can match it and go further." They acknowledge that "[o]ur problem is that we do not fully understand Putin's calculus, just as he does not understand ours" and that, as a consequence, from Putin's perspective "any concession or compromise he makes will encourage the West to push further." To assume "Putin's wartime rhetoric is a bluff is making a very risky assumption." Rather than force Putin to the negotiation table, the delivery of U.S. offensive military aid to Ukraine would "fuel this escalatory cycle" as well as fracture transatlantic unity (Gaddy and Hill, 2015). Graham Allison, former assistant U.S. secretary of defense, and Dimitri Simes also warned of the willingness of Russian hard-liners to use nuclear weapons if a conventional conflict got out of hand: "In these debates, many ask whether President Obama would risk losing Chicago, New York and Washington to protect Riga, Tallinn and Vilnius" (Allison and Simes, 2015).

Does President Putin have a risk ceiling – a level of escalation he does not want to go beyond because in his view the risk of his miscalculation and mistakes becomes unacceptable? For example might the possibility that all-out conventional war with the United States could escalate to a nuclear conflict qualify as a scenario that would breach Putin's escalation ceiling? Or, precisely in order to prevent this wider conflict, might battlefield or tactical nuclear weapons be deployed? What of the development of non-nuclear precision weapons, which increase the possibility of non-nuclear conflict? If there is a notional escalation ceiling in Putin's mind, how close does he consider Russia to be to it? Is the threshold for the use of force being lowered as time goes on? By 2021, has President Putin become more confident and does he have a greater tolerance for what he considers manageable risk? Is the notional ceiling permeable in that under certain conditions or certain issue areas the tolerance increases as President Putin feels exposure would be temporary and contained?

In the military sphere, Putin can leverage his 10:1 tactical nuclear superiority in Central Europe and quick decision-making, and geography allows Russia to mobilize faster than NATO can respond. Russia has maintained a meaningful second-strike capability. It has advanced cyberwarfare capabilities and can leverage the militarization of space (which offers a non-nuclear escalatory option). Does Putin see escalation dominance in the military sphere as compensatory for Western escalation dominance in the economic sphere, where the greater West has a 21:1 advantage? We can see that Western sanctions clearly have a disproportionate effect on Russia, particularly when compared to the impact of Russian counter sanctions. The potential of the West to increase economic pressure far outstrips Russia's economic retaliatory potential. As many analysts have noted, countries in decline accept greater risk to uphold the status quo.

Subject, scope and structure of the book

When analyzing Russian strategic behavior, what are the determining forces and factors we should focus upon? If we consider the influence of the *Tsarist* and Soviet ideational political and strategic cultures on shaping "Putinism" and Putin's agency today, we need not go further than Putin himself for an assessment. In May 2021 at the 43rd meeting of the Russian *Pobeda* (Victory) Organising Committee, Putin condemned foreign distortions of "the role played by the Red Army in the routing of Nazism and the liberation of European nations from the Nazi plague." Putin understands such "slander and distortions" as part of perennial "attempts to hamper the development of this country, regardless of its name, be it the Russian Empire, the Soviet Union or Russia, were made in different times and historical epochs and under different political systems." Putin neatly suggests that there is only one historical Russia and that the golden thread of continuity is an existential struggle for survival and resistance to constant and unremitting external pressure. The logic is unrelenting:

> There is one principle or rather, one reason for containing Russia: the stronger and more independent Russia becomes, the more consistently it defends its national interests, the greater the striving of foreign forces to weaken it, to discredit the values uniting our society and sometimes to slander and distort what people hold dear, the things that are instilled in the younger generations of Russians and which help them acquire a strong character and their own opinions.
>
> *("Meeting of the Russian Pobeda," 2021)*

In an interview following the submission for approval of Russia's latest NSS, its Secretary Nikolai Patrushev commented:

> The actions against Russia aimed at weakening Russian statehood, internal unity, and defence potential are becoming more obvious. In order to contain Russia, political and economic pressure is intensifying, there are attempts to destabilise the social and political situation in the country, to inspire and radicalise the protest movement, and erode traditional Russian spiritual and moral values.
>
> *(Interview, 2021)*

It follows that only a strong leader can "Make Russia Great Again" and then defend Russia against the inevitable backlash. Thus, rather circuitously, Russia would only be besieged if it had a strong leader; unless Russia is besieged, its leader is not capable of making Russia great. Besiegement, encirclement and containment become performance indicators: the worse the situation the better.

This book notes that given the weight of Russian ideational and economic history, any given president in Russia might reasonably be viewed as a simulacrum – a reflection of the nation they lead, its worldview made flesh, a person who rules through bureaucratic consensus. Andrei Kovalev, who served as a diplomat and official in the Soviet Union under Mikhail Gorbachev, Yeltsin and Putin, argues: "What would Russia be without Putin? Putin himself is nothing. He is merely a facade concealing the special services and the oligarchs. They can easily replace him with another representative of the secret services" (Kovalev, 2017). In this sense, is President Putin the handmaiden of the elite, shaped by national discourses? A "selectorate" puts a "collective Putin" in place and can remove him should the president fail to observe the sacred strictures, bureaucratic protocols and public expectations embedded in this tradition. Gleb Pavlosky has argued that 100 or so people in the inner circle around Putin constitute the "collective Putin" label for the Kremlin's decisions, a conclusion reached also by Russian journalist Mikhail Zygar, who uses the metaphor of "monarchial court" in his study titled *All the Kremlin's Men: Inside the Court of Vladimir Putin* (Zygar, 2016; Lewis, 2020, 68–69). According to this understanding, the "collective Putin" is more important than Putin himself, whose status is reduced to that of a convenient figurehead. Indeed, Putinism is merely the behavioral sum of the parts. As innumerable "'little Putins' try to guess how the 'big Putin' in the Kremlin would behave in their place," loyalty manifests itself in a system of aggressive conformism:

> Cruelty and pettiness have now become the norm and officials need no order from above to outdo each other with initiatives that are obsequious in their aggressiveness. This system, with its judges, investigators, officials, FSB agents, Kremlin-orchestrated volunteer brigades, United Russia party members, trolls, bots, snoops, riot police, etc. now works on autopilot.
>
> *(Kolesnikov, 2019)*

This contention can certainly be evidenced by President Putin's own experience of coming to power in 1999. Vladimir Putin was a largely unknown and uncharismatic entity selected by the "Family" group around Yeltsin, who thought that Putin was strong enough to protect them from prosecution after the presidency of Yeltsin had ended but weak enough to be dependent and controllable. Indeed, Putin in fact could be said to represent their "Plan B," selected as a pushback by the family against the former head of Russia's Foreign Intelligence Service (SVR), Evgeni Primakov, who along with powerful mayor of Moscow Yuri Luzhkov and Yuri Maslyukov, former head of the State Planning Committee (*Gosplan*), the Prosecutor-General Yuri Skuratov, mid-ranking army officers and support from the Moscow FSB, looked set to be the security services' first choice – "Plan A." *Kanditat-Resident* (candidate-spy) Putin represented a younger more ruthless cadre within the security services able to preempt the older generation by deploying *kompromat* and utilizing a national emergency (apartment bombings and the second Chechen War) to demonstrate Putin's ability to take decisive action, reverse national humiliation and project a new strong regime (Belton, 2020). "Operation Successor" represented a peaceful transfer of power, but the struggle beneath the surface was anything but, with overt violence displaced to apartment bombings and military conflict in the North Caucasus, which served to highlight the absence of a self-regulating political system in Russia, a condition that has only deteriorated after 21 years of Putin as president.

The notion that the past imposes a straightjacket on the present and binds contemporary actors to pre-ordained behavior within a preset destiny appears compelling. According to a historically determinist understanding, President Putin is bound to create an authoritarian system based on nationalist populism – this is the Russian historical default position that in turn reflects an enduring political cultural code that Putin channels and directs to ensure he personally remains in power and over what he imagines is a stable, strong and restored Great Power. As Oleg Kashin argues:

> The superpresidential constitution, the Presidential Staff as the real supreme organ of power, the special role of the federal television channels, the Kremlin-controlled system of electoral commissions – all the basic principles of the Putin regime took shape long before Putin's arrival in power, and they will probably remain in place even without Putin. It is far easier to imagine a post-Putin Russia whose leader reviews the main slogans and publicly declared values of the Putin era but at the same time does not question the actual structure of the state than it is to imagine a Russia that has undergone full-blown political reform, established real separation of powers, federalism, local self-government, and other features of democracy.
>
> *(Kashin, 2017)*

Vladimir Putin's personal experiences, particularly as a young counter-intelligence officer in the KGB's Chief Second Directorate in Dresden 1985–1990, are surprisingly relevant in a number of ways. Putin was himself a "first person" witness to the speed at which order in the German Democratic Republic (GDR) descended into chaos, as the most seemingly stable and Stalinist of the Soviet satellites crumbled and fell in 1989. As Putin recounts: "I got the feeling then that the country [the Soviet Union] no longer existed. That it had disappeared. It was clear that the Union was ailing. And it had a terminal disease without a cure – a paralysis of power" (Putin et al., 2000, 76). The need to avoid paralysis and prevent the disintegration of order are clear motivations that drive Putin. It was also in Dresden, Catherine Belton argues, that Putin learned to work through clandestine-organized criminal networks to achieve operational objectives. The value of an *obshchak*, or off-the-books slush fund, not subject to accountability, oversight or transparency, to where the personal and strategic are blurred, was also reinforced (Belton, 2020). In the Putinite mind-set, encroachment upon Russia has taken many forms, including an ideational contest in which West would instrumentalize its political system to undermine, weaken and ultimately control Russia. According to this perspective, democracy, the rule of law and human rights are contemporary tools of Western power that Russia should resist:

NATO is the hard power backstop of soft power tools designed to enable a post-modern "color revolution"-type *coup d'état*. Thus, if Russia accepts Western constraints, limits and control, then Russia becomes, in Putin's words, a "colonial democracy."

Twenty-two years after Dresden, an older Putin experienced a similar crucible of fire in the intense period between 6 December 2011 and the inauguration of Putin on 6 May 2012 for a third term. Just as security imperatives had shaped Stalin's strategic calculus by 1937, so too had it Putin's in 2011, as both: "Perceived security imperatives and a need for absolute unity once again turned the quest in Russia to build a strong state into personal rule" (Wood, 2019). Mass protest in 2011 was triggered by then Prime Minister Putin's decision to reverse the "tandem": Putin and Medvedev would swop roles, with Putin once again president and Medvedev once again prime minister. Stolen ballots in the state *Duma* election provided the proximate trigger of protest. If we look to a historical analogy, by 29 June 1941, Hitler's *Wehrmacht* had stormed into Minsk within a week of the surprise attack on the Soviet Union (Operation *Barbarossa*). Soviet military formations were either smashed, overrun or in full retreat. Stalin sat isolated in the Kremlin with a Soviet elite divided and in panic, and his regime's survival hung in the balance. Stalin addressed the Soviet people with the rallying cry of "Forward to Victory!" For Putin, the "Moscow Maidan" of December 2011 represented his own "Minsk moment." The evident tears in Putin's eyes at a political rally to celebrate the victory ("We have prevailed!") once the results were announced and his thanks to the patriotic workers of a tank-making factory (Uralvagonzavod) were both genuine and heartfelt. Society was now to be radicalized, foreign agents identified and the besieged fortress narrative given new life.

An inferiority complex had been sublimated by growing vanity and grandiosity his entourage sought to feed, but 2011 stripped Putin's psyche bare: fear, shame, anger, relief and catharsis, compressed into a few weeks, with the prospect of his political and perhaps even physical elimination, reinforced instinctive paranoia and solidified Putin's worldview (*Weltanschauung*), resonating as it did with global events of this time. As Political Techniques Center Director General Igor Bunin notes, Putin's objective when being president was to "transform an uncontrollable oligarchic republic into a state controlled by the president" and so gain Western respect, acceptance and approval. However, three shocks changed Putin's attitude:

> Qaddafi's gruesome death was the first. I think that Putin took it as a personal tragedy. I think that it was right then that he realized that Medvedev was weak and that left to its own devices, the West would one day try to pull off something like that in Russia. Mass protests in Moscow after the parliamentary and presidential elections became the second event. Putin decided that they had been organized by the West which was out to get him. And thirdly, the crisis in Ukraine. Putin became the president for the third time with a new program of post-Soviet integration . . . and no such integration is possible without Ukraine. . . . I believe that the Maidan was initially an

impromptu event . . . but Putin saw the hand of the West in it. He perceived what was a heartfelt reaction of the Ukrainian youth . . . as a cabal.

(Zubov, 2015)

As a result, Putin stepped into the presidency again in 2012 with a fixed and certain worldview:

[N]o longer afraid of provoking a confrontation with the West because he is stone-cold confident that the West needs no provocations or excuses for an attack. The West will attack any opponent regardless of what this opponent does or does not do.

(Zubov, 2015)

President Putin's deputy chief of staff Vyacheslav Volodin, speaking at the Valdai Club in October 2014, asserted: "If there is Putin, there is Russia: no Putin, no Russia." Volodin's "no Putin, no Russia" thesis was advanced in the context of post-Crimean annexation sanctions, a besieged fortress mentality narrative and a shift from legal–rational to historical and charismatic legitimation of Putin's political authority. This slogan highlighted that there was a relationship between the agency of Putin and structure of Russia, but how to understand it?

Putin has led Russia longer than Leonid Brezhnev (18 years) or Yuri Andropov, Konstantin Chernenko, Mikhail Gorbachev and Boris Yeltsin combined. Stalin ruled for 28 years, Putin is set for 36, passing in this respect at least, Catherine the Great's 34 years. Putin's presidency has promoted an official state discourse that builds bridges to a glorious past, based on a foundational myth of a rich thousand-year history. This narrative weaponizes history. If Moscow inherited the lands and peoples of *Kievan Rus'* and a golden thread of glory runs from the eighth to twelfth centuries, onto Muscovy, Imperial *Tsarist* and then the Soviet period to contemporary times, then Russia is an imperial center. As such, Russia has a historically legitimized sphere of influence, and any Russian revanchism represents a defensive move to restore the *status quo ante.* Understanding the relationships between President Putin and Russian elite strategic decision-makers and the wider economic and cultural (norms, customs, traditions and ideologies) structures that shape how those decisions are framed is an important key to unlocking Russian strategic behavior.

An alternative way to understand the relationship between structure and agency in contemporary Russia, one that does not dismiss Putin's agency and role as a systems-forming figure, is to think in terms of the "means and ends" dichotomy. Structures in the shape of an enduring tradition (norms, customs and ideologies) set national objectives (e.g. Russia as a regional hegemon and key global great power player) and so frame its foreign policy goals. But this is not a wholly deterministic proposition. Different Russian leaderships (agency) can redefine and highlight different examples as both positive and negative from this rich Russian tradition. Any given ruling regime can choose to identify or de-emphases particular conservative or liberal traits, values interests. The regime can enact policies that increase the power of the military but reduce economic development or vice versa: Russian interests and values under Catherine the Great were not synonymous with those under Alexander III; those of the Soviet Union and President Yeltsin's first-term administration were incompatible and irreconcilable. Ruling regimes can then select and determine the means and policies to achieve these goals. While every Russian president would see Russia as the arbiter and guardian of Ukraine's own national interest, President Putin chooses to annex Crimea and launch and support active subversion in the Donbas. President Yeltsin chose to recognize Ukrainian independence. Any Russian president would want Russia to have a voice and veto in global hotspots; President Putin sends an armed operational group to conduct coalitional expeditionary warfare in Syria to that end. President Medvedev chose not to intervene in Kyrgyzstan in April 2010 or Libya in 2011. Any Russian president wants parity and equality with the United States; for Putin, this translates into a discourse around a "new Cold War" and performative rhetoric ("knock your teeth out"), as for the next president co-equal status with the United States may be understood and expressed differently.

Russia should not be judged by Western standards, even if the United States constitutes its own strategic benchmark, and its own understanding of strategic relevance and avoiding pariah status is in reference to the West. Russia's own long-term development, the intrinsic logic of its historical evolution and, most importantly, how Russia views its own past (strategic empathy) must be the starting point of this investigation. A better understanding of Russian political and strategic thinking and behavior is essential to provide a valid framework through which to understand Russian foreign and security policy. To this end, we need to unpack the relationship between Russia's political and strategic culture and President Putin's operational code. This book addresses a number of themes at the heart of understanding Russian strategic behavior:

- What is the influence of the *Tsarist* and Soviet ideational political and strategic cultures on shaping "Putinism" and Putin's agency today?
- Given the undoubted influence of the weight of history, how might we characterize Putinism in terms of Russian governance practices and strategic behavior? Does Putin determine or does he shape strategic decisions and the decision-making process in Russia? How does his influence or direction occur?
- What are the particular decision-making processes that underpin Russian policy formulation and implementation? Who makes the decisions, where, when, how and why? What are the elements that contribute to President Putin's risk calculations? How can President Putin's "red lines" be discerned?
- What is the geostrategic reach of Russia? As Russia steps up its global engagement and increases its influence, how should we judge its statecraft – that is its ability to align its ways and means with its strategic objectives?

• Putin can run to 2036 after resetting the presidential term clock in 2020. What are the alternative power transition scenarios, and how might they stress-test our assumptions about power in Russia?

Chapter 2 defines the notion of strategic culture, identifying the relationship between structure, strategic culture, its drivers and Russian strategic behavior. This conceptual overview argues that the mind-set of Russia's national security decision-makers reflects Russia's political and strategic culture: "Russia's decision-making framework is bounded by an entirely different understanding of history, geography, social policy and relations between countries means that Moscow's decisions routinely surprise and dismay the West" (Giles, 2021, 25). Parallels in Russian history suggest continuities and Soviet legacy carry overs, especially with regard to the geopolitical mind-set of the Russian elite, the autocratic tradition with centralization of power; the sacralization and personification of power (the belief in a "Good *Tsar*") able to act as arbiter and mediator and so maintain an equilibrium and stability; the instrumentalization of repressive apparatus and military power; the presence of *de facto* dual power centers and competition between normative and prerogative procedures, rules and regulations. This chapter highlights the ability of those that own Russia and who run Russia to shape societal attitudes and how "the ways in which autocratic governance produces not just political behaviors but also more deeply engrained social incentives and preferences, which in turn lend internal coherence – and this durability – to authoritarian systems" (Greene, 2019, 182). It also stresses the importance of domestic determinants on Russian foreign policy and strategic culture (McFaul, 2020; Adomeit, 2019).

Chapter 3 examines the "inner logic" of *Tsarist* imperial history, focusing on the selective "lessons" that Russia's current elite draw from Russian history, and how past legacies and heritage are communicated to Russian society. In his June 2021 "Direct-Line" phone-in, President Putin noted:

> Some time ago, unfortunately, our common fatherland, the Soviet Union, fell apart. It is well known that the core of that common state was formed by historical Russia, the Russian Federation itself. As is well known, it lost almost half of its industrial potential, half of its economy, about 50%, about the same share of population and a significant part of territory. Those were important territories in terms of industry and the economy, infrastructurally developed territories, in which historical Russia invested its resources not just for decades but for centuries.
>
> *(BBC Monitoring, 2021b)*

President Putin, like *Tsars* before him, including proletarian *Tsars* in the Soviet period, faces the choice: modernize and change or stabilize and stay the same.

When examining Russia's political culture, three interlocking factors appear as constants that reinforce themselves and grow stronger through time: a return to great power status; a well-founded fear of instability and an understanding that respect is generated, ultimately, through fear. These "lessons" have been attributed to a number of factors, not least the fusion of history and geography, the development of the Russian economy, the emergence and consolidation of a service state, a strong leader defending a besieged fortress against external adversary's intent on destruction of the Russian people, their sacred beliefs and inalienable values.

The focus of Chapter 4 is the impact of Soviet legacies on the present, highlighting in particular domestic governance and foreign policy linkages and parallels between Stalin and Brezhnev and Putin. What are the Soviet influences on contemporary Russian political and strategic cultures? By 2024, President Putin will have led a system he himself has created for 24 years – this will fall exactly between the length of Stalin's and Brezhnev's reigns. In domestic terms, this chapter suggests that Putinism resembles the USSR of the 1970s under Leonid Brezhnev. Economic stagnation, a stability of cadres' (in effect, elite stagnation) policy and domestic political demobilization of the population are all apparent, and a neo-Brezhnevite tinge infects the body politic. We can also make comparisons with Joseph Stalin's USSR of the 1940s and early 1950s. In Russian foreign policy terms, a "sphere of influence" and balance of power thinking reflect a desire for a "Vienna system" projected to the global level and a "Yalta–Potsdam II" restoration along their northern, western and southern flanks. We can also observe military-patriotic mobilization of the population against externally directed threats and the formation of a cult of personality. In these respects, Putin's regime takes on a neo-Stalinist hue. The weight of history is an important structural factor, as Sergei Medvedev, author of *The Return of the Russian Leviathan*, notes:

> In the history of Russian statehood, there are periods of expansion and contraction of the empire, which take place at intervals of 30–50 years. In the 1980s, with the collapse of the USSR, there was a period of resignation and reform of Russian statehood, but from the 21st century onwards, "Russian Leviathan is again pouring out of the sea and trying to suppress the freedoms that have arisen over the years."
>
> *(Sprude and Medevdev, 2021; Medvedev, 2020)*

Indeed, Andrey Kozyerev, the Russian Federation's first foreign minister, concluded:

> After all the U.S.S.R. did not materialize out of thin air; it came in the wake of the former Russian Empire and bore many of its birthmarks. It will be long before many of those blemishes cease to affect the fate of those countries that have now inherited the expanses of the former U.S.S.R.
>
> *(Kozeyrev, 1992)*

Chapter 5 brings us to the contemporary period, noting continuities with the past in order to highlight the extent to which Putin and Putinism represent change from the past. The interplay between the two is represented by the Soviet anthem with new lyrics, the Russian tricolor flag and *Tsarist* eagles on the Kremlin's towers, with Lenin's mausoleum and simulated or imitative democratic institutions and market economy. Important differences with *Tsarist* and Soviet heritages, complete with their inherent structural flaws, can be identified. However central the Soviet legacy in shaping contemporary norms, attitude and worldview of Russian elites and society be, "Putinism" cannot simply be understood in terms of an amalgam or sum of Brezhnev and Stalin – stagnation at home and great power projection abroad – with a sprinkling of Andropov, a dash of Khrushchev and "anything but Gorbachev" to taste.

First, the economic context was transformed. While in the Soviet period, fluctuations in the currency markets were an irrelevance for the average citizen, today's international economic environment is one in which capitalism is the global default system, and the ruble and inflation rate responds to changes in the oil market and government policy. Second, unlike the Stalinist period with its purges and gulag archipelago, the scale, scope and style of repression in Putin's Russia are in no way comparable. Third, President Putin is much less restrained by checks and balances than Soviet leaders. Fourth, in an unprecedented break from Soviet and Russian historical past, every key sector and resource – from finance, to economics, the media, military, energy and foreign policy sectors – are controlled by the security services, not least oligarchs in the Kremlin entourage with security service backgrounds and the "combination of the new redistribution of property with a rather archaic ideology is a unique feature of Putin's regime" (Khvostunova, 2021).

This chapter also argues that the analytical construct of "hybrid state" has a better purchase on reality than "dual state" or even "patrimonial state." "Hybrid state" should not be confused with "hybrid war" or "hybrid regimes," which combine democratic forms and authoritarian practices (electoral authoritarianism), although these terms can be compatible. Hybrid state combines state legitimacy based on formal hierarchy with informal networked organizations, overseen by trusted custodians, gatekeepers and controllers of information and access to the president. The critical determinant of a person's ability to achieve preferred policy outcomes is not rank or institutional position but one's network position and connectedness to Putin, which itself is determined by political loyalty and utility to Putin – not simply friendship or past associations. Power in Russia is a measure of an individual's network connectedness to Putin (rather than his official position), and this reflects the individual's purpose-fulfilling value for the network.

By 2020/21, the hybrid authoritarian regime appeared to be superseded by a one that was gradually shrinking free space (culture, enlightenment, religion, morality and science), abolishing politics as an institutional realm and becoming more totalitarian in nature,

> with a monopoly of power by one party and ideology that is maintained by bodies of repression. Any dissenter is not an opponent with whom one

should debate and whose opinion should be heard, but an enemy and criminal to be eliminated if he does not surrender.

(Vishnevsky, 2021; Latynina, 2021)

While opposition to the state is criminalized and *de facto* constitutes "terrorism," *siloviki* takeover of the Federal Tax Service and Courts renders court rulings Kremlin directives, and the law can be applied selectively and retroactively. Russia is run by people who own it and seek to preserve their position. However, the lack of self-regulating institutions means that political infighting characterizes late Putinism. The need for Putin to balance elite factions and mediate intra-elite disputes over power, property and money is constant. Arbitration is complicated in the context of failing performance legitimacy.

Chapter 6 now turns to the question of how these national security decisions and the decision-making process work, focusing in on President Putin's observable operational code. An operational code consists of two sets of beliefs that structure and shape perception and diagnosis of how conflictual or cooperative one perceives the world to be (philosophical beliefs), and, given this, points to the acceptable courses of action, affordable tools with which to respond, and appropriate responses (instrumental beliefs). With regard to philosophical beliefs, one clear and recurrent feature is that Russian strategic calculation is based on poor threat analysis and understanding of the strategic environment. The notion of "Trojan Horses," "Fifth Columnists," "Color Revolutions" and a Russian opposition, which allegedly operates under "orders from the West," are the logically predestined outcomes of such thinking. So too is the fixation on great power status, with the United States as Russia's strategic benchmark, and hence the need to explain policy choices in terms of affirmation, validation, acknowledgment and the need for respect. These philosophical beliefs are very much shaped by Russia's strategic culture, which rests on a blurred distinction between war and peace (Jonsson, 2019) and internal and external threats, and the never-ending quest for status.

With regard to Putin's instrumental beliefs, we can discern three recurring features. First, Putin's understanding of risk, his perception of costs and benefits and tipping points determine when decisions are made and define the intent of the decisions. This goes to a defensive-reactive mentality. Russia is under siege; therefore, any action taken to counter or deter the siege can only be understood as being defensive and reactive, an attempt to uphold the status quo. A second feature is the issue of manual control (*ruchnoye upravleniye*) of Putin personally with only a small group of advisors, with few, if any checks and balances, making key strategic decisions that appear as improvised responses to changing circumstances. Third, a style of indirect interpretation and ambiguity characterizes the communication of the decisions. While the philosophical beliefs of national security decision-makers map onto the prevailing strategic culture, their instrumental beliefs are also shaped by what has been termed the "Code of Putinism" or "Putin's Code," that is the particular emotions, habits and ideas, which are shared by other members of Putin's team who are of his generation and background. Contemporary

Russian strategic behavior is generated by the fusion of its enduring strategic culture with particularities of President Putin's operational code.

Chapter 7 offers a statecraft assessment of Russia's global reach, a phenomenon that gathered speed after 2014 and post-Crimea sanctions. Russia's global activism is often characterized as opportunistic, transactional, all vision but no strategy. Russia has global ambitions and aspirations but lacks the resources to institutionalize gains and attain goals. Reality is somewhat different. First, Russia aims to be a sovereign or strategically autonomous great power with global reach. This aspiration has systemic consequences. Second, Russia seeks to promote a global system compatible with its interests and in opposition to the "totalitarian West," which Russia claims promotes one set of values and norms and one power – "one master, one sovereign," as President Putin asserted in 2007 – the United States. Thus, Russia's conception of world order is fundamentally incompatible with the interests of the United States, its friends and allies. Third, Russia seeks through linkage to leverage its global activism to break Russia's strategic isolation and increase support for Moscow's assertion of primacy and the strengthening of its own strategic depth in its neighborhood. Interestingly, over the first there decades of the post-Soviet period, Russia had first road tested many of its influence tools in its near and abroad, not least perfecting its use of corruption, kickbacks and access to render key interlocutors complicit and controllable. Russia now deploys these tools globally to shore up its position in its neighborhood. In terms of ways and means, Russia attains strategic relevance through hot-spot engagement, mediation efforts, presenting itself as an alternative partner to the United States (and China), as a sovereignty and security provider and economic collaborator. Increasingly, Russia uses engagement in one conflict to project power and influence into the next. Russia's construction of a global imaginary is work in progress, and "tactical globalism" allows for incremental gains at low cost.

Chapter 8 focuses on alternative power transition scenarios not to predict the future – this is mission impossible given the number of intervening variables – but to make explicit and then stress-test our assumptions about power and how it is exercised in Russia today, as elaborated in Chapter 5. To that end, this chapter first notes that President Putin had reset the presidential clock in January 2020 and was therefore likely to run for the "first" time in 2024, before it then identifies other alternative scenarios: "Putinism with Paramount Putin": *Densyaopinizatisitskya* Scenario or a "Kazakh way forward"; "Putinism with Partial Putin" or as an "Enhanced Brezhnev" Collective Leadership Scenario; "Putinism without Putin" or a "post-Stalin 1953–56" Scenario; "Neither Putin nor Putinism," or a "Liberal Dictatorship" Scenario and, "Neither Putin nor Putinism" or "Populist People Power 2011–12" Scenario. Putin-dictated scenarios suggest continuities in strategic culture and operational code. The "Collective Putin" or selectorate-led scenarios suggest strategic culture continuity but operational code change. The radical rupture from the past scenarios suggests that both strategic culture and operational code change, along with the current regime and political system. Continuity of Putin in power suggests continuity in foreign policy, but a successor, by definition, will be a weaker candidate. In less-controlled or even breakdown and "loss of control" scenarios, the risks of miscalculation and unintended escalation increase as Russian responses are less calibrated and coordinated. In addition, we note that institutions and organizations that constitute the regime have competing preferences. Though they are strategically aligned in support of Putin, they are tactically divided, with some adopting more statist and some more ideological stances.

In Chapter 9, rather than attempting to offer a unified field theory that accounts for Putin, Putinism and its practical expression in policies, practices and procedures in Russia, this chapter has three aims. First, it highlights the paradoxes that characterize Putin's Russia, exploring the tensions between stability and the need to develop and modernize. Despite the fact that Putin's popularity is high and he receives overwhelming societal and elite support, "Putinism" can only be considered sustainable if Putin's regime can manage the destabilizing gaps and contradictions that it itself generates. Second, it identifies the carriers of Russian strategic culture, their function in relationship to the use of force and their competitive goals. Although a succession crisis in 2024 appears to have been averted, can we speculate on other mini-crises, generated by tensions in the system, and how these may promote and advance or sideline and render redundant the different carriers of Russian strategic culture? It is in current elite self-interest to instrumentalize Russia's strategic culture to suggest that threats are ever present. After 21 years of power (and with a possible fifteen still to go), this is the most efficient and effective means of continuing to legitimize President Putin's political authority. The need to uphold the status quo in the name of stability compound dysfunctionality generates the very threats the system is designed to avoid. Russia is characterized by competing subcultures that promote their own future institutional relevance within a system that is full of paradoxes based on contradictions. The latter generates the crises the former will ineffectively address.

At the end, the chapter looks forward to 2036 and outlines three alternative world order paradigms: Russia's preferred and official future, a Global Concert of great powers; Russia's understanding of the current world order paradigm, U.S. neo-containment of Russia within a Cold War 2.0 paradigm and, a G-Zero world order. The book contends that a G-Zero world order best aligns with the hybrid nature of the Russian state, its strategic culture and president's operational code. Russia's strategic behavior is a function of its strategic culture and Putin's operational code. A G-Zero world order, the book concludes, stabilizes an anti-fragile Russia, which, paradoxically, is vulnerable to tranquility.

Selected bibliography

Adomeit, Hannes. 2019. "Domestic Determinants of Russia's anti-Western Campaign." London: Institute for Statecraft. May 24, 2019. https://medium.com/@instituteforstatecraft.

Albats, Yevgenia. 2021. "Chasing Muons in Geneva." *The Moscow Times*. June 23, 2021. www. themoscowtimes.com/2021/06/23/chasing-muons-in-geneva-a74315.

Allison, Graham, and Dimitri K. Simes. 2015. "Russia and America: Stumbling to War." *Text*. *The National Interest*. April 20, 2015. https://nationalinterest.org/feature/russia-america-stumbling-war-12662.

Arquilla, John, and Nicole Peterson, eds. 2019. *Russian Strategic Intentions*. Boston, MA: NSI, Inc. https://nsiteam.com/social/wp-content/uploads/2019/05/SMA-TRADOC-Russian-Strategic-Intentions-White-Paper-PDF-1.pdf.

BBC Monitoring. 2021a. "Russian Minister Accuses West of Trying to Influence Upcoming Elections." July 9, 2021.

———. 2021b. "Putin Mourns USSR's Collapse." *Rossiya 1 TV*, Moscow. June 30, 2021.

BBC Report. 2021. "Russian Defence Minister Warns of 'New Confrontation' in the World." *BBC Monitoring*. June 23, 2021.

Belton, Catherine. 2020. *Putin's People: How the KGB Took Back Russia and Then Took on the West*. London: William Collins.

Bershidsky, Leonid. 2018. "Putin Wants Modern Weapons, Not a Modern Russia – Bloomberg." *Bloomberg Opinion*. March 1, 2018. www.bloomberg.com/opinion/articles/2018-03-01/putin-s-speech-he-wants-modern-weapons-not-a-modern-russia.

Charap, Samuel, Elina Treyger, and Edward Geist. 2019. "Understanding Russia's Intervention in Syria." *RAND Corporation*. 2019. www.rand.org/pubs/research_reports/RR3180.html.

Eleftheriou-Smith, Loulla-Mae. 2015. "Fox News 'Expert' Thinks It's Time to Start 'Killing Russians', Russia Disagrees." *The Independent*. September 23, 2015. www.independent.co.uk/news/world/americas/fox-news-expert-claims-only-way-turn-tide-ukraine-us-start-killing-russians-10110558.html.

Gaddy, Clifford G., and Fiona Hill. 2015. "How Aiding the Ukrainian Military Could Push Putin into a Regional War." *Brookings* (blog). February 6, 2015. www.brookings.edu/opinions/how-aiding-the-ukrainian-military-could-push-putin-into-a-regional-war/.

Galeotti, Mark. 2021. "Moscow Turns Up the Volume Over HMS Defender." *The Moscow Times*. June 25, 2021. www.themoscowtimes.com/2021/06/24/moscow-turns-up-the-volume-over-hms-defender-a74326.

Giles, Keir. 2021. "Russia and the West Want the Same Thing." In *Myths and Misconceptions in the Debate on Russia: How They Affect Western Policy, and What Can Be Done*, 23–27. London: Chatham House. www.chathamhouse.org/2021/05/myths-and-misconceptions-debate-russia.

Greene, Samuel A. 2019. "Homo-Post-Sovieticus: Reconstructing Citizenship in Russia." *Social Research: An International Quarterly* 86 (1): 181–202.

Interview with Nikolai Patrushev, Secretary of the Russian Security Council. 2021. "Without Fear and Reproach." *Rossiyskaya Gazeta Website*. May 31, 2021. https://rg.ru/2021/05/31/patrushev-raskryl-neizvestnye-podrobnosti-zhenevskoj-vstrechi-s-sallivanom.html.

Jonsson, Oscar. 2019. *The Russian Understanding of War: Blurring the Lines Between War and Peace*. Washington, DC: Georgetown University Press. ISBN: 978-1-62616-734-6.

Kashin, Oleg. 2016. "It Will Be Fun and Scary. What to Expect From New Russian Nation." *Slon*. November 1, 2016.

Khvostunova, Olga. 2021. "Lev Gudkov: 'The Unity of the Empire in Russia Is Maintained by Three Institutions: The School, the Army, and the Police'." *Institute of Modern Russia*. May 3, 2021. https://imrussia.org/en/opinions/3278-lev-gudkov-.

Kolesnikov, Andrei. 2019. "How 'Loyalty' Ensnared Russia's Journalists and Media Owners." *Carnegie Moscow Center*. May 28, 2019. https://carnegie.ru/commentary/79206.

Kovalev, Andrei. 2017. "Putin's Hand Can Clearly Be Seen in the Chaos of a Destabilized West." *Newsweek.* September 3. https://www.newsweek.com/putins-hand-can-clearly-be-seen-chaos-destabilized-west-658667.

Kozeyrev, Andrey. 1992. "Russia: A Chance for Survival." *Foreign Affairs* 71 (2): 1–16.

Latynina, Yulia. 2021. "Three-Letter Government." *Novaya Gazeta.* May 1, 2021.

"Lavrov Accused the US and the EU of Planting Totalitarianism." 2021. *RIA Novosti.* May 7, 2021. https://ria.ru/20210507/totalitarizm-1731411397.html.

Lavrov, Sergei. 2021. "The Law, the Rights and the Rules." *Ministry of Foreign Affairs Website,* Moscow. June 27, 2021.

Lewis, David. 2020. *Russia's New Authoritarianism: Putin and the Politics of Order.* Edinburgh: Edinburgh University Press.

McFaul, Michael. 2020. "Putin, Putinism, and the Domestic Determinants of Russian Foreign Policy." *International Security* 45 (2): 95–139. https://doi.org/10.1162/.

Medvedev, Sergej Aleksandrovič. 2020. *The Return of the Russian Leviathan.* Cambridge: Polity Press.

"Meeting of the Russian Pobeda (Victory) Organising Committee." 2021. *President of Russia.* May 20, 2021. http://en.kremlin.ru/events/president/news/65618.

National Security Strategy. 2021. "National Security Strategy of the Russian Federation." *President of the Russian Federation Website.* July 2, 2021. http://publication.pravo.gov.ru/Document/View/0001202107030001?index=0&rangeSize=1.

Oliker, Olga, Michael J. McNerney, and Lynn E. Davis. 2015. "NATO Needs a Comprehensive Strategy for Russia." *RAND Corporation.* March 25, 2015. www.rand.org/pubs/perspectives/PE143.html.

Pfifer, Steven, and Strobe Talbott. 2015. "Ukraine Needs America's Help." *Washington Post.* January 29, 2015. www.washingtonpost.com/opinions/ukraine-needs-more-help-from-the-west/2015/01/29/462b1ea4-a71b-11e4-a7c2-03d37af98440_story.html.

Putin, Vladimir, Nataliya Gevorkyan, Natalya Timakova, and Andrei Kolesnikov. 2000. *First Person: An Astonishingly Frank Self-Portrait by Russia's President Vladimir Putin.* New York: PublicAffairs.

Seligman, Lara, and Andrew Desiderio. 2021. "Russian Spy Unit Suspected of Directed-Energy Attacks on U.S. Personnel – POLITICO." *Politico.* May 10, 2021. www.politico.com/news/2021/05/10/russia-gru-directed-energy-486640.

Sengupta, Kim. 2016. "Former Nato Commander's New Book Predicts Invasion of Baltic as Putin Bids to 'Make Russia a Great Power Again' | The Independent." *Independent.* May 18, 2016. www.independent.co.uk/news/world/europe/former-nato-commander-s-new-book-predicts-invasion-baltic-putin-bids-make-russia-great-power-again-a7036911.html.

Shagina, Maria. 2021. "Don't Underestimate Importance of Joe Biden's First Sanctions Move." *The Moscow Times.* April 27, 2021. www.themoscowtimes.com/2021/04/27/dont-underestimate-importance-of-joe-bidens-first-sanctions-move-a73754.

Shlapak, David A., and Michael Johnson. 2016. "Reinforcing Deterrence on NATO's Eastern Flank: Wargaming the Defense of the Baltics." *RAND Corporation.* https://www.rand.org/pubs/research_reports/RR1253.html.

Sprude, Viesturs, and Sergei Medvedev. 2021. "There Is a Return to Public Control and Efforts to Celebrate 9 May Continuously." *Latvijas Avize.* May 9, 2021.

Vishnevsky, Boris. 2021. "The New Disqualified." *Novaya Gazeta.* May 6, 2021. https://novayagazeta.ru/articles/2021/05/06/novye-lishentsy.

"What You Need to Know about Russia's 2021 National Security Strategy." *Meduza.* July 5, 2021. https://meduza.io/en/feature/2021/07/05/what-you-need-to-know-about-russia-s-2021-national-security-strategy.

Wigell, Mikael. 2021. "Democratic Deterrence: How to Dissuade Hybrid Interference." *The Washington Quarterly* 44 (1): 49–67. https://doi.org/10.1080/0163660X.2021.1893027.

Wood, Andrew. 2019. "Putinist Rule Minus Putin?" *The American Interest.* July 29, 2019. www.the-american-interest.com/2019/07/29/putinist-rule-minus-putin/.

Yegorov, Ivan. 2021. "Where US is and Where Black Sea Is." *Rossiyskaya Gazeta.* April 14, 2021. https://rg.ru/2021/04/14/patrushev-rasskazal-ob-opasnyh-provokaciiah-kieva-i-ssha-u-granic-rossii.html.

Zapesotsky, Alexander. 2021. "Why It Is Necessary to Expel US Ambassador from Moscow." *Moskovsky Komsomolets.* April 20, 2021. www.mk.ru/politics/2021/04/20/pochemu-nuzhno-bylo-vygnat-iz-moskvy-posla-ssha.html.

Zubov, Mikhail. 2015. "Fifteen Years: A Different Putin." *Moskovsky Komsomolets.* March 26, 2015. https://russian.rt.com/article/90340.

Zygar, Mikhail. 2016. *All the Kremlin's Men: Inside the Court of Vladimir Putin.* New York: PublicAffairs.

2

RUSSIAN STRATEGIC CULTURE

Conceptualization and evolution

Introduction

Is Putin running Russia or is Russia running Putin? Does the political West have a Putin problem or a Russia problem? In other words, are confrontational relations with Russia tied to the person, personality and policy preferences of Putin himself, in his presidential capacity as Russia's strategic decision-maker? If so, stronger more cooperative interactions between Russia and the West can be expected after 2024 or 2036. If not, then whether Putin departs the presidency or not, we can assume that the preexisting structural conditions, which shape Putin's thinking and range of policy options and courses of action, continue to be decisive. As a result, relations with Russia under any successor will remain the same, if not deteriorate further.

"Strategic culture" provides a conceptual frame to address these questions. The concept highlights the relationship between foreign and security policy pronouncements and written doctrines and patterns of Russia's actual strategic behavior and its use of strategic instruments. In essence, a focus on strategic culture highlights Russia's geography, its national historical experiences, and political and organizational cultures (multiple competing subcultures). There is a general consensus that

> Russian strategic culture is a product of several key factors: a long history of wars and adversarial relations with other European powers; an open geographic landscape that puts a premium on strategic depth; and an elite given to embracing a narrative of implacable Western hostility toward Russia.
>
> *(Rumer and Sokolsky, 2020)*

In particular, we can explore how these elements are understood and made to matter by those who draw lessons and control the propagation of interpretations. States are not simply

> functionally undifferentiated units that seek power to optimize their utility" but "elites socialized in different strategic cultures will make different choices

DOI: 10.4324/9780429261985-2

when placed in similar situations. Since cultures are attributes of and vary across states, similar strategic realities will be interpreted differently"

(Johnson, 1995)

Conceptualizing strategic culture

When seeking the genesis of the concept "strategic culture," we can start with Colin Gray (1971). Gray examined the relationship between nuclear weapons and statecraft. He focused on how the concepts of, for example, escalation and escalation ladders, deterrence, limited war, arms control and disarmament, first and second strike and assured destruction were understood by U.S. strategists. Was the rational-actor logic that informed U.S. behavior globally valid and timeless, shared by all adversaries, or did cultural explanations center on fundamental, distinct and particular national histories, values, politics and traditions? If so, did these different mental constructions and contexts matter (Heuser, 2007)?

Building on the insights of Gray (1971), Jack Snyder (1977) developed the term "strategic culture" in an analysis of how American and Soviet competing strategic cultures influenced nuclear rivalry, strategic thinking and decision-making. Snyder adapted the definition of "political culture" offered by Almond and Verba (1963) to account for strategic behavior. A political culture is the totality of the unconscious, widely and commonly held political ideas and basic norms (i.e. rules, regulations and behavior that are considered normal, acceptable and appropriate), beliefs, values, habits, emotions and assumptions that are unique to a given group or country. Snyder argued that a distinctive Soviet strategic culture provided the context for understanding the intellectual, institutional and strategic-cultural determinants that bind Soviet decision-making in a crisis, as well as the behavioral propensities that would motivate and constrain Soviet leaders.

Strategic culture is conventionally characterized as the set of beliefs, assumptions, attitudes, norms, worldviews and patterns of habitual behavior held by strategic decision-makers regarding the political objectives of war and the best way to achieve them. Snyder defined it as "the sum total of ideas, conditioned emotional responses, and patterns of habitual behaviour that members of a national strategic community have acquired through instruction or imitation and share with each other" (Snyder, 1977), which reflect a more generalized understanding as to which coercive responses to threats are most appropriate and effective.

A state's strategic culture is influenced by a number of factors, including distinct cognitive styles or reasoning traits, preferences in ways of waging war, the structure of a given military system and its leadership, the role of technology and approaches to the development of military knowledge, weapons' procurement and organization. Reasoning styles are shaped by differences between societies in their social structures, communication styles and time orientations. These three differences produce decision-making that is on a continuum. The continuum falls between holistic–dialectic deductive field-dependent reasoning that finds explanations through looking at implicit and indirect relationships between focal points in a given field and logical–analytical inductive reasoning that explains behavior by looking at direct and explicit relationships (Aristotelean/Anglo-Saxon thinking). The former reasoning is found in high context hierarchical and collectivist group-based interdependent societies and the latter in more fragmented and individualistic societies. Studies show scientists from different cultural backgrounds approach the same given problem differently and come to different conclusions (Adamsky, 2010, 20, ftn 17). For this reason, the holistic–dialectical reasoning style is better able and predisposed to recognizing emergent RMA ("serendipity effect'), and the latter less able (Adamsky, 2010, 22).

Alistair Ian Johnson (1995) argues that the weight of subjective and deeply rooted formative histories and experiences, geography and philosophical, political, cultural and cognitive characteristics of the state and its elites, combined with more objective ahistorical realities centered on the external context (e.g. polarity, the distribution of capabilities and technological advances), constitute a range of structural factors that shape a state's strategic preferences. Strategic preferences reflect historically rooted core assumptions about most effective options to address threats. These structural factors set national interest and core objectives and so frame foreign policy goals. Structure creates the paradigm within which agency operates.

Ruling regimes can select and determine the means and policies to achieve these goals. Different elites are socialized within different cultures, educational systems and military and security institutions, which ensure that their responses to different external threats will vary significantly. Different elites will make different choices when faced with the same context, as they will understand the significance of the same strategic reality differently: "So the problem for culturalists is to explain similarities in strategic behavior across varied strategic cultures. Conversely, the problem for structuralists is to explain differences in strategic behavior across strategic cultures when structural conditions are constant" (Johnson, 1995, 35). Strategic culture provides a distinct and critical explanation for the way different groups of people think and act when it comes to the use of force. Cultural, ideational and normative influences explain the motivations and causes of state behavior and that of their leaders. Thus,

> strategic culture is compatible with notions of limited rationality (where strategic culture simplifies reality), with process rationality (where strategic culture defines ranked preferences or narrows options), and with adaptive rationality (where historical choices, analogies, metaphors, and precedents are invoked to guide choice).
>
> (Johnson, 1995, 34)

An opposing view advanced by Colin Gray (1999) holds that it is important to study strategic culture as it provides a useful causal and discursive context for understanding decisions but does not dictate strategic behavior: 'other domestic and external variables' – for example dominant ideational beliefs, political and physical geography, as well as the material (economic and military) balance of power and structure of the international system – also shape behavior. These structures shape an understanding among the elite and society as to the national interest, long-term goals and foreign policy objectives of any given state. Thus, as different states wage war and make different strategic decisions in the same kinds of situations, the rational actor model does not offer a full explanation of state behavior.

How do we discern the nature of a given state's strategic culture? We can analyze its strategic guidelines set out within official documents (e.g. an NSS, Military Doctrine or Foreign Policy Concept) and identify the agreed national security threats against which coercive force could be used, references to concepts and capabilities to address these threats, relevant institutional machinery that highlights a capacity to act and the norms that give coercive action legitimacy. This is a starting point. More broadly, official and unofficial discourse can identify the wider worldview of key elites and how they interpret events in the world, including speeches at events such as the general assembly of the Academy of Military Science, Ministry of Defense Collegium or Putin's annual address to the Federation Assembly. We need then to identify real-life examples of strategic action to determine whether documented official words and stated intent match actual deeds and outcomes. With regard to threats against which to act, we can distinguish between two types in the Russian context: officially recognized and declared pro-forma threats identified in official documents and foreign policy pronouncements and even popular propaganda shows on TV and actual threats to the corporate interests, values and culture of carriers/keepers and their role, status and function and power relative to other political players and institutional actors. The two sets of threats are not necessarily synonymous or even compatible with each other. Mapping change over time reveals the evolution of that culture.

Grand strategy is long term, addresses the state's highest priorities and utilizes all spheres of statecraft (military, diplomatic and economic) and all resources (Silove, 2018). The development of "new concepts, strategies and doctrines that attempt to frame plans in a long-term horizon, to 2020 and beyond" (Monaghan, 2013), supported by a planning process (Cooper, 2012), is indicative of the existence of strategy. An effective grand strategy suggests a coherent, balanced and holistic approach. Grand strategy is a pattern of consistent behavior over time that is the result of grand strategic choices, a set of ideas, organizing or overarching principles, detailed plans (linking means to ends), policies, values, goals and tradeoffs designed to advance state's most important interests. In Russia's case, these interests tend to center on elite security, upholding Russia sovereignty and defending territorial integrity, even while exercising an order producing and managerial role in its self-declared sphere of influence (a hinterland over which Russia has gravitational pull). Even as Russia's power is increasingly mono-dimensional (military-nuclear) compared to other centers of global power, Russia still maintain a voice and veto in global hotspots thorough mediation, geopolitical arbitrage or adopting a spoiler role. Russia repositions itself as a great power in an emerging global order, with an entente or alliance with China, a military cooperation-based pivot to Africa, the Middle East and the Arctic.

We can infer the existence of organizing principles from the purposive efforts and activities of state agents, their statements and behavior ('what leaders think and want' and shared strategic vision). Given 'money is policy' and 'personnel is policy', decisions concerning budgetary and staffing allocations reflect priorities. To give an example, Peter I's actions are said to have spoken for themselves – we can see through the directed action and behavior of state instruments that he sought 'hegemony within the Heartland' (Le Donne, 2003, 6). President Putin's actions since 2014 (perhaps even 2007) can also be said to speak for themselves. But what are they saying: that stability in Russia and a sense of security at home can only be attained through Russia exercising strategic influence over neighbors – through the export of instability if needs be? We can infer intent from observed behavior, actions, statements, policies or plans. On the basis of official Russian discourse and foreign policy practice, the strategic goals of Putin appear to be twofold. First, Putin insists that Russia be acknowledged as a strategically independent, autonomous actor in the international system. Second, Russia seeks to uphold its exceptional great power identity and the status, honor, respect, prestige and equality this secures. Achieving the first two goals enables the third and most important: internal stability, elite status quo, and Putin's continuity in power in Russia.

However, multiple factors may account for them, and this raises the problem of equifinality: how certain can we be that we have inferred the real causes of a demonstrated pattern of behavior? Thus, while we may identify a Russian grand strategy and strategic goals, the causes and drivers of that strategy may be misidentified. In addition, with regard to Russian grand strategy under Putin, it did not emerge fully formed in 2000 but evolved organically in an *ad hoc* manner. It did not adhere to a closely held rigid strategic blueprint. At the end, strategic culture is not coterminous with military culture, though Russia's strategic culture is an amalgamation of military culture ('war-fighting') and bureaucratic culture (Kofman, 2017). Moreover, given Russia's political culture itself is heavily securitized, supporting the notion of Russia itself as constituting a counterintelligence state, and given the military-strategic culture is heavily bureaucratized, the blurring and overlap between political and strategic cultures in Russia make distinctions harder to sustain. Strategic culture is not unitary. It consists of multiple cultural identities, including public, political and military cultures, and the organizational cultures of the bearers or keepers of national strategic culture.

In terms of the word "coercive force," a broad understanding could include not just the use of conventional or nuclear coercive force by the Russian military against external state actors but might include three other dimensions. First is the use of sub-conventional shadow strategic proxy forces alongside the conventional in foreign policy. GRU Unit 29155 is primarily responsible for sabotage, acts of terrorism and contract killings in foreign countries. Since 2018, it has been headed by Admiral Igor Kostyukov, and "his direct manager is Gen Valery Gerasimov, chief of the General Staff, and Sergei Shoigu, the defence minister. Above them is only the president. As the saying goes, the trio plans, the fourth executes" (Dapkus, 2021). Second is the use of conventional and even sub-conventional coercive force against internal dissent and opposition. Third is the threat of the use of force. As Sergei Medvedev noted with regard to "unfriendly states" concept that Russia developed in April 2021:

> The Kremlin wants to demonstrate that it can use such a "stick". This does not mean that it will be used. It is a maximisation of risk, threat and uncertainty policies. That is the main thing the Kremlin can do now.
>
> *(Sprude and Medvedev, 2021)*

The notion of "strategic" use should focus on the intended outcome and impact of the use of force in that we would expect outcomes to be long term, be directed toward Russia's highest priorities and utilize if necessary all resources. The impact or outcome would likely maintain or change the strategic balance and so shape the strategic environment.

Strategic historical continuities

Like all cultures, Russian strategic culture reflects both long-standing historical elements that prove resistant to change and contemporary imperatives that emerge from shifts in the external and domestic environment. The dominant norms, attitudes and assumptions are embedded in a cultural matrix and can evolve and change, but they often do so only slowly, unless impacted by a major internal or external crisis such as war, revolution and crisis: 1598–1613 (Time of Troubles), 1917–1920 (Revolution and Civil War) and 1989–1991 (revolutions and collapse of the Soviet Union). The latter – the direct impact of the Soviet legacy – created an oven-ready foreign policy agenda for the Yeltsin administration, one President Putin still addresses (Kramer, 2019–20; Adomeit, 1982). Despite Russia's often cataclysmic history, Russian strategic culture has maintained at least six major inter-enabling elements that demonstrate strong continuity to the present day.

First, Russia insists that it plays a primary role in international relations as a 'great power'. Russian contemporary national security decision-makers argue that a rules-based balance of power system, exemplified by the Congress of Vienna (1815) and the Yalta–Potsdam conferences (1945), brought stability, predictability and peace to international relations, as Russia in the process twice saved Europe from itself. This basic premise that Russia was, is and must remain a 'great power' was widely accepted across the political spectrum. In 2000, Putin asserted in an interview that "Russia is not claiming a Great Power status. It is a Great Power by virtue of its huge potential, its history and its culture." He concluded that this was an existential question for Russia: "Either Russia will be great, or it will not be at all" (Shevtsova, 2003, 175). This advocacy of 'greatpowerness' is popular and translates into a willingness to use military power, the retention of a sphere of influence and a preference for bilateral relations with other major powers over multilateral institutions. At a "Direct Line" question-and-answer session, President Putin referenced Alexander III's famous dictum:

> I would like to remind you Alexander III, our emperor, once said that Russia has just two allies, the armed forces and the navy. In a message addressed to his son he warned that everybody feels scared at the vastness of Russia.
>
> *("Putin Agrees with Emperor,"* 2015)

Today, Putin ensures that Russia's power is ultimately predicated on maintaining an independent nuclear triad and modernized conventional forces. As Dmitry Kiselev, a propagandist on state TV Channel 1, pointedly remarked: "Russia is the only country in the world that is realistically capable of turning the United States into radioactive dust" (Kelly, 2014).

If, historically, great powers boasted empires, today they exercise ideological, economic, and influence over these residual hinterlands. These spheres create distance and buffer space between the great powers, so avoiding great power war. Russia's sphere of influence or "privileged interest" highlights a two-tier Russian understanding of statehood (sovereignty and territorial integrity): great powers have strategic autonomy; lesser states that fall in their orbits have limited sovereignty. Relations between each tier are negotiated, contested and subject to change. David Lewis suggests that for Russia, spheres of influence are viewed as spatial zones within which three threats should be countered: the threat that states might join foreign military alliances or – in some cases – economic blocs, the threat of the establishment of permanent foreign military bases or operations and the threat of political interference that undermines regime stability (Lewis, 2021). As a result, liberal democratic ideologies cannot flourish, while authoritarian ideologies can thrive.

Contemporary authoritarian governance practices in post-Soviet space are inter-enabling, using for example regional international organizations such as the Collective Security Treaty Organization, Eurasia Economic Union and Shanghai Cooperation Council to diffuse a common worldview and share learning and best authoritarian practice among the state members and their regime elites. Lewis posits this as a 'Moscow Consensus', a set of norms and practices with takers in post-Soviet space and beyond. A 'sovereign leader' is supported by imitation-independent institutions such as the media (which is state-owned and controlled) and state-funded civil society. Hard power instruments, such as the intelligence services, can enforce a 'sovereign leader's' arbitration and mediation efforts. A 'sovereign leader's' acceptance of extra-territorial practices insulates "his" elite from domestic protests, enabling the leader to retain support within a *sistema* – the fusion of business and political elites (Lewis, 2016). This geopolitical sphere of interest can be imagined variously as a *Russkii mir* ('Russian World'), a new post-sovereign cultural and civilizational space; as "Eurasia" encompassed as the supranational governance and regulatory frameworks (Eurasian Economic Union model) and as a militarized imperialist anti-Western space subject to Russian coercive control or as the echoes of a 'Post-Soviet Space 2.0', based on Belarus, Abkhazia, South Ossetia, the Donetsk People's Republic (DNR) and Luhansk People's Republic (LNR), and Transnistria and potentially even Kyrgyzstan.

President Putin has stated that Russian borders do not end anywhere. Russia, though, views and values different geographical space and the risks and dangers associated with it, differently. These spatial imaginaries provide cognitive frames that filter information and provide meaning for events, while legitimizing particular policy decisions. They play an important role in asserting boundaries between "them" and "us," thus constructing and shaping national identities constituted by difference (Lewis, 2018, 2021). What are these different strategic spaces? Russia constructs and engages with five "spatial imaginaries." First is Belarus and Ukraine as part of an East Slavic Orthodox foundational core of "one people," one language, one history, one culture and one religion. They are "territories of historical Russia," not independent sovereign states; as such, they constitute the central to core non-negotiable national interest, over which Russia will go to war to prevent loss. Second, the wider hinterland of former Soviet space, over which Russia should have influence, demonstrates that Russia is a center of global power in a multi-polar world order. In 2021, Putin codified a *de facto* doctrine of limited sovereignty in his July 12 "historical" article and July 13 interview "On the Historical Unity of Russians and Ukrainians" (Putin, 2021b, 2021c). Though marred by presentism and phobias, the thrust of Putin's thinking is clear: the post-Soviet settlement is illegitimate and that "anti-Russian platform" states (states that create "problems or threats to Russia") would never host foreign bases or join military alliances unless they themselves were foreign controlled or influenced. As Putin stated at the Valdai Club meeting in October 2021:

> One gets the impression that the Ukrainian people are not allowed and will not be allowed to legally form the bodies of power that would uphold their interests. The people there are even afraid to respond to polls. They are scared, because the small group that has appropriated the victory in the fight for independence holds radical political views. And that group actually runs the country, regardless of the name of the current head of state.
>
> *('Text of Report', 2021).*

As such, in Putin's view, these states are not and so should not be treated as sovereign. Third, Europe's function in Russian strategic identity is to validate Russia's exceptional civilizational identity as a besieged fortress and alternative governance model. This narrative argues that Europe consists of U.S. vassal states, puppet states incapable of strategic autonomy. The fourth imaginary is the United States. From a Russian perspective, its own nuclear triad gives it parity, equality and reciprocity with the United States. The United States serves as Russia's strategic benchmark, and because of its own great power status, the United States represents for Russia a "dignified foe." The power-status disparities between Russia and the United States and Russia's perception of the leader-subordinate nature of transatlantic relations make sense of Russia's strategic calculus. Russian status-based activism and presence in the fifth imaginary, the wider globe, evidence its first-tier global power.

Second, elites and society have a shared understanding that Russia can transition from stability to collapse, disorder and anarchy extremely quickly, that the sources of instability are multiple and that when Russia is weak, external actors take advantage. *Tsar* Ivan III (1462–1505) tripled the size of Muscovy in the late fifteenth and early sixteenth century, and under the reign of Ivan IV (1533–1584), Muscovy could be considered a paradoxical predator state and prey nation, in that the state was strong enough to terrorize society, but too weak to provide protection from external threats. This strategic vulnerability was compounded by geography, with Moscow easily reached over accessible steppe-land, the ubiquitous "boundless Russia plain." V.O. Klyuchevskiĭ, a historian of the Moscow School writing in the late imperial period, noted that in the seventeenth century, Russia under the early Romanovs was constantly invaded – the Polish-Lithuanian Commonwealth, Swedish empire, Tartars, Ching dynasty and Ottoman empire all launched attacks, with only thirteen years recorded in that century when Russia was at peace. War and foreign invasion were the norm, and in their most extreme form caused chaos and anarchy in Russia. Regime implosion (1598–1613) resulted in foreign troops (Polish) occupying and burning the Kremlin complex in the heart of Moscow (1611), while Sweden annexed and then held the city of Novgorod until 1618 (Klyuchevskiĭ, 1970). This trauma inculcated the belief that the end of a regime results in a cataclysm rather than providing a source of hope and renewal and that it would be foolish indeed to trade the uncertainties of change with the certitudes of order. The Cossack peasant rebellion of Stepan Razin (1670–71) and Yemelyan Pugachev (1773–75) and the Siberian revolt in the twentieth century provided a different source of insecurity. The persistence of crises and catastrophes has lowered Russia's tolerance for instability.

Following the October 1917 Russian Revolution, the Russian Civil War witnessed 'Whites' versus 'Reds', with an Anglo-American expeditionary force landed in Archangel while Japanese, Chinese and U.S. military contingents occupied the Maritime Provinces in the Russian Far East. The lesson was clear: internal weakness encouraged external intervention. During the Cold War, Soviet leaderships firmly understood that the United States sought to destroy the Soviet Union and that the 'Dulles' Plan' would achieve this end (Allen Dulles was head of the CIA). According to this plan, the United States would subvert and influence a 'fifth column' within the USSR to undermine Soviet values and morals and ultimately betray the majority (Snegovaya, 2016). At the end of the Cold War, while serving in Dresden between 1985 and 1990 as a counter-intelligence officer in the KGB's Chief Second Directorate, President Putin was himself a 'first person' witness to the speed at which order in the German Democratic Republic (GDR) descended into chaos, as the most seemingly stable and Stalinist of the Soviet satellites crumbled and fell in 1989. As Putin himself remarked: "It was hard to imagine that such abrupt changes could take hold in the GDR. No one could ever have imagined it! And we didn't know how it would end" (Putin et al., 2000). The prevailing notion is that throughout Russian history:

Russia practically has not lost any wars against its opponents until its destruction began from within. Our enemy understands this well. To resist Russia by military means is too difficult for them. Therefore, the informational and psychological impact on the enemy now comes to the fore.

(Bozhyeva, 2021)

Third, respect for Russian great power status ensures stability, and respect is ultimately generated through a healthy regard, even fear, of Russian power. President Putin's passionate "Listen to us now!" *crie de couer*, at his address to the Federal Assembly on 1 March 2018, when he unveiled five new weapons systems that could destroy the United States, held an underlying message: "Love me or I will punch you in the face" (BBC Monitoring, 2018). Putin unveiled a monument to *Tsar* Alexander III of Russia at Livadiya, the *Tsar*'s summer palace near the Crimean resort of Yalta, extolling Alexander III as an ideal leader:

His contemporaries called him the Peacemaker *Tsar*. But as [*tsarist* minister] Sergei Yuryevich Vitte noted, the 13 years of peace that he gave to Russia were not the result of concessions but of his just and unshakeable firmness. He considered that a strong, sovereign, independent state should rely not only on economic and military might, but also on tradition.

According to Putin, Alexander III also thought that "no progress is possible without respect for your history, culture and spiritual values" ("Putin Unveils Tsar," 2017; Aptekar, 2017). While in the late imperial period, Russia's only two allies may have been its "army and its fleet" in the words of *Tsar* Alexander III, today Russian power is ultimately predicated on maintaining an independent nuclear triad and modernized conventional forces. The pervasiveness of military themes, military patriotism and militaristic policies in the state's framing of Russianness helps forge social consensus, though there are limitations to its unifying effects (Bækken, 2021). Thus, the role of fear in generating respect is a central feature of Russian strategic culture. Sergey Medvedev, a political science professor at the National Research University Higher School of Economics, television host and columnist, contends that Russia's most successful export commodity was not hydrocarbon energy but fear. Russia is not afraid that neighbors are afraid of Russia; it fears that its neighbors do not fear Russia (Novoprudskiy, 2017). As Alexander Golts notes:

The main problem is that for three centuries (with short intervals from 1860–1880, 1905–1914, 1925–1935, 1987–2014) the primary, if not the only mission of the Russian state was to sustain a huge military machine . . . Russia practically did not know any other way of concentrating state resources than military mobilization. A genetic link between the decrees of Peter the Great, the military settlements of Alexander I, Trotsky's labor armies, and the Soviet construction battalions is undeniable. For three centuries, a man was interested in the Russian state first of all as a future soldier and second of all as a source of funds to support the army.

(Golts, 2019)

This fear of not being feared helps account for perception differences: Russia genuinely understands its actions as defensive, while external actors interpret them as being offensive.

Fourth, Russia's view of space is conditioned by threat perception and strategic psychology born to strategic vulnerability and anxiety. Russia's strategic culture has been shaped by the indefensibility of its natural borders, resulting in a fear of external intervention and a complex dynamic between offense and defense that has characterized Russian military campaigns for centuries. Russia's imperial past, ethno-linguistic ties and the lack of clarity over Russia's borders have all contributed to a complex relationship between Russia and its neighbors and an unwillingness to consider its post-1991 frontiers as necessarily legally binding. According to this lens,

> Ukraine and Belarus are artificial and inferior states, whose independent existence is only officially justified if they are strategically subordinate to Moscow. The drift of Ukraine and Belarus towards the West is perceived as an encroachment on Russia's national identity and a dangerous challenge to the country's security.
>
> *(Solovey, 2019)*

In reality,

> For 17 years, from the signing of the Russia – Ukraine State Treaty of May 1997 to Yanukovych's fall from power in February 2014, Russia lodged no official complaint against Ukraine with respect to the latter's treatment of Russian "compatriots," despite presenting this ostensible justification for war.
>
> *(Sherr, 2021, 17)*

A contemporary effort to revise borders in the Black Sea region looks to turn it into a "Russian lake."

Fifth, Russian strategic culture has been strongly influenced by a contested relationship with the West, with Russia both being a part of Europe and apart from Europe. Despite Russia's strong historical and cultural involvement in European history, the ambivalence of its relationship with Europe has continued to affect Russian strategic thinking. President Putin channels this "traditional and instinctive Russian sense of insecurity" (Department of State, 1946), convinced as he is that Western intelligence agencies and economic sanctions combine to actively destabilize Russia as the West's main geopolitical rival. In response to perceived failings in its relations with Europe, Russia has repeatedly turned to the east to attempt to find a new orientation in ties with Asia. While nineteenth-century intellectuals challenged Europe through the Slavophile movement, in the twenty-first century Russian strategic ideas have become bound up with other spatial visions, such as the 'Russian World', or various incarnations of Eurasianist ideas (Lewis, 2018). In the aftermath of the breakdown in relations with the West following Russia's annexation of Crimea in 2014, Russia once again turned to Asia and especially China as a potential ally to balance hostile relations with the United States and most EU member states. These other strategic orientations only mask the essential challenge for Russia in finding a working relationship with the West.

As Maria Engström acutely observes, national image building after Crimea

> posits Russia as the main ally, guardian and shield of the "true" classical European Christian heritage and civilization rooted in Greek and Roman culture, one that protects this classical tradition from decadent, liberal multicultural, dysfunctional and secular West, bereft of "civilisational memory."
>
> *(Engström, 2016)*

The 5 May 2016 open-air concert in Palmyra by the Mariinsky Theater Orchestra, conducted by Valery Gergiev,

> was a symbolic act designed to demonstrate the triumph of Russia's civilizing force over a new barbarism, the Islamic State. Pieces by Bach, Prokofiev and Shchedrin were played at the concert, an event christened "Pray for Palmyra. Music Revives Ancient Ruins". All of a sudden, the antiquity embodied in the second century Monumental Arch of Palmyra – well-known to millions of Russians from their (Soviet) fifth-grade textbooks on ancient history – became animate and tangible, and (according to the official version) Russia had acted as its main and only defender.
>
> *(Engström, 2016)*

In this sense, Russia becomes a country with a global horizon, not bounded by geographical borders or limited by historical timeframes. Russia certainly has a very well-developed sense of historical entitlement, centered on its role at the heart of an exceptional world civilization and what President Putin has characterized as an individual cultural code and historical experience. A central pillar of Russia's sense of itself as a distinctive century's old unbroken great power status was its integral role in shaping European culture and politics for over 300 years, while itself remaining distinctive.

Sixth, Russian strategic culture has been characterized by a messianic element that has taken on different forms over the centuries but continues to frame Russian military campaigns in moral and ideological language (Duncan, 2000; Østbø, 2016). Religious and counter-revolutionary ideas of nineteenth-century *Tsarism* were followed by the Soviet Union's Communist ideology in the twentieth century with, paradoxically, "militant atheism" in its 'messianic' vanguard.

Messianism coupled to the self-perception that Russia is a providential great power with a civilizational mission has been a trait in Russian strategic mentality and national narrative during the *Tsarist* and Soviet times. Messianism surges when Russian leaders propagate its central elements. In the sixteenth century, the notion of a 'Third Rome' became the foundation stone of Russian imperial identity. A letter of the Russian monk Phlotheus of Pskov in 1510 to Grand Duke Vasili III proclaimed: "Two Romes have fallen. The third stands. And there will be no fourth. No one shall replace your Christian Tsardom!" (Crawford, 2014). Russia was savior of the world – the Russian language had supra-national status and that Russian traditions were normative yardsticks for less stable and duly grateful neighbors – and acted "as a unique restraining factor in the world of increasing chaos" (Engström, 2014, 362). David Lewis analyzes brilliantly the influence of Carl Schmitt on Russian conservative thought: contemporary Russia is the biblical *katechon*, the heroically tragic figure able to hold back and restrain the anti-Christ and delay the advent of chaotic darkness and the *apocalypse* (Lewis, 2020, 193–214). Putin himself notes: paraphrasing Russian philosopher Nikolai Berdyaev, states:

> Conservatism is not something preventing upward, forward movement, but something preventing you from sliding back into chaos.

'Text of report "Valdai Discussion Club meeting"', President of the Russian Federation website, October 25, 2021. As Andrey Kozyrev, Russia's first post-Soviet foreign minister, warned:

> Communist ideology, like the tsarist ideology before it, has run its course. Russia already knows those two ideologies for their true value and will never step for a second time into either of these dried-up rivers of its past. However, the centuries-old, carefully cultivated and genetically encoded hopes for a messiah may still give rise to new forms of stultifying ideology, particularly in these difficult times of economic crisis.
>
> *(Kozyrev, 1992)*

This finds contemporary expression in the notion of "Orthodox geopolitics" and "nuclear Orthodoxy." "Orthodox geopolitics" suggests that Russia is the leader of a Slavic-Orthodox world, able to promote Russian culture and values across a supra-national Orthodox space that encompasses the Balkans, the Black Sea and the Eastern Mediterranean, from Serbia to Syria (Sidorov, 2006). Russia is able to practice "Orthodox geopolitics" within the borders of the canonical territory of the Russian Orthodox Church. This territory covers 16 states: Russia, Ukraine, Belarus, Moldova, Azerbaijan, Kazakhstan, China, Japan, Mongolia, Kyrgyzstan, Tajikistan, Turkmenistan, Uzbekistan, Estonia, Latvia and Lithuania. In addition, it incorporates all those who have joined the Russian Orthodox Church. Russia now frames the "struggle for Crimea as Russia's Mount Sinai, its own Jerusalem, a cradle of Russian civilization and of its Orthodox leadership in the wider world" (Khrushcheva, 2015). In this narrative, Russia defends the Christian traditional family values heritage of the West better than the West itself, and the Russian Orthodox Church exercises influence through para-diplomacy and its role as a "neutral" mediator in conflicts.

Russia's 'civilizational turn' since 2012 has been accompanied by more assertions of Russian exceptionalism in international relations and a greater emphasis on the special role of the Russian Orthodox Church. Indeed, Messianic ideas in religious philosophy have merged with national ideology, and the synthesis of the two is used to legitimize and justify foreign policy gambits both at home and abroad. This finds expression in the role of the Church in the draft and mobilization and, once recruited, in morale building through Russia's Ministry of Defense's Political Directorate. The Russian Orthodox Church has a longer-term influence on conflict duration, escalation dynamics and effectiveness of deterrence, including "nuclear Orthodoxy" (Adamsky, 2020a). Indeed, at the plenary session of the 2018 Valdai Club, Putin referenced heaven and hell in the context of nuclear deployment:

> [W]hen we confirm an attack on Russia, only then will be strike back. . . . An aggressor must know that retribution is inevitable, that he will be destroyed. And we, the victims of aggression will go to heaven as martyrs, and they will simply perish because they will not even have time to repent.
>
> *("Vladimir Putin's Speech," 2018)*

Strategic instruments

There is also continuity in Russia's commitments to particular mechanisms of foreign and defense policy. The balance of power has been a consistent instrument of Russian foreign policy and a highlight of Russia's heyday as a European power in the nineteenth century. Contemporary Russian strategic thought has also emphasized the concepts and theoretical assumptions of realist theories such as great power management, balance of power and spheres of influence. Putin has remarked on such mechanisms of international competition as an eternal element in international relations. In 2017, he told the Valdai conference:

> Of course, the interests of states certainly do not always coincide. This is normal, natural, this was always the case. Leading powers have different geopolitical strategies, [different] visions of the world. Such is the unchanging essence of international relations, constructed on the balance of interaction and competition.
>
> *("Meeting of the Valdai," 2017)*

In the Cold War, the balance of power not only returned in Europe but also escalated to a global strategy of mutual deterrence. The USSR and the United

States adopted strategies of deterrence, but there is a mismatch in how the two are understood. Deterrence in the West is understood as the ability to persuade an opponent that the risks outweigh the benefits of a given course of action. For Russia, strategic deterrence (*sderzhivanie*) is a much broader concept, a "multi-domain, cross-cutting effort to shape the strategic environment to serve Russia's objectives using a range of both soft and hard power tools of statecraft in peace-time and during conflict" (Charap, 2020a). Strategic deterrence can occur in three ways. First, there is deterrence by "intimidation or fear inducement" (Kofman et al., 2020, i). Second, there is deterrence "by denial," that is by preventing an adversary from achieving its goals by reducing one's own vulnerabilities and so denying the conditions that enable attacks. Third, "deterrence by punishment" is an option. Here, a state seeks to impose unacceptable costs on an adversary through counter force (attack an opponent's military infrastructure) and counter value (attack an opponent's civilian population to threaten its socioeconomic base). In classical Cold War deterrence theory, U.S.–USSR state conventional military/nuclear deterrence took place along a well-understood linear spectrum of conflict. This spectrum was marked by rungs on an escalation ladder. These rungs reflected measurable and quantifiable respective strengths and weaknesses of a well-understood correlation of forces.

Russia is a deterrence by intimidation and then punishment power, prepared to inflict unacceptable damage and cost in defense of "Russia and allies" by the forceful nuclear demonstration for deterrence and intimidation purposes in a conventional conflict (the so-called escalate to de-escalate or Ivanov Doctrine 2003) and use "non-strategic nuclear weapons" (low yield artillery shells) for non-strategic effect (Fink and Kofman, 2020). Col (ret.) Viktor Murakhovsky, a member of the Expert Council of the Board of the Military-Industrial Commission, and chief editor of the *Arsenal of Fatherland* magazine noted that Russia develops long-range hypersonic high-precision non-nuclear weapons such as *Kinzhal* and *Tsirkon*, new-generation air launch cruise missiles such as *Kalibr* and Kh-101 and anti-satellite missiles, which allow for strategic nonnuclear (i.e. conventional) deterrence (Bozhyeva, 2021). Russia adopts flexible deterrence options in which "escalation management concepts are not tied to matching yield or payload of adversary weapons" (Kofman et al., 2020, iii).

Russia blurs the distinction between war and peace (Jonsson, 2019), internal and external threats, nuclear and conventional forces and military and non-military means. In contemporary Russian thought, strategic deterrence has expanded as a concept to incorporate both military and non-military components. It is a concept that is still grounded in traditional ideas of nuclear deterrence, but it also includes the use of conventional military force and non-military tactics such as diplomacy, peace talks, "information warfare" and politics (Ven Bruusgaard, 2016; Louki-anova Fink, 2017). This emphasis on non-military tactics in strategic deterrence highlights similarities with the more common – but now highly politicized – concept of 'hybrid war' in that it demonstrates a characteristically holistic approach to warfare that uses the full spectrum of methods available to the state (Bērziņš,

2020). Yet, it also continues a long Russian tradition of seeking to establish a balance of power, even when Russia is clearly in an asymmetric relationship. To that end, notions of 'reasonable sufficiency' give way to 'reckless redundancy' as new hypersonic missiles are used to signal the unviability of Russian statehood, but real readiness lags behind rhetoric, and the risk of accidents increases.

Historically, Russia's strategic culture has also embraced the use of a mix of covert and sub-conventional instruments for strategic advantage. This strategic tradition stems in part from historical experience – a tradition of partisan warfare against invaders, the relative weakness of Russian military power forcing improvisation and a Soviet tradition of both revolutionary warfare and the extensive use of intelligence services in overseas operations. As Chapter 1 noted, Putin's Russia, particularly since 2007, has engaged in political warfare and hybrid interference against the political West. Russia attempts to undermine the strategic center of gravity, that is the belief and trust of elites and society in the utility of democratic values, norms, practices and principles. If the strategic center of gravity of the political West is the belief of elites and societies in democratic ideals (checks and balances, transparency, free and independent media, vibrant civil societies) and functioning law-based institutions and diverse identities and shared norms and values, then its operational center of gravity is the functioning of these very democratic institutions.

Russia uses cross-domain coercion to attack the functioning of these institutions, attempting to widen preexisting seams between local and national, civilian and military, ethnicities, language, religion, supporting communities of grievance and resentment, and weakening the resilience of societies to uphold democracy. The necessary tools are at hand (indeed, they are infinite and inexhaustible), including networks of intelligence officials ('active measures' and coordination function), organized crime groups, warlords, oligarchs and corrupted business elites and institutions, protracted conflicts, energy, cyber/information warfare tools, the weaponization of migrants and private armies and militias and other strategic proxy forces and illicit power structures, allowing a semblance of deniability. These tools are ideal for raiding – state-directed campaigns based on coercion and cost imposition as well as brigandage. Brigandage can be defined as problematic confrontational behavior that may not be centrally directed but is sanctioned (Kofman, 2018). In the modern world, interconnected and fragmented, such activities can have a disproportionate impact, and this complicates any discussion of the correlation of forces. It makes it harder to measure and quantify strengths and weaknesses: non-military means can have the same or even greater effect than military means for less cost and greater deniability. Inherent ambiguities in intent and attribution (means and method) mean that deterrence by punishment is problematic and deterrence by denial much less effective.

At his address to the Federal Assembly on 21 April 2021, Putin articulated an anti-Western narrative designed to appeal to his core supporters (pensioners and public sector employees). Putin first highlighted Russian exceptionalism: "They may think that we are like them, but we are different, with a different genetic, cultural and moral code. We know how to defend our interests" (Troianovsky, 2021). Putin promises that an innocent Russia will take "swift and hard" action and act "rapidly, asymmetrically and sharply" against opponents determined to impose their will through threats of the use of force, economic sanctions and provocations. Russia will react to provocations and any violation of its "red lines," so that provocateurs will "regret their actions like they have never regretted anything before." He defines "red lines" in terms of "interests," "interference" and "insults" and "infringements":

> [T]hese are our national interests, our external security interests, our internal security interests as regards not allowing anyone to interfere from the outside, be it our elections or other internal political processes. These [also] are not allowing insults in conversations with our country and not allowing infringement of our country's economic interests and "in each case we shall decide for ourselves where it lies"
>
> *(Putin, 2021a)*

Russia determines the extent of retaliation and where, when and to whom they should be applied, highlighting demonstrative, damage-inflicting and retaliatory deterrence.

A "red line" is a policy tool used by policy makers to distinguish acceptable from unacceptable actions, to set limits of what will be tolerated and what not (Tertrais, 2014); drawing "red lines" involves accepting tradeoffs between, for example, a "commitment trap" and a "reputational credibility trap" (Altman and Miller, 2017). Those that set "red lines" must take punitive action if the declaration has no deterrent effect but then lose freedom to maneuver or lose credibility in the eyes of domestic audience, adversary and allies (Fearon, 1994; Schultz, 2001). There is an inherent tension between the benefits of clarity, resolve and flexibility:

> A clearer red line means greater reputational damage from failing to uphold it. By providing a way to avoid carrying out a threat when a red line is crossed, ambiguity creates both a cost – undermining credibility – and a benefit – reducing the risk of entrapment into unwanted escalation.
>
> *(Altman and Miller, 2017, 321)*

However, if "red lines" are incomplete and unverifiable they are not credible, and then too sharp "red lines" may simply encourage action below the "red line," where by implication everything is permitted (Tertrais, 2014, 8).

On the eve of the Putin–Biden Geneva Summit on 16 June 2021, and, following a call between President Biden and President Zelensky of Ukraine, President Putin returned to the theme of "red lines." He stated that: "As for NATO's enlargement and the advancement of NATO infrastructure towards Russia's borders, this is a matter of paramount significance as far as the security of Russians and Russia goes." He noted that the flight time of NATO missiles to Moscow will drop to just 7–10 minutes if Ukraine joins the alliance: "Let's imagine that Ukraine becomes a NATO member. The flight time from, let's say, Kharkov and, I don't know, Dnepropetrovsk to central Russia, to Moscow, will shrink to 7–10 minutes. Is it a redline for us or not?" Putin then drew parallels with Russia's strategic bench-mark – the United States – and drew attention back to the Cold War deployment of Soviet missiles in Cuba with only 15 minute missile flight U.S. industrial cen-ters, including Washington: "To lower this flight time to 7–10 minutes, we should station out missiles on Canada's southern border or Mexico's northern border. Is it a redline for the US or not?" ("By Enlarging NATO," 2021)

Force multipliers

Russia can utilize a number of force multipliers in its great power competition context, including first-use nuclear weapons, the political will to take greater risk, its geographical proximity to Eurasian hotspots, rapid deployment ability, UN Security Council veto, organizational creativity, cheap operational costs, as well as "de-institutionalized decision-making, no allied interests to constrain action, and no shortage of imagination on what is possible (Kofman, 2017). In purchasing power parity terms, effective military expenditure

> is more in the range of $150–180 billion per year, with a much higher per-centage dedicated to procurement, research and development than Western defense budgets. . . . There is well over 1 trillion rubles of military expendi-ture in Russia outside of the regular defense budget.
>
> *(Kofman, 2019)*

Thus, the pursuit of narrow objectives at low cost, utilizing *kompromat* and cor-ruption to suborn politicians, and "active measures" to exert covert influence can make Russia strategically relevant.

From at least the attempted Montenegro coup (16 October 2016) attempt onward, the effectiveness of such destabilization activities has decreased with higher costs imposed on Russia for less and less benefits. In the case of the Wagner Group debacle in Syria in February 2018, the United States pretended to believe Russia's denial that the Wagner Group represented a non-Russian albeit pro-Assad force, before proceeding to 'annihilate', in the words of U.S. Secretary of Defense Mattis, a detached battalion. The UK's attribution of Russia's involvement in the attempted assassination of the Skripals – there was "no other plausible explanation" with regard to "means, motive and record" – has been subsequently vindicated with the image of GRU professionalism tarnished in the process. Russia's con-tinued use of 'plausible deniability' has less and less salience and, in some cases, can be a strategic vulnerability turned against itself and as a tactic appears to have passed its sell-by date. Russian actions to control the Azov Sea indicate that Russia seeks to apply just enough conventional force to achieve its ends and enable cross-domain coercion, while not so much as to make acquiescence politically untenable for Western governments (Åtland, 2021; Herd, 2019). Russia thereby avoids financial-economic or military escalation, which would seriously undercut Russian foreign-exchange earnings, state revenues and GDP; risk regime stability and potentially even render all-out catastrophic nuclear war more likely.

The terms "nonlinear", "gradualist", "cross-domain", "complex strategic" and "multi-dimensional" coercion are used to capture the asymmetric tactic used by Russia to avoid direct military confrontation against an adversary whose military power projection capabilities are superior. Chief of the Main Operations Directorate of the General Staff, Lt.-General Andrei Kartapolov, speaking at the IV Moscow Conference on International Security in April 2015, noted:

> [N]on-standard forms and methods of using our armed forces are being developed, which will help to level the enemy's technological superiority. To do this it is necessary to . . . develop "asymmetric" methods to confront the enemy. Asymmetric actions are inherent in a conflict situation in which the weaker [side] uses economic, diplomatic, informational, and direct military measures to conduct an asymmetric strategy (tactics) in accordance with his limited resources to mitigate the military-technological advantages of the stronger side.
>
> *(Kartapolov, 2015, 35)*

An asymmetric strategy thus compensates for and mitigates technological and economic weaknesses relative to adversaries, such as the United States and NATO, and hybrid interference can prevent the West from creating a "cordon sanitaire" around Russia through NATO expansion, a concern raised by Gen Kartapolov.

Such coercion is holistic in that it can merge and so unite "military and non-military forms of influence across nuclear, conventional and informational (cyber) domains" (Adamsky, 2018a, 33). Russian coercion employs systematic pressure across 5Ds (disinformation, destabilization, disruption, deception and implied destruction) "to systematically undermine the command authority and the political and social cohesion of adversary states and institutions" (Lindley-French, 2019). Such coercion seeks to narrow, limit and restrict the West's responses to a binary choice: unacceptably risky escalation or acquiescence in the form of accommodation or conciliation. Coercion is achieved when it triggers an acquiescent rather than escalatory response. When is cross-domain deterrence of cross-domain coercion achieved? If coercion is achieved when it triggers an acquiescent rather than escalatory response, cross-domain deterrence is achieved when the adversary is no longer able to risk that coercion leads to acquiescence rather than escalation.

In Russian eyes, there is no illegitimate form of deterrence, compellence or escalation management: "The war is being fought on multiple levels simultaneously and with all means available, if not in every way" (Goure, 2019, 33). Michael Kofman notes a paradox at the heart of Russia's strategy for great power competition. Russia's effective conventional and nuclear deterrence creates an escalation ceiling adversaries do not want to breach, thereby providing Moscow with

> [the] confidence to pursue an indirect approach against the United States. This is a strategy of cost imposition and erosion, an indirect approach which could be considered a form of raiding. As long as conventional and nuclear deterrence holds, it makes various form of competition below the threshold of war not only viable, but highly attractive.

He concludes:

> Ultimately, Russia seeks a deal, not based on the actual balance of power in the international system, but tied to its performance in the competition. That deal can best be likened to a form of detente, status recognition, and attendant privileges or understandings, which have profound geopolitical ramifications for politics in Europe.
>
> *(Kofman, 2019)*

Andrey Mikhaylovich Ilnitsky, an adviser to Defense Minister Shoigu, has called "informational war" with its focus on the psychological impact on the adversary a "type of war a mental war. The purpose of this new war is to destroy self-consciousness, to change the mental, civilizational basis of the enemy's society" (Bozhyeva, 2021). It follows that Western political–legal constructs derived from a Western philosophical-normative tradition are designed to constrain Russian behavior and prevent its attainment of great power status.

The logic of 'Putinism' can be understood in part as a foreign policy doctrine to divide and destabilize through raiding and brigandage (Kofman, 2018). Russian conflict strategy consists of 1) hybrid operations in peacetime, 2) the threat of short fait accompli "land grab" conventional war facilitated by regional escalation dominance and (3) the threat of nuclear retaliation that targets the resolve and determination of Western decision-makers. Russia pursues a competitive strategy against the 'political West', using asymmetric disinformation, subversion and political warfare operations to destabilize and exercise reflexive control (Jensen and Doran, 2018). Russia can exploit a permissive and predictable Western operating environment and leverage its ability to better manage the psychology and politics of disorder. This strategy is entirely rational. If Russia cannot strengthen itself, it can weaken its adversaries. Maintenance of the status quo is critical to regime's survival. These internal imperatives are predicated on an anti-fragile regime-building strategy: the regime thrives on ordered disorder and controlled chaos but is vulnerable to tranquility. Russia's pariah status and the state's spoiler role ensure continued state strategic relevance and regime survival (defers disruptive reform, reinforces the status quo). A constructive foreign policy allows Russia only limited strategic relevance, given its influence would reflect its diminishing power outside of the military-nuclear realm.

On 2 March 2019, Gen. Valery Gerasimov, the Russian Armed Forces' General Staff Chief and First Deputy Defense Minister, argued that:

> The Pentagon has begun devising a fundamentally new strategy of warfare, which has already been baptized the Trojan Horse. Basically, it consists in the active use of a protest potential of the fifth column in the interest of destabilization while simultaneously carrying out precision attacks on most critical facilities.
>
> *(Johnson, 2019)*

This echoed his 2013 article, which referenced what he, the General Staff and wider Russia's strategic community understood to be the Western way of coercive war: the use of political warfare, information technologies, conventional military and precision-guided munitions to effect color revolutions (post-modern *coup d'états*) leading to the strategic reorientation of states from Russia to the West (Gerasimov, 2013). As Gerasimov notes: "It happened in Iraq, Libya and Ukraine. Similar actions are currently being observed in Venezuela." In response, Russia's "active-defense strategy" has sought to use military and nonmilitary means to address and proactively neutralize threats before they accumulate. To that end, Russia adopts and utilizes a "limited action strategy," which entails

> the establishment of a self-sufficient task force based on a unit of a type of the Armed Forces, which is highly mobile and capable of making the greatest contribution to the fulfillment of the set objectives. The units of the Aerospace Forces play this part in Syria.
>
> *(Gerasimov, 2019; Johnson, 2019)*

TABLE 2.1 Historical Lessons, State Discourse and Russia's Evolving Political and Strategic Cultures

Historical "Lessons"	*State Discourse – the kind of past Russia's future needs?*	*Implications for Russia's Political and Strategic Cultures?*
Russian weakness invites external attack	(1) **Necessity of strong leader for 'besieged fortress':** Putin's wise, bold, far-sighted authority is sacred; strong military and 'service state' – *Tsar* as solution, not the problem; 'West loves Russia when Russia weak, fears Russia when it is strong'; "moral fortress"; West "genetically" disposed to be anti-Slav; 2) **Enemy within paradigm:** vigilance versus '5th columnists', 'foreign agents' and 'national traitors' – Western values are 'false-flag' operations for post-modern *coup d'état*; (3) **Traditional values:** single power vertical with popular leader promotes network coordination and stability – competing power networks create chaos;	(1) **Charismatic and historical legitimation of political authority:** state-sponsored conservatism, censorship, military-patriotic mobilization; Soviet *intelligentsia* statist modernity replaced by *siloviki*-statist *Chekistocracy*, confrontational counter-intelligence state; 2) **Exceptionalism:** redress historical injustices; Soviet grandeur nostalgia, anti-Americanism and conspiracy theories exalt Russia influence over neighborhood – legally sovereign neighbors part of Russia's "exceptional" past; 3) **Patronal path dependency:** anti-patronal revolutions (Trotsky, Bukharin, Yeltsin first term) fail as incentives for status quo too strong; *silovarchic* networks hijack via predatory raids and property expropriation; regime projects image of political permanence but 'bad Nash equilibrium'; 'crony capitalism' morphs into 'sentry capitalism'

(Continued)

TABLE 2.1 (Continued)

Historical "Lessons"	State Discourse – the kind of past Russia's future needs?	Implications for Russia's Political and Strategic Cultures?
Great power eternal Russia	(1) **Russia's special path, mission and values:** consensus-based, collectivist, patriotic, authentic political and strategic cultures generate stability through centralized uninterrupted power; Gumiliev's *passionarnost* ("a nations' capacity to make sacrifices"); (2) **Status quo as stability**: USSR collapse as "greatest geopolitical catastrophe of 20th C." – syndrome of "lost motherland" national consciousness shock; (3) **"Victory" as status projection**: Congress of Vienna, 1815; Yalta-Potsdam 1945; Russia as arbiter of great power affairs; Russia saves Europe from tyranny; strong military generates fear, respect and national pride in past and so in future	(1) **Deferred modernization:** prevailing idea is anti-modern: openness/ competition understood as chaos, breakdown; social contract under stress: elites pretend to govern (informal rules); society pretend to be governed (formal law); traditional values, societal stability and order privileged over individual rights and justice; (2) **Weaponized history:** monopolization of memory and language, culture and ethnicity as justification for intervention; dissenters as enemy of the state; irrationalize roots of power to undercut rational analysis; (3) **Historical language as touchstone of political psychology**: "invention of tradition" conservative rather than liberal Russia: "How can we walk forward while looking backward all the time?" (Andrey Kortunov); reality of indistinct civilizational self-identity, weak geopolitical and geo-cultural arsenal, psychological alienation – no coming to terms with the past (*vergangenheitsbewältigang*)
Russia on the right side of history – creator of history	1) **New system; new rules; Russia as change leader:** liberal democracies dysfunctional; Russia as rule-maker; privilege order above justice; 2) **'Neo-modern' 'civilizational state':** historical order-producing role; trans-ethnic Orthodox unity; 3) **'Moscow consensus'**: 'sovereign leader', imitation institutions, strong intelligence services, fusion of business and political elites – "everything inside the State, nothing outside the State, nothing against the State" – viable model	1) **Vulnerable great power**: "working poor" are teachers, doctors, engineers; grievance litany not reform; "[t]he state grows fat but the people grow lean"; 2) **'Sovereign globalization'**: "aggressive isolationism" achieves 'post-imperium' equilibrium; *silovarchy* collective action problem; 3) **Enduring dilemmas, paradoxes**: pivot to Asia/catch-up competition with West; destabilize neighbors to stabilize Russia; gaps/ divisions between *de jure pravovoye gostudarstva* (law-based state), "Good Tsar" and *sistema*, electoral *stoligarchy* and "Bad *Boyars*"; internet/youth generation protests versus TV-based "Crimean majority"

Thus, the most appropriate branch or combat arm is placed in the lead, with limited support grouping of forces. In this way, conflicts like Ukraine or Syria fall beneath the threshold of regional war and remain local and limited.

Conclusions

This conceptual overview has highlighted how Russia's broader strategic culture sets national interest and core foreign policy goals, fixes strategic benchmarks and incubates the enduring ideas that inform it. Strategic culture constitutes an important structural factor that influences decision-making around the use of force. Strategic culture shapes how Russian strategic decision-makers view the world, their philosophical beliefs and hence threat perceptions. See Table 2.1 above. Strategic cultures are subject to slow changes, though incremental and slow cultural transformations reflected, for example, the interplay of three subcultures within the military – "bureaucratic, warfighting, and arms-parading" – the latter "blends the propensity for showing off with the desire to modernize and obtain most modern weapons" (Baev, 2019).

Rapid accelerated strategic culture changes can be brought on by war-fighting operations and especially crisis. The Syrian operations drive changes in Russian military theory, concepts of operations, organizational structures and force build-up, promoting "(1) conceptualization of new forms of warfare and features of operational art, (2) force modernization around the reconnaissance-strike complex, and (3) the emerging concept of operations known as 'the strategy of limited actions'" (Adamsky, 2020b, 2020c). Expeditionary coalitional warfare is a new feature of Russian warfighting, as is in effect using the Russian military to "deter the West from manipulating the threat of revolutions" (Baev, 2019b). Undeclared operations in Donbas, Ukraine, are unique in that they are governed by "a senior-level policy decision to pursue a persistent but indecisive conflict – as opposed to a decisive 'big war' – type military operation or a truly 'frozen' conflict (i.e. without regular bloodshed)." Samuel Charap characterizes this approach as "*calibrated coercion*" and argues it

> represents a departure from the Russian strategic-cultural emphasis on the big-war approach of seeking a decisive, rapid, and overwhelming victory. Russian military leaders are being told that they cannot fight to win, and the fighting they can do is strictly limited to holding the line with a highly circumscribed set of capabilities made available.
>
> *(Charap, 2020b)*

Operations may lead to changes that are limited to the operational theater in question – the issue of decentralized delegated mission versus central command in Syria and calibrated coercion versus "big war" in Ukraine are cases in point – whereas crisis can generate new system-wide change.

As Russia insists that it has a 1,000-year history and so deep historical roots, we can infer that Russia's strategic culture owes much to its formative and foundational pre-Westphalian period. Russia's own understanding of its past as interpreted by an elite and state-controlled media is a primary source of its strategic behavior. As a result, Russia's strategic culture will be subject to only very slow, gradual, evolutionary change and transformation, not sudden elimination of key tenets or accepted guiding norms and their replacement. A post-Putin president will likely continue to focus on current strategic goals. There are two caveats: first, even strategic culture can change after a catastrophic crisis and, second, the means to achieve these goals – Churchill's Russian "national interest" – may change, depending on who is the successor and which operational code is dominant.

Selected bibliography

Adamsky, Dmitry. 2010. *The Culture of Military Innovation; The Impact of Cultural Factors on the Revolution in Military Affairs in Russia, US and Israel*. Stanford: Stanford University Press.

———. 2018a. "From Moscow with Coercion: Russian Deterrence Theory and Strategic Culture." *Journal of Strategic Studies* 41 (1–2): 33–60.

———. 2020a. *Russian Nuclear Orthodoxy: Religion, Politics, and Strategy*. Stanford: Stanford University Press. https://doi.org/10.1515/9781503608658.

———. 2020b. "Russian Lessons from the Syrian Operation and the Culture of Military Innovation." *MC Security Insights*. No. 47, February 2020. www.marshallcenter.org/en/publications/security-insights/russian-lessons-syrian-operation-and-culture-military-innovation.

———. 2020c. "Discontinuity in Russian Strategic Culture? A Case Study of Mission Command Practice." *MC Security Insights*. No. 49, February 2020. www.marshallcenter.org/en/publications/security-insights/discontinuity-russian-strategic-culture-case-study-mission-command-practice-0.

Adomeit, Hannes. 1982. *Soviet Risk Taking and Crisis Behavior: A Theoretical and Empirical Analysis*. Studies of the Russian Institute, Columbia University. London: Allen and Unwin.

Almond, Gabriel A., and Sidney Verba. 1963. *The Civic Culture: Political Attitudes and Democracy in Five Nations*. Princeton, NJ: Princeton University Press.

Altman, Dan and Nicholas L. Miller. 2017. "Red Lines in Nuclear Nonproliferation." *The Nonproliferation Review* 24 (3–4): 315–342. https://doi.org/10.1080/10736700.2018.1433575.

Aptekar, Pavel. 2017. "What Vladimir Putin Needs to Know About Alexander III. President and His Inner Circle See the Empire of that Epoch as Optimal Model State and Image of Rule." *Vedemosti Online*, in Russian, November 20.

Åtland, Kristian. 2021. "Redrawing Borders, Reshaping Orders: Russia's Quest for Dominance in the Black Sea Region." *European Security* 30 (2): 305–324. https://doi.org/10.1080/09662839.2021.1872546.

Bækken, Håvard. 2021. "Patriotic Disunity: Limits to Popular Support for Militaristic Policy in Russia." *Post-Soviet Affairs* 37 (3): 261–275. https://doi.org/10.1080/1060586X.2021.1905417.

Baev, Pavel K. 2019. "The Impacts of the Syrian Intervention on Russian Strategic Culture." *MC Security Insight*. No. 33, June 2019. www.marshallcenter.org/en/publications/security-insights/impacts-syrian-intervention-russian-strategic-culture-0.

BBC Monitoring. 2018. "Commentary: Putin Address Declaration of New Cold War." *Yezhednevny Zhurnal Website*, in Russian. March 12, 2018.

Bērziņš, Jānis. 2020. "The Theory and Practice of New Generation Warfare: The Case of Ukraine and Syria." *The Journal of Slavic Military Studies* 33 (3): 355–380. https://doi.org/10.1080/13518046.2020.1824109.

Bozhyeva, Olga. 2021. "Interview with Military Expert Viktor Murakhovsky by Olga Bozhyeva: Doctrine of Mental Wars and Hybrid Operations." *Moskovsky Komsomolets.* April 3, 2021.

"By Enlarging NATO, West 'Spat Upon' Russia's Interests Despite Good Relations, Putin Says." *TASS.* June 9, 2021. https://tass.com/politics/1300975.

Charap, Samuel. 2020a. "Strategic Sderzhivanie: Understanding Contemporary Russian Approaches to 'Deterrence'." *MC Security Insight.* No. 62, September 2020. www.marshall center.org/en/publications/security-insights/strategic-sderzhivanie-understanding-contemporary-russian-approaches-deterrence-0.

———. 2020b. "Moscow's Calibrated Coercion in Ukraine and Russian Strategic Culture." *MC Security Insights.* No. 63, September 2020. www.marshallcenter.org/en/publications/security-insights/moscows-calibrated-coercion-ukraine-and-russian-strategic-culture-0.

Cooper, Julian. 2012. "Reviewing Russian Strategic Planning: The Emergence of Strategy 2020." *NDC Research Review.* https://research.birmingham.ac.uk/portal/en/publications/reviewing-russian-strategic-planning(67dac507-9e3e-4c2c-8e58-1bba40db1087).html.

Dapkus, Liudas. 2021. "Severe Hangover in the Kremlin." *Delfi.* April 28, 2021.

Department of State. 1946. "Telegram, George Kennan to George Marshall ['Long Telegram']. February 22, 1946. Harry S. Truman Administration File, Elsey Papers." *Department of State.* https://upload.wikimedia.org/wikipedia/commons/6/68/The_Long_Telegram.pdf.

Duncan, Peter. 2000. *Russian Messianism: Third Rome, Revolution, Communism and After.* London: Routledge.

Engström, Maria. 2014. "Contemporary Russian Messianism and New Russian Foreign Policy." *Contemporary Security Policy* 35 (3): 356–379.

———. 2016. 'The New Russian Renaissance', Why the Kremlin is fascinated by classical antiquity', Warsaw, *Intersection,* 4 April 2017: http://intersectionproject.eu/article/russia-europe/new-russian-renaissance

Fearon, James D. 1994. "Domestic Political Audiences and the Escalation of International Disputes." *American Political Science Review* 88 (3): 577–592.

Fink, Anya, and Michael Kofman. 2020. "Russian Strategy for Escalation Management: Key Debates and Players in Military Thought." www.cna.org/CNA_files/PDF/DIM-2020-U-026101-Final.pdf.

Gerasimov, Valeriy. 2013. "The Value of Science Is in the Foresight: New Challenges Demand Rethinking the Forms and Methods of Carrying out Combat Operations." *Voyenno-Promyshlennyy Kuryer.* February 26, 2013.

———. 2019. "Pentagon Devising New Trojan Horse Military Strategy." *Interfax.* March 4, 2019.

Golts, Aleksandr. 2019. "Why Militarization of Russian Minds Happens and Why It Is Dangerous." *Ekho Moskvy.* February 19, 2019.

Goure, Daniel. 2019. "How Does Russia Perceive Deterrence, Compellence, Escalation Management, and the Continuum of Conflict?" In *Russian Strategic Intentions,* edited by John Arquilla and Nicole Peterson. Boston, MA: NSI, Inc. https://nsiteam.com/social/wp-content/uploads/2019/05/SMA-TRADOC-Russian-Strategic-Intentions-White-Paper-PDF-1.pdf.

Gray, Colin S. 1971. "Strategists: Some Views Critical of the Profession." *International Journal* 26 (4): 771–790.

———. 1999. "Strategic Culture as Context: The First Generation of Theory Strikes Back." *Review of International Studies* 25 (1): 49–69.

Herd, Graeme. 2019. "The Annexation of the Sea of Azov: Russian Strategic Behavior and the Role of Cross-Domain Coercion." In *NATO at 70 and the Baltic States: Strengthening the Euro-Atlantic*, edited by Mark Voyger, 140–154. Tartu: Baltic Defence College.

Heuser, Beatrice. 2007. "Clausewitz's Ideas of Strategy and Victory." In *Clausewitz in the Twenty-First Century*, edited by Hew Strachan and Andreas Herberg-Rothe, 138–162. Oxford: Oxford University Press.

Jensen, Donald N., and Peter B. Doran. 2018. "Chaos as a Strategy: Putin's Promethean Gamble. Findings and Recommendations." Washington, DC: Center for European Policy Analysis. https://cepa.org/cepa_files/2018-CEPA-report-Chaos_as_a_Strategy_findings_and_recs.pdf.

Johnson, Alistair Iain. 1995. "Thinking about Strategic Culture." *International Security* 19 (4): 32–64.

Johnson, Dave. 2019. "Review of Speech by General Gerasimov at the Russian Academy of Military Science." *Russian Studies Series. 4/19*. March 2, 2019. www.ndc.nato.int/research/research.php?icode=585.

Jonsson, Oscar. 2019. *The Russian Understanding of War: Blurring the Lines Between War and Peace*. Washington, DC: Georgetown University Press. ISBN: 978-1-62616-734-6.

Kartapolov, Andrey V. 2015. "Lessons of Military Conflicts and Prospects for the Development of Means and Methods of Conducting Them, Direct and Indirect Actions in Contemporary International Conflicts." *Vestnik Akademii Voennykh Nauk* (2): 28–29.

Kelly, Lidia. 2014. "Russia can turn US to radioactive ash – Kremlin-backed journalist", Reuters, March 16, 2014. https://www.reuters.com/article/ukraine-crisis-russia-kiselyov-idUSL6N0MD0P920140316

Khrushcheva, Nina L. 2015. "The Tsar and the Sultan." *Quartz*. December 4, 2015. http://qz.com/565276/vladimir-putin-fancies-himself-a-tsar-standing-up-to-turkeys-new-sultan/.

Klyuchevskiĭ, V. O. 1970. *History of Russia. Vol. 3: The Rise of the Romanovs*. London: Macmillan.

Kofman, Michael. 2017. "A Comparative Guide to Russia's Use of Force: Measure Twice, Invade Once." *War on the Rocks*. February 16, 2017. https://warontherocks.com/2017/02/a-comparative-guide-to-russias-use-of-force-measure-twice-invade-once/.

———. 2018. "Raiding and International Brigandry: Russia's Strategy for Great Power Competition." *War on the Rocks*. June 14. https://warontherocks.com/2018/06/raiding-and-international-brigandry-russias-strategy-for-great-power-competition/.

———. 2019. "Russian Defense Spending Is Much Larger, and More Sustainable than It Seems." *Defense News*. May 3, 2019. www.defensenews.com/opinion/commentary/2019/05/03/russian-defense-spending-is-much-larger-and-more-sustainable-than-it-seems/.

Kofman, Michael, Anya Fink, and Jeffrey Edmonds. 2020. "Russian Strategy for Escalation Management: Evolution of Key Concepts." www.cna.org/CNA_files/PDF/DRM-2019-U-022455-1Rev.pdf.

Kozyrev, Andrey. 1992. "Russia: A Chance for Survival." *Foreign Affairs* 71 (2), Spring. www.foreignaffairs.com/articles/russia-fsu/1992-03-01/russia-chance-survival.

Kramer, Mark. 2019–20. "The Soviet Legacy in Russian Foreign Policy." *Political Science Quarterly* 134 (4), Winter: 585–610.

Le Donne, John P. 2003. *Grand Strategy of the Russian Empire, 1650–1831*. Oxford; New York: Oxford University Press.

Lewis, David. 2016. "The Moscow Consensus: Constructing Autocracy in Post-Soviet Eurasia." *The Foreign Policy Centre*. May 24, 2016. https://fpc.org.uk/moscow-consensus-constructing-autocracy-post-soviet-eurasia/.

Lewis, David G. 2018. "Geopolitical Imaginaries in Russian Foreign Policy: The Evolution of 'Greater Eurasia'", *Europe-Asia Studies*, 70:10, 1612–1637.

———. 2020. *Russia's New Authoritarianism: Putin and the Politics of Order*. Edinburgh: Edinburgh University Press.

———. 2021. "Russian Diplomacy and Conflict Management." In *Russia's Global Reach: A Security and Statecraft Assessment*, edited by Graeme Herd. Garmisch-Partenkirchen: George C. Marshall European Center for Security Studies. www.marshallcenter.org/en/publications/marshall-center-books/russias-global-reach-security-and-statecraft-assessment/chapter-13-russian-diplomacy-and-conflict-management.

Lindley-French, Julian. 2019. "Briefing: Complex Strategic Coercion and Russian Military Modernisation." *The Lindley-French Analysis*. January 9, 2019. http://lindleyfrench.blogspot.com/2019/01/briefing-complex-strategic-coercion-and.html.

Loukianova Fink, Anya. 2017. "The Evolving Russian Concept of Strategic Deterrence: Risks and Responses." *Arms Control Today*. August 2017. www.armscontrol.org/act/2017-07/features/evolving-russian-concept-strategic-deterrence-risks-responses.

"Meeting of the Valdai." 2017. "Vladimir Putin Meets with Members of the Valdai Discussion Club. Transcript of the Plenary Session of the 14th Annual Meeting." October 19, 2017. https://valdaiclub.com/events/posts/articles/putin-meets-with-members-of-the-valdai-club/.

Monaghan, Andrew. 2013. "Putin's Russia: Shaping a 'Grand Strategy'?" *International Affairs* 89 (5): 1221–1236.

Østbø, Jardar. 2016. *The New Third Rome: Readings of a Russian Nationalist Myth*. Foreword by Pål Kolstø. Stuttgart: Ibidem-Verlag.

"Putin agrees with emperor that Russia's only allies are Army and Navy", TASS News agency, Moscow, April 16, 2015. https://tass.com/russia/789866

"Putin Unveils Tsar Alexander III Monument in Yalta." 2017. *Rossiya 24 Television*, in Russian, November 20, 2017.

Putin, Vladimir, Nataliya Gevorkyan, Natalya Timakova, and Andrei Kolesnikov. 2000. *First Person: An Astonishingly Frank Self-Portrait by Russia's President Vladimir Putin*. New York: PublicAffairs.

Putin, Vladimir. 2021a. "Presidential Address to the Federal Assembly." *President of Russia*. April 21, 2021. http://en.kremlin.ru/events/president/transcripts/65418.

———. 2021b. "On the Historical Unity of Russians and Ukrainians." *President of the Russian Federation Website*. July 12, 2021. http://kremlin.ru/events/president/news/66181.

———. 2021c. "Vladimir Putin Answered Questions on His Article 'On the Historical Unity of the Russians and Ukrainians'." *President of the Russian Federation Website*. July 13, 2021. http://en.kremlin.ru/events/president/news/66191.

Rumer, Eugene, and Richard Sokolsky. 2020. "Etched in Stone: Russian Strategic Culture and the Future of Transatlantic Security." *Carnegie Endowment for International Peace*. September 8, 2020. https://carnegieendowment.org/2020/09/08/etched-in-stone-russian-strategic-culture-and-future-of-transatlantic-security-pub-82657.

Schultz, Kenneth A. 2001. *Democracy and Coercive Diplomacy*. Cambridge: Cambridge University Press.

Sherr, James. 2021. "Russia and the West Are as 'Bad' as Each Other." In *Myths and Misconceptions in the Debate on Russia: How They Affect Western Policy, and What Can Be Done*, 18–22. London: Chatham House.

Shevtsova, Lilia. 2003. *Putin's Russia*. Carnegie Endowment for International Peace. https://carnegieendowment.org/2003/04/03/putin-s-russia-pub-9081.

Sidorov, Dmitrii. 2006. "Post-Imperial Third Romes: Resurrections of a Russian Orthodox Geopolitical Metaphor." *Geopolitics* 11 (2): 317–347.

Silove, Nina. 2018. "Beyond the Buzzword: The Three Meanings of Grand Strategy." *Security Studies* 27 (1): 27–57.

Snegovaya, Maria. 2016. "What Explains the Sometimes Obsessive Anti-Americanism of Russian Elites?" *Brookings*. February 23, 2016. www.brookings.edu/blog/order-from-chaos/2016/02/23/what-explains-the-sometimes-obsessive-anti-americanism-of-russian-elites/.

Snyder, Jack L. 1977. "The Soviet Strategic Culture: Implications for Limited Nuclear Operations." *R-2154-AF*. Santa Monica: RAND Corporation. www.rand.org/pubs/reports/R2154.html.

Solovey, Valeriy. 2019. "The True Story of How Russia's Foreign Policy Process Evolved." *Text. The National Interest*. The Center for the National Interest. February 28, 2019. https://nationalinterest.org/feature/true-story-how-russias-foreign-policy-process-evolved-45812.

Sprude, Viesturs, and Sergei Medvedev. 2021. "There Is a Return to Public Control and Efforts to Celebrate 9 May Continuously." *Latvijas Avize*. May 9, 2021.

Tertrais, Bruno. 2014. "Drawing Red Lines Right." *The Washington Quarterly* 37 (3): 7–24. https://doi.org/10.1080/0163660X.2014.978433.

'Text of report "Valdai Discussion Club meeting"', President of the Russian Federation website, October 25, 2021.

Troianovsky, Anton. 2021. "We Know How to Defend Our Interests': Putin's Emerging Hard Line." *New York Times*. April 20, 2021. www.nytimes.com/2021/04/20/world/europe/putin-biden-ukraine-navalny.html.

Ven Bruusgaard, Kristin. 2016. "Russian Strategic Deterrence." *Survival* 58 (4): 7–26.

"Vladimir Putin's Speech at Valdai Forum." 2018. *Politkom.ru*, in Russian. October 22, 2018.

3

THE "INNER LOGIC" OF *TSARIST* IMPERIAL HISTORY

Introduction

What are the common threads that link *Kievan Rus'*, a medieval political federation situated on what now constitutes Belarus, Ukraine and the western portion of Russia, to the rise of Moscow, Muscovy, and the *Riurikhid* and Romanov dynasties, Bolshevism (the "Red dynasty"), post-Soviet Yeltsin's and then Putinist Russia? For President Putin, the very idea of Russia is rooted in the past. The Russian Ministry of Foreign Affairs website proudly notes continuity in Russian institutions first created in the *Tsarist* period. Although Russia is the legal successor state to the Soviet Union, a number of Russian official institutions have extended their claims of origin to the structures of the Russian Empire:

> The Industry and Trade Ministry says it was born in 1905 when Tsar Nicholas II signed the creation of an eponymous Russian ministry into law. The Russian Defense Ministry tells its story starting in 1802, the date when, under Tsar Alexander I, Russia's first Military Infantry Ministry was formed. The Interior Ministry begins its remembrances at an even earlier moment in time: in 1718, when Peter the Great appointed his first police chief, Anton Devier. The champion is the Foreign Ministry. Russia's Foreign Service traces its origin to the moment when, in 860 AD, *Kievan Rus'* concluded its first known peace treaty with the Byzantine Empire. That was the moment *Rus* was recognized internationally.
>
> *(Trudolyubov, 2017)*

Links that bind the present with the past are not just institutional, but also individual. In an interview, Sergei Ivanov, Russian presidential envoy on environmental and transport issues and former head of the presidential administration, objected to paint being poured on a Mannerheim plaque in St. Petersburg, commenting:

> you probably need to explain to people elementary things linked to a knowledge of history. Our people, unfortunately, often either do not know their history or even when they recognize certain facts they do not want to accept

DOI: 10.4324/9780429261985-3

them completely . . . The main falsification was that the plaque had been put up for the Finnish Marshal Mannerheim. Complete lies! It is a memorial to the Russian Lt-Gen Mannerheim. It cannot be denied that Mannerheim did an awful lot for the Russian Empire. He was a knight of St George. And all the knights of St George are immortalized here on plaques in the St George Hall at the Kremlin. Of course, Mannerheim is a controversial figure. But this is an example of how people's lives, and not only the lives of ordinary people, changed fundamentally, were ruined by October 1917. . . . We are not saying that Finnish citizen Mannerheim (and he became Finnish after 1918) was of great benefit to the Soviet Union. Of course not. But we are saying that he was of great benefit including because he carried out crucial intelligence missions for the Main Intelligence Director of the Russian Empire's General Staff and, ultimately, he was a Soviet military pensioner. Many people did not know about this.

(Ivanov, 2016)

Other examples can also illustrate the notion of linkages, ties and traditions that binds the contemporary Russian Federation to an invented tradition. Oleksandr Zakharchenko, leader of the so-called "Donetsk People's Republic," in an interview with *Komsomolskaya Pravda* distils the essence of patriotic struggle with morally justified resistance and heroism in the face of external immorality and aggression:

A feeling has now awakened in our people, an inner spirit that is inherent in us alone. The spirit that helped to break the neck of the French [in 1812], the spirit that walked in Vanya Susanin [hero who gave his life for the czar in 1613], the spirit that was present in the defenders of Brest [in 1941], the spirit that plunged into the embrasures of gun emplacements, that turned aircraft towards the fascist echelons, Poltava [in 1709], the battle of Kulikovo [in 1380] . . . The thousand-year-old spirit of freedom is back with a bang. Imagine all Russia being "infected" with this. And we will say: "Stop, we really are the descendants of those glorious predecessors who handed all this down to us. And we can do it." And we will hand down to our children what our forefathers left to us. And then this country is indestructible. That is all there is to it!

(Kots and Steshin, 2016)

The underlying message that unites contemporary military–patriotic political discourse in Russia today is: the future is fear – the present unstable and unpredictable – and the past glory. President Putin has both instilled fear in a future without him at the helm of the Russian ship-of-state and, at the same time, propagated a great and glorious Russian past which only he can uphold and sustain if only because of its eternal vulnerability.

Sergei Lavrov noted that President Putin published an article on 22 June 2021 titled: "Being Open, Despite the Past." In this article, Putin noted:

> We simply cannot afford to carry the burden of past misunderstandings, hard feelings, conflicts, and mistakes. He also discussed the need to ensure security without dividing lines, a common space for equitable cooperation and inclusive development. This approach hinges on Russia's thousand-year history and is fully consistent with the current stage in its development.
>
> *(Lavrov, 2021)*

The fixation of current elites with "Russia's thousand-year history" can be explained through the need to create a stable sense of self (self-identity), a response to the "ontological anxiety" caused by the disintegration of the Soviet Union or the "greatest geopolitical tragedy of the 20th century" in the words of Vladimir Putin. "Ontological security" places an emphasis on continuity, consistency and order and also dislocation, trauma and tragedy and how this is interpreted (Chrzanowski, 2021; Steele, 2021). President Putin's references to "time bombs" embedded in the Soviet Constitution (the right of former Soviet Republics to withdraw from the Union) or the over-reliance on the Communist Party as unifying actor highlight two sources of "ontological anxiety" and "ontological insecurity." Russian history is politicized and made to matter.

This chapter identifies some of the key "lessons" that Russia's current elite draw from Russian history and communicate to Russian society. When examining Russia's political culture, three interlocking factors appear as constants that reinforce themselves and grow stronger through time: a return to great power status; a well-founded fear of instability and an understanding that respect is generated, ultimately, through fear. These "lessons" have been attributed to a number of factors, not least the role of geography, the development of the Russian economy and the role of the elite and emergence and consolidation of a service state, a strong leader defending a besieged fortress against external adversary's intent on destruction of the Russian people, their sacred beliefs and inalienable values.

Cycles in Russian history

The Holy Grail for Russian historians is to correctly discern patterns of historical development, which allows for a grand unified theory that explains the "inner logic" of how the present is shaped by the past. Reoccurring patterns and parallels suggest a rhyme and reason that underpin Russian historical evolution, implying that the weight of history and heritage constitutes a powerful determinant of Russian history. If only properly understood, this reasoning goes, and these faint echoes allow us to discard historical stereotypes and identify how and when contemporary official narratives propagated by state-controlled media instrumentalize Russian history by cherry picking examples of success or failure in any given period to support and legitimize contemporary foreign and security policy preferences:

> Attempts to draw parallels always seem to me a very foolish method of scientific analysis. The similarity which you note is mainly superficial, you lose sight of what is most important since what is most important are not similarities but differences. I am against the drawing of historical parallels – they mislead us.
>
> *(Shulman, 2017)*

Vladislav Surkov argues that Russia will experience "a hundred years (or possibly two hundred or three hundred) of geopolitical loneliness", and that Russia with its "doubleheaded statehood, hybrid mentality, intercontinental territory and bipolar history" would no longer oscillate between the East and West (Surkov, 2018). Vladimir Ryzhkov, having surveyed the latest history text book issued to Russian school children, argues that its purpose is to forge "obedient servants" in thrall to the idea of the supremacy of the state, with state interests privileged above those of the individual citizen and to that end:

> Ivan the Terrible is a "reformer," Stalin is a "modernizer," the democratic achievements of Gorbachev and Yeltsin are ignored, and Putin is a hero who restored Russia's greatness. . . . Simply put, it suggests that all tsars and Communist Party general secretaries were enlightened autocrats, no matter what they did to their own people. The text overlooks the fact that this pantheon of leaders did little or nothing to improve the lives of their citizens, develop the economy or introduce personal freedoms, and it lavishly praises them for the far more important accomplishment of strengthening and expanding the state.
>
> *(Ryzhkov, 2013)*

When accounting for both change and continuity in Russian history, the prevalence of apparent "cycles" has been widely noted, though Igor Guberman's famous verse regarding the influence of the 'bald' and the 'hairy' on Russia's political regime – ". . . things ease up when the bald are in charge, and then things become harder again when the hairy take over" – suggests, to say the least, that correlation should not in every case be confused with causation (Pastukhov, 2018). Historical parallels can be illustrative and allow for comparisons, but they can also obscure important differences between the present and the past, given Russia's elite is more educated than Soviet predecessors and the economy much more flexible.

The theory of cyclical recurrence is, at least, an enduring feature of Russian historical development. It suggests that periods of decentralization, relaxation and reform are followed or preceded by periods of centralization, conservatism and repression. Advocates of this view point to the reformist and counter-reformist cycles exemplified by the reigns or rule of, for example, *Tsar* Alexander II, the Communist Party of the Soviet Union (CPSU) General Secretary Khrushchev, Gorbachev and Russian Federation President Yeltsin on the one hand, and the reigns of Alexander III, Nicholas II, CPSU General Secretary Stalin and now President Putin. Stalin replaced Lenin's New Economic Policy of the 1920s with the "Great Terror" of the 1930s; Gorbachev's reforms of the 1980s ended Brezhnev's stagnation of the 1970s. In short,

> Reform in Russia: over the centuries has always failed, sometimes to be replaced by a reactionary regime (Alexander III's reversal of Alexander II's "great reforms" of the 1860s and 1870s), and sometimes culminating in the collapse of the system (1917 and 1991).
>
> *(McDaniel, 1996)*

As Alexey Kudrin, a liberal economist and former Finance Minister wryly noted: "You know, when everything stagnates, when something needs to be moved forward, they call the liberals. Because, as a rule, they cross those conservative boundaries, give a new movement, a new fresh stream" (Loshak, 2021). In foreign policy cycles alternative periods of détente and confrontation can be punctuated by romanticism and resets. This pattern is evident, for example, in Russian–US relations, which in the contemporary Biden–Putin era are characterized by an action–reaction, escalation–retreat cycle. (Tsygankov, 2021; Baunov, 2021)

There are at least three points of interest that this schema raises. First, as there is no consensus as to how either reform or counter reform efforts are associated with stability or instability, we can ask: do reforms constitute forced development that damage stability and equilibrium? Can counter reforms be understood as short-term stability, followed by political and economic stagnation and then eventually instability? Putin's fourth presidential term certainly poses that question, even as it has yet to answer it. Second, should reforms be associated with pro-liberal, pro-western domestic and foreign policies? If so, are counter reforms synonymous with reactionary conservative, nationalist and xenophobic turns in Russian history? Given the numerous attempts at reformist breakthroughs since the mid-sixteenth century, many prominent Russian leaders were both reformers and counter-reformers: Ivan Groznyy, Peter I, Alexander I, and Lenin embody this phenomena. Had Putin's fourth term recaptured his first term reformist drive (2000–2003), his rule may have been added to this list as well. Third, what is the catalyst that accounts for radical and all-encompassing profound shifts in any prevailing sociocultural national tradition, mentality and psyche at any given time? For Solovey, "mutation, metamorphosis, and modifications" are driven by breakdown and discord associated with the "Time of Troubles," such as 1598–1613, the 1917–23 (Revolutions and Civil War – which actually continued another ten years in Soviet Central Asia) or, according to Putinist somewhat self-serving and legitimizing narratives, the years 1989–2000. These years witnessed the Revolutions in Central and Eastern Europe, the collapse of the USSR in 1991 and then the Yeltsin years, which Putin labels as the new "Time of Troubles" (Solovey, 2004).

Other cycles are notable, not least the competition for indirect, mediated, influence on political decisions between military bureaucracies and those in the civilian spheres, such as police and security services. Pastukhov again argues that the

> political role of the civilian bureaucracy is manifested at the surface only in periods of crisis, when the system is in need of restructuring. For the rest of the time more importance attaches to the rivalry between the two main detachments of the security forces bureaucracy – the army and the police (in the broad sense of the word). The choice in favor of a particular political strategy often depends on which of these two security services blocs is politically dominant at a given moment in time.
>
> *(Pastukhov, 2018)*

According to Pastukhov's argument, approximately every 12 years since 1917, one or the other bureaucracy has exercised political control: the military bureaucracies' influence was predominant from 1917 to 1929; the secret police until 1941; the military through to the anti-Beria coup of 1953; young KGB cadres undertaking de-Stalinization under Khrushchev; USSR KGB Chairman Yuriy Andropov's appointment as CPSU Central Committee secretary oversaw the army's resurrection until *perestroika*. In the early 1990s, Yeltsin relied more on the military; but by 2001, the security service was back in vogue as democratization efforts were rolled back. At the start of Putin's third term in 2012, conflict in Ukraine (2014–), Syria (2015–) and concurrent military-patriotic mobilization propelled the army back to political predominance. By the fourth term, SVR and FSB coordinated cyber-hacking, GRU active measures and other undeclared hybrid operations and put the spotlight on both the intelligence services and Russian military.

Similarly, a motor of Russia's own cultural identity and historical evolution is shaped by patterns of alienation and attraction toward European civilizational identity, with Russia alternatively being a part of Europe and apart from Europe. Russia views Europe as a development model to be emulated or a source of military threat, reflecting both commonalities between the two as well as differences. The French historian Georges Sokoloff argues that from the tenth century onward, Russia, paradoxically, has gradually moved further from Europe every time it tried to "catch up" (Sokoloff, 2014). Russian–European relations are characterized by strategic cycles: first, Western influences through borrowing and adaptation spread within Russia; second, such influence became associated with attempts to undermine the integrity of Russian statehood (territorial integrity and sovereignty) either directly through invasions (Charles XII, 1700–1721; Napoleon, 1803–15; Hitler, 1941–45) or indirectly through the sponsorship of political dissent, with the contemporary expression of the notion of a "Color Revolution" or post-modern *coup d'état*. Westernization dynamics and impulses are followed by a backlash against and a rejection of the West. Russian society is polarized. The determination of Russia's elite to maintain a balance of power in Europe, gaining Western acknowledgment of Russia's great power status while expanding territory to the east, destabilizes Russian self-conceptions of its status, honor, prestige and pride (Tsygankov, 2014). In the Putinist period, particularly after 2014, Russia poses as champion of a conservative Europe, almost lost: "the Europe of tradition, modernity, cultural hierarchies and purity of form," not a "fallen" Europe, "with its dictatorship of minorities, its disintegration of strong ties and a whole set of its perversions" (Firsov, 2021).

Implicitly embedded in the metaphor of cycles is the notion that Russia's political culture has an underlying adaptability, persistence and strength, as its core essential features and characteristics are present in both periods of reform and repression. Russia's political culture withstood the Alexandrine reforms of 1861–74 (emancipation of the serfs, local government, judicial and military reforms); the 1917 Revolution and its aftermath – the Civil War, Stalin's 'Revolution from Above'; Gorbachev's *perestroika* and *glasnost* reform efforts; and the disintegration of USSR. Its core characteristics continued to endure through the Yeltsin years of the 1990s, Putin's seven golden years of economic growth (2000–2007), President Medvedev's modernization efforts and now, in the late Putin period, Russia's current economic stagnation, military-patriotic mobilization and the securitization of "spiritual" values. President Putin explicitly views his regime in terms of restoration, and his worldview encapsulates the notion of cyclical theory: it is founded on the myth that liberal reformers and a weak state brought a "time of troubles" in the 1990s, whereas "effective managers" in his regime, by contrast, have established stability, order and prosperity and rescued Russia from failing state status, restoring its great power identity, pride, prestige and honor. If the idea of cycles holds, then for Putin the significance lies in what comes after: the presumption being that Putinism (anti-Westernism, anti-liberalism and anti-pluralism) would be followed by the opposite. In other words, Putinism will not outlast Putin.

The influence of structural factors

Throughout Russian history, the physical survival of the Russian state has been an overriding objective. To that end, a premium has been placed on social control and order as this ensured predictability and so stability. Nadezhda Arbatova highlights the enduring impact of thirteenth-century Tatar–Mongol conquest (1236–38) of what is Russia today on Russian political and strategic culture, noting that "before the Mongol–Tatar invasion, Russian principalities were developing much like the rest of Europe." Novgorod, Vladimir, Suzdal, Pskov and other "cities in *Kievan Rus'* all had a town assembly (*veche*) comprising all free male citizens, who met to discuss and resolve the community's most important problems." After the Mongol invasion, this *veche* self-government system of early feudal monarchy was replaced by the Horde system, which "laid the foundations for Muscovite autocracy through its emphasis on the centralization of power, personal loyalty to a single ruler, strict social hierarchies, the militarization of the nation and a huge repressive apparatus" (Arbatova, 2019, 10). The shock and humiliation of slaughter, enslavement and subjugation shattered preexisting political authority in *Kievan Rus'*, which facilitated the role of the Russian Orthodox Church as the "embodiment of both religious and national identity while filling the gap of lost political identity" (Riasanovsky, 2000, 57). The Tatar–Mongol "yoke" reinforced the notion that different ethnicities had to live "symbiotically" and that a strong power was a necessity (Shlapentokh, 2020). Echoes of the Mongol–Tatar past resonated in the Russian empire, divided as it was among 10 governor-generals (*Voeovoda*), each appointed by the *Tsar*. In Chechnya today, Ramzan Kadyrov is referred to as *padishah*, a Mongol and Ottoman empire monarchical title that derives from the Persian *shahanshah*, meaning "king of kings" (Yakovenko, 2020).

Ivan III Vasilyevich ('the Great') ruled from 1462 to 1505 as Grand Prince of Moscow and Grand Prince of all Rus'. His reign saw the end of the Mongol–Tatar dominance and restoration of independence after a victory over the Great Horde in 1480, though Tatars sacked Moscow as late as 1571. Moscow moved from tribute-paying client state status to a tripling of the size of its territory in this period. Ivan III created the foundations of a Russian-centralized state, establishing the practice of core governance concepts, such as the patriarchal order of succession, notion of the state as *votchina* (patrimony, that is estates owned by hereditary right) and *symfoniya* (Russian Orthodox Church–state relations), the divine origin of power and authority.

However, before a Russian identity rooted in a common conception of nationhood based on shared ethnicity and history was formed, by necessity Russia began to expand its territory both east and west. In this sense, Russia did not become an empire but was born an empire (Abalov and Inozemtsov, 2019). There is no foundational ethnicity or nation at its core. While to be Russian is to speak Russian and to be raised in a Russian cultural context, in the *Tsarist* and Soviet times, most Russians were Orthodox Christians and Muslims of Turkic origin. This ingrained imperial identity became the unifying inner logic linking *Tsarist* history and the Soviet institutional matrix to a contemporary revisionist Russia:

> The idea of an empire, on the other hand, implies expansion – seizure of vast territories and projection of strength – which forms the basis of an individual's self-respect and dignity and people's collective pride, but only as subjects of a great power. Under chronic poverty, especially during deepening crises and mass hopelessness, this feeling of greatness serves as a compensatory mechanism for lifting the chronic feeling of humiliation, dependence, poverty, and shame for one's existence – all these are typical features of a society that is catching up with modernization. There is no other foundation for collective pride in Russia.
>
> *(Khvostunova, 2021)*

This explains an enduring sense of state vulnerability and fragility and why territorial expansion rather than development or democratization is perceived to be a source of stability and unity. In the post-Soviet period, a new Russian identity was enshrined in the Constitutional changes of 2020: ethnic Russians ("*Russkiye*") are declared to be the dominant state-forming group, and Russia has a right and responsibility to protect Russian-speaking communities in post-Soviet space.

Russia's first empire – what we would now term as "historical Russia" – was created between 1480 and 1721, built around Moscow and Muscovy and *Rossiya* (a term first used in the 1490s) and consisted of territory colonized by the Muscovite empire. Expansion was rapid: between 1644 and 1650, Russian settlers reached the Pacific; in 1649 they reached the Chukotka Peninsula. In 1567, the terms Muscovy or Muscovy *Tsardom* entered official use. The second "inner" empire was created between 1722 and 1914. Importantly, this empire consisted of conquered territories where Russians had never been in a majority: Poland, Finland, Bessarabia, the North and South Caucasus and Central Asia. The third "outer" empire was created between 1917 and 1991, with the Molotov–Ribbentrop Pact allowing for forced annexation, and the Yalta–Potsdam conferences for Stalinization of eight polities in Central and Eastern Europe and imposed neutrality on Finland and Austria (Abalov and Inozemtsov, 2019). Does Putin create a "Post-Soviet space 2.0" – which we can characterize as the fourth empire? Or is Russian policy really post-post imperial, that is, pragmatic, interest-based, unemotional, and non-ideological?

Foreigners, with alien disruptive ideas and practices, were to be feared. A risk-averse culture centered on *sobornost* ("togetherness") and consensual collective decision-making was a feature of village life (Keenan, 1986). Individual initiative was discouraged as it threatened the *status quo,* and political, religious and other nonconformists were outlawed. As a result of a mismatch between resources available to be mobilized against threats to group survival, stability and order were placed above individual initiative, justice and accumulated wealth. Given the immense size of Russia, sparse settlements and poor communications, elites focused on a limited agenda centered on regime survival. Indeed, Vladislav Surkov in essence argued that the Mongols left, but the yoke remained: "high internal tension associated with the retention of vast heterogeneous spaces, and constant presence in the midst of geopolitical struggle make the state's military – police functions the most important and decisive" (Surkov, 2019). *Sobornost* could also manifest itself in spontaneous social protest against the "Bad *Boyars*," if not the "Good *Tsar*." This notion continues to have relevance today, not least as Putin himself has *Tsar*-like status (Myers, 2015).

For example with the creation of the National Guard (*Rosgvardiya*) in April 2016, the Federal Drug Control Service of the Russian Federation (FSKN) was amalgamated with the Ministry of Interior (MVD), and President Putin promised that jobs would be protected. However, of the 300 officers in the FSKN's Transbaikal branch, only 14 subsequently found employment in the MVD. One unemployed officer, reflecting on his predicament, expressed well the pervasive belief in a "good *tsar*, bad *boyar*" syndrome:

There is no help coming our way from the central unit of the Federal Drug Control Service. Our former bosses have withdrawn and abandoned us all. We are alone, and the Ministry of Internal Affairs does whatever it wants with us. And the leadership of the country is probably unaware of what is going on. Our president is a decent person, whom we all love and respect. I think that he is simply being lied to and does not know that our food is being taken out of our mouths and that we are on the verge of living life as if it were the Siege of Leningrad.

("A Hard Goodbye," 2016)

In economic terms, Russia has always embodied a semi-integrated periphery to Europe, which for the last 500 years constituted the global imperial capitalist core. In the early modern period, Muscovite diplomacy sought to obtain diplomatic recognition and acknowledgment of Muscovy's Christian and European credentials from major European powers. In return, foreign commercial companies, such as the London-based Muscovy Company, (founded after the "discovery of Russia" in 1553) and their rivals, the Dutch Company, competed against each other to secure the privilege of trading with Russia and in the process reduce Russian dependence on Swedish and Polish trade. In this period, Russia exported a range of primary commodities – not least, timber, hemp, potash, whale oil and fur – while today oil, gas, grain, minerals, metals and armaments are dominant export commodities. In the late *Tsarist* period, trade surplus, foreign finance and investments fueled reform and modernization efforts to "catch-up" with the West, a realization underscored by Russia's defeat in the Crimean War (1853–56) by Great Britain and France and exacerbated further by Russia's peripheral "closed" status. A pattern of coercive state-led industrial growth was followed by periods of stagnation. By the twentieth century, Stalin expropriated money and resources from *"kulak class"* through forced collectivization to finance a crash-industrialization program. By contrast, Brezhnev accepted interdependence, exporting hydrocarbons in return for grain and foreign loans. The theme is clear: to overcome economic weakness and maintain internal stability and political order, Russia had either to trade and accept dependencies and vulnerabilities which came with external interaction or had to turn in on itself and use its indigenous resources at great human cost.

Russia's geographical size and the absence of a strong mercantile class and market towns generated spatial inefficiencies and statist and mercantilist policies. The interplay of geography, limited resources and constant threats highlighted the need for a unified command, a single power center, a strong military and an ability to create buffer zones on the periphery. This in turn affected the relationship between the elite, the state and the economy, and it created a "service nobility" that serviced a "service state." Russia's elite was militarized and mobilized and regulated state resources to defend the state. This entailed forced extraction of raw materials, constraints placed on the *Boyar* (noble) elite through the conditionality placed on their privileges (suppression of the right to private property prevented independent power bases that could challenge the *Tsar*) and on society through serfdom. This created an institutional structure or matrix particular to Muscovy and then the Russian Empire, Soviet and post-Soviet Federation. (Hellie, 2005; Hedlund, 2006)

Major threats to Russia mounted by foreign adversaries shaped ways in which the Russian elite and society served the state and mobilized resources. Russia's elite constituted the service class of the service state, and defensive reactive responses to external aggression triggered what historian Richard Hellie has identified as three service class revolutions. The first service class revolution occurred in 1480, following the annexation of the city of Novgorod by Russia in 1478, when newly acquired Novgorodian territory could be distributed as service land (*pomestie*) to the old Muscovite elite, which consisted of provincial cavalrymen totally dependent on *Tsarist pomestie* patronage. In order to enforce *Tsarist* power, in 1565, Ivan IV (the Terrible) created an administrative system whereby the *oprichnina* (literally, "the place apart") consisting of territory under the control of the state and separated from *boyar* lands (*zemshchina*), allotted it to a personal guard (*oprichniki*), which he also created (Hellie, 1971, 1987). This coercive structure was prepared to use terror against the *Tsar's* opponents within the *boyar* elite and dispossess them of lands and was under his direct control.

The second service class revolution occurred during the Great Northern War (1700–1721) and was codified through the Petrine "Table of Ranks" in 1721, which created a merit-based hierarchy as the Baltic cities Narva, Reval (Tallinn) and Riga were incorporated into the Russian Empire, and with them the land that could be reallocated and distributed among the Petrine *boyar* elite. The Russian Orthodox Church had formerly controlled one third of the land as Church land, but in 1721 the Holy Synod was created as a department of government. Peter the Great's service state defeated Charles II of Sweden and pushed back against the Crimean khanate and *Rzeczpospolita* (Polish-Lithuanian Commonwealth). The bearers of Russia's strategic culture in the first two service class revolutions were the *Tsar*, the military leadership, cavalry class and the wider *boyar* elite (Hellie, 2006).

The third service class revolution occurred in 1927/28 and aimed at the elimination of the *institution* of property rights. This service class revolution can be understood as an attempt to consolidate a Soviet institutional matrix and create and then consolidate a Soviet service state class. The Stalin "revolution from above" bound peasants to the land through its nationalization, the process of collectivization and industrialization. These three processes were overseen by the Communist Party of the USSR which controlled the top 400,000 *nomenklatura* positions, that is to say the core influential administrative positions in the state bureaucracy (Tucker, 1992). While collectivization in the 1930s has been labeled Russia's 'second serfdom', following the serfdom that existed between 1725 and 1861 and was experienced by 80 percent of the Soviet population, which even by the early twentieth century was peasant. This means most Russians are "two to four generations removed from their peasant ancestors" (Trudolyubov, 2018). Alexander Nikulin, head of the Center of Agrarian Studies at the Academy of National Economy, notes that:

> Three Soviet generations were not enough to kill off the rural streak in the citizens of the formerly great peasant power. We see the fragments of the former peasant worldview in the ways people tend to their country plots of land, to their dachas. We see the lifestyle of a people who are atomized, powerless, deprived of any real self-rule or communal cooperation.
>
> *(Trudolyubov, 2018)*

Collectivization enabled the state to exert control over the economy and society to receive a minimum wage, social welfare, benefits and pensions (Pipes, 1974). Though property was nationalized, power and status offered the *nomenklatura* a compensatory alternative:

> A party boss did not own a factory personally – he could not even buy a flat – but his position in the party gave him access to the collective property of the state, including elite housing and special food parcels. The word "special" was a favorite one in the Soviet system, as in "special meeting," "special departments" and "special regime."
>
> *(Russia: The Long Life of Homo Sovieticus, 2011)*

In the Soviet period, a very narrow understanding of the bearers, carriers or keepers of Russia's political and strategic culture attributed such status to the leadership in the communist party, Soviet military and wider military-industrial complex and the security services. A wider strategic community of experts existed within the leading Academy of Sciences Institutes addressing international political and economic affairs. The collapse of the Soviet system can be in part attributed to the decision of the Soviet elite "to 'monetize' their privileges and turn them into property." In the Yeltsin era, the "word 'special' was also commercialized to become *eksklusivny* (exclusive) and *elitny* (elite)." Under President Putin, "special" regained its Soviet meaning without losing its commercial value. "A black Mercedes with a blue flashing light, ploughing its way through pedestrians, became the ultimate manifestation of power and money" ("The Long Life of *Homo Sovieticus*", 2011).

Is President Putin instituting a fourth service class revolution "2003–" ? In 2014, President Putin

> created a parallel system of power from people personally devoted to him, on whom he relied when resolving any issues. For almost 500 years that system of power in Russia has been called the oprichnina system. Its structure is uncomplicated, but it operates effectively.
>
> *(Pastukhov, 2018)*

Putin's creation of the National Guard (*Rosgvardia*), the imprisonment of Mikhail Khodovovsky, the creation of a corporate state and 10-year hard penal colony for former Economic Development Minister Aleksey Ulyukayev indicate that in budgetary and judicial terms a division between *zemshchina* (institutionalized normative-state based "Collective Putin") and the *oprichnina* (Putin's networked prerogative state) appears to exist, with Rosneft and the FSB part of Putin's *oprichnina*. The *oprichnina* is able to terrorize the politically neutered and loyal *zemshchina*, increasing their influence through over fulfilling the mandate, raiding in the name of economic crimes ("fraud" and "criminal association"), when attempts at extortion and brigandage fail:

> To understand what is happening it is important to know not which prominent figures are being jailed but which of them cannot yet be jailed. Joining the secret caste of untouchables and staying in it as long as possible is the Russian political and business elite's highest and essentially only aim. And to somehow preserve what they have acquired for their children in a country where *de facto* there is no private property.
>
> *(Novoprudskiy, 2019)*

As Vladimir Pastukhov observes:

> Under the *oprichnina*, state bureaucracy does not disappear, but it is assigned a secondary, technical, role. Political and control functions are concentrated in the hands of a narrow circle of figures close to the head of state and organized according to a medieval ranking system. Today's mafia structures are organized in a similar manner.
>
> *(Pastukhov, 2018)*

Necessity of a strong leader and "besieged fortress'" syndrome

Statehood is sacrosanct, sacred and unqualified and to be defended at all costs. As a result, such a state must be ruled by a strong leader if it is to survive as an independent and sovereign entity. In addition, a relationship between Russia's size not only influenced its economy, but also shaped its governance system. Vladimir Pastukhov argues that:

> the size of the country has always been a powerful stabilizing force for political power, and as a consequence, the most important condition for the preservation of sovereignty and independence of the Russian state (thanks in part, of course, to the resources that can be "dug up" on this territory).

However, he notes that

> it was precisely the grandiosity of this space (which had to be settled and controlled), the impossibly long land and sea borders (which had to be serviced and defended), and the variety of geographical, economic, and cultural

conditions (which had to be reduced to a common denominator), that served to hinder the successful evolution of the country's social and political systems, and, in part, the conversion of the empire into a nation-state. Under these conditions, any transformational impulse quickly ran out of steam and dissolved without a trace.

(Pastukhov, 2016)

The Russian political system and default political doctrine have been state-centered. At times statism has manifested itself in attempts at absolutism. Russian history has never experienced a popular secular constitutional tradition. Neither the ordinary mass of society or independent institutions have at any point taken part in the national, still less national-security, decision-making process. This function was the preserve of designated or unelected leaders, an elite inner circle clustered around a strong leader, whether that be *Tsar*, *Vozhd*, or President. As Lilia Shevtsova notes, leadership "continues to be Russia's major political institution – in fact, it's only one" (Shevtsova, 2003). Russia's theory of rule – a Russian equivalent of the "divine right of kings" – dates back to the reign of Grand Prince Ivan III: "In his person, the ruler is a man, but in his authority he is like a God" (Hellie, 2005). Indeed, in Stalin's view, the Russian people needed a "czar whom they can worship and for whom they can live and work." Valentina Matvienko, a Putin ally, former governor of St. Petersburg and now Speaker of the Russian Senate, believes that a parliamentary republic headed by a prime minister would fail in Russia: "No, this doesn't fit us. We are not ready for such an experiment. The Russian mentality needs a baron, a czar, a president . . . In one word, a boss" (Starobin, 2005). A circular logic was at work. If the Russian people obey their leader, they create a strong motherland. Vasily Yakemenko, head of the Russian Federal Agency for Youth Affairs, perhaps unwittingly through his telling use of metaphor, captures well the notion that a subservient and paternalist society is to be protected by a strong patriarch:

> Imagine that the government is the husband, that state power is the husband, and that all of us – society – is the wife. In 2000 our society married Vladimir Vladimirovich Putin. Society voted for him and said: Vladimir Vladimirovich, be our husband, care for us, protect us, give us work.
>
> *(Boyes, 2014)*

Historically, Russia has demonstrated a preference for an autocratic monarchical façade that cloaks an oligarchic bureaucratic reality (Hellie, 1977; Pomper, 2012). In this reality, decision-making, as in the village, was collegial, even if dynastic *Boyar* clans and their extended families were reluctant to discuss the inner workings of the system. The *Tsar* balanced, aligned, reconciled and harmonized the interests of an elite to maintain stability. This elite was clustered around him in a hierarchy of concentric circles. The closest circle was familial, consisting of maternal uncles, cousins and other familial relations. A *Boyar* elite accepted the idea of a strong leader as the leader gave both legitimacy to their position and protection of their clan against other clans that conspired against them.

The lack of a clear and institutionalized succession process has led to succession crises. At such moments, military units could play decisive roles, despite Russia's tradition of civilian control of the military. In the seventeenth century, numerous *streltsy* (old style musketeer regiments created by Ivan IV a century before) revolts were triggered by Miloslavsky–Naryshkin *boyar* clan factionalism, not least in 1682, 1689 and especially 1698 (Herd, 2001). In the eighteenth century, Peter the Great's new style *Gvardiya* (guards' regiments) played a decisive role in determining the outcome of both Catherine the Great's overthrow of Peter II by *coup d'état* in 1762 and the murder of Paul I on 23 March 1801 (by dismissed officers), opening the way for his son Alexander I to accede to the throne. Following Alexander's death in 1825, the Decembrist revolt broke out in St Petersburg, involving some 3000 troops and heavy artillery. The February Revolution of 1917 was precipitated by military defeats and potential mutiny, with the armed forces unable to suppress revolt, resulting in the abdication of Nicholas II. An armed insurrection of Bolshevik-led soldiers and workers ushered in Communist rule, and the Civil War itself was mid-wife to the Soviet Union in December 1922.

In the Soviet period, a leadership crisis followed Stalin's sudden death in 1953. Former Marshall of the Soviet Union, but then Defense Minister Zhukov, allied with Georgy Malenkov and Nikita Khrushchev, opposed, arrested and shot Lavrenti Beria. Beria was the first deputy prime minister, head of the ministry of the interior (which had merged with the ministry of state security) and the second most powerful man in the Soviet Union, poised to become its leader. A late Soviet *coup d'état* attempt in August 1991 by a self-declared State Committee on the State of Emergency precipitated the end of the Communist Party of the Soviet Union and collapse of the Soviet Union itself. The *coup* involved the deployment of the Tamanskaya and Kantemirovskaya divisions and paratroopers – around 4,500 troops, 350 tanks and 300 armored personnel carriers – in Moscow itself in its support. During the Constitutional Crisis of 1993, the army stormed the Supreme Soviet on 4 October in events that appeared to herald civil war in Moscow, if not throughout the Russian Federation.

Thus, rather than a pyramid of power, an informal network structure may provide a clearer conceptual map that better reflected the reality of Russian power practice in history and today:

> Orbiting around Putin are powerful figures connected to his person: former colleagues in the KGB/FSB, civic colleagues from St. Petersburg, relatives, friends and their children, and his close buddies from the Ozero dacha collective. All of these people are bound to Putin as *svoi* – people in his personal circle.
>
> *(Ledeneva, 2013)*

A premodern symbiosis between strong informal personalized interest-based elite networks and weak formal state administrative institutions creates a *sistema* which exists today. Elite networks infiltrate the weak and inefficient normative state, hold high-ranking positions, dominate policy-making and secure their special interests without being held to account (Kononenko and Moshes, 2011). *Sistema* is tenacious: "Peter the Great tried to systematize it. Nicholas I tried to regularize it. Stalin tried to simply chop off its head and begin anew. Each failed because *sistema* looms too large" (Guillory, 2013). State officials in public administration interact with counterparts in politics, business, law enforcement and the judiciary and legislative system within this *sistema*. As Gleb Pavlovskiy observes:

> In actuality, there has been no state in Russia ever since then (1993); there only exists a "system" in which the government is tied to society on the one hand and to business on the other. The foundation of this system does not lie in the assets of the state but rather in the act of taking power. It is only once you hold power that you may gain control of said assets, which are necessary in order to maintain loyalty by handing out loans and subsidies.
>
> *(Pavlovskiy, 2015)*

Pavlovsky goes on to develop this argument by noting: "*Sistema* is a deep-seated facet of Russian culture that goes beyond politics and ideology." *Sistema* "combines the idea that the state should enjoy unlimited access to all national resources, public or private." Within such a system, business and the state "have merged in a union of total and seamless corruption" (Pavlovsky, 2016). Alena Ledeneva brilliantly uncovers the logic of *sistema*: no one leader can reform *sistema* as they are too entrapped by it.

> The more leaders try to change *sistema*, the more they have to rely on the informal means of execution of power and decision-making outside of formal procedures. The more they rely on them, the more they get entangled and eventually tied up with *sistema*'s power networks. The more reliant on institutions, and thus less interventionist, leaders are, the less credit they receive for their leadership. It is almost as if informal leadership is a key characteristic of leadership in Russia, unachievable without instruments of informal governance.
>
> *(Ledeneva, 2013)*

Within this construct, and as with every Russian leader, President Putin mediates elite clan and factional economic interests: "Putin's role in this system remains the same: His role is that of an arbiter and moderator. Truth be told, he is an influential arbiter, who, at least in conflict situations, still has the final say" (Kasciunas et al., 2014). This arbitration function is particularly challenging in a context where resources available for redistribution (for example, via major infrastructure projects) become scarce and competition increases. Before 2012, these interests were understood to represent *siloviki* (security service elite headed by Rosneft President Igor Sechin) clans pitted against system liberals (globalized oligarchs headed by former President and Prime Minister Sergei Medvedev). Putin's personalized loyalty networks within his elite shared the same objectives – a great power-resurgent Russia – but differed on the best means to realize this vision. According to a report titled *Politburo 2.0 in the Post-Crimea Russia* published by Minchenko Consulting, based on interviews with more than 60 experts with close ties to the government, Russian governance model evolved on Putin's return to the presidency. By 2015, Putin's system of control had shifted from a binary or "bipolar model" that balanced the two broad factions toward a sectoral approach in which President Putin exercises power through determining how resources are distributed between key sectors, including energy, the Defense Industrial Complex (DIC), financial sector, security structures and foreign policy. Given that Putin rather than the market or other less personalized forms of rationality decides resource distribution, a populist corrupt kleptocracy ("mafia state") has emerged (Kosnya, 2014).

As Russia historically lacks an independent judiciary and a culture of public scrutiny of decision-making (which national security decision-makers would view as destabilizing and dangerous), the relationship between rulers and ruled (subjects rather than citizens) was characterized by paternalism and patrimonialism. That is to say, direct personal relations and exchanges occur and take place within extended networks of patrons and clients in the context of patronage politics, a weak rule of law, nepotism and corruption and low levels of social capital (Hale, 2017). Under these conditions, the "service state" has primacy over the individual, that is to say, subjects provide service to the state rather than the state provides citizens with public services. The persistence of patrimonialism is evident in Putin's Russia today as Putin: "makes no distinction between public and private property and is seen by his followers as having authority to dispose of all property as he sees fit." In return for loyalty, submission and obedience, "the followers receive material and political benefits and prestige from the ruler. Patrimonialism has thrived in Russia for hundreds of years, but rarely has it been as entrenched as over the past sixteen years" (Kramer, 2005). Vladimir Yakunin, the former head of state-owned Russian Railways, has cautioned that rotations in the inner circle around Putin suggest that "Putin has yet to form a stable ruling class like Russia had during czarist times" and as a consequence "some insiders are making the mistake of viewing their property and privilege as inalienable rights, but everything they have hinges on Putin's shifting views of what's good for Russia" (Trudolyubov, 2016). The service state is alive and well, even if Putin has proved unable to institute a fourth service state class revolution.

Manufactured consent and the invention of tradition

Widely held core assumptions, values and preferences have shaped Russian foreign policy over the last 700 years. Within this Russian tradition, the interplay of ideology, identity and interests has resulted in changing rather than static fixed sets of strategic relations, postures and orientations. In our century, a well-developed sense of Russian cultural exceptionalism combines with a deep sense of insecurity and vulnerability. Compensatory official accounts emphasize stable continuities in "cultural and historical codes", "cultural matrix", "genes" and a Russian "ethnos." As Igor Zevelev goes on to note: "Another constant feature of history in this narrative is the centuries-old Western policy of containment of Russia" (Zevelev, 2014). "The notion of a Russian 'civilization' can be understood as "an attempt to construct unity across ideological, spatial and societal cleavages, associated with the disintegration of the Soviet Union and earlier critical points in Russian history."' (Khazarski, 2020).

"Ontological insecurity" and "ontological anxiety" created an "ontological drive" to invade Donbas. A traumatic interruption of routinized relations took place in 2014: the sudden fall of President Yanukovych as a controllable malleable and dependently corrupt asset and the breakup of the Moscow-friendly Party of Regions. However, 7 years of by now routinized low-level but ongoing conflict creates an "ontological security" dilemma: "Where conflict persists and comes to fulfill identity needs, breaking free can generate ontological insecurity, which states seek to avoid" (Chrzanowski, 2021). A new *status quo* is consolidated. Economic ties between Donetsk and Luhansk reorientate away from Ukrainian oligarchs (Rinat Akhmetov) to Moscow where "representatives of Russian financial-industrial groups are simply informed that they and their companies are now responsible for developing certain enterprises." A "Russian Donbass" emerges (Skorkin, 2021). This implies that a new greater dislocation will overturn this "new normal," leading to a breakthrough or paradigm shift in the shape-renewed real conflict resolution efforts or, more likely, further escalation. President Putin's radical language in his article "On the historical unity of Russians and Ukrainians" ("time bomb", "violent assimilation", "robbed", "WMD") promotes, without evidence, the fabricated idea of a *de facto* ongoing cultural genocide against Russians in Ukraine. Might Putin's "speech acts" signifying a clear ontological disruption to the "new normal" be used to justify a Russian policy shift to escalation, even further intervention? (Putin, 2021b)

Realpolitik pragmatism has also driven strategic behavior. The Russian empire's role at the Congress of Vienna (1815) and Joseph Stalin at the Yalta–Potsdam conferences (1945) are emblematic of this reality. The idea of a *Russkii Mir* centered naturally on a national conservative anti-liberal and anti-Western Russia demonstrates identity-driven strategic orientations. Ideology, interests and identity are of course present to differing extents in all periods of Russian history, and their centrality to Russian foreign policy is clear. The founding of St. Petersburg in 1702 – "the European Venice of the North" as Russia's new imperial capital – provided a strategic balcony through to the West. Peter the Great's defeat of Charles XII of Sweden at the battle of Poltova in 1709 and ultimate victory in the Great Northern War best exemplify a westernizing tradition in Russian history. Fyodor Dostoevsky expresses well a profound and shared disillusionment with this orientation that also exemplifies a Russian historical tradition: "Russia was a slave in Europe but would be a master in Asia" (Lieven, 1999). Contemporary expressions of Slavophile and Eurasianist orientations are at play today as an anti-Western foreign policy encourages domestic self-reliance (Slavophile) and a pivot to Asia (Eurasianist). The Syrian expeditionary intervention signals Russia's global rather than regional power aspirations and coincides with the notion of a non-Western, ideally anti-Western, BRICS-based multipolar international order, with Russia looking to strengthen relations with Brazil, Vietnam, India, Indonesia, Iran, Cuba, Pakistan and South Africa as main partners (Trenin, 2016).

In reality, when compared to other "centers of global power," Russia's power is one dimensional, resting as it does on its military–nuclear triad power component, rather than on a multidimensional power complex. Human capital is the critical capability that shapes the economic strength and technological development of Russia. Those that emigrate to the West are scholars, college students and independently wealthy Russians, including former government officials, families of politicians and members of the financial and bureaucratic elite. As a result, development within Russia slows.

The common thread running through Russian foreign policy is its status-seeking nature, one that values respect, recognition and acknowledgment above all. Igor Zevelev captures the different historical dynamics and logics in Russia's changed strategic calculus well:

> By spring 2014 Moscow had developed a seemingly irrational combination of the logic and rhetoric borrowed from the discourses concerning three spheres: (1) national identity (involving the ideas of "compatriots abroad," "the Russian world," "a divided people," and "a greater Russian civilization"); (2) international security; and (3) domestic stability. In all these spheres, the Kremlin sees threats emanating from the West.
>
> *(Zevelev, 2014)*

The notion of righting "outrageous historical injustice" and reuniting "historically Russian land" is used to justify intervention, as is Russia's historical great power role in the region to use the metaphors of President Putin:

> The ox may not be allowed something, but the bear will not even bother to ask permission. Here we consider it the master of the taiga, and I know for sure that it does not intend to move to any other climatic zones – it will not be comfortable there. However, it will not let anyone have its taiga either. I believe this is clear.
>
> *("Meeting of the Valdai", 2014)*

According to this perspective, encroachment takes many forms, including the physical encirclement of Russian territory, as well as an ideational contest in which West would instrumentalize its political system to undermine, weaken and ultimately control Russia.

Belarus, Ukraine and Russia stood as the three core fraternal pillars of a Slavic Orthodox empire, and President Putin views the second and third most populous Slavic republics as part of one historical Russian space and mission (Motyl, 2014). In a conversation with President Bush at April 2008 Bucharest NATO Summit, President Putin remarked: "You don't understand, George, that Ukraine is not even a state. What is Ukraine? Part of its territories is Eastern Europe, but the greater part is a gift from us" (Marson, 2009). On 27 July 2013 at the 1025th anniversary of the conversion of *Kievan Rus'* to Christianity, President Putin highlighted centrality of a "single people" in the *Russkii Mir*:

> we know today's reality of course, know that there are the Ukrainian people and the Belarusian people, and other peoples too, and we respect all the parts of this heritage, but at the same time, at the foundations of this heritage are the common spiritual values that make us a single people.
>
> *("Orthodox-Slavic Values", 2013)*

Five years later, on 28 July 2018 in a sermon in Moscow to mark the 1030th anniversary of the Baptism of *Rus*, the head of the Russian Orthodox Church, Patriarch Kirill, underlined this understanding, explaining that when using the term "Russian culture" he refers to Ukraine, Russia and Belarus, "because they are the Holy Rus and the Byzantines used to call our people 'Rus,' that is Russians, in the days of the Holy Knyaz Vladimir" (BBC Monitoring, 2018).

President Putin held his 2021 annual phone-in with the nation, known as "Direct Line with Vladimir Putin," and repeated the "single nation" assertion. For Putin, Moscow is both somehow central to *Kievan Rus'* or "Ancient Rus,'" as Putin calls it, and Muscovy, *Tsardom*, the Soviet Union and contemporary Russia are its unbroken linear descendants. On 12 July 2021, the president's website published his article titled: "On the historical unity of Russians and Ukrainians" (Putin, 2021a). In a follow-up interview, Putin claims that it is "analytical material based on historical facts, events and historical documents" (Putin, 2021b). In it, Putin states that "Both Russians, Ukrainians, and Belarusians are the heirs of Ancient Rus, which was the largest state in Europe" and that "The Kiev princely table occupied a dominant position in the Old Russian state." He repeats previous references to one (triune) people, one religion, one language. However, in reality, no single unified language or culture ever existed on the historical lands of Ukraine, Russia and Belarus. There was no "Ancient Rus," and an "Old Russian State" never existed: erecting a statue to Vladimir I in Moscow does not make it so.

The weight of this imperial tradition on contemporary thinking in Russia is profound. The year 1917 did not represent a historical watershed and chance for the Bolshevik Party to wipe the historical slate clean and build a 'brave new order': *Tsarist* imperial Russian heritage Russified communism as much as Communism communized Russia. A strong and enduring pre-Soviet Muscovite and Russian political imperial tradition and political culture heavily influenced and facilitated the transfer from a Russian to a Soviet empire. The Bolsheviks inherited the land and the peoples of the continental Russian Empire. Thus, a vast multiethnic and multinational, multi-faith territory had a Slavic Orthodox majority populace deeply imprinted by long experience of absolutism and a tradition of dominance and subjugation between imperial centers – Moscow, St. Petersburg/Petrograd and Moscow – and the periphery. One state (European Russia) effectively controlled the political sovereignty of other subordinated political societies (the non-Russian republics east of the Urals in the Arctic Circle and "Deep South" – the North Caucasus).

Conclusions

It is clear that:

> the foundations of Russian statehood have been in place for centuries: rigid authoritarian rule; the subordination of the economy to political and military goals; a repressive law-enforcement system; the merging of the state with the church; a messianic ideology; an imperial foreign policy; and militarism.
>
> *(Arbatova, 2019, 12)*

State-regulated elite discourses and narratives in Russia argue that Russian weakness invites external attack, with Charles XII, Napoleon and Hitler all able to evidence this reality. From this, it follows in the state narrative that to survive Russia needs a strong leader to defend the besieged fortress. Russia's conservative historical tradition is mined to highlight the notions that Russia has a special and unique path, mission and values – it is an exceptional power. Russia's imperial history, symbols and ceremonies are weaponized by current elites in order to project and buttress state narratives to legitimize current policies. Russian identity – language, culture and ethnicity – is instrumentalized as potent and popular justification for intervention. This weaponization of identity and its constituent components is itself a symptom of an "imperial subaltern syndrome" and the need for simulated sovereignty.

How does official state discourse in Russia today instrumentalize the *Tsarist* legacy? Nikolai Patrushev, Russian Security Council secretary, commenting on Russia's new NSS, made it clear that Russian history and historical memory are vital strategic assets that must be protected:

> In order to neutralise the threats associated with the distortion of history, the destruction of basic moral and ethical norms, and attempts to introduce alien ideals and values in the areas of education, culture, and religion, the strategy includes a new strategic national priority – protection of traditional Russian spiritual and moral values, culture and historical memory.
>
> *(Interview, 2021)*

The NSS stated that "Traditional Russian spiritual, moral and cultural and historical values are under intense attack from the United States and its allies, as well as by transnational corporations, foreign non-profit non-governmental, religious, extremist and terrorist organizations." As a result,

> Information and psychological sabotage and the "westernization" of culture reinforce the threat of the Russian Federation losing its cultural sovereignty. Attempts to falsify Russian and world history, distort the historical truth and destroy historical memory, incite inter-ethnic and interfaith conflicts, and weaken the state-forming people have increased their efforts to falsify Russian and world history.
>
> *(National Security Strategy, 2021)*

Putin's 12 July 2021 article ("On the historical unity of Russians and Ukrainians") attempts to consolidate a new official concept of the history of the relations between the two states. For the official state narrative, a 1,000-year "uninterrupted" history binds today's *Russkii Mir* (Russian World) and *Novorossiya* (New Russia/eastern Ukraine) to its linear descendant – *Kievan Rus'* – despite the historical realities of subordination, timelines and orientation.

> To illustrate this tendency, at the Valdai Club in October 2021, Putin stated: "Russia is also "a melting pot." Since the formation of a united Russian state – the first steps were made, probably in the 8th–9th centuries, and also after Conversion of Rus', the Russian nation and a centralised Russian state began to take shape with a common market, common language, the power of a prince and common spiritual values.
>
> *('Text of Report', 2021).*

The political aim is to argue that independent Ukraine is an anti-Russian project: "In the "anti-Russia" project there is no place for sovereign Ukraine, as well as for political forces that are trying to defend its real independence" (Putin, 2021a). This could be reformulated to mean there is no place for a sovereign Ukraine unless it is pro-Russian in strategic orientation. For Putin, "complete external management" becomes a euphemism for "independence." In other words, Putin's assertion of "historical destiny" means he thinks "historical choice" is predetermined, and if the wrong "historical choice" is made, Russia reserves the right to take action to rectify it:

> In Ukraine today the situation is completely different, since we are talking about a forced change of identity. And the most disgusting thing is that Russians in Ukraine are forced not only to renounce their roots, from generations of ancestors, but also to believe that Russia is their enemy. It would not be an exaggeration to say that the course towards violent assimilation, towards the formation of an ethnically pure Ukrainian state, aggressively disposed towards Russia, is comparable in its consequences to the use of weapons

of mass destruction against us. As a result of such a crude, artificial divide between Russians and Ukrainians, the total Russian people may decrease by hundreds of thousands, or even millions.

(Putin, 2021a)

This assertion represents the continued codification of a shift in Russian neighborhood policy, which began in practice in 2014, and provides the ideological underpinnings for an Orthodox "just war." Putin's predilection for "presentism," that is the application of present-day concepts, ideas and perspectives onto the past results in his interpretations and analysis of Russian history become a clear guide to contemporary Russia attitudes, justifications and policy toward neighbors, especially Ukraine and Belarus. The weaponization of Russian history to support contemporary policy preferences receives pushback, and memory politics has become a factor in interstate relations. In an "Address by President Volodymyr Zelenskyy on the occasion of the Day of Christianization of Kyivan Rus' – Ukraine," Zelensky stated that:

Ukraine is the successor of one of the most powerful states in medieval Europe. In its capital, which is the capital of modern Ukraine, the history of Christianity in Eastern Europe began, when 1033 years ago Grand Prince Volodymyr of Kyiv christened Kyivan Rus'. Kyivan Rus' – Ukraine. This is not part of our history, this is our history itself.

In case the pont was missed, Zelensky went on to note: "Kievan Rus' is the mother of our history" and that the

24 regions of Ukraine and the Crimean peninsula are her own children, and they are rightfully her heirs. And cousins and very distant relatives should not encroach on her legacy. They should not try to prove their involvement in the history of thousands of years and thousands of events, being from the places where they took place thousands of kilometers away.

(Zelensky, 2021)

Historical language has become a touchstone of political psychology, a proxy indicator for how Russians view contemporary politics, the very nature, roots and destiny of the state. As such, Russian history becomes more unpredictable, with "historical truth" whatever Putin says it is. Russia is posited as a distinct "neo-modern" "civilizational state," with a historical gravitational, order-producing and managerial role in a neighborhood characterized by trans-ethnic Russian language and Orthodox unity, a Slavic civilization and *Russkii Mir* in shared community (*obshchii Mir*) (Laruelle, 2016). This asserted shared imagined identity balances the centripedal forces few geographic boundaries and the reality of the "boundless Russian plain." The physical geography of *Russkii Mir* is ambiguous: is it primarily synonymous with Russian Orthodox geography ('Holy Rus'), Slavic ethnicity, imperial history (based on contiguous territories, underscored by contemporary Russian 'passportization' and 'borderization' practices in Abkhazia, South Ossetia Nagorno-Karabakh and Donbas) or does it, in addition, include any Russian compatriot community or even individual Russian speaker, wherever their location, be that in London, Geneva or Dubai, and whatever their citizenship? The pillars of neo-modernist thinking in the twenty-first century consist of nationalism, transactionalism, holism, historicism – reminiscent of Count Sergei Uvarov's nineteenth-century trinity of "Orthodoxy, Autocracy, Nationalism" which constituted the Russian Empire's state ideology – back to the future indeed (Yurgens, 2014).

In reality, Russians have an indistinct civilizational self-identity and weak geo-political and geo-cultural arsenal. Putin's assertions of one language, one people, one culture, religion and history drew a sarcastic response from Ukraine's President Zelensky:

> Let us finally dot the I's and cross the t's. We are definitely not one people. Yes, we have a lot in common. We have some shared history, memory, neighbourhood, relatives, the joint victory over fascism and common tragedies. But if Ukrainians and Russians were one people, the [Ukrainian national currency] *hryvnya* would, in all likelihood, circulate in Moscow, and a yellow and blue flag would be flying over the State Duma.
>
> *(BBC Monitoring, 2021)*

The myths and manipulations pedalled by Putin are phantom pains of a lost empire and identity, reflecting the experience of psychological alienation and isolation, which is exacerbated by a failure "to come to terms with the past" – what the Germans call *vergangenheitsbewältigung*. A "secret speech" in 1956 is no substitute for a "truth and reconciliation" commission in the 1990s. State narratives with an overemphasis on the importance of stability and the *status quo* and demonization of change and reform as the harbinger of chaos and a new time of troubles mean that Russia substitutes a bright and glorious past for a modernized future. This in turn indicates that in Russia, path dependency and patrimonial patterns are strongly ingrained in the political culture of the state. The overwhelming need for a *status quo*-based "order and stability" trumps any reform, developmental and modernization agenda. If it is true that *Tsarist* deep history has had a profound impact on contemporary strategic thinking in Russia, influencing how elites and society view and frame contemporary national interests, foreign policy goals and political and strategic culture, then period of 1917–1991 does the same, only more so.

Selected bibliography

Abalov, Alexander and Vladislav Inozemtsev. 2019. "Russia: The Everlasting Empire?" *Israel Journal of Foreign Affairs* 13 (3): 329–338.

Arbatova, Nadezhda. 2019. "Three Faces of Russia's Neo-Eurasianism." *Survival* 61 (6): 7–24.

Baunov, Alexander. 2021. "Escalation and Retreat: The New Model for U.S.-Russian Relations?" *Carnegie Moscow Center.* April 29, 2021. https://carnegie.ru/commentary/84432.

BBC Monitoring. 2018. "Russian Patriarch Calls Russians, Ukrainians, Belorussians 'One Nation'." *RIA Novosti. Moscow,* in Russian. July 28, 2018. https://monitoring.bbc.co.uk/product/c2004cxs.

———. 2021. "President Zelensky Rips Putin's Phone-in Comments on Ukraine." *Interfax-Ukraine News Agency.* Kyiv. July 1, 2021.

Boyes, Roger. 2014. "Mother Russia Takes a Lover." *The Times (London).* January 25, 2014.

Chrzanowski, Brendan. 2021. "An Episode of Existential Uncertainty: The Ontological Security Origins of the War in Donbas." *Texas National Security Review* 4 (3), Summer. https://tnsr.org/2021/05/an-episode-of-existential-uncertainty-the-ontological-security-origins-of-the-war-in-donbas/.

Crawford, Malcolm E. 2014. *The Rise of Russia: Putin's Place in Prophecy.* Bloomington, IN: WestBow Press.

Firsov, Alexei. 2021. "There Is No Such Thing as Eurasianism." *Vedomosti.* March 29, 2021.

Guillory, Sean. 2013. "Sistema: How Power Works in Modern Russia." *Russia Direct.* September 17, 2013. https://russia-direct.org/reviews/sistema-how-power-works-modern-russia.

Hale, Henry E. 2017. "Russian Patronal Politics beyond Putin." *Daedalus* 146 (2): 30–40.

"A Hard Goodbye for the Narcs Former Staff of Russia's Federal Drug Control Service Talk about Unemployment and a Collapse of Policing." 2016a. *Meduza.* August 2, 2016. https://meduza.io/en/feature/2016/08/03/a-hard-goodbye-for-the-narcs.

Hedlund, Stefan. 2006. "Vladimir the Great, Grand Prince of Muscovy: Resurrecting the Russian Service State." *Europe-Asia Studies* 58 (5): 775–801.

Hellie, Richard. 1971. *Enserfment and Military Change in Muscovy.* Chicago: University of Chicago Press.

———. 1977. "The Structure of Modern Russian History: Toward a Dynamic Model." *Russian History* 4 (1): 1–22.

———. 1987. "What Happened? How Did He Get a Way With It? Ivan Groznyi's Paranoia and the Problem of Institutional Restraints." *Russian History* 14 (1): 199–224.

———. 2005. "The Structure of Russian Imperial History." *History and Theory* 44 (4): 88–112.

———. 2006. "The Economy, Trade and Serfdom." Chapter. In *The Cambridge History of Russia,* edited by Maureen Perrie, 1:539–558. Cambridge: Cambridge University Press.

Herd, Graeme P. 2001. "Modernizing the Muscovite Military: The Systemic Shock of 1698." *Journal of Slavic Military Studies* 14 (4): 110–130.

Interview with Nikolai Patrushev, secretary of the Russian Security Council. 2021. "Without Fear and Reproach." *Rossiyskaya Gazeta Website.* May 31, 2021. https://rg.ru/2021/05/31/patrushev-raskryl-neizvestnye-podrobnosti-zhenevskoj-vstrechi-s-sallivanom.html.

Kasciunas, Laurynas, Marius Laurinavicius, and Vytautas Kersanskas. 2014. "The Basis of Putin's Power: Russian Clans and Their Members." *Delfi.* August 4, 2014. www.delfi.lt/multimedija/putino_rusija/v-putino-galios-pagrindas-rusijos-klanai-ir-ju-hero-jai.d?id=65409760.

Keenan, Edward L. 1986. "Muscovite Political Folkways." *The Russian Review* 45 (2): 115–181.

Khazarski, Aliaksei. 2020. "Civilizations as Ontological Security? Stories of the Russian Trauma." *Problems of Post-Communism* 67 (1): 24–36.

Khvostunova, Olga. 2021. "Lev Gudkov: 'The Unity of the Empire in Russia Is Maintained by Three Institutions: The School, the Army, and the Police'." *Institute of Modern Russia.* May 3, 2021. https://imrussia.org/en/opinions/3278-lev-gudkov-.

Kononenko, Vadim, and Arkady Moshes, eds. 2011. *Russia as a Network State: What Works in Russia When State Institutions Do Not?* New York, NY: Palgrave Macmillan.

Kosnya, Anastasia. 2014. "Awaiting Purges." *Vedomosti.*

Kots, Alexander, and Dmitry Steshin. 2016. "DNR Leader Oleksandr (Alexander) Zakharchenko: We Will Without Fail Demand a Reckoning for Our Fallen Friends." *Komsomolskaya Pravda.* April 21, 2016.

Kramer, Mark. 2005. "High-Level Corruption in Russia." *PONARS Eurasia.* November 20, 2005. www.ponarseurasia.org/high-level-corruption-in-russia/.

Laruelle, Marlene. 2016. "Misinterpreting Nationalism: Why Russkii Is Not a Sign of Ethnonationalism." *PONARS Eurasia.* January 27, 2016.

Lavrov, Sergei. 2021. "The Law, the Rights and the Rules." *Ministry of Foreign Affairs Website,* Moscow. June 27, 2021.

Ledeneva, Alena V. 2013. *Can Russia Modernise? Sistema, Power Networks and Informal Governance.* Cambridge: Cambridge University Press.

Lieven, Dominic. 1999. "Dilemmas of Empire 1850–1918. Power, Territory, Identity." *Journal of Contemporary History* 34 (2): 163–200.

"The Long Life of *Homo Sovieticus.*" 2011. *The Economist.* December 10, 2011. www.economist.com/briefing/2011/12/10/the-long-life-of-homo-sovieticus.

Loshak, Viktor. 2021. "When Everything Stagnates, Call the Liberals." *Kommersant.* July 17, 2021. www.kommersant.ru/doc/4898660?from=other_spec.

Marson, James. 2009. "Putin to the West: Hands off Ukraine." *Time.* May 25, 2009. http://content.time.com/time/world/article/0,8599,1900838,00.html.

McDaniel, Tim. 1996. *The Agony of the Russian Idea.* Princeton: Princeton University Press.

"Meeting of the Valdai International Discussion Club." 2014. *President of Russia.* September 19, 2014. http://en.kremlin.ru/events/president/news/19243.

Motyl, Alexander. 2014. "Is Russia Artificial?" *World Affairs.* November 7, 2014.

Myers, Steven Lee. 2015. *The New Tsar: The Rise and Reign of Vladimir Putin.* New York: Knopf Doubleday.

National Security Strategy. 2021. "National Security Strategy of the Russian Federation." *President of the Russian Federation Website.* July 2, 2021. http://publication.pravo.gov.ru/Document/View/0001202107030001?index=0&rangeSize=1.

Novoprudskiy, Semen. 2019. "Spektr Press: You Jail Them or They Will Jail You. Why Former Minister Abyzov Came Back, and How His Arrest Exposes Russia's Domestic Policy." *Ekho Moskvy.* March 27, 2019.

"Orthodox-Slavic Values: The Foundation of Ukraine's Civilisational Choice Conference." 2013. *President of Russia.* July 27, 2013. http://en.kremlin.ru/events/president/news/18961.

Pastukhov, Vladimir. 2016. "The Hamlet Question: Autocracy or Federation? Part 1." *Institute of Modern Russia.* May 19, 2016. https://imrussia.org/en/analysis/law/2556-the-hamlet-question-autocracy-or-federation-part-1.

———. 2018. "Perimeter Protection. What Is the Danger of Replacing Putin's Friends with Putin's People's Commissars?" *Republic.* January 24, 2018. https://republic.ru/posts/89091.

Pavlovsky, Gleb. 2015. "The Kremlin is Living without Sensing the Country Beneath It: Effective Policy Foundation Head Gleb Pavlovskiy on the Russian System of Management." *Gazeta.Ru.* December 26, 2015.

———. 2016. "Russian Politics under Putin: The System Will Outlast the Master." *Foreign Affairs.* May/June 2016. www.foreignaffairs.com/articles/russia-fsu/2016-04-18/russian-politics-under-putin.

Pipes, Richard. 1974. *Russia Under the Old Regime.* New York: Charles Scribner's Sons.

Pomper, Philip. 2012. "The Evolution of the Russian Tradition of State Power." *History and Theory* 51 (4): 60–88.

Putin, Vladimir. 2021a. "On the Historical Unity of Russians and Ukrainians." *President of the Russian Federation Website.* July 12, 2021. http://kremlin.ru/events/president/news/66181.

———. 2021b. "Vladimir Putin Answered Questions on His Article 'On the Historical Unity of the Russians and Ukrainians'." *President of the Russian Federation Website.* July 13, 2021. http://en.kremlin.ru/events/president/news/66191.

Riasanovsky, Nicholas Valentine. 2000. *A History of Russia.* 6th ed. New York: Oxford University Press.

Ryzhkov, Vladimir. 2013. "Putin's Distorted History." *The Moscow Times.* November 18, 2013. www.themoscowtimes.com/2013/11/18/putins-distorted-history-a29683.

"Sergei Ivanov: On Arrests of Officials, State Security Super-Ministry, and Mannerheim Plaque." 2016. *Komsomolskaya Pravda.* October 18, 2016.

Shevtsova, Lilia. 2003. "Putin's Russia." *Carnegie Endowment for International Peace.* https://carnegieendowment.org/2003/04/03/putin-s-russia-pub-9081.

Shlapentokh, Dmitry. 2020. "New Russian Identity Makes Way into the Constitution." *Institute of Modern Russia.* June 26, 2020. https://imrussia.org/en/analysis/3126-new-russian-identity-makes-way-into-the-constitution.

Shulman, Ekaterina. 2017. "Reduced Calorie Campaign. How Putin's Last Term Started." *Snob Online.* December 19, 2017. https://snob.ru/entry/155893/.

Skorkin, Konstantin. 2021. "All Change: Donbas Republics Get New Russian Business Boss." *Carnegie Moscow Center.* June 29, 2021. https://carnegie.ru/commentary/8485.

Sokoloff, Georges. 2014. "Livre Le Retard russe – Histoire et développement 882–2014." *France Inter.* May 8, 2014. www.franceinter.fr/oeuvres/le-retard-russe-histoire-et-developpement-882-2014.

Solovey, Valeriy. 2004. "Russia on the Eve of Discord." *Svobodnaya Mysl.* December 1, 2004. https://socialhistoryportal.org/serials/issues/180867.

Starobin, Paul. 2005. "The Accidental Autocrat." *The Atlantic.* March 2005. www.theatlantic.com/magazine/archive/2005/03/the-accidental-autocrat/303725/.

Steele, Brent J. 2021. *Ontological Security in International Relations: Self-Identity and the IR State.* London: Routledge.

Surkov, Vladislav. 2018. "Vladislav Surkov. The Loneliness of the Half-Caste." *Russia in Global Affairs.* April 10, 2018. https://eng.globalaffairs.ru/articles/the-loneliness-of-the-half-breed/.

———. 2019. "Putin's Long State." *Nezavisimaya Gazeta.* February 11, 2019. www.ng.ru/ideas/2019-02-11/5_7503_surkov.html.

"Text of report "Valdai Discussion Club meeting"", President of the Russian Federation website, October 25, 2021.

Trenin, Dmitri. 2016. "Russia's Foreign Policy in the Coming Fiver Years: Goals, Stimuli." *Carnegie Moscow Center.* April 29, 2016. https://carnegie.ru/2016/04/28/ru-pub-63462.

Trudolyubov, Maxim. 2016. "Panama Reaction Reveals Russia's 2 Value Systems." *The Moscow Times Online.* April 6, 2016. www.themoscowtimes.com/2016/04/06/panama-reaction-reveals-russias-2-value-systems-op-ed-a52440.

———. 2017. "The Russian State's Lost Birth Certificate." *The Moscow Times.* November 3, 2017. www.themoscowtimes.com/2017/11/03/the-russian-states-lost-birth-certificate-a59468.

———. 2018. "The Hidden, Self-Reliant Russia." *The Moscow Times.* August 21, 2018. www.themoscowtimes.com/2018/08/21/the-hidden-self-reliant-russia-a62583.

Tsygankov, Andrei P. 2014. "The Frustrating Partnership: Honor, Status, and Emotions in Russia's Discourses of the West." *Communist and Post-Communist Studies* 47 (3): 345–354.

Tsygankov, Andrei. 2021. "Russia and US in Search for Admissible Confrontation Limits." *Vedomosti Website*, in Russian. July 11, 2021.

Tucker, Robert C. 1992. *Stalin in Power: The Revolution from Above, 1928–1941.* Robert C. Verlag, New York: W.W. Norton & Company.

Yakovenko, Igor. 2020. "His Excellency Governor General Kadyrov." *Yezhednevny Zhurnal.* July 24, 2020.

Yurgens, Igor. 2014. "It is Not Possible to Turn the Country Back. The Course of History Will Crush This Sort of Algorithm- How Putin Fell Out with the West, Why This Occurred, and What It Threatens." *Novaya Gazeta Online.* November 14, 2014. https://novayagazeta.ru/articles/2014/11/14/61943-igor-yurgens-171-razvernut-stranu-nazad-nevozmozhno-hod-istorii-somnet-takoy-algoritm-187.

Zelensky, Volodymyr. 2021. "Ukraine. Kyivan Rus'. 1033". Address by President Volodymyr Zelenskyy on the Occasion of the Day of Christianization of Kyivan Rus' – Ukraine." *President of Ukraine Official Website.* July 28, 2021. www.president.gov.ua/en/news/ukrayina-kiyivska-rus-1033-zvernennya-prezidenta-volodimira-69757.

Zevelev, Igor. 2014. "The Russian World Boundaries: Russia's National Identity Transformation and New Foreign Policy Doctrine." *Russia in Global Affairs.* 2014. https://eng.globalaffairs.ru/articles/the-russian-world-boundaries/.

4

SOVIET LEGACIES

Stalin, Brezhnev and Putin

Introduction

In 2016, President Putin has argued that Lenin planted a "historical time bomb" on the ashes of the *Tsarist* Empire, drawing administrative borders with no regard to ethnic realities:

> With that, the borders were being defined absolutely arbitrarily and far from always based on reason. Donbass, for example, was transferred to Ukraine under the following pretext: to increase the percentage of proletariat in Ukraine in order to obtain stronger social support there. This is nonsense.
>
> *(Arkhangelskiy, 2016)*

This "bomb" exploded in 1991, triggering the collapse of the Soviet Union. In 2020, Putin again condemned the 1922 declaration on the Formation of the USSR and 1924 Constitution of the USSR for giving Soviet Republics the right of free withdrawal with what he declared were "traditional" Russian territories. Putin repeated the metaphor of "time-bomb" and claimed that the secession clause later "migrated" to other versions of the Soviet constitution, creating a threat for Russia: what if, he asked:

> a republic had joined the Soviet Union receiving in its baggage a huge part of Russian land, traditional, historical Russian territory – and then suddenly decided to leave? At least it could leave with what it came with. It should not drag with it presents from the Russian people. None of this was stipulated" in the Soviet 1977 Constitution.
>
> *(Putin, 2020)*

Putin's thinking on "time bombs" was further clarified by Putin in his July 12, 2021 article "On the historical unity of Russians and Ukrainians" when he noted that "the right of free withdrawal of the republics from the Union" resulted in "the most dangerous "time bomb" was laid in the foundation of our statehood. It exploded as soon as the safety and security mechanism disappeared in the form

DOI: 10.4324/9780429261985-4

of the leading role of the CPSU, which eventually collapsed from within" (Putin, 2021a). In a follow-up interview a day later, Putin expanded further:

> And the second time bomb, which I also mentioned, was the leading role of the Communist Party of the Soviet Union, its directing and primary role. Why? Because it turned out that the party was the only thing that kept the entire country together as a single state. As I wrote in the article, as soon as the party started to fall apart from the inside, the whole country shattered. There were other time bombs as well. Perhaps we will talk about this later on.
>
> *(Putin, 2021b)*

Despite such sentiments, as a KGB officer, Vladimir Putin was very much a part of the Soviet regime. Indeed, Putin was a poster-boy for Soviet upward mobility and patriotism. For Putin, August 1991 represented a psychological humiliation and defeat, rather than a victory of the Russian people over a communist occupation. President Putin can be considered as being the successor to Stalin's regime. As philologist and cultural historian Evegeny Dobrenko observed:

> If Peter the Great was the "father" of the Petrine nation and Stalin of the Soviet nation, then Putin is to Stalin what Catherine the Great was to Peter. Peter is said to have "opened the window on Europe," but I would suggest that he merely cut a hole, while it was Catherine who made it into a framed window, i.e. modernized the country. Within the same vein, Putin tries to modernize the Soviet nation and its institutions, which is why there is so much déjà vu in his actions.
>
> *(Khvostunova, 2020)*

The Soviet Union educated the Russian ruling elite, along with mid- and senior-level officials, providing global superpower status, strategic benchmarks, worldviews, sets of assumptions and frames of reference. The Soviet experience profoundly shapes President Putin and those of the Russian elite, including the largely males over 60 years old, with law enforcement, secret service and military backgrounds, who constitute the decision-makers within the ruling bureaucracy (Schulmann, 2017). This bureaucracy can be considered as a class that is now "aware of its status, linked by internal connections, and economically self-contained. The more time that passes, the more strongly it is encroaching on the social space of other social groups. Because the bureaucracy is growing quantitatively and enjoys impunity" (Grozovskiy, 2017). Soviet grandeur and nostalgia fuse together in the present to birth a Russian national anthem, which incorporates the Soviet musical score with revised contemporary words.

When we examine more closely the Soviet period and contemporary parallels between then and the present, three parallels between President Putin's regime of the 2010s and that of Stalin in the 1940s are apparent: a 'sphere of influence', balance of power ("Yalta–Potsdam II") thinking; military-patriotic mobilization of the population against externally directed threats and, the formation of a cult of personality. There are also three parallels that one can draw between Putin's Russia in the 2010s and 2020s and Brezhnev's Soviet Union in the 1970s: economic stagnation; stability of cadres (in effect, elite stagnation) and, domestic political demobilization of the population. A foundational element of Putinism is the appropriation of the memory of the Great Patriotic War, the legitimizing event of the Soviet period. Putin has made it the duty of the President to determine, define and then defend "historical truth," as enshrined in the Constitution of 2020 and Russia's forthcoming NSS (Kurilla, 2020).

Yalta–Potsdam Grand Bargain

The first and perhaps most obvious parallel between the late Stalinist and contemporary Putin era is the notion of a Yalta–Potsdam-like 'Grand Bargain' and the sense of identity and status seeking validation this construct embodies. For President Putin, the current *status quo* represents the open and determined containment, confrontation and encirclement of Russia by the West. Mikhail Troitskiy notes that status is defined as a "collective beliefs about a given state's ranking on valued attributes" such as "wealth, coercive capabilities, culture, [or] demographic position." Status is assumed to consist of two main components: "honor" and "authority." Honor is generated by the symbolic recognition of a given state's place in a certain hierarchy. Authority "is the commonly accepted right of that state to use its power or have a say on a range of issues that arguably affect its interests." Troitskiy argues that Russia's

> demands for "honor" and concurrent emotions have included: expressions of gratitude to Moscow by the West for agreeing to end the Cold War; abstention by the West from raising legitimacy issues about various aspects of Russian politics; symbolic trappings of an "equal partnership," such as high-profile bilateral meetings between top Russian and U.S. leaders; and "alliance jealousy" – attempts to outbid NATO and the EU in attracting members to Russian-led blocs.
>
> *(Troitskiy, 2016)*

However, a status dilemma exists between Russia and the United States. Does Russia seek recognition of its great power status as an end in-and-of itself or as a means of generating "authority" that can then be used to achieve other more threatening ends? For example Russia understands that its ability to both break the rules that govern the post-Cold War order that it dislikes and introduce its own rules and norms is in-and-of itself a sign of its status as near peer competitor rather than peer pretender. A refusal to engage with Russia through negotiations concerning global hotspots is a status-diminishing signal, "effective in exerting psychological pressure and pushing Moscow toward costly, risky, and at times erratic maneuvers" (Paul et al., 2014; Tsygankov, 2014).

In the face of such perceived iniquity, Russia feels duty bound to concentrate and mobilize its resources to achieve strategic breakout from imposed isolation and, to that end, must use the tools at its disposal to disrupt and prevent such operations against it. Thus, the Russian military enjoyed rapid increase in defense expenditures through the 2010s. By 2015, defense, national security and law enforcement authorities account for 34 percent of the state budget, and this represents a two-fold increase since 2010. Key features of rapid military modernization include a greater use of high technology, a move from divisions to more combat-ready brigades and from conscript to professional. Eight snap and preplanned military exercises were held in 2013, 5 in 2014 and 10 in 2015. Russia's black budget (authorized but not itemized expenditure) stands at $60 billion. In addition to exercises, Russia's military has effectively enjoyed years of live-fire training in Donbas and Syria. The Russian military has constantly tested Western operational effectiveness through irresponsible and aggressive military behavior designed to intimidate and provoke – as it is outlined later. In the process it has: "demonstrated a capability and organization and logistics skill-set that we have not seen before" (Farkas, 2015).

An insight into the Russian security elite worldview is provided by Investigations Committee Chairman Alexander Bastrykin in an April 2016 article in *Kommersant-Vlast* magazine. Here, Bastrykin claimed that a "hybrid war" unleashed by the United States and its allies against Russia is underway:

> Obvious examples of this were the outcome of the Yukos case, the judgment on the murder of former FSB officer Alexander Litvinenko, the report of the Security Council of the Netherlands on the investigation into the downing of the Malaysian Boeing MH17, the FBI's investigation into the legitimacy of Russia and Qatar being awarded the right to host the world championships in 2018 and 2022, the United States' kidnapping, forcible transfer and sentencing to long prison terms of our citizens Viktor Bout and Konstantin Yaroshenko and so on.
>
> *(Zheleznova and Epple, 2016)*

Sergey Karaganov also captures a contemporary mindset well *when arguing that* the major cause of "Russia's confrontation with the West" was Western behavior and Russia's reaction to this: the West imposed a *de facto* 1919 Versailles-like *diktat* on Russia, albeit in "velvet gloves" (Karaganov, 2014). While limiting Russia's freedom, spheres of influence and markets, the West expanded political, military and economic interests through NATO and EU enlargement (Shevtsova, 2015).

When on 29–30 March 2016, Belarus President Alyaksandr Lukashenka received U.S. Deputy Assistant Secretary of Defense Michael Carpenter in Minsk to achieve a "new stage of interaction" through developing trade and economic cooperation, it suggested the possibility of a thaw in relations. The Russian press reported this meeting in terms of "betrayal" and the crossing of "red lines" (Yanka, 2016). Ukraine's 'Budapest Memorandum' guarantees do not hold, the argument goes, if the Ukrainian President is deposed in a *coup d'état*, a status or interpretation that only Moscow alone can make. As Krzysztof Szczerski, minister at the Polish Presidential Chancellery responsible for foreign affairs, notes:

> Poland's border with Ukraine is the last peaceful frontier in Europe in the eastern direction. The next frontier is already a war frontier. This means that we are not just a flank for the alliance but the last safe border that must be defended.
>
> *(Macierewicz, 2016)*

In 2015, many anniversaries occurred. It was the 200th anniversary of the Congress of Vienna, 70th of end of the Second World War, 40th of the Helsinki Final Act and 25th of the Charter of Paris for a New Europe. For President Putin, the "Vienna model" and "Yalta system" constructs illustrate a key lesson of history – power balance creates order and stability. The Congress of Vienna of 1814–1815 established a "concert of nations," and in the "golden age" of European diplomacy, a century of peace ensured. Spheres of military and political interest and noninterference in the internal affairs of the victorious powers after the Second World War – as brokered by Stalin, Roosevelt and Churchill at the Yalta Conference (8–11 February 1945) and by Stalin, Truman and Churchill at the Potsdam Conference (17 July to 2 August 1945) – ensured that the Cold War between competing blocs did not become hot. The Soviet Union and the United States recognized each other as equal actors and were prepared to play by the rules of the game. To avoid war, powerful states but reach agreement: if only the politics of strength, secret agreements and spheres of influence prevail then stability follows. Russia believes "International law applies to regions in the Russian influence space precisely to the extent of what Russia considers to be international law" ("Postimees," 2020).

It is within this winning tradition that President Putin suggests that a similarly stabilizing anti-Hitler coalition against *Da'esh* would create a lasting peace – a great power agreement would enshrine a fixed balance of power and rules of the game. The Syria settlement, Putin posited, could become a model for future international cooperation that would reduce instability in Syria and create an "effective risk management system" ("Vladimir Putin at the Valdai", 2015). President Putin has placed what he considers a "positive sum" proposition on the table: a stabilizing, predictable interest-based balance of power restoration thrashed out by great powers – Russia–the United States–Germany as the 'big three' – acting as co-equals and proposed by Russia from a position of strength will follow. U.S. participation is crucial as the United States is the strategic benchmark against which Russia measures its successes and failures.

Former Soviet states have become hostage to Russia's paranoid anti-Western encirclement rhetoric and "strategic breakout" practice and a temporizing transactional approach:

> We do not believe in principles or in long-term coalitions based on ideology or friendship and we are not trying to create them. The Russian Federation arose in a period when it had no allies left in the precise sense of the word, even the former USSR republics wanted to cut loose. And the system learned to survive alone at the expense of the rest of the world by an original method.
>
> *(Pavlovskiy, 2015)*

Attempts to demonstrate autonomy by acting as intermediaries between Russia and Ukraine (President Nursultan Nazarbayev of Kazakhstan) and Russia and Turkey (President Lukashenko of Belarus and President Aliyev of Azerbaijan) are not offset by their own ability to remain non-aligned as Russia's anti-Americanism and anti-Westernism increase. Thus, the state of relations between FSU states and the West will be more a function of Russia's deteriorating relations than their own strategic choices and intent. Russia continued to limit its neighbor's ability to pursue independent policies and join other institutions and to reassert an empire of influence (if not territorial conquest) by coercion through to 2021. Russia does not want to incorporate Belarus, Kazakhstan, Moldova and Ukraine into a neo-Soviet multiethnic construct as such an entity would be too destabilized, and Russia lacks the capacity to exert control. Rather, indirect control through a veto on key foreign and security policy decisions is the aim, thereby enjoying security while projecting a buffer zone while minimizing direct borders with Europe and China. The strategic autonomy given by Russia to Belarus is an interesting case in point, as are the nature of the 'red lines' that both Belarus and the West must not cross.

Russia's rhetoric in support of *Novorossiya* and the *Russkii Mir* generated disquiet in Central Asia. Central Asian states are uneasy at Russian use of force against a former *Tsarist* territory with a limited history of statehood and internal divisions. As Alexander Cooley noted with regard to Kazakhstan:

> Though officially supportive of Crimea's referendum, Kazakh authorities are concerned about the potential for Russia to similarly interfere in Kazakhstan on the pretext of defending the rights of the country's sizable Russian minority (many of who hold Russian passports), as well as the potential damaging impact of Russian media campaigns.
>
> *(Satke, 2014)*

Indeed, President Nazarbayev used his Annual Address in 2014 to underline Kazakh statehood and right to make its own strategic choices – China and the Silk Road were highlighted, and the EEU was not mentioned ("The Address of President", 2014). States in the region also resist being dragged into political battle between Russia and the West and will look to use China to hedge and balance, while at the same time exploit opportunities to frustrate or drive up costs of integration with Russia to gain concessions. In addition, China combines neo-liberal economics with political authoritarianism and consistently states that it rejects "interference in the domestic affairs" and gives unqualified support to statehood and sovereignty. This brand has much greater appeal than a Russia-heavy super-imperial identity, undercut by a failing economy.

Military-patriotic mobilization and the cult of victory

The second parallel and continuity between the late Stalinist and contemporary Putin era is the notion of military-patriotic mobilization against an external enemy that poses an existential threat. Indeed, President Putin has declared 'patriotism' to be the core unifying Russian idea and officially celebrated as the highest civic virtue. For Stalin, the invasion of the USSR by an erstwhile ally in June 1941 initiated the Great Patriotic War. The period starting from 1941 to 1945 was of suffering, deprivation and loss and endurance followed by ultimate victory, as Soviet troops stormed into Berlin. The USSR had defeated the most militarily advanced state in Europe, and the victory re-legitimized the Soviet system, becoming in the process a touchstone within Russia's historical fabric. President Putin channels victory in the Great Patriotic War and champions late Stalinist (1945–55) narratives based on the perception of a stable and unified internal order, external respect and fear. This inculcates a mental matrix in society that incubates and reproduces psychological and political traumas (victimhood), phobias (inferiority, humiliation) and paranoia, as well as feelings of superiority and heroic patriotic self-grandeur.

During the war, strategic breakouts from encirclement were epitomized by the battles for Leningrad, Stalingrad and Kursk, with the Battle for Moscow the first Allied victory. The Soviet Union had spared Europe from Nazi tyranny, just as the Russian empire had defeated the hegemonic ambitions of Napoleon and Muscovy was thrown off the 'Mongol yoke', acting as a shield for European Christianity. The Russian Federation, so this discourse argues, is the spiritual, politico-military, sociocultural linear descendent of this tradition, and so Russia today deserves Europe's enduring respect and profound gratitude for having fulfilled this 'sacred' role. The memory of the Great Patriotic War legitimizes the political authority of the Putin regime, and so the state creates official narratives that cannot be contested: the Molotov–Ribbentrop Pact is now considered a "diplomatic triumph" – not a source of shame but one of pride (Kolesnikov, 2021)

President Putin poses as the linear successor to this tradition, opposing a 'fascist neo-Nazi Junta' in Kyiv and calling for 'anti-*Daesh* Hitler-like coalition' to defeat Islamic State. Lev Gudkov, head of the Levada Centre, has highlighted a 2-week-long propaganda and disinformation campaign, unprecedented in post-Soviet times, aimed at manipulating public opinion. This campaign is built on several simple ideas and techniques. First, that the rights of Russians and the Russian-speaking population are constantly infringed and that their well-being and lives are threatened. Second, it labels the supporters of the Euromaidan pro-European protest movement bandits, Nazis and Banderites in an effort to discredit them. Ukraine is leaderless and in chaos ever since the opponents of Yanukovych took power. These ideas enable the negative mobilization of Russian society and revive "its dormant imperial complexes" ("The Situation in Ukraine," 2014). In the context of the 70th anniversary of victory in the Great Patriotic War (1941–45), the ongoing Ukrainian crisis was increasingly reified through the lens of endurance, suffering and sacrifice before final victory – helping consolidate a societal base in a time of economic hardship. Nerijus Maliukevicius, lecturer at the International Relations and Political Science Institute of Vilnius University (TSPMI), argues that the Second World War is a foundational axis of Kremlin policy:

> The whole subject of the Second World War victory is important to the whole great narrative of Putin about the Soviet Union victory against fascism. It is a certain taking over of the achievements by the current Russia, a sort of the current fight of Putin's Kremlin against today's neo-Nazis, neo-fascists.
>
> (Jackevicius, 2016)

In June 2020, Putin stated that the USSR's annexation of Latvia, Lithuania and Estonia was based on "contractual terms, in coordination with [local] elected authorities." According to this argument, when Soviet Russia signed treaties with Latvia and Estonia in 1920, its government was not recognized. The treaties were therefore void, and a legitimate separation from the Russian Empire did not take place. As a result, and legally speaking, the status of the Baltic states in the inter-war period was that of temporary devolution. It logically follows, then, that their annexation in 1940 represented the restoration of "historical justice" (Jushkin, 2020). Indeed, on 14 July 2020, Russia's embassy in Tallinn published a social media post referencing the annexation of Estonia in 1940 as "the June coup." In Riga, the Russian embassy asserted that the Baltic states joined the Soviet Union voluntarily (Kopotin, 2020). Moreover, today's Russia, as the legal successors of historical Russia (Soviet and *Tsarist*), "have an indisputable right to this territory in line with international law, specifically the 1721 Nystadt agreement." Indeed, by "signing the Helsinki Final Act, Europe recognised the territorial integrity of all post-war states according to the borders agreed in Yalta and Potsdam, in other words the fact that the Baltic states belong to the Soviet Union" (Jushkin, 2020).

President Putin can pose as a president on the 'frontline', a geopolitical strategist *par excellence*, able to defend Russia's historical borders and uphold its great power interest, while his government addresses the 'rear' – that is the increasingly volatile domestic agenda. The capture of Crimea was the jewel in the crown of imperial great power restoration, a validation of Russia's spiritual core, a celebration of collective interests trumping the individuals and the defiance of an external Western enemy. Power legitimation via military triumphalism and patriotism is as much a feature of the late Stalinist period as is of Putin's from 2014, through Crimea, Donbas and Syria – and beyond. Negative militant and militarized patriotism has mobilized the Russian population and contributed to a sense of pride and the personal popularity of the president. Russia's internal perception and official (increasingly stereotypical) strategic narratives highlight the embattled bear caught in an existential trap – to fight or be conquered. Russia's imperial history, ethnicity and identity, as well as a blurring and instrumentalization of the distinction between opposition and treason are now tools in the service of power.

Putin's support rests on a broad constituency consisting of middle income, conservative nationalists, the politically timid and apathetic and the exhausted who either yearn for, or at least are prepared to tolerate, a strong hand and authoritarian stability against less certain and predictable alternatives. Putin's approach and agenda chime with a traditional political culture supportive of the notion that Russia under Putin is restored to great power status with its associated emotion-laden (patriotic pride, dignity, respect) values and fearful of disorder and chaos (humiliation and terror). This in turn allows for a new informal social contract to emerge: 'socio-economic decline in return for geo-strategic grandeur'. Between 2013 and 2014, public trust in Russian power institutions, particularly the presidency, military and security services, increased – a dynamic carried through the third term presidency and into the fourth. Indeed, the popularity of the special services in Russia has increased in line with the besieged fortress propaganda: in 2000, 35 percent viewed the work of special services positively and 34 percent negatively; by January 2018, 66 percent were in the positive column, 12 percent in the negative and 45 percent "would like their children and grandchildren to become security officers (the figure was 29 percent in 2001)" (Aptekar, 2018). In addition, Russia's Defense Ministry announced that it would create the Main Military-Political Directorate (*GlavVoyenPUR*) by 1 December 2018, in order to develop patriotism among military personnel. Subunits were subsequently established in the MChS (Emergencies Directorate), FSB [Federal Security Service] and *Rosgvardiya* (Federal Service of National Guard Troops). This mirrored a Soviet period Main Political Directorate (*Soviet GlavPUR*), which itself had its genesis in the Russian Civil War in the shape of the Political Directorate of the *Revvoyensovet* (Revolutionary Military Council – PUR). Vladimir Scherbakov, a military specialist at the *Nezavisimaya Gazeta* daily, questioned the resurrection of the Soviet-era directorate:

> The main question is this. In the Soviet era, the directorate in practice worked in the interests of the Communist Party's central committee. It's not completely clear what military-political work the resurrected directorate will do and more importantly in the interests of which political party.
>
> *(Reuters, 2018)*

The post-Crimea mobilization and consolidation of society were in part based on the notion that President Putin "makes the world admit that Russia matters" and, as focus groups attest, Putin ensures that: "They [EU and US] have stopped wiping their feet on Russia" (Dmitriyev, 2015). The state has promoted such thinking, with the reintroduction of Pioneers, popularization of St. George's ribbons, retro-chic nostalgia and propagated militaristic memes: "Don't mess with my Iskanders", "polite people", "we can do it again" (Novoprudskiy, 2018). A patriotic 'Stop List' of foreign-funded NGOs serves to protect Russian society from 'encroachments from abroad' and 'State Department projects in disguise' eager to turn "fifth columnists" (anyone who disagrees with the government) against the state. As a result, societal beliefs equate anti-Americanism with patriotism: one of the long distance lorry drivers who went on strike over a new tax introduced in December 2015 stated: "We are not a fifth column. I love my country and I hate America" (Greene, 2015). Another example of public psychology is found in a focus group where a working class respondent: "spent a long time complaining about the hard life, the unbearable working conditions, the declining standard of living" only to suddenly exclaim: "But when I remember how the Caspian Flotilla launches missiles, my heart immediately rejoices!" (Zubov, 2015).

Andrey Arkhangelskiy, the cultural editor at the prominent *Ogonek* weekly magazine, observes that ordinary Russians are captivated by crusades launched by the state media:

> Geopolitics are a lot like childhood, when you feel on top of the world and there's no need for compromises. The past 25 years haven't changed those 40–50 years old people – they just decided not to grow up. And those who are 20–25 now . . . were looking for something to believe in, and for them the Soviet Union became that something – a dream of a lost paradise, the time when 'everyone was afraid and respected us.
>
> *(Litvinova, 2015)*

Be this as it may, Russian society exhibits widespread Russian pride in the exploits of the "polite little green men" and Russia's nuclear triad – the military has been normalized in the eyes of society. State propaganda features decisive thrusts of Russian military power which neutralizes opponent's strengths and capitalizes on their weaknesses. The Syria operation is portrayed on Russian TV as a complete and unmitigated success.

Moreover, as Russian economic performance deteriorates and the social protest potential increases, President Putin even contends that not only is the Russian military the last best hope for Russia to maintain its strategic autonomy, but also that: "the development of the military-industrial complex provides both combat readiness of the Russian armed forces and the country's economic recovery" (Sharkovskiy, 2015). A 'military first' approach will reinvigorate the state itself: "guns before butter," and defense of the Motherland is the mantra. Military patriotic-mobilization can also be targeted against 'internal enemies' and 'extremists.' The key message of "Victory Day" (May 9) celebrations – which in 2016 were celebrated outside of Russia's borders (Crimea, Transdneistr, Abkhazia, South Ossetia and Syria) – is that Russia is ready and able to use force against any enemy: "We protected our country against Nazism before. Now we will protect it against extremism." Given that extremism under Russian legislation is whatever the government decides on any given day, domestic political mobilization against the current regime is corralled and suppressed in the name of military-patriotic pride (Fishman, 2016).

Cult of personality

The third emerging parallel between the late Stalinist and contemporary Putin era is the notion of a personality cult. In 1956 on the final day of the 20th Congress of the Communist Party of the Soviet Union, secretary Nikita Khrushchev denounced Stalin, quoting Lenin to the effect that Stalin was "excessively rude, lacked tolerance, kindness and considerateness toward his comrades," further accused Stalin of perpetuating "a grave abuse of power . . . which has caused untold harm to our party" and denounced the "cult of the individual," a core characteristic of the Stalinist period (Lenon, 2016). Putin, like Stalin, is presented in Russian state-controlled media as a world-historical leader, a strong patriot, a *pater patria* married to the state.

Political science experts suggest that charismatic legitimation is rare: "it would be a serious mistake to confuse such an engineered idolatry with genuine charismatic leadership" (Dogan, 1992). Engineered idolatry can of course transmute into genuine charismatic leadership, particularly in a popular autocracy where an individual channels the wider beliefs of society. Leadership cults thrive under certain conditions: where there is little or no freedom of expression; rights are suppressed; state media manipulates information (and so citizens suffer from 'false consciousness') and, where charismatic personalities first achieve power through the structures of modern legal–rational authority and then adapt and shift the basis of regime and political system legitimacy toward one based on charismatic legitimacy.

Mikhail Sholokhov, a Soviet/Russian novelist and winner of the 1965 Nobel Prize in Literature, once said of Stalin's 'personality cult': "OK, there was a personality cult, but there was also a personality" (Roy, 2004). President Putin has managed to go one better and present multiple personalities for the Russian people to select:

> First, all 15 years [of Putin's presidential term] have been spent narrowing down alternative political candidates to only one figure, because this figure is politically encompassing and many-sided – he is the main communist, the main liberal or the main nationalist, the rest of the political forces are like supporting blocks.
>
> *(Koshkin and Kolesnikov, 2015)*

The Words that are Changing the World: Key Quotes of Vladimir Putin, a 400-page must-read for the 1000 senior leaders of the Russian Federation published in January 2016, is characterized as being 'prophetic' by the pro-Kremlin youth group *Set*

('Network') which published the book, in conjunction with Vyacheslav Volodin, the presidential deputy chief of staff at the time. Although Putin assumed power in 2000 through the noncharismatic route – he was selected from within the system and had risen without a trace – he now emerges primarily as a leader with a national mission, the only individual able to protect and safeguard a patriotic electorate and so regenerate and strategically renovate the nation.

As Volodin stated in October 2014: "If there's Putin – there's Russia, if there's no Putin – there's no Russia" (Sudakov, 2014). Putin was projected as Russia's crisis manager, a lone heroic individual who stands between order and chaos. Military interventions in Crimea and Syria only appear to enhance Russian power and hence President Putin's stature as Commander-in-Chief. State-sponsored TV documentary films and 'memoir interviews', such as 'The President' and 'Crimea: Path to the Motherland,' glorify his role as 'father of the nation.' As one analyst notes:

> Emotions are at the core of the Kremlin's message; indeed, they are the tie that binds Putin to his subjects. This is why Surkov portrays Putin, who recently divorced his wife of 30 years and is rumored to have fathered several children with a former Olympic gymnast, as an avatar of conservative values, with the Orthodox Patriarch constantly at his side.
>
> *(Khrushcheva, 2015)*

Psychology can also explain why President Putin's high popularity ratings are genuine rather than fixed or manipulated. His popularity reflects a Russian national "cultural code," a societal reflex for self-preservation, rather than public relations undertaken by 'political technologists' and spin doctors. The recent memory of the 1990s as a "time of troubles" reinforces the belief in the necessity of a strong leader. At the 'Direct Line' annual phone-in session, Putin is portrayed as a capable effective and wise leader, who is the epitome of a nonconfrontational, pragmatic and honest ruler, "the father of a large family, who will punish whom necessary, solve all problems and give salutary advice." The phone-in appears to be a continuation of the centuries-old tradition in which petitions (*chelobitnyye*) were presented to the *Tsar*, with a twenty-first century twist of comparing Russian progress to European failures:

> One phone call to Putin and 'problems that have been accumulated for decades' have been resolved in a flash. Is that not a miracle? Is that not a well-functioning vertical chain of command? The tsar ordered his boyars without wasting his time . . . Peoples' needs are his priority, at least once a year.
>
> *(Petrovskaya, 2021)*

Timing worked in Putin's favor, as did a popular predisposition to believe in a national hero or savior:

> After a litany of disappointing Soviet leaders – such as Leonid Brezhnev, who was senile; Yuriy Andropov, who was only half-living; Konstantin Chernenko,

who was already half-dead; Mikhail Gorbachev, who spoke well but led poorly; and power-hungry but drunken Boris Yeltsin – the Russian people hoped to finally "win the lottery" and land a leader in whom they could place their full confidence. Most Russians were sincerely convinced that Putin was the only man capable of implementing "national projects", getting fifth-and sixth-generation combat aircraft off the drawing board and into the air, raising pensions to European levels, resolving the demographic problem, eliminating corruption, commencing the drilling of Arctic oil and so on.

(Romanov, 2014)

Stagnation

The first and perhaps most obvious parallel between the late Brezhnev and contemporary Putin era is one of political and economic stagnation. The regimes of Leonid Brezhnev, the third General Secretary of the Central Committee of the Communist Party of the USSR, and President Vladimir Putin of the Russian Federation both enjoyed a 'golden age' of stability and sensible governance. Both regimes oversaw growth in the well-being of the population for the first 12 years of their rule. By 1976, Leonid Brezhnev had planned to retire in 1977, when the USSR would mark the 60th anniversary of the 1917 Bolshevik Revolution. The 25th Party Congress had other ideas and after reelection, Brezhnev died in office in 1982. Vladimir Pastukhov suggests that similarly in 2006–7, Putin sought a transition through a "division of power into "inward," which would remain with Putin, and "outward", which should pass to the successor." However, Kremlin elites moved to prevent this:

> The thought that Putin would go away and leave them alone with each other seriously alarmed the Kremlin elites. Left alone, they would only eat each other. Putin began to come under pressure from all sides. They wanted him to amend the constitution and stay on for a third term.
>
> *(Pastukhov, 2021)*

Putin proposed a "castling" compromise. In 2020, Putin's amendments to Russia's 1993 constitution mirrored Brezhnev's ritual to "create the illusion of a modernized, law-based state, but it is as detached from Russian reality as was the 1977 constitution from Soviet life" (Barber, 2020).

Under Brezhnev, oil and gas constantly grew as a share of the USSRs exports. Under President Putin, non–oil exports fell from 21 percent in 2000 to 8 percent in 2014 and gigantic, inefficient state monopolies predominated with small and medium businesses constituting only 20 percent of Russia's GDP. Between 2012 and 2020, Russia's economy grew by 1 percent per annum. Remarkably, and ominously, this "growth" represents only half the rate that the Soviet Union's economy grew between 1977 and 1985 ("Under Siege", 2021).

Both the Brezhnev and Putin eras boasted of economies whose growth was reliant on hydrocarbon exports rather than diversification, and both regimes entered a period of 'stable stagnation' after 12 golden years. While it is only in 2012 that the notion of economic stagnation has been applied to Putin's economy, President Gorbachev referred to the Brezhnev period as the 'era of stagnation,' inheriting as he did a series of chronic systemic problems. Both regimes appear to use energy as a diplomatic tool to obfuscate the need for structural reform at home. In the case of Brezhnev, economic reform only occurred when it was too late. Rhetoric aside, President Putin's Russia has yet to initiate structural reform and anti-corruption measures, having missed the opportunity afforded by the 2009 global financial crisis. However, as with Brezhnev, under President Putin early economic growth undermined a perceived need and rationale for reform.

President Putin is quick to note that Russia under his leadership has paid all external debts, and reserves, in 2016, stood at $366bn, with state spending 22 times higher in 2014 than 1999, living standards increased three times in this period and took pride in Russia registering 51/189 in the 'Doing Business Report 2016'. The official rhetoric of Putin's government is as upbeat as it is possible to be. President Putin himself noted at the 2015 Valdai Club Meeting in October and then again on his 3 December address to the Federal Assembly and Annual Reporters Interview on 17 December that the peak of crisis has been reached and that adaptation occurs. The crisis provides Russia the opportunity to develop a new socioeconomic development model based on rebalancing its economy through import substitution, self-reliance and a pivot to Asia. In addition, the economic crisis allows Russia to pay off devalued pension obligations with dollar-denominated oil income and bring companies and elites into greater dependence on Putin, so allowing his control of state structures, personnel and policies to increase. This is understood in and of itself to be a positive, as according to such thinking, control is synonymous with order and stability.

Respected economists offer a much more critical and pessimistic assessments of the ability of companies in the Russian state sector to make a profit, or to restructure and modernize. The fundamental flaw in the Russian economy is its structural imbalance. The 'Dutch disease' aside, when we look to the rest of the Russian economy, successful structural reform efforts, which are the necessary precursor for economic growth, are limited by '*sistema,*' institutionalized corruption, red tape, weak market and legal institutions and a lack technology and investment capital.

Construction, logistics, transport, infrastructure and modern business services (e.g. design, marketing, engineering, IT legal, architectural, finance) are the major long-term drivers of Russian economic growth, and all require investment (Dmitriev, 2015). The productivity of labor can only be increased if structural reforms occur. A declining middle class and labor force reduces demand and contributes towards a consumer. These tendencies hinder the diversification of Russia's economy and inhibits increases in direct foreign investment (DFI). Russia lacks scale and capacity to build full industrial clusters (heavy robotics, metallurgy, military equipment and aerospace).

Stability of the cadres – elite stasis

Prior to Brezhnev, in 1961, Khrushchev adopted rules on mandatory reselection of party officials and time limits on terms in office. The resultant upheavals and reorganizations destabilized the bureaucracy and threatened to sideline the careers of party officials in the *nomenklatura* – an elite subset of the Communist party that held administrative posts throughout the Soviet Union. *Nomenklatura* resistance and lack of support were factors in Khrushchev's downfall. Brezhnev dropped these rules and promised the elite a policy of 'trust in the cadres' and 'stability of the cadres.' Opportunists, careerists and corrupt officials – a Communist oligarchy – emerged. These officials, fearful of losing power and responsibility and predisposed to being risk-averse and anti-innovation, embraced the notion that change was destabilizing and the *status quo* represented stability, the prerequisite of order. Andrei Fursov notes that Soviet society was urbanized under Brezhnev and that with growing oil prices a middle class began to prosper alongside the *nomenklatura*. Once the economy contracted, a struggle emerged between "a part of the *nomenklatura* (including criminal operators and foreign capital associated with it) and the Soviet (and then ex-Soviet) middle class." Beneath a superpower façade, the Communist Party disintegrated into a "collection of satrapies or 'mafias,' as they were more popularly known: the Krasnodar mafia, the Uzbek mafia, the Georgian mafia, the Baku mafia, the Dnepropetrovsk (Brezhnev's original power base) mafia, the Moscow mafia, etc. The 'mafias' were loose, informal collections of individuals linked by ties of personal loyalty and power and financial interests, consisting of long, intersecting and convoluted chains of corrupt Party apparatchiks, other officials, underground businessmen, criminal kingpins, their henchmen, and so on" (Roy, 2004).

One feature of President Putin's first two terms was constant reshuffles with little prior warning. This enabled Putin to maintain primacy in Russian politics. In this regard, Putin was more like Khrushchev than Brezhnev in his relationship with subordinates. As one former government official put it in 2007: "Russia's federal decision-making center has contracted to the size of President Putin's head." In a calculated manner:

> President Putin erodes any teams that take shape within the authorities. He forces all the major players to act on their own. As soon as they make any serious attempt to form a group, Putin makes a move and it all falls apart.
>
> *(Rostovsky, 2007)*

On Putin's return to the presidency in 2012, he embraced a 'stability of cadres' policy. When asked if any changes in the government-line up could be expected, not least in response to the economic crisis, President Putin replied:

> Well, as you may know or could have noticed throughout the years I've been in office, I a) value people highly and b) believe that staff reshuffles, usually, but not always, are to be avoided and can be detrimental. If someone is unable to work something out, I think that I bear part of the blame and responsibility. For this reason, there will be no changes, at least no major reshuffles.
>
> *(Radzikhovskiy, 2012)*

The post-Crimea Putin no longer criticizes oligarchs and the bureaucracy – he had become part of the system he leads. The charismatic president, standing alone above party and bureaucracy, able to speak directly to the people and channel their wishes and desires as protector and savior, was focused again on elite meeting interests in conditions of socioeconomic decline.

De-politicization of the population

Gleb Pavlovsky explains that:

> De-politicization is the process of denuding the political landscape to leave all decisions and authority in the hands of a single leader. By stripping away all other players and maintaining a monopoly over the political agenda, such regimes effectively hide most of their workaday policies from the populace, leaving society unprepared for the changes that must inevitably come.
>
> *(Pavlovsky, 2016)*

In the Brezhnev era, as with today's Russia, an alternative to overt expressions of loyalty was 'exit', either internal (withdrawal to private life) or external (emigration) (Kolesnikov, 2015). The prevailing social contract captured well this state of affairs: "you pretend to pay and we pretend to work." The Brezhnev era was characterized by past ideas, formulas and illusions recycled *in lieu* of fresh proposals and policies to tackle underlying problems. The ideological grammar of state-backed illiberalism or Putinist conservatism consists of traditional values (despite transactional realities), patriotism, religion, sovereignty, centralization, and isolation, as opposed to the destabilizing delights of supranational institutions, globalization, multiculturalism and minority-rights protections (Laruelle, 2020).

For the first two terms of the Putin presidency, a social contract was guaranteed by rising commodity prices – rising living standards in exchange for the unaccountability of corrupt elites (Guriev, 2015). Foreign holidays, mortgages and good salaries in return for the passive majority not involving itself in political activism were the centerpiece of a demobilization with regard to domestic affairs. The new social contract of 'security and great power pride and geopolitical grandeur for loyalty' may begin to grate with Russia's middle class (defined by

Russian sociologists as those with higher education, nonmanual labor, and above average salary), but traditionalist society is prepared to endure, barter and adopt self-help survivalists strategies – and such rhetoric is appealing. According to official Russian statistics, however, which experts say underplay the reality, 350,000 people emigrated from Russia in 2015, a ten-fold rise from 2011 (Bennetts, 2016).

Maxim Trudolyubov argues that: "The country's conservative rebound is real. The question is the degree to which he [Putin] can manipulate social change" (Biryukova, 2014; Stanovaya, 2013). According to this understanding, the 'Russian spring' offers the world values:

> These are the values of conservatism – family, faith, and tradition. The freedom to have more than two children and go to church every Sunday. The right to bring up children in one's native culture, to celebrate one's own, and not other people's, holidays, and to live according to one's own laws.

This idyll is contrasted starkly with life in the decadent West:

> The dictatorship of minorities in the West has left no room for tradition and has perverted the norms of morality. Parents no.1 and no.2, more than 50 definitions of gender, and the legalization of incest have changed Western consciousness, leaving normal traditionalists in the minority. In Europe, any demonstration of the norm becomes a target of persecution. The Church is subjected to even greater repression in this society. Wearing a cross has more than once become an occasion for firing employees in various companies.
>
> *(Bondarenko, 2014)*

Since mass protests in Moscow following falsifications of the *Duma* elections in December 2011, President Putin has demonstrated well the extent to which social change can be manipulated in Russia. Russian national ultra-conservative Christian traditional family values and respect for authority become Russia's core code and can be contrasted with the secular, soulless, morally relativist (*Gayrope*) and permissive, liberal, predatory and morally bankrupt code of the West. At the Valdai Club in 2013, President Putin stated that:

> The Euro-Atlantic countries are actually rejecting their roots, including the Christian values that constitute the basis of Western civilization. They are denying moral principles and all traditional identities: national, cultural, religious and even sexual. . . . People in many European countries are embarrassed or afraid to talk about their religious affiliations. Holidays are abolished or even called something different; their essence is hidden away, as is their moral foundation. And people are aggressively trying to export this model all over the world. I am convinced that this opens a direct path to degradation and primitivism, resulting in a profound demographic and moral crisis.
>
> *("Meeting of the Valdai", 2013)*

Alexander Lukin explained that in Putin's mind, "western society is more than imperfect; it is the very centre of sin" (Trudolyubov, 2014; Snyder, 2014; Kaylan, 2014). Worst still, the liberal West, decadent and dysfunctional as it is, seeks to export such values through color-revolutions, and with the help of western-leaning liberal "fifth columnists" in Russia. Putin stoked suspicion of the *intelligentsia* as a source of instability, drawing parallels to the role of *intelligentsia*-led opposition to the government in the late Romanov and Soviet periods and regime and political system collapse: "Too often in our national history, instead of opposition to the government we have come into conflict with opposition to Russia itself, and we know how that ended – with the destruction of the state itself" ("Meeting of the Valdai," 2013).

Russia's economic crisis has cut household budgets and shrunk the Russian middle class, helping to isolate society from foreign travel. As the economy shrunk, a greater emphasis has been placed on maintaining 'social consensus' – Russia's 'Day of Unity' is more actively promoted than ever in previous years. Social consensus ensured stability and order and continuity in terms of enduring Russian values and tradition. The public stigmatization of NGOs (particularly 'foreign funded' with a 'Patriotic Stop List') and the sidelining of civil society institutions by ensuring they are 'state-aligned' are all symptomatic attempts to diminish, manage and control civic activism in Russia. A passive, conformist, conservative majority mostly living in the provinces constitutes the bedrock of Putin's support. The focus is on keeping this segment of the population from being politicized.

A state-controlled pro-Kremlin media and informational regime ('we-against-them') has emerged, with the opposition given very limited access to the media. Vyacheslav Morozov argues that conservatism in Russia today translates into no more than an offensive against a so-called fifth column understood as western collaborators seeking to undermine Russian traditional values (Morozov, 2016). Russia's newly elected Human Rights Commissioner Tatyana Moskalkova, a member of the 'A Just Russia' party and former Major-General in the MVD, underscored such thinking by warning that human rights are used to pressure and threaten Russia. She appeared less concerned with defending individual people against the tyranny of power as defending the regime's political interests against "foreign agents of influence" ("Read Us Our Rights", 2018). The annual report from the Club of NGO Lawyers on the activities of organizations deemed to be "foreign agents" notes that pressure from state authorities on the NGOS is increasing. Maksim Olenichev, head of the legal service of the Club of NGO Lawyers, says: "A process of replacing civil society is under way – independent organizations are to die out, while more and more presidential grants are allocated to NGOs that imitate civil society" (Mukhametshina, 2016).

As a result, alternative principles and ideas to the Putin regime are not generally aired, and where dissident voices do appear, their function is to inoculate society against full-blown 'contagion' and the forced 'implantation' of 'alien' ideas and 'disruptive foreign practices', ill-fitted to thrive on Holy Russia's sacred soil. Armies of bloggers and troll factories complement this demobilization approach, as does legislation designed to curtail freedom of the press and freedom of speech and assembly. The Russian media is considered less diverse than it was in the year 2000. In Putin's Russia, compromise, negotiation, mutual concessions – the life blood of a democratic order and discourse – are portrayed by state media and understood in public perception as weakness, instability and disorder. The *Duma* acts as part of the democratic façade. Within the *Duma*, the 'systemic opposition' to the government, the Communist Party of the Russian Federation under Gennady Zyuganov and the ultranationalist Liberal Democratic Party of the Russian Federation Chairman Vladimir Zhirinovsky do not in fact oppose the government.

Chairman of the Russian Investigation Committee, Alexander Bastrykin, citing an information war waged by the West against Russia, argues that besieged fortress Russia should respond by eliminating the last vestiges of democracy and civil rights:

> We have had enough of playing at pseudo-democracy and following pseudo-liberal values. After all, democracy or rule by the people is nothing other than the power of the people themselves enacted in their interests. These interests can be attained only by means of the greater good, not absolute freedom and the tyranny of individual representatives of society. It is extremely important to create a concept for the state's ideological policy. Its basic element could be the national idea, which would truly rally the unified multi-ethnic Russian people"
>
> *(Zheleznova and Epple, 2016)*

His program essentially advocates a restoration of the Soviet-type extreme authoritarian system, with a clear government – imposed ideology, criminal punishment for "falsifications of history," greater censorship and control ("ideological education") over youth organizations, foreigners and the movement of capital, as well as, apparently without irony, a broader interpretation of the term 'extremism' (Rostovsky, 2016). In 2021, the defense of "historical truth" and prosecution of "falsehoods" were written into Russia's NSS.

The continued suppression of political activism and autonomy generates an aggressive apathy felt by society:

> Russian society as a whole does not care if its leading scholars and scientists have a way to publish their research and discoveries and that nobody has the power to prevent abuses and torture by the police . . . Russians have been more united during these last 18 difficult months than during the whole of the post-Soviet period. As they say, the person who holds the flag determines what is written on it.
>
> *(Sukhov, 2015)*

Andrey Demidov, a history and natural science teacher at a private school in St Petersburg, told *Gazeta.ru* news website:

> They are seriously tightening the screws anyway: introducing single text-books, one uniform, coming up with a single programme of classroom dis-cussions. There are concerns that they will recruit [people] not quite volun-tarily for the new Pioneer system and pressure will be put on teachers so that they enroll children into this forcefully.
>
> *(Vinokutov et al., 2015)*

Levada Centre Deputy Director Alexei Grazhdankin notes:

> If no campaign is mounted, the complaints against the state will grow, but if a local conflict arises again and it is successfully attributed to certain forces, then the trend will change again. What is important is not how badly people are living, but who is blamed and what the prospects are.

Although Russian society is becoming more depressed, it has a reserve of patience and according to political analyst Alexei Makarkin: "People can feel the crisis, but they retain the hope that the situation will change: Any good news is received with enthusiasm, while bad news is perceived as temporary" (Mukhametshina, 2016). Tatyana Maleva, director of the Institute of Social Analysis and Forecast-ing at the Russian Academy of National Economy and Public Administration (RANEPA), argues:

> Some people fear social unrest. What I fear more is social apathy, infantilism, indifference. With a society like that, it will be even more difficult to lift our-selves out of crisis, and it will be impossible to make a new start.
>
> *(Hille, 2016)*

Conclusions

The Soviet past poses two core challenges to Putin's regime. First, the current regime fears all things revolutionary, whether "color revolutions," the Arab Spring or the Ukrainian Maidan movement of 2013–14:

> The paradox is that, historically, Russia's current political regime was born out of a peaceful bourgeois revolution, the liberal political and economic reforms of the early 1990s. This dissonance shapes the regime's ambiguous relation-ship to the past. Although the current leadership ultimately hails from a revo-lution in the population's mind-set, in the country's economic system, and in its political structures, the Kremlin is obsessed with its own self-preservation, and it cannot stand anything revolutionary.
>
> *(Kolesnikov, 2017)*

Second, and as Charles Robertson, Global Chief Economist at Renaissance Capital, argues, without the Bolshevik revolution in 1917 and forced industrialization, Russia may have been able to converge its per-capita GDP and democracy score with Italy or Spain, rather than with Mexico (Russia's human development benchmark in 1900). Furthermore, Russia, like China, may only have suffered from three rather than five major declines in industrial or agricultural output in the twentieth century: "two prolonged invasions, a civil war, two famines plus the collapse of all trading links and an economic system." Robertson notes some startling developmental parallels between Russia of 2017 and 1917:

> Two-thirds of Russia's exports were raw materials pre-1917. Today, it's roughly the same. Pre-1917, Russia was the world's biggest exporter of grain. From 2015 to 2017, the countries that made up imperial Russia were again the world's largest exporters of grain. Pre-1917, foreigners owned nearly one-third of Russian debt. Today, foreigners own nearly one-third of Russian debt. Pre-1917 foreigners got 5 to 8 percent dividend yields from Russian utility shares. Today, it's just the same, 5 to 8 percent for utility shares. The capital account was opened in 1897 and is open again. The state still owns the railways and still has a dominant role in banking. Brazil and Mexico were Russia's peers then – and they are again now. The most literate parts of the Imperial Russia in 1897 are also the most successful in 2017.
>
> *(Robertson, 2017)*

We can see that these parallels between dominant characteristics and trends in the Soviet period and the contemporary political environment of today generate certain tensions and contradictions. How to manage military-patriotic mobilization against a fabricated and phantom external threat emanating from the demonized West (NATO) while seeking to demobilize and depoliticize the population with regard to a domestic agenda? This challenge is compounded by the difficulties of securing popular and elite support and loyalty, or at least acquiescence, in the context of economic stagnation and growing social dissatisfaction. The Putin regime and its Soviet predecessors both suppress political opponents and curtail civic freedom and develop a legitimizing narrative justifying such actions in the name of preserving national freedom from Western encroachment and encirclement (Radchenko, 2021). While the 'cult of personality' and military-patriotic mobilization are compatible (indeed, are self-reinforcing), to what extent are these two Stalinist-era features dependent on the realization of the third? Does President Putin's regime need a 'Yalta–Potsdam-II'-type Grand Bargain and then stable and predictable international relations? Does Putin need a clear visible "victory" as an end to justify the means? For now, Putin is able to communicate well the myth of Western aggression among the Russian people, thereby consolidating the charismatic and historical or traditional basis for his political authority, substituting for a legal–rational deficit. But for how long?

What of other Soviet parallels? Yuri Andropov could also be viewed as a role model for Putin in terms of the type of modernization both have embraced and their *chekist* worldview chimed, in particular Andropov's "Hungarian complex" of 1956 as a precursor of Putin's "Dresden syndrome" of 1989 and subsequent fixation on "color revolutions" and "producers hand" (Pringle, 2001). The consolidation of a service state, with a particular emphasis on the mind-sets, cultural norms and organizational experience of a counter-intelligence state, provides another parallel and resonance (Pringle, 2000). Both of these leaders perceive international politics in terms of special operations by another name. In addition, and most importantly, the net effect of such "Chekist distortion of Russian security policy turns the Kremlin's quest for regime security into grand strategy, meaning the essence of Russian securitry policymaking" (Skak, 2016, 2019). As Mark Galeoti notes,

> Putin's generation of siloviki are, after all, Andropov's children. As the cere-bral and coldly analytical head of the KGB between 1967 and 1982, Yuri Andropov ushered in a new style of repression, one of "minimum effort for maximum effect," in which psychiatric incarcerations, forced emigration and "prophylactic chats" largely replaced the mass actions of the past.
>
> *(Galeotti, 2021)*

However central the Soviet legacy in shaping contemporary norms, attitude and worldview of Russian elites and society is, 'Putinism' cannot simply be under-stood in terms of an amalgam or sum of Brezhnev and Stalin – stagnation at home and great power projection abroad – with a sprinkling of Andropov, a dash of Khrushchev and 'anything but Gorbachev' to taste. 'Putinism' is not just a composite or crude amalgam: the sum of 'Putinism' is more than the parts of the past. Putinism is shaped by the weight and burden of *Tsarist* imperial past and contains the structural flaws inherent in the Soviet legacy, but security-thinking processes and Russia's strategic behavior is not justified or explained in terms of Marxist–Leninist ideology (Aliyev, 2019). Moreover, Russia now operates in a new globalized, transnational and technologically enabled present. Can Putin's Russia step into the same river of autocracy, orthodoxy and nationalism twice? If the Soviet Union was led by a proletarian *Tsar*, what of Russia today? 'Putinism,' in all its glory, is the focus of the next chapter.

Selected bibliography

"The Address of President of the Republic of Kazakhstan. N. Nazarbayev to the People of Kazakhstan. Nyrly Zhol – The Path to the Future." 2014. *Official Site of the President of the Republic of Kazakhstan.* November 11, 2014. https://web.archive.org/web/20150419084304/www.akorda.kz/en/page/page_218343_.

Aliyev, Nurlan. 2019. "Determinants of Russia's Political Elite Security Thought: Similarities and Differences between the Soviet Union and Contemporary Russia." *Problems of Post-Communism* 67 (6): 467–477. https://doi.org/10.1080/10758216.2019.1689827.

Aptekar, Pavel. 2018. "How Special Services Became Prestigious. Almost Half of Russians Would Like Their Children to Become Intelligence Officers." *Vedemosti*. February 6, 2018.

Arkhangelskiy, Andrey. 2016. "Out From the Underground: Russia's New Propagandists." *Carnegie Moscow Center*. March 6, 2016. https://carnegie.ru/commentary/63725.

Barber, Tony. 2020. "Vladimir Putin Has Just Done a Brezhnev." *FT.Com*. London: The Financial Times Limited. July 2, 2020.

Bastrykin, Alexander. 2016. "Time to Start Fighting Back in Information." *Kommersant-Vlast*. April 18, 2016.

Bennetts, Marc. 2016. "Russians Facing Brain Drain as Executives Flee." *The Times*. June 9, 2016. www.thetimes.co.uk/article/russians-facing-brain-drain-as-executives-flee-v86k8m0m7.

Biryukova, Liliya. 2014. "Spiritual Ties to be Exported. For First Time Defence of Traditional Values Becomes Official Aim of Russian Propaganda Abroad. Several Ministries and Departments to Coordinate this Work." *Vedomosti*. January 13, 2014.

Bondarenko, Oleg. 2014. "Ideology of the Russian Spring. On the Awakening of the Political Nation and the Revival of Conservative Values." *Izvestiya*. April 14, 2014.

Dmitriev, Mikhail. 2015. "Protective Patriotism. Continuation of Foreign Policy Conflict in Acute Form May Keep Ratings High for While to Come." *Vedomosti*. March 31, 2015.

Dogan, Mattei. 1992. "Conceptions of Legitimacy." In *Encyclopedia of Government and Politics*, edited by Mary Hawkesworth and Maurice Kogan. 1st ed., 116–128. London: Routledge.

Farkas, Evelyn. 2015. "Russia's Sergei Shoigu: Master of Emergencies." *The Economist*. November 7, 2015. www.economist.com/europe/2015/11/07/master-of-emergencies.

Fishman, Mikhail. 2016. "Victory Day in Moscow: 'Yes, We Can Do It Again'." *The Moscow Times*. May 11, 2016. www.themoscowtimes.com/2016/05/11/victory-day-in-moscow-yes-we-can-do-it-again-a52851.

Galeotti, Mark. 2021. "The Great Turn in Putin's Post-Post-Modern Authoritarianism." *The Moscow Times*, May 1, 2021. https://www.themoscowtimes.com/2021/05/01/the-great-turn-in-putins-post-post-modern-authoritarianism-a73802.

Greene, Sam. 2015. "Road Rage Redux." *Moscow-on-Thames*. December 4, 2015. https://moscowonthames.wordpress.com/2015/12/04/road-rage-redux/.

Grozovskiy, Boris. 2017. "Taking to the Street on Your Own Will Get You Nowhere. What Will Bring Change to Russia?" *Republic*. June 5, 2017.

Guriev, Sergei. 2015. "Deglobalizing Russia." *Carnegie Moscow Center*. December 15, 2015. https://carnegie.ru/2015/12/16/deglobalizing-russia-pub-62294.

Hille, Kathrin. 2016. "Russia: Putin's Balance Sheet." *Financial Times*. April 7, 2016. www.ft.com/content/cbeae0fc-f048-11e5-9f20-c3a047354386.

Jackevicius, Mindaugas. 2016. "Grandson's Surprise: Letter to Grandmother Sent by Vladimir Putin Himself." *Delfi*. May 3, 2016. www.delfi.lt/news/daily/lithuania/anuko-nuostaba-mociutei-laiska-atsiunte-pats-v-putinas.d?id=71168006.

Jushkin, Vladimir. 2020. "Putin's June Thesis." *Postimees*. July 8, 2020.

Karaganov, Sergey. 2014. "The Watershed Year: Interim Results." *Russia in Global Affairs*. December 18, 2014. https://eng.globalaffairs.ru/articles/the-watershed-year-interim-results/.

Kaylan, Melik. 2014. "Kremlin Values Putin's Strategic Conservatism." *World Affairs* 177 (1): 9–17.

Khrushcheva, Nina L. 2015. "The Tsar and the Sultan." *Quartz*. December 4, 2015. http://qz.com/565276/vladimir-putin-fancies-himself-a-tsar-standing-up-to-turkeys-new-sultan/.

Khvostunova, Olga. 2020. "Evgeny Dobrenko: 'The WWII Victory Cult Is Meant to Legitimize the Regime' (Part II)." *Institute of Modern Russia*. July 1, 2020. https://imrussia.org/

en/opinions/3131-evgeny-dobrenko-%E2%80%9Cthe-wwii-victory-cult-is-meant-to-legitimize-the-regime%E2%80%9D-part-ii.

Kolesnikov, Alexander. 2017. "A Past That Divides: Russia's New Official History." *Carnegie Moscow Center*. October 5, 2017. http://carnegie.ru/2017/10/05/past-that-divides-russia-s-new-official-history-pub-73304.

Kolesnikov, Andrei. 2015. "Totalitarianism 2.0." *Project Syndicate*. June 16, 2015.

———. 2021. "Russia's History Wars: Why is Stalin's Popularity on the Rise?" *Carnegie Moscow Center*. July 19, 2021. https://carnegie.ru/commentary/84991.

Kopotin, Igor. 2020. "The Kremlin May Attempt a New June Coup in Estonia, This Time It Is Targeting NATO." *Eesti Paevaleht. In Estonian, BBC Monitoring*. July 21, 2020. https://monitoring.bbc.co.uk/product/c201wpxv.

Koshkin, Pavel, and Andrei Kolesnikov. 2015. "Why the Kremlin Neglects Strategic Thinking." *Russia Direct*. September 14, 2015.

Kurilla, Ivan. 2020. "Reusing Soviet History Books: The Role of World War II in Russian Domestic Politics and Academia." *The Journal of Slavic Military Studies* 33 (4): 502–507.

Laruelle, Marlene. 2020. "Making Sense of Russia's Illiberalism." *Journal of Democracy* 31 (3): 115–129.

Lenon, Troy. 2016. "The Day Khrushchev Decried Stalin for Abuses of Power." *The Daily Telegraph*. February 25, 2016. www.2gb.com/podcast/day-khrushchev-decried-stalin-abuses-power/.

Litvinova, Daria. 2015. "Inoculated against Russian Propaganda." *The Moscow Times*. December 4, 2015.

Macierewicz, Antoni. 2016. "The Threat from Moscow is Serious." *Rzeczpospolita*. April 19, 2016.

"Meeting of the Valdai." 2013. "Meeting of the Valdai International Discussion Club." *President of Russia*. September 19, 2013. http://en.kremlin.ru/events/president/news/19243.

Morozov, Viatcheslav. 2016. "What Is the Meaning of 'National' in the Russian Debate about the National Interest?" *Ponars Eurasia*. January 19, 2016. www.ponarseurasia.org/what-is-the-meaning-of-national-in-the-russian-debate-about-the-national-interest/.

Mukhametshina, Elena. 2016. "Agents under Pressure: Experts Consider All Heads of Independent NGOs to be at Risk of Criminal Prosecution." *Vedomosti*. May 27, 2016.

Novoprudskiy, Semen. 2018. "Do the Russians Want War?" *Gazeta.Ru*. January 18, 2018. www.gazeta.ru/comments/column/novoprudsky/11877925.shtml.

Pastukhov, Vlafimir. 2021. "Heavenly Praskoveyevka." *Novaya Gazeta Website*, in Russian. March 19, 2021.

Paul, T. V., Deborah Welch Larson, and William C. Wohlforth, eds. 2014. *Status in World Politics*. Cambridge: Cambridge University Press. https://doi.org/10.1017/CBO9781107444409.

Pavlovskiy, Gleb. 2015. "The Kremlin is Living without Sensing the Country Beneath It: Effective Policy Foundation Head Gleb Pavlovskiy on the Russian System of Management." *Gazeta.Ru*. December 26, 2015.

———. 2016. "Russia's New Politicization: How Putin Trumped Politics." *The Moscow Times*. June 3, 2016. www.themoscowtimes.com/2016/06/02/russias-new-politicization-how-putin-trumped-politics-op-ed-a53135.

Petrovskaya, Irina. 2021. "Tsar Orders His Boyars." *Novaya Gazeta*. July 2, 2021. https://novayagazeta.ru/articles/2021/07/01/tsar-velel-svoim-boiaram.

Postimees. 2020. "Putin's Ambitions." *Postimees*. June 25, 2020.

Pringle, Robert W. 2000. "Andropov's Counterintelligence State." *International Journal of Intelligence and CounterIntelligence* 13 (2): 193–203.

————. 2001. "Putin: The New Andropov?" *International Journal of Intelligence and Counter-Intelligence* 14 (4): 545–558.

Putin, Vladimir. 2020. "Putin Condemns Time-Bomb of Soviet Constitution Secession Clause." *Rossiya 1 TV.* July 5, 2020. www.rbc.ru/politics/05/07/2020/5f01ab049a794 700be0883d1.

————. 2021a. "On the Historical Unity of Russians and Ukrainians." *President of the Russian Federation Website.* July 12, 2021. http://kremlin.ru/events/president/news/66181.

————. 2021b. "Vladimir Putin Answered Questions on His Article "On the Historical Unity of the Russians and Ukrainians." *President of the Russian Federation Website.* July 13, 2021. http://en.kremlin.ru/events/president/news/66191.

Radchenko, Sergey. 2021. "Putin's Regime and Its Soviet Predecessor Are Dark Comedies." *The Moscow Times.* May 6, 2021. www.themoscowtimes.com/2021/05/06/ putins-regime-and-its-soviet-predecessor-are-dark-comedies-a73823.

Radzikhovskiy, Leonid. 2012. "With One Stone. Putin's New Political Style Is Gradually Coming to Light." *Nezavisimaya Gazeta.* November 8, 2012.

"Read Us Our Rights: Will MVD General be Able to Change from Law Enforcer to Rights Defender." 2018. *Gazeta.Ru.* April 22, 2018.

Reuters. 2018. "Putin Recreates Soviet-Era Patriotic Directorate in Russia's Army." *The Moscow Times.* July 31, 2018. www.themoscowtimes.com/2018/07/31/putin-recreates-soviet-era-patriotic-directorate-russias-army-a62402.

Robertson, Charles. 2017. "Why the 1917 Bolshevik Revolution Was Bad for Russia's Economy Today (Op-Ed)." *The Moscow Times.* October 4, 2017. www.themoscowtimes. com/2017/10/04/why-the-1917-bolshevik-revolution-was-bad-for-russia-a59146.

Romanov, Pyotr. 2014. "Putin's Popularity Masks an Uncomfortable Reality." *The Moscow Times.* August 28, 2018. https://www.themoscowtimes.com/2014/08/28/putins-popularity-masks-an-uncomfortable-reality-a38833.

Rostovsky, Mikhail. 2007. "Behind the Scenes Everything Is Decided: Why Putin Rules Everything Alone." *Moskovsky Komsomolets.* October 24, 2007. www.mk.ru/politics/ article/2007/10/24/73716-za-kadryi-reshayut-vse.html.

————. 2016. "Where Bastrykin is Wrong; and What Does His Fellow Student at the Leningrad Law Faculty Vladimir Putin Think of His Former Group Monitor's Calls?" *Moskovsky Komsomolets.* October 5, 2016.

Roy, Sergei. 2004. "Perestroika 1985–1991." *The Moscow News.* February 4, 2004.

Satke, Ryskeldi. 2014. "Kazakhstan Opposition Fears Ukraine's 'Russian Spring'." *The Diplomat.* April 12, 2014. https://thediplomat.com/2014/04/kazakhstan-opposition-fears-ukraines-russian-spring/.

Schulmann, Ekaterina. 2017. "Babushkas Rule." *Chatham House.* July 28, 2017. www.cha-thamhouse.org/publications/the-world-today/2017-08/babushkas-rule.

Sharkovskiy, Aleksandr. 2015. "Russia Does Not Intend to Get Involved in an Arms Race." *Nezavisimaya Gazeta.* November 12, 2015.

Shevtsova, Liliya. 2015. "Review of the Year. 2014. The End of the Illusion?" *Yezhednevny Zhurnal.* January 1, 2015. https://monitoring.bbc.co.uk/product/00038676.

"The Situation in Ukraine and Crimea." 2014. *Levada Centre Press Release.* March 13, 2014. www.levada.ru/2014/03/13/situatsiya-v-ukraine-i-v-krymu/.

Skak, Mette. 2016. "Russian Strategic Culture: The Role of Today's *Chekisty.*" *Contemporary Politics* 22 (3): 324–341. https://doi.org/10.1080/13569775.2016.1201317.

————. 2019. "Russian Strategic Culture: The Generational Approach and the Counter-Intelligence State Thesis." In *Routledge Handbook of Russian Security*, edited by Roger E. Kanet, 109–118. London: Routledge.

Snyder, Timothy. 2014. "Fascism, Russia, and Ukraine." *The New York Review of Books*. March 20, 2014. www.nybooks.com/articles/2014/03/20/fascism-russia-and-ukraine/.

Stanovaya, Tatyana. 2013. "In an Attempt to Understand the President's Intentions." *Politcom. ru*. December 16, 2013. http://politcom.ru/16919.html.

Sudakov, Dmitry. 2014. "If There Is No Putin, There Is No Russia." *Pravda Report*. October 23, 2014. https://english.pravda.ru/society/128877-putin_russia/.

Troitskiy, Mikhail. 2016. "The Need to Massage Egos: Status Politics as a Crucial Element of US-Russia Relations." *PONARS Eurasia*. October 16, 2016. www.ponarseurasia.org/ the-need-to-massage-egos-status-politics-as-a-crucial-element-of-us-russia-relations/.

Trudolyubov, Maxim. 2014. "Russia's Culture Wars." *The New York Times*. February 8, 2014. www.nytimes.com/2014/02/08/opinion/trudolyubov-russias-culture-wars.html.

Tsygankov, Andrei P. 2014. "The Frustrating Partnership: Honor, Status, and Emotions in Russia's Discourses of the West." *Communist and Post-Communist Studies* 47 (3): 345–354.

"Under Siege: The Kremlin Has Isolated Russia's Economy." 2021. *The Economist* 439 (9242): 18–19.

"Vladimir Putin Meets with Members of the Valdai Discussion Club. Transcript of the Final Plenary Session of the 12th Annual Meeting." 2015. Valdai Club. October 22, 2015. https://valdaiclub.com/events/posts/articles/vladimir-putin-meets-with-members-of-the-valdai-discussion-club-transcript-of-the-final-plenary-sess/.

Yanka, Hryl. 2016. "Courier from the Pentagon." *BelGazeta*. April 4, 2016.

Zheleznova, Mariya, and Nikolay Epple. 2016. "Pens of the Motherland: Why High-Ranking Officials Are Fighting the United States in the Russian Media." *Vedemosti*. April 18, 2016.

Zubov, Mikhail. 2015. "Fifteen Years: A Different Putin." *Moskovsky Komsomolets*. March 26, 2015. https://russian.rt.com/article/90340.

5

"PUTINISM" AND RUSSIA'S HYBRID STATE

Policies, practice and performance

Introduction

Carl J. Friedrich and Zbigniew K. Brzezinski (1956) in their seminal book *Totalitarian Dictatorship and Autocracy* identified six basic features: an ideology, a single party, a terroristic police, a communications monopoly, a weapons monopoly and a centrally directed economy. Distinctions between totalitarian dictatorships as defined by Friedrich and Brzezinski and contemporary autocracy in Russia are not just one of degree (20 percent of the economy is not under state control, the police are not "terroristic"), but also the issue of ideology – Russia is said to lack one. While Putinism cannot be understood as a clearly defined belief system, there are: "sufficient agreement across parts of the elite to talk about shared elements of a worldview, a collective agreement on the meanings of concepts, a paradigm that imposed meaning on the world and structured Russia's potential responses" (Lewis, 2020, ix). Putinism's *leitmotif* is a stark binary division between Putin and the Russian people on the one side and foreign Russo-phobic interference that seeks to disrupt Russian internal stability on the other. Putinism began with the promise of a "dictatorship of the rule of law" in 2000 which became the ideal of a "sovereign democracy" in 2005. By 2007, Putin identified the scourge of "one master, one sovereign" in foreign affairs like the United States, and in 2012 he provided the antidote in the shape of charismatic-historical "no Putin no Russia" conception of leadership within a besieged fortress. By 2021, in the face of a "totalitarian West," vigilance, strength, stability and continuity are four pillars of Putinism, impossible without the guidance of Putin himself, married and eternally faithful, as he is, to Mother Russia.

All ideologies represent patterned thinking (with clusters of ideas, beliefs, opinions, values and attitudes) presenting an internalized worldview. All ideologies offer a problem diagnosis (provide an explanation for the cause of problems, issues or grievances), provide responsibility attribution (point to scapegoats or actual causes of problems – individuals, groups or state policies) and offer a solution though prognostic and motivational framing (ideologies suggest viable solutions to the problems and call individuals to action and offer a future vision

DOI: 10.4324/9780429261985-5

of society). According to Russian official discourse, two problems need to be addressed: Western liberal democratic values are decadent and destabilizing; liberal international order is a construct designed to exclude Russia. The responsibility and blame lies with the "totalitarian West" and its messianic coercive promotion of demonic democratic universalism. Only strong autocracies led by sovereign leaders who can avoid instability and promote statehood and, at some undefined future date, prosperity, provide the solution. Thus, an ideology of Russian autocracy is born and able to propagate not just through post-Soviet space but also resonates and cements partnerships with other autocracies in a global context.

For 20 years, Putinism has been understood variously as:

> *managed democracy, illiberal democracy, competitive authoritarianism, electoral authoritarianism, semi-authoritarianism,* and *patronal regime,* as well as newer concepts like informational dictatorship (in which the dictator convinces the public that they are competent and wise) and plebiscite democracy (where the leader periodically renews the legitimacy of their enormous power using elections).
> *(Trudolyubov, 2021)*

Putinism is "post-modern authoritarianism" because it relies more on narrative control than fear and force. For Bálint Magyar and Bálint Madlovics content that Western democratic concepts of "politician," "private property," and "political party," for example, have a different meaning in post-communist countries, where there is no clear separation or dividing line between political power, business ownership, and public activities, with formal institutions act as façade for informal relations and corruption the norm, not the exception:

> the current system differs from the systems of the past in one key way – it's heterogeneous and it's not totalitarian. Therefore, people living in Russia today have the opportunity to choose which Russia they live in – whether to accept the statements of the *informational dictatorship* on faith, whether to participate in the *plebiscite democracy,* or whether to become part of the *mafia state.*
> *(Magyar and Madlovics, 2020)*

The state was prepared to invest in an effort to both create and reflect majority popular opinion and sentiment. An effective means to creating an identity is to identify a common enemy and convince the Russian population that alternatives were even worse. The reproduction of Soviet myths, conservative revanchism and the mantra of external threats and emergency keeps society vertically unified in support of Putin but horizontally fragmented (Khvostunova, 2021). Samuel Greene qualifies this understanding by highlighting the performative element involved in support of Putin. Russians view national-level politics as primarily symbolic and are attracted to Putin for his perceived "agreeableness," his role as "lubricant in social relations" and a sense of "emotional inclusion" (Greene, 2019, 199). As David Lewis notes,

> For a short period following the annexation of Crimea, all these efforts to build unity came together to form the 'Crimean Consensus', which successfully combined Russian nationalist sentiment (both ethnic and statist), a majoritarian agreement over values and beliefs, and a general identification of an existential enemy that posed a threat to the well-being of Russians, their identity and the Russian state more widely.
>
> *(Lewis, 2020, 114)*

However, might this construct be under threat due to a major Russian policy shift which has occurred in 2020–21? Policy is now characterized by the application of much more openly repressive measures following the criminalization of the non-systemic opposition and signifying the "political decay and intellectual debasement of late Putinism" (Galeotti, 2020). For Galeotti, this shift was triggered by an elite consensus (Security Council Secretary Nikolai Patrushev, FSB director Alexander Bortnikov, Investigatory Committee head Alexander Bastrykin and *Rosgvardiya* commander Viktor Zolotov) that a Western campaign of subversive *gibridnaya voina* (hybrid war) was targeting Putin himself. For the purposes of this chapter, we can ask: Is this fundamental policy shift the logical outcome of Putinism, conceived at the consummation of Putin's assumption to the presidency in 2000?

Soviet and *Tsarist* precursors

Twice before in Russian history, new regimes have been created following clear-cut politico-military victories – in 1613 when the *Tsar* Mikhail, first of the Romanov dynasty, assumed the throne and in 1917 when the Bolshevik revolutionary Vladimir Lenin declared a Communist revolution. When the Russian Federation emerged as the legal successor state to the Soviet Union on 1 January 1992, adopting the borders of the Russian Soviet Federative Socialist Republic (RSFSR), it did not do so after a politico-military victory but rather as a result of the lack of will of Soviet elites to self-reproduce and sustain themselves and the Soviet system. The Soviet system was delegitimized through the late 1980s and effectively imploded. Its territory, economic system and the prevailing certitudes, foundational assumptions and attitudes of a demoralized Soviet strategic community were shattered (Odom, 2000). All that had underpinned a Soviet strategic culture appeared to have become irrelevant. As Igor Zevelev astutely observed:

> The collapse of the Soviet Union meant much more for Russia than just the loss of colonies. It was the loss of identity. Political, historical, cultural, ethnic boundaries, as well as a subjective mental map held by most Russians, share

no congruence. There have been no clear and historically consistent criteria for distinguishing "we" from "they" in the Russian consciousness. Confusion over the boundaries of the Russian people has been the major factor of Eurasia's historical development for at least three hundred years.

(Zevelev, 2016, 7)

When Vladimir Putin was elected President of the Russian Federation and inaugurated on 6 May 2000, he declared that the 'Time of Troubles' of the 1990s was over and that his presidency would recentralize state authority around a 'power vertical' chain of command, ensure progress through the emergence of Russia as a globally integrated and economically competitive power, raise living standards and restore international respect for Russia, returning it to *velikaya derzhava* (Great Power) status. On 29 March 1999, FSB head Putin was appointed Secretary of the Security Council of the Russian Federation in a position where he was able to coordinate the activities of all security-related institutions and work on a day-to-day basis with power ministries, including Interior, Defense, Foreign Affairs, Emergencies and Disaster Relief and Justice, as well as the security services. On becoming president in 2000, Putin was a little-known supreme pragmatist, one who wanted to build a strong and effectively functioning centralized state that was integrated into and competitive within a globalized economy.

Although Putin presided over a constitutional order from President Yeltsin that had the institutional prerequisites for further democratic development, as well as an urban, educated population, Putin has created an autocracy. With the collapse of the Soviet Union came the new symbols of the state, including a flag, anthem and ideology, and institutions had to be constructed and built. A pluralist polity, with a vibrant civil society, multiparty competitive political system and a market economy were all promised. The Yeltsin Constitution enshrined 'five freedoms': freedom of speech, freedom of movement, freedom of assembly, freedom of religion and freedom of the press. The oligarchs of the Yeltsin era "were not old friends of Yeltsin" (Kamakin, 2015). President Yeltsin began a process of state-building. His yardstick was the notion of legal and rational legitimation. He assumed that Russia would abandon a command-control economy within a one-party state. It would embrace market-democratic transition and then enjoy the benefits of market-democratic consolidation.

President Putin's official state-sponsored and propagated narrative has consistently argued that democratic transition in the 1990s represented a period of administrative chaos, the decentralization of power, corruption and criminalization, decay, disintegration and disorder. As Aleksander Kolesnikov notes, "without this historical window dressing the image of Putin as the savior of a nation pales. There can be no phoenix if there are no ashes" (Kolesnikov, 2017). The challenges of transition were immense – reshaping state–society and center–periphery relations; adapting an authoritarian political culture and overcoming corruption, cronyism and predatory elites. The era began with a failed *putsch* in August 1991 and led to the Constitutional crisis in October 1993 and open warfare in the North Caucasus in 1994 which threatened territorial collapse and ended in a financial meltdown in 1998. Democratic transition endangered the very existence of statehood – the territorial integrity and sovereignty of the Russian Federation.

When Putin first became president in 2000, he assumed a legal–rational ("dictatorship of the rule of law") legitimation of his political authority. President Medvedev promoted socioeconomic modernization in cooperation with the West, up to and including the "modernization partnerships" with first Germany, then other European countries and the EU, as well as cooperation with the United States. Following the mass demonstrations for a "Russia without Putin" after the parliamentary election in December 2011 and in March–May 2012 following the presidential election, Putin embraced national–patriotic mobilization and confrontation with the West. The term modernization was reserved for the military/technical spheres, as in "modernization of the armed forces." Putin's political authority was now clearly based on historical–charismatic ("No Putin, no Russia") legitimation, and in 2014 Crimea and Donbas and the notions of *Russkii Mir* and *Novorossiya* became the observable outcomes of this shift (Adomeit, 2016, 685–710, 2017, 2019).

By 2020–21, an aging Putin presides over a fully fledged authoritarian regime and police state. Core characteristics of the regime can be listed. First is an absence of a rotation of power and lack of any liberal or democratic impulses or even an authoritarian modernization project beyond the military. Late Putinism lacks a positive agenda: repression of the opposition and wider civil society is not the same as mobilizing supporters around a compelling vision of the future. Second, the marketing of external and internal threats binds a passive, conformist, indifferent and apathetic majority of the population to the state to legitimize the regime and keep it safe. Third, the all-pervasive presence of the state manifests itself by Praetorian Guard capitalism, an economy marked by low dynamism, reflecting the lack of a law-based state, high levels of raiding, and, a disproportionate allocation of resources for prestige state projects.

Prior to Putin's first presidential inauguration on 6 May 2000, carefully staged events juxtaposed his youth, physical vigor and sobriety with that of the outgoing president, Boris Yeltsin. The centrality of President Putin to stability in the state – an idea propagated by his political technologists to boost his power – is unprecedented. Vladislav Surkov asserts that "Putinism" is a "functioning ideology of the everyday, with all its social innovations and productive contradictions" and a "global political lifehack for governing" (Surkov, 2019). By contrast, Konstantin Gaaze argues:

> The sovereign or regime in Russia is not sitting inside the head of an enormous mechanical being. It is not at all to be found in the same order of existence as this being. Putinism is a doctrine of the erosion of statehood as an idea and the destruction of the state as a stable ensemble of people, practices and institutions. In some sense Putinism is repeating the move the Bolsheviks made: having seized power, they ruled not from within this power, but from without, from a secretive headquarters called the Politburo.
>
> *(Gaaze, 2019)*

Putinism – a qualitatively new post-Soviet context?

As well as continuities with the legacies of the past, there are important differences that shape the Putin presidency. The 2020s represent an increasingly multipolar strategic environment. Has Putin sacrificed modernization on the false altar of security and stability? Is the system Putin has constructed able to adapt to the strategic, economic and technological drivers of the international system, with its non-state transnational actors, interdependencies and supply chains? How will this era be defined: Putinite, Putinist, an era of Putinism? What is the ideology, priorities and policies of President Putin and his system of government? Let us examine five principal differences between present and past.

First, the economic context is transformed. Whereas in the Soviet period, fluctuations in the currency markets were an irrelevance for the average citizen, today's international economic environment is one in which capitalism is the global default system and the ruble and inflation rate responds to changes in the oil market and government policy. As former Russian Ambassador to the United States Vladimir Lukin noted: "We are all living in real world time, in a real-world economy and real world information environment" (Lukin, 2016). Because of these realities, Russia has no real prospect of economic autarky. The failure of 'sovereign globalization' project underscores this point. If Russia today embodies state capitalism and propagates an ideology based on statism and neo-mercantilism in post-Soviet space, the USSR symbolized an alternative global economic model of growth and an ideology based on equality and social justice. The differences in scale, scope and ambition between the Soviet period and contemporary Russia are palpable:

> the contours of the social and political system now unfolding before our eyes are far harsher, the political taboos preventing society from degenerating into primitive obscurantism far fewer and the barriers separating the country from the rest of the world far higher.
>
> *(Sukhov, 2015)*

But economic continuities are also apparent, not least Russia as a petro-state is suffering from the 'natural resource curse' or 'Dutch disease'. State corporatist command and control mechanisms can create a "middle income" society, but the transition to high-income per capita county demands that

> all the energies of civil society and workforces have to be harnessed to create great self-standing organizations. These, by developing their own purpose and cultures, can marshal the immense amounts of information that are at the core of the modern economy – and then produce at scale. Russia can use command-and-control economics to create a Gazprom. It can never create a Google, an Apple, a BBC, a Siemens or even the Anglo-Saxon rock'n'roll culture. For that, it would need the rule of law and all the open democratic structures that support it.
>
> *(Hutton, 2016)*

Loren Graham, a professor at MIT, highlights this dissonance when examining the relationship between invention and innovation in Russia: "To Putin, like past Soviet and tsarist rulers, modernization means getting his hands on technologies but rejecting the economic and political principles that pushed these technologies elsewhere to commercial success. He wants the milk without the cow" (Kirin, 2015).

President Putin has attempted to use market means to mercantilist ends. He has sought to attract investment and economic gains that make the state stronger while limiting the influence of investors and the potential political vulnerability that comes with international interdependence. In this way, he uses economic statecraft to ensure he can autonomously use the power of a stronger state. Nigel Gould-Davies suggests that this approach represents a strategy of "sovereign globalization." He notes that during Putin's first two administrations (2000–2008), Putin used "positive-sum economic cooperation to achieve zero-sum political goals of influence and domination. For the first time, Russia began to use economic power as a source of strength in its foreign policy" (Gould-Davies, 2016). Putin and his elite sat within a besieged fortress, made fiscally resilient to insulate Russia from external shocks. In mid-2008, a decade after the 1998 economic meltdown, Russia had accumulated $570 billion (around one-third of GDP). By 2020 the National Welfare Fund of Russia had $183 billion and Russia's total international currency reserves had reached $596 billion, as currency holdings diversified to hedge against sanctions. In addition, Russia debt is low, standing at 20 percent of GDP, and four-fifths of this is held by Russians. Moreover, in 2020, Russian average incomes were 10 percent lower than they had been in 2013 ("Under Siege," 2021). Russia faces a protracted economic stagnation, and its economy only expanded at an average annual rate of just 0.7 percent. As Anders Åslund notes:

> Though Putin has utterly squandered the country's abundant human capital through corrupt cronyism and systematic deinstitutionalization, his politicization of the courts and law enforcement has eliminated any pretext of rule of law – a prerequisite for private investment and business development.
>
> *(Åslund and Gozeman, 2021)*

If Putin's regime cannot legitimize its political authority on the basis of quality-of-life improvements, then more censorship, propaganda and foreign adventurism can become substitutes.

Second, repression in Putin's Russia is much less and more indirect than in the Stalinist era. Unlike the Stalinist period with its purges and gulag archipelago, the scale, scope and style of repression in Putin's Russia are in no way comparable:

> Today's Russian propaganda combines quintessentially Soviet-style heavy-handedness and state-of-the-art technique. There have been no mass purges and few large rallies. Western values may be under assault, but Western goods (food apart) are welcome. A common sight in Russia is a shiny German-

made car with a bumper sticker recalling the glories of World War II: "On to Berlin" or "Thank you, grandfather, for the victory, and grandmother for the tough bullets.

(Khrushcheva, 2015; Orttung, 2015)

While political trials (e.g. Khodokovsky, Pussy Riot and Navalny) and censorship are features of the current system, gulags, political terror and mass repression are not:

> In order to intimidate society, one show trial, which is covered by all television channels and about which all news media and social networks write, is sufficient. In addition, interim autocracies, as distinct from the totalitarian structures of the past, do not endeavor to keep a hold on disgruntled citizens – they never restrict departure for abroad. They put a scare into the part of society which is simultaneously told: "Get out! It will be quieter without you!
>
> *(Shulman, 2017)*

President Putin is still considered a serious political figure within Russia, and, again unlike Brezhnev but in the tradition of Stalin, he still enjoys majority popular support, though this is waning.

The National Guard includes the interior ministry troops and aviation, the Special-Purpose Mobile Detachment (OMON) riot police, the Special Rapid-Reaction Detachment (SOBR), the Federal State Unitary Enterprise (FGUP Okhrana), the weapons licensing department of the Interior Ministry (providing Zolotov control over all private military and security firms in Russia) and the external protection service. It reports directly to the president and guarantees his personal safety:

> The idea of personal security is becoming one and the same thing as the idea of state security as a whole. It is not for nothing that the concept of "Putin is Russia" was invented. Putin does not entirely trust a single security agency structure and that is why he needs, alongside the armed forces that already exist and mainly perform tasks abroad, a personal army that solves problems inside the country.
>
> *(Yevstifeyev and Petelin, 2016)*

The *coup d'état* attempt in August 1991 failed in part because Soviet generals refused to shoot at protesters. The October 1993 'events' managers in the Kremlin had to personally identify and bribe tank commanders in the Moscow garrison to open fire on the State Duma, as communication with the Defense Ministry and Minister broke down. The way the National Guard is structured gives President Putin maximum assurance that his orders would be carried out under any circumstance (MacKinnon, 2016).

Another anxiety concerns preventing or controlling an intra-*siloviki* war as resources that can be distributed cannot support the present clan structure. The formation of the National Guard (NG) and with it the elevation of the Federal Protection Service group under Zolotov at the expense of the Federal Security Services (FSB) and Ministry of Internal Affairs (MVD) create a 'Third Force' in Russia. Two agencies formally independent, the Federal Migration Service (FMS) under Konstantin Romadanovsky and the Drug Trade Control Service (FSKN) under Viktor Ivanov, are integrated into the MVD but an MVD which "has lost the capacity to wield armed instruments of power – and much political influence coming from such muscle" (Baev, 2016; Nikolskiy et al., 2016). In the process, the creation of the strong National Guard also balances FSB power, thereby in the process preventing Putin becoming hostage to FSB factions through his over-dependence on their coercive capacity. The FSB proves a counterweight to the Russian military under Defense Minister Shoigu, whose reputation has increased after the Crimean and Syrian campaigns. Most importantly, it is Putin who has initiated this process and sets the agenda and arbitrates between the clans. He holds the balance of power and demonstrates his ability to undercut the formation of independent power bases.

The formation of this new group, explicitly created, armed and equipped to suppress internal unrest, also preserves the image of the "FSB as sword and shield" and prevents the army, which is constitutionally prohibited from being used inside the country, from tarnishing its image as defender of the state by turning it into a praetorian regime defense force (Rakela, 2018). This force, with its special rapid-reaction detachments and special-purpose detachments located (with HQs) in each region, may also provide a stick to beat recalcitrant regional leaders who may feel the need to exert greater autonomy as distributed revenues from the center dry up. The implications for Chechnya are 'colossal' as the reform "takes the most combat-capable forces out of the sphere of influence of the republic's leadership and makes them directly subordinate to the director of the National Guard and the president of Russia" which will enable "an extensive and civilized purge" thereby ensuring "the Chechen force loyal to the head of Chechnya has been truncated." In a televised meeting with Chechnya's leader Ramzan Kadyrov, President Putin indicated that immunity from prosecution has limits, sending signal to the wider elite:

> I would like to draw your attention to the need for closer cooperation with the federal authorities, in particular this concerns security issues. You and future leaders of the republic must of course do all that is necessary to observe Russian laws in all spheres of our life, I want to stress that, in all spheres of our life.
>
> *("How Putin Closed", 2016)*

Third, President Putin is much less restrained by checks and balances than Soviet leaders and in turn is able to exert control through updated sticks-and-carrots. After all, Brezhnev and other Soviet leaders did at least have a 600-person Central Committee of the Communist Party of the Soviet Union to take into account. Indeed, a plenary session of the Central Committee removed

Nikita Khrushchev (1953–64) from power. Patron client relations did exist in the Soviet period, but bureaucratic institutions tempered the decisions of individual leaders, at least after Stalin, and the Communist Party balanced the KGB. Though Anders Åslund is able to infer that President Putin may not fully control the composition of the National Security Council (General Viktor Zolotov was appointed a permanent member on 5 April but then demoted on 11 April 2016 to "a mere member, of whom there are dozens, telling us that Putin was unable to defend him"), President Putin works through informal personalized decision-making processes rather than collegial decision-making bodies (Åslund, 2016). Chrystia Freeland highlights the personalistic nature of the regime, noting:

> Russia's transformation into what political scientists call a sultanistic or neo-patrimonial regime is a break both with Russian history and with the global trend. The Kremlin has been home to plenty of murderous dictators. But the czars drew their legitimacy from their blood and their faith. The general secretaries owed their power to their party and their ideology. Mr. Putin's rule is based solely on the man himself.
>
> *(Freeland, 2011)*

Fourth, in an unprecedented break from Soviet and Russian historical past, every key sector and resource, from finance to economics, the media, military, energy and foreign policy sectors, is controlled by the security services. The role of this *siloviki* group is unique:

> There is no historical precedent for a society so dominated by former and active-duty internal-security and intelligence officials; men who rose up in a professional culture in which murder could be an acceptable, even obligatory, business practice. . . . Those who operated within the Soviet sphere were the most malevolent in their practices. These men mentored and shaped Putin and his closest friends and allies. It is therefore unsurprising that Putin's Russia has become an assassination-happy state where detention, interrogation, and torture, all tried and true methods of the Soviet KGB, are used to silence the voices of untoward journalists and businessmen who annoy or threaten Putin's FSB state.
>
> *(Gerecht, 2007)*

When looking to security services and their ability to police the domestic scene, we see their influence over key Russian institutions that shape societal attitudes and expectations, not least: the media, the educational sector, cultural affairs and youth policy, the Russian Orthodox Church and the legal system. Collectively, these institutions serve the function of buffer and insulate the Russian elite from society, and society from the elite. Close control of these institutions enables the Russian leadership to ensure that a contemporary interpretation and meaning can be attached to a set of inherited cultural assumptions that have been passed on from generation to generation. Taking each in turn, let us first focus on the role of the Russian media.

The media, particularly television and mainstream newspapers, give the appearance of variety, but a unity of pro-Kremlin message (a mixture of Soviet nostalgia, xenophobia, homophobia and anti-Americanism) betrays their tight control by the government (Wilson, 2015; Yerofeyev, 2016). As Glunaz Sharafutdinova notes, "The authoritarian toolkit for 'manufacturing consent' has been expanding in the age of information technologies that allow political elites to manipulate public opinion more efficiently and more effectively" (Sharafutdinova, 2021). Vladislav Surkov states that Kremlin propaganda delivered through state TV and social media meets a public need:

> People need it. Most people need their heads to be filled with thoughts. You are not going to feed people with some highly intellectual discourse. Most people eat simple foods. Not the kind of food we are having tonight. Generally, most people consume very simple-meaning beliefs. This is normal. There is haute cuisine, and there is McDonald's. Everyone takes advantage of such people all over the world.
>
> *(Foy, 2021)*

The degree of state control was vividly illustrated in April 2016 when the Kremlin's dislike of RBK media holding's editorial policy, in particular stories concerning Innopraktika Foundation director Katerina Tikhonova and Kirill Shamalov, whom Reuters sources described as "Putin's daughter" and son-in-law respectively, forced the billionaire Mikhail Prokhorov to relinquish ownership and sell. ONEXIM group, which manages Prokhorov's Russian assets (assessed at $7.7 billion), had its headquarters raided to accelerate sale negotiations (Galimova et al., 2016). State control of television is paramount as data from the Levada Center obtained in March 2014 (the report 'Russian Media Landscape: Television, Press, internet) indicates that 90 percent of Russians names TV as their main source for obtaining news about Russia and the world. This study suggested: "there is a lack of any interest among the overwhelming majority of people in a detailed study of the news and obtaining a true picture of the world on a daily basis" (Pozdnyakova, 2016). As Gleb Pavlovsky observes, "Neoprop" is the contemporary equivalent of Soviet Agitprop:

> In Russia there is 'neoprop' – the machinery of stultifying television propaganda. It pumps up the population's loyalty by keeping the mass consciousness in a state of hysteria. Russia's people are being moved to the world of a sinister political serial, and that is where they live.
>
> *(Pavlovsky, 2015)*

The world is presented as a contest between a heroic Russian government successfully battling evil foreigners. In his book, *Nothing Is True and Everything Is Possible:*

The Surreal Heart of the New Russia, Peter Pomerantsev writes that he was told by a Russian Television and Radio Broadcasting Network executive: "The news is the incense by which we bless Putin's actions, make him the President" (Ostrovsky, 2016; Pomerantsev, 2015). As political authority in Russia is now legitimized through charismatic-historical means, Putin needs to secure continuous "victories." Charismatic leaders do not preside over defeats, and in the Russian media, Putin will never suffer such a fate (Petrovskaya, 2016).

Education, culture and youth policy support the media messaging and can further foster Russia's "spiritual and moral traditions" by providing a vehicle to inculcate a worldview among Putin's generation. President Putin consistently argues that it is vital that Russia follows its own cultural orientation rather than "blindly imitating foreign clichés" as this "inevitably leads to a nation losing its identity. Cultural criteria are part of state sovereignty." At the same time:

> cultural and spiritual identity [vernacular: *samobytnost*] has never hindered anyone establishing a country that is open to the world. Russia itself has made an enormous contribution to European and world culture. Historically, our country has been established as a union of many peoples and cultures. The foundation of spirituality of the Russian people themselves has, since the dawn of time, been the idea of common peace, peace for people of different ethnic and religious groups.
>
> *(Putin, 2007)*

In Putin's Federal Assembly Address in 2013, he noted: "We know the all-encompassing, unifying role of culture, history, and the Russian language for our multi-ethnic people, and we must build our state policy with this in mind, including in the sphere of education." It is notable, for example, that one state approved school textbook, *A Book for Teachers: The Modern History of Russia, 1945–2006*, which characterizes Stalin as "the most successful leader of the USSR," in keeping with President Putin's admonition to the effect that Russia "has nothing to be ashamed of" and that it was time to "stop apologizing" (Mathews, 2007).

State control of education is a means to control the past. Pavel Aptekar highlights how this phenomenon plays out in practice, analyzing the subordination of the Federal Archives Agency under the president's direct management:

> The country's leaders do not consider history to be an independent academic discipline. It is seen as part of an ideology, as a battlefield against foreign enemies and their supporters inside the country. The Kremlin intends to control the past and myth-making related to it and direct research in such a way as to confirm authority as sacred and emphasize the state's priority over personal interests.
>
> *(Aptekar, 2016)*

Sergei Mironenko, the director of the Russian State Archive of Ancient Acts since 1992, was demoted to its head of research for uncovering documentary evidence that demonstrated that the "Panfilov's guardsmen" (28 members of the Red Army's 316th Rifle Division) were not wiped out heroically derailing a German armored advance on Moscow, but rather that this dramatic exploit was the invention of a war journalist subsequently woven into Soviet propaganda. Mironenko gave short-thrift in response to those that prefer the heroic myth of "Panifolv's guardsmen" to the reality: "I don't care what you want. There are historical facts backed by documentary evidence, and let psychologists deal with the rest" (Hobson, 2016).

The Russian Orthodox Church (ROC) is the second of the three key institutions which shape societal attitudes and expectations. The ROC promotes and propagates traditional values, 'Patriotic Orthodoxy' in the guise of 'spiritual security', and itself embodies the idea of a strong ruler, hierarchy and centralized order and Russia's unique historical trajectory. According to Patriarch of Moscow and All Russia Kirill (f), Prince Vladimir (*Kievan Rus'*, 980–1015) chose Christianity but not Europe and so Russia is in but not of Europe: "Russia has a special path." Kirill presents Orthodox civilization as a special geopolitical formation consisting of the countries where orthodoxy decisively influences political cultures in Bulgaria, Belarus, Greece, Cyprus, Macedonia, Russia, Romania, Serbia, Montenegro and Ukraine. A psychological compatibility is also at play: "the basic tenet of Patriotic Orthodoxy – that only Russia can help Russia – is akin to his personal conviction that strength comes from within, that he can count only on himself" (Starobin, 2005). In return, the line between sacred and secular is blurred, with the church exercising palpable influence over public policy and spaces. However, at the same time, the Russian Orthodox Church is becoming more dependent on and instrumentalized by the state. This reflects the traditional handmaiden status of the Russian Orthodox Church from its subordination to the state by the Holy Synod, a government bureau, in 1721 to 1991 through the Soviet period when it was organized "by Department Z of the KGB" (Hellie, 2005). The *Tsarist* trinity of "Orthodoxy, Autocracy, Nationality" of 1916 gave way to the grand national ideals and goals of socialism and communism by 1926. Communism served the function of the state religion, with Marx-Lenin-Stalin as the Father, Son and Holy Ghost, the General Secretary of the Communist Party as the High Priest and a *Tsarist* Empire became a Soviet one (Surkov, 2008). Today, orthodoxy has a central role in domestic policy and helps propagate patriotism, the contemporary substitute for modernization.

The regime is populist. Putin

> is for the empire, a traditional, autocratic leader who understands that preserving Russia in a current geographical format does not allow him to be a Russian nationalist. Because Russian nationalism is disintegration, it means "it is enough to feed Caucasus", Russian nationalist demands to separate from Caucasus, Bashkirs and Tatars, and finally to create a Russian national state.

But this is the end of the Russian Federation, which Putin cannot allow. . . . He tried to blindly use Russian nationalism and Girkin-Malofeyevs to preserve the empire. Because what he did in Ukraine was to preserve the Russian Federation, the empire. Using nationalism to save the empire is a pretty original solution. But he understood that he could not develop the idea of the Russian world any longer, because everything was falling apart, Lukashenko and Nazarbayev are horrified. And Putin left, retreated. In principle, he betrayed the idea of the Russian world.

(Shevtsova, 2015)

Indeed, Igor Girkin (whose *nom de guerre* is "Strelkov"), a rebel commander in the Donbas, offers this critique himself, noting that Putin: "crossed the Rubicon, but then stopped unexpectedly and illogically. He didn't retreat, but didn't go forward either. He has no ideas and seems to be waiting for a miracle. He's stuck in the middle of a swamp" (Walker, 2016).

The legal and judicial system is a means control. The *Tsar* was the personification of the law and had impunity from the law. As a result, property was not an inalienable right and so source of hereditary power and a temporary and conditional asset as well. Power resided in the nature of one's personal familial relationship to the *Tsar*, and this in turn determined whether law would be applied or not. The *Tsar* granted land to and could take land away from his nobility – rule *by* law rather than the rule *of* law was in operation. President Yeltsin's tanks shelled the State *Duma* in October 1993, and he was not censured. President Putin is virtually unimpeachable under the Constitution, which is in keeping with Russian historical tradition. In Russia today, the operating principle appears to be: "for my friends everything, for my enemies the law!" Patriotism is expressed as paranoid xenophobia and policed by a politicized judiciary, adept at using the law selectively to punish critics and protect loyalists through selective enforcement. This undermines the credibility of the law and the concept of justice in Russia (Slabykh, 2021). This form of control is complemented by state-sponsored murders of independent journalists and critics. At its most extreme expression, named members of the *intelligentsia* and non-parliamentary opposition in Russia are "target marked" through castigation as "enemies of the people" and "traitors to the Motherland" who "are seeking to profit from the complex economic situation in the country" and who must therefore be "punished for subversive activity" ("How Putin", 2016).

In Russia today, the institution of private property was eliminated, and owners are "temporary users" of the land with permission in Soviet times given by the state, and today "by the amorphous semi-mafiosi syndicate that lacks precise legal status but *de facto* governs the country." The Soviet *nomenklatura* tradition continues, with one important difference: "The Communist *nomenklatura* collectively controlled property that theoretically belonged to the state, while the present-day *nomenklatura* jointly controls property that is in theory registered to a multitude of individuals and corporate entities, as if there are the 'private owners.'" To illustrate the reality of ruling clan syndicate or corporate ownership, Vladimir Pastukhov uses the comparison of the collective farm household, where members "held their property jointly – that is everything belonged to all of them but was not divided into shares," rather "the collective farm household's property was managed in strict compliance with the internal hierarchy, the head of the household made the decisions on its behalf and all the members were responsible for its obligations" (Pastukhov, 2021). In other words, traditional patrimonialism was at work.

After two decades of winnowing, filtering and sifting, Putin's elite are by now hard core loyalists, or at least profess to be, and share the same worldview in line with Russia's Great Power tradition. There are, however, tensions and differences of view, based in part on personal, political and pragmatic interests and in part on belief – that is genuine policy differences on how best to achieve commonly shared goals. Russian society's belief in the state's omniscience is misplaced, as the reputation of sapping corruption cases against members of the security services reflect more a typically chaotic *Game of Thrones* episode than a strategic blueprint. Intra-*siloviki* competition is also generated by groups having largely the same legal functions which legitimize struggles to prove a greater utility to Putin in order to maintain and increase access to budgets, privileges and precedence and so advance their agendas and corporate identities. In analyzing promotions and demotions in the *siloviki*, Alexei Makarkin argues that

> there are no clans at all in present-day Russia; they existed only in the 90s and the early "noughties." If a political clan is seen as a coalition of several players who are equal in terms of their resources and are part of the president's close entourage, there is no such phenomenon in present-day Russia. Contempo-rary Russian politics are atomized: several dozen individual major players who have their own clienteles, enter into situational coalitions with each other in order to achieve certain objectives, fall out and make peace with each other, and fight with each other, while the president is the arbiter and demiurge of this entire construct.
>
> *(Makarkin, 2016; Anayev, 2018)*

The Putin system in practice: power vertical hierarchies and networks

Efforts to characterize the nature of political power in Russia have explored the notion of Russia as a 'dual state' and focused on the defining role of neo-patrimonialism in regulating relations between the elite and society. In 2010, political scientist Richard Sakwa (2010, 185–186) developed the concept of a Russian dual 'normative' and 'administrative state', in which the former was constituted by a formal legal constitutional order and the latter, the 'dominant power system', by an informal and diffuse entity characterized by 'factional conflict', 'bureaucratic managerialism' and 'para-constitutional practices', where para-constitutionalism was enabled by institutions created by Putin, such as federal districts, the state and legislative councils and the Presidential Council for the Implementation of National Projects. Sakwa argued that the resultant regime system was 'more than personalized leadership or neo-patrimonialism, but less than an institutionalized law-governed system' (Sakwa, 2010, 187). Political order under Putin was defined by the constant interaction and resultant tensions between the two pillars of the dual state. By 2016, Neil Robinson viewed Russian political developments through the prism of neo-patrimonial relations, noting that such systems are always "trying to manage the tensions that they contain," including stresses generated by the notion of Russia as a "state-civilization" (Robinson, 2017, 351).

For David Lewis, the Western binary of democracy versus authoritarianism fails to characterize the reality of Russian political order. Instead, a Russian conceptual understanding based on a struggle between "order" or control and "chaos" better reflects reality. In this understanding, the state is a bulwark of order, defender of values and statehood (Lewis, 2020). Sakwa discusses the primary challenge Putin's leadership faces in similar terms, as a struggle between chaos and control, as exemplified by Putin-ordered vertical hierarchies which compete with horizontal factors (Sakwa, 2021). Vladislav Surkov presents himself as the founding father of "a new type of state" and key enabler of Putinism. As Surkov himself notes,

> People need to see themselves on stage. In this masked comedy, there is a director, there is a plot. And this is when I understood what needed to be done. We had to give diversity to people. But that diversity had to be under control. And then everyone would be satisfied. And at the same time, the unity of the society would be preserved...It works, this model works. It is a good compromise between chaos and order.

Using analogy from Roman imperial history, Surkov argues:

> Octavian came to power when the nation, the people, were wary of fighting. He created a different type of state. It was not a republic any more...he preserved the formal institutions of the republic – there was a senate, there was a tribune. But everyone reported to one person and obeyed him. Thus, he married the wishes of the republicans who killed Caesar, and those of the common people who wanted a direct dictatorship. Putin did the same with democracy. He did not abolish it. He married it with the monarchical archetype of Russian governance. This archetype is working. It is not going anywhere...It has enough freedom and enough order.
>
> *(Foy, 2021)*

A closer look at the nature of power (access to Putin) and its distribution in Russia indicates that the analytical construct of 'hybrid-state' has a better purchase on reality than "dual state," accounts for "patrimonism" and the struggle between order and chaos. "Hybrid state" is not synonymous with the notion of a "hybrid civilization." Nor should "hybrid state" be confused with "hybrid war" or "hybrid regimes," which combine democratic forms and authoritarian practices (electoral authoritarianism), although these terms can be compatible. Rather, as Mark Galeotti noted in 2016, a "hybrid state" is characterized by the "rejection of ideological constraints and the complete elimination of institutions" and so "the permeability of boundaries between public and private, domestic and external" (Galeotti, 2016a) and combines state legitimacy based on formal hierarchy with informal networked organizations. The critical determinant of a person's ability to achieve preferred policy outcomes is not rank or institutional position but one's network position and connectedness to Putin, which itself is determined by political loyalty and utility to Putin – not simply friendship or past associations (e.g. Leningrad University Law Faculty, KGB service in Dresden, Mayor's office in St. Petersburg, Ozero *dacha*, or FSB). Power in Russia is a measure of an individual's network connectedness to Putin (rather than his official position), and this reflects the individual's purpose-fulfilling value for the network.

The leadership regime of Russia's hybrid state consists of a parallel power network that combines the heads of large economic conglomerates, some government ministers, leaders of regional political machines and key administrators and oligarchs, wielded together in a parallel power network. Intra-regime competition and infighting for shrinking resources will continue to be managed by unwritten rules and norms enforced by whole group but guaranteed by Putin. Igor Sechin; Arkadiy and Boris Rotenberg; the Kovalchuks, particularly Yuriy, Gennadiy Timchenko, Sergey Chemezov, Viktor Zolotov, Nikolay Patrushev, Dmitriy Medvedev and also German Gref appear to constitute the inner court – some of whom are on the informal *Politburo*. As a result, Putin: "is not free in his actions, being hostage to a group of close friends in and around the Kremlin – businessmen and top officials who need him more than he needs them" (Torop, 2017).

In this sense, the defining feature of the hybrid state is how informal networks interconnect and intersect with hierarchies and influence decision-making. To help illuminate this network, it can be envisaged as being distributed across three pillars of power (see Table 5.1). The first pillar is very visible, tangible. It is based on the official formal, impersonal, centralized, constitutional-based and functioning legitimate Russian 'normative state' which represents a stable institutional framework. This pillar consists of individuals in regular conventional institutions, such as the presidential administration, Cabinet of Ministers, State *Duma* and Federation Council, courts and the state bureaucracy. According to the U.S. Department of the Treasury's January 2018 'Kremlin Report', this group of 'senior political leaders' consist of 73 individuals, with 43 from the presidential administration and 30 from the Cabinet of Ministers ("Treasury Releases", 2018). In Russian constitutional theory, these individuals are guided by and operate according to checks and balances, the logics of hierarchy and subordination, democratic accountability and transparency. In this sphere, political and diplomatic formalities and legal standards and norms are adhered to, thereby maintaining the legal–rational legitimacy of the state and so the regime. This pillar has a clear leadership in a formal hierarchy. Its duty is to maintain political order and economic development and efficiency and conduct day-to-day business and large tasks.

The second pillar is semi-official and consists of 29 individuals who are heads of 'parastatal entities,' that is large state-owned corporations (SOEs), where the state has 25 per cent or more of investments ("Treasury Releases", 2018). According to Russia's Federal Anti-Monopoly Service, SOEs generate 70 per cent of Russia's GDP and account for one-third of all jobs in Russia (in the year 2000, private enterprise was responsible for 70 per cent of Russian GDP), dominating Russia's economic landscape (Szakonyi, 2018, 12). Unlike the Yeltsin era, Putin-era oligarchs are friends of Putin, and Putin has in effect revived the historical tradition of granting patrimonial estates, with high-ranking senior officials managing state corporations that dominate strategic sectors of the economy, the definition of which has also expanded. In this sense, dynasticism ('princelings' promoted) and the creation of post-Soviet aristocracy (neo-*Boyar* elite) are ongoing processes.

A neo-feudal system appears to be emerging under Putin, with key resources in hands of five to seven families. Putin-era oligarchs renationalized strategic industries, creating state conglomerates (a 'state–private partnership') in which costs, risks and responsibilities are in effect nationalized and are met by the formal state institutions, while profit and privilege flows to the domestic power networks are privatized. As a result, even by 2014, Bloomberg argued that 110 Russian oligarchs controlled 35 percent of Russia's GDP ($420 billion), and in 2015 *Credit Suisse* reported 10 percent of the population controlled 87 percent of the wealth, representing the highest levels of wealth inequality among major economies globally (Shulman, 2017).

On Putin's watch and under "Sechin's leadership, Rosneft has become a state within a state, with quarter-million employees, United States' $65 billion in revenue, and 50 subsidiaries at home and abroad – as many as Gazprom" (Khrushcheva, 2015). Defense analyst Ruslan Pukhov highlights this phenomenon by noting that Sergey Chemezov, current head of huge state corporation Rostec and *de facto* minister of the defense industry,

> has never occupied high posts in the executive branch. But is this really a weakness? The head of the FSB [Federal Security Service] is responsible if an explosion has occurred somewhere and people have died, the defense minister may have a submarine sink. But nothing can sink for Chemezov.
>
> *(Bekbulatova, 2016)*

Political consultant Evgeny Minchenko expands on this notion: "How do you regulate [lobbying] if the people involved in making certain decisions often don't hold any formal office? Rotenberg is more influential than a lot of federal ministers. But who is Rotenberg?" (Bekbulatova, 2016). A *Meduza* source noted that in "conversations about lobbying, you often hear the phrase 'The best lobbyist is Sechin,' implying that corporate CEOs strike the best deals with the state. Industry insiders say this misses the picture. 'Anyone who can get a meeting with the president isn't a lobbyist but a player himself . . . By default, lobbyists are second-tier players.'" (Bekbulatova, 2016) Compare the power and influence of Chemezov and Sechin to that of Prime Minister Dmitry Medvedev. Indeed, former KGB general Aleksey Kondaurov argues that the Ulyukayev prosecution highlights Sechin's ability to privatize the FSB's Internal Security Administration's (USB) special forces (*spetsnaz*):

> Sechin's *spetsnaz* testifies to the degeneracy not of the special services in particular but of the state as a whole. A situation in which an influential person like him [Sechin] in effect "privatizes" an FSB administration in his own interests would have been absolutely impossible during my years of service and is completely unacceptable.
>
> *(Romanova and Korbal, 2017)*

In addition, during gubernatorial elections in 2017, the 'Chemezov Group' was understood to have influenced the appointments of governors to regions in which Rostec is heavily involved. Political analyst Rostislav Turovskiy noted that: "The Chemezov group played a big, if not decisive, role in shaping this trend – the appointment of young technocrats. Apart from Azarov and Nikitin, Sevastopol' Governor Dmitriy Ovsyannikov and Kaliningradskaya Region Head Anton Alikhanov have links to Rostech" (Kuznetsova et al., 2017).

The hybrid state's third pillar is constituted by a set of personal, unofficial, informal clans and networks. Putin's inner circle or court is identified by the U.S. Treasury Department as consisting of 96 oligarchs (including the Kovalchuk brothers, Gennadiy Timchenko and Arkadiy Rotenberg), with a net value of more than $1 billion. These individuals have gained wealth and power through association with Putin according to *Forbes* magazine's "Kings of State Contracts" ranking (Schreck, 2016). Indeed, 2015 could well be called the 'Year of the Rotenburgs,' given Arkadiy Rotenberg's Stroygazmontazh company received R228.3 billion to build the Kerch straits bridge and five other contracts worth R197.7 billion from state-owned Gazprom, all without competition (Roldugin, 2016). By inference, these oligarchs have maintained their wealth and power through ongoing demonstrations of political loyalty, utility and involvement in corrupt practices ("Treasury Releases", 2018). Mikhail Khodorkovskiy has created a 'Dossier' project, which gathers information about businessmen and officials in Putin's entourage allegedly involved in criminal activity. The 'Dossier' has over 50 names, 19 being major Russian corporation owners or members of boards of directors, including: "Ziyavudin Magomedov, Andrey Akimov, Viktor Vekselberg, Suleyman Kerimov, Aleksey Miller, Aleksey Mordashov, Iskander Makhmudov, Yevgeniy Prigozhin; Arkadiy, Boris, and Igor Rotenberg, Andrey Skoch, Igor Sechin, Gennadiy Timchenko, Kirill Shamalov, and others" (Gorbachev, 2018).

While second pillar individuals can exercise parallel decision-making functions, the oligarchs in the third pillar fund the luxurious lifestyle of the elite, finance domestic infrastructure projects (the Kerch Strait Bridge being a case in

TABLE 5.1 Russia's Hybrid State: Pillars, Functions and Working Assumptions

'Collective Putin'	*Normative State*	*Parastatal Entities*	*Non-State Oligarchic Actors*
Who? **What?**	Formal state institutions, Senate/ Duma, courts, bureaucracy; leadership dynastic but prey for parastatal and oligarchic economic entities	Economic: 40 SOEs, 70% GDP, 1/3 jobs; Political: federal Districts, public chamber, presidential councils; societal: state-sponsored civil society	Billionaire oligarchs: financial prowess (kings of state contracts); inner circle, personalistic court; criminalized – nonsystem shadow power ambiguity
Role and Function	State legitimation, formal IR actor; maintain order; force structures and prosecutorial power; isolates society from globalized world – "Besieged Fortress" narrative	Use state admin. resources against business competitors; Ineffective/corrupt but guarantee social stability and strategic autonomy; global economy dependent (*Gazprom, Rostec, Rosatom*) – *Rosneft* as "pseudo-corporate shadow MFA"	Fund luxurious elite lifestyle, finance domestic projects; foreign policy tool: foster foreign lobbies, finance; illicit activity as resilience; destabilization *kurators* provide plausible deniability for "exploitation military"
Working Assumptions	Limited by law, electorate, risk susceptibility; rational actor, undertakes hybrid war as an equalizer; as reduced resources, accept greater risks and responsibilities	'Friends of Putin' operate in parallel administrative reality; not beholden to electorate, privileges and rewards but not risks or responsibility.	Acts of political loyalty in return for state protection; deterrence hard as decentralized, disaggregated and sanctions a badge of honor.

point), foster foreign lobbies and provide funding and coordination (*kuratory*) and the promise of plausible deniability for external disruption and destabilization operations. The minority of businesses personally and ideologically attached to Putin "to a significant extent controls the mechanisms for allocating benefits between the state and the private sector [and receive] unconditional protection and guarantees from the state" (Stanovaya, 2017). In December 2017, for example, Putin met oligarchs (with a combined wealth of $213 billion) in the Kremlin to ensure their loyalty (Dobrokhotov, 2017).

Putin referees and balances these tensions. The stability and tenacity of Putin's political regime can be attributed to the promotion of "informal, often semi-criminal and criminal communities in the place of institutions" which "used quite long and sophisticated 'unwritten rule chains' (collections of informal rules of conduct rooted in tradition) instead of laws." In this context, Putin is

> simultaneously both the head of state and the leader of an organization that did not exist officially but was powerful and extremely diverse, living in accordance with its own code of conduct, non-compliance with which, in contrast to non-compliance with the laws, was fraught with the most serious difficulties. This unique Putin universality, his ability to be simultaneously a prince of the light and a prince of the darkness, to a significant extent explains the success of his long rule.
>
> *(Pastukhov, 2018)*

Putin has carrots and sticks at his disposal.

Sticks are wielded by the FSB's counter-intelligence and economic security departments who, through surveillance, can manage elite hedging behavior. As former Economic Development Minister Alexey Ulyukaev bitterly noted, *kompromat* ('compromising material') is damaging information about a politician or other public figure used to create negative publicity for blackmail or to ensure loyalty –

> is very easy. A bag, a basket, a poorly recorded video, and it's done. Imagine a familiar state official who's worn out his welcome. You invite him for a walk, and tell him to hold your briefcase, while you tie your shoes. And then the good guys pop out from the bushes. They grab the bureaucrat right there and it's off to the detention center.
>
> *("An Elderly Gladiator", 2017)*

As William Browder observes:

> Putin is in power. [Yuri] Chaika [the Prosecutor General] is in power, [Alexander] Basrtrykin [the head of the Investigative Committee] is in power, [Sergei] Shoigu [the Defense Minister] is in power. Lavrov, Medvedev are in power . . . The power goes to the people who have the power to arrest other people.
>
> *(Orlova, 2016)*

Carrots consist of favored access, sanctioned corruption and "familial ties, personal relationships, long-term acquaintances, informal transactions, mafia-like behavior codes, accumulated obligations, and withheld compromising materials [*kompromat*]" (Umland, 2017). Systemic corruption became the glue to bind Putin's elite and generate loyalty across the business, security service and political elite. This new aristocracy or nobility have a vested interest in the *status quo* as regime leadership change would break the compact and contract between themselves and Putin.

Their businesses would be harassed or expropriated by law enforcement officials, and their property would be seized. Thus, in Russia "corruption is a way to get and keep the political power that is so much more important than mere wealth" (Galeotti, 2016b). Determining which clans have taken control of which investigative bodies in Russia and then identifying who is investigated and who is not and by whom – Prosecutor Generals' Office, Investigation Committee or Presidential Monitoring Directorate – serves as a barometer of elite power. The fight against corruption becomes a means of controlling the bureaucracy, seizing the assets of rival clans, scapegoating, blaming and disciplining rivals, while embedding one's own networks, power and influence.

Putin delegates domestic policy to a wider Putinite institution-based *gosudarstvenniki* elite – the 'Collective Putin' – that rules in Putin's name. In his informal role, Putin is the 'Oligarch-in-Chief', operating through a networked 'prerogative state,' and maintains his own sovereignty and autonomy over and within his elite power network through sanctioned 'brigandage." Here, Putin focusses on his own and his entourage's personal enrichment and security. Putin is the central node within this network. Connectedness to Putin is a function of the inner circle's loyalty and, more importantly from Putin's perspective, their utility to him and his interests. Putin as both president and oligarch-in-chief has the tools to effectively manage his elite (Herd, 2018). Putin can control personnel changes/rotation and has a decisive role in allocating the distribution of administrative rent flows, budgets and property, adjudicating disputes (such as disruptive intra-elite corporate raiding or *raiderstvo*) over access to these flows. Putin can, in other words, determine and, through the FSB as the ultimate single "roof" (*krysha*), regulate and enforce the level of corruption (i.e. the administrative rent flows associated with particular posts) that will be tolerated. Putin can direct prosecution bodies to use surveillance, start investigations and initiate selective prosecutions to keep elite factions in balance. The Federal Protection Service (FSO), reporting directly to Putin, can use intelligence to gather *kompromat* in order to punish and deter non-compliant elite behavior. Ultimately, the type of "active measures" used against the nonsystemic opposition in Russia can be deployed to silence elite dissent. Putin has also used the "successor's race" and the prospect of favoring one successor or the other to keep the elite off balance, competing for his favor. By hollowing out independent institutions and fermenting administrative battles and inter- and even intra-agency factionalism, Putin maintains an equilibrium and prevents elite consolidation and the emergence of a collective leadership capable of collective action and so preserves his strategic autonomy against a "siloviki state capture" that would restrict Putin.

Conclusions

An understanding of Putin and Putinism can be refined through an analysis of Russian responses to the strategic challenge of COVID-19. In March 2020, Putin delegated day-to-day management of the crisis responses to COVID-19 to Mayor

Sobyanin, Prime Minister Mishutsin and regional governors. Putin appeared indecisive and inconsistent, the polar opposite of state narratives around "strong leader." How can we account for his ambiguity and a "muddling through" COVID-19 response? Putin is a rational actor: Putin acts decisively but is risk-averse when he cannot judge likely outcomes; what appears to be paralysis is in fact a well-considered strategic pause to allow Putin to assess responses in the face of COVID-19 unpredictability and uncertainty; he realizes the gravity of the situation and delegates in order to politically immunize himself against the COVID-19 legitimation trap. Putin extends "authority but not power" to Major Sobyanin, who lacks Putin's "unambiguous backing" (Galeotti, 2020). In this way, Putin can shift blame and responsibility onto the shoulders of domestic managers to preserve his father-figure reputation and image for competence and cunning. This allows President Putin to step back in as a neutral arbitrator, decisively fire unpopular governors and even offer constructive course corrections.

Putin's pronounced reluctance to mobilize and deploy Russia's accumulated strategic reserves can be explained by his desire to push the costs of COVID-19 onto the SME "creative entrepreneur class," a group that was generally unsupportive of Putin's agenda but politically neutered (with a ban on mass demonstrations), while protecting the state-owned enterprises run by his loyal inner circle and entourage. In addition, Putin saves strategic reserves for what he might consider a more "real" emergency worthy of his personal attention, such as a global depression. Thus, Putin's responses may also be able to be explained by his predictive thinking. At the end, Putin is animated by the need to uphold the myth of the power vertical. While democratic leaders may resist lockdowns and quarantines given the need to balance civil liberties and democratic oversight and accountability with the need for restrictions and control, Putin may resist the same. In his second COVID-19 address to the nation, Putin, remarkably, did not mention once the National Guard, Interior Ministry or Federal Security Service. Again, Putin's predictive thinking may be on display; Putin understands that mobilization for and then mismanagement of a COVID-19 state of emergency would expose the lack of a functioning power vertical and the incompetence of the bureaucracy and fatally undermine the Putin brand as security guarantor. In reality, paradoxically, after 20 years of President Putin, the greater the centralization and control, the less the security bloc can manage (Herd, 2020). By mid-2021, with COVID-19 numbers sharply increasing, the prime minister and mayor of Moscow are the public face of Russia's COVID-19 responses. The declaration of a state of emergency would necessitate effective coordination and cooperation between the defense-security bloc and public health and social services. This stress test of the Putin system is resisted.

Russian rhetoric is increasingly challenged by reality. By 2021, as the third wave of delta variant COVID-19 circled the world, Russia's approach is characterized by "obfuscation, deflection, and trolling," one that deploys "a toolkit of political technologies to divert criticism and sow distrust through propaganda, disinformation, and smear campaigns that also target the West." Russian mixed messaging highlights the "Russian government's paradoxical approach to dealing with the pandemic, in which statistics are unclear, government-aligned speakers voice contradictory information – some downplaying the pandemic's effects, others calling for people to get vaccinated – and the state media ridicule strict measures imposed by Western countries." To give one example, during his March 2021 trip to China, Foreign Minister Lavrov was photographed with a face mask sporting the letters: "FCKNG QRNTN" (Michlin-Shapir, 2021). There is a five-fold increased difference between excess mortality in Russia over the year 2020–2021 and official government-released COVID-19 death statics. Putin's policies in practice (Putinism) increasingly stress the trust between the Russian public and Putin.

Selected bibliography

Adomeit, Hannes. 2016. *Imperial Overstretch: Germany in Soviet Policy from Stalin to Gorbachev – An Analysis Based on New Archival Evidence, Memoirs, and Interviews*. 2nd ed. Baden-Baden: Nomos.

———. 2017. "Innenpolitische Determinanten der Putinschen Außenpolitik." *Sirius: Zeitschrift für Strategische Studien*. March 2017. www.degruyter.com/document/doi/10.1515/sirius-2017-0002/html.

———. 2019. "Domestic Determinants of Russia's anti-Western Campaign." *London: Institute for Statecraft*. May 24, 2019. https://medium.com/@instituteforstatecraft.

Anayev, Maxim. 2018. "Inside the Kremlin: The Presidency and the Executive Branch." In *The New Autocracy: Information, Politics and Policy in Putin's Russia*, edited by Daniel Treisman, 29–48. Washington, DC: Brookings.

Aptekar, Pavel. 2016. "Russian Investigations Committee Held Captive by FSB; How Arrest of Three High-Ranking Investigators Alters the Special Services' Disposition of Forces." *Vedomosti*. July 21, 2016.

Åslund, Anders. 2016. "Why We Need Kremlinology Again." *The American Interest*. August 18, 2016. www.the-american-interest.com/2016/08/18/why-we-need-kremlinology-again/.

Åslund, Anders, and Leonid Gozman. 2021. "Russia after Putin: How to Rebuild the State." *The Atlantic Council*. February 24, 2021. www.atlanticcouncil.org/in-depth-research-reports/report/russia-after-putin-report/.

Baev, Pavel K. 2016. "Newly Formed National Guard Cannot Dispel Putin's Multiple Insecurities." *The Jamestown Foundation*. April 2016. https://jamestown.org/program/newly-formed-national-guard-cannot-dispel-putins-multiple-insecurities/.

Bekbulatova, Taisiya. 2016. "Effective Old Comrade – Meduza Tells the Story of Sergey Chemezov, One of the Most Influential People in Russia." *Meduza*. December 22, 2016. https://meduza.io/feature/2016/12/22/effektivnyy-staryy-tovarisch.

Dobrokhotov, Roman. 2017. "How Putin Became a Problem for Russian Oligarchs." *Al Jazeera*. December 24, 2017. www.aljazeera.com/opinions/2017/12/24/how-putin-became-a-problem-for-russian-oligarchs.

"An Elderly Gladiator and His Cardboard Sword Alexey Ulyukayev's Closing Statement." 2017. *Meduza*. December 7, 2017. https://meduza.io/en/feature/2017/12/07/an-elderly-gladiator-and-his-cardboard-sword.

Foy, Henry. 2021. "Vladislav Surkov: 'An Overdose of Freedom is Lethal to a State." *Financial Times*. June 18, 2021. https://on.ft.com/3iSRzqn.

Freeland, Chrystia. 2011. "Putin's Autocracy Has a Shaky Foundation: Oil – The Globe and Mail." *The Globe and Mail*. September 29, 2011. www.theglobeandmail.com/report-on-business/rob-commentary/putins-autocracy-has-a-shaky-foundation-oil/article4199348/.

Friedrich, Carl J., and Zbigniew K. Brzezinski. 1956. *Totalitarian Dictatorship and Autocracy*. Cambridge, MA: Harvard University Press.

Gaaze, Konstantin. 2019. "The True Nature of Putinism." *The Moscow Times*. October 21, 2019. www.themoscowtimes.com/2019/10/21/the-true-nature-of-putinism-a67820.

Galeotti, Mark. 2016a. "Russia's Hybrid War as a Byproduct of a Hybrid State." *War on the Rocks*. December 6, 2016. https://warontherocks.com/2016/12/russias-hybrid-war-as-a-byproduct-of-a-hybrid-state/.

———. 2016b. "The Panama Papers Show How Corruption Really Works in Russia." *Vox*. April 4, 2016. www.vox.com/2016/4/4/11360212/panama-papers-russia-putin.

———. 2020. "Moscow's Mayor, Not Putin, Is Leading Russia's Coronavirus Fight. Will He Be Allowed to Do the Job?" *The Moscow Times*. March 26, 2020. www.themoscowtimes.com/2020/03/26/moscows-mayor-not-putin-is-leading-russias-coronavirus-fight-will-he-be-allowed-to-do-the-job-a69759.

Galimova, Natalia, Elena Platonova, Olga Alekseeva, and Elizaveta Maetnaya. 2016. "Prokhorov sells assets." *Gazeta.Ru*. April 24, 2016. www.gazeta.ru/business/2016/04/24/8193059.shtml.

Gerecht, Reuel Marc. 2007. "A Rogue Intelligence State?" *American Enterprise Institute – AEI*. April 6, 2007. www.aei.org/research-products/report/a-rogue-intelligence-state/.

Gorbachev, Aleksey. 2018. "Khodorkovskiy Expands Kremlin Dossier." *Nezavisimaya Gazeta*. April 12, 2018. www.ng.ru/politics/2018-04-12/1_7210_hodor.html.

Gould-Davies, Nigel. 2016. "Russia's Sovereign Globalization: Rise, Fall and Future." *Chatham House*. January 6, 2016. www.chathamhouse.org/2016/01/russias-sovereign-globalization-rise-fall-and-future.

Greene, Samuel A. 2019. "Homo-Post-Sovieticus: Reconstructing Citizenship in Russia." *Social Research: An International Quarterly* 86 (1): 181–202.

Hellie, Richard. 2005. "The Structure of Russian Imperial History." *History and Theory* 44 (4): 88–112.

Herd, Graeme P. 2018. "Russia's Hybrid State and President Putin's Fourth-Term Foreign Policy?" *The RUSI Journal* 163 (4): 20–28.

———. 2020. "COVID-19, Russian Responses, and President Putin's Operational Code." *050. Security Insights*. Garmisch-Partenkirchen: George C. Marshall European Center for Security Studies. www.marshallcenter.org/en/publications/security-insights/covid-19-russian-responses-and-president-putins-operational-code.

Hobson, Peter. 2016. "Battle in the Archives – Uncovering Russia's Secret Past." *The Moscow Times*. March 24, 2016. www.themoscowtimes.com/2016/03/24/battle-in-the-archives-uncovering-russias-secret-past-a52254.

"How Putin Closed Down Kadyrov's Army." 2016. *Novaya Gazeta*. April 9, 2016.

Hutton, Will. 2016. "Litvinenko's Murder Shows Why Putin's Russia Will Never Prosper." *The Guardian*. January 24, 2016. www.theguardian.com/commentisfree/2016/jan/24/litvinenko-murder-putin-russia.

Kamakin, Andrey. 2015. "A Kind of Fashion for Yeltsin is Arising- Revelations of First President's Aide, Georgiy Satarov." *Moskovskiy Komsomolets*. November 23, 2015.

Khrushcheva, Nina L. 2015. "The Tsar and the Sultan." *Quartz*. December 4, 2015. http://qz.com/565276/vladimir-putin-fancies-himself-a-tsar-standing-up-to-turkeys-new-sultan/.

Khvostunova, Olga. 2021. "Lev Gudkov: 'The Unity of the Empire in Russia Is Maintained by Three Institutions: The School, the Army, and the Police'." *Institute of Modern Russia.* May 3, 2021. https://imrussia.org/en/opinions/3278-lev-gudkov-.

Kirin, George. 2015. "Invention vs. Innovation in Russia." *Spicy UP.* March 1, 2015.

Kolesnikov, Alexander. 2017. "A Past That Divides: Russia's New Official History." *Carnegie Moscow Center.* October 5, 2017. http://carnegie.ru/2017/10/05/past-that-divides-russia-s-new-official-history-pub-73304.

Kuznetsova, Yevgeniya, Natalya Galimova, and Mariya Istomina. 2017. "Rostechnocrats Head for the Regions." *RBK Online.* September 28, 2017. https://1prime.ru/INDUSTRY/20170928/827951760.html.

Lewis, David. 2020. *Russia's New Authoritarianism: Putin and the Politics of Order.* Edinburgh: Edinburgh University Press.

Lukin, Alexander. 2016. "Russia in a Post-Bipolar World." *Survival* 58 (1): 91–112.

MacKinnon, Mark. 2016. "Putin Sends Warning to Domestic Enemies; This Year's V-Day Parade in Moscow Features National Guardsmen, a New Force Meant to Crush Protests by the President's Opponents." *The Globe and Mail.* May 10, 2016.

Magyar, Bálint, and Bálint Madlovics. 2020. *The Anatomy of Post-Communist Regimes.* Budapest and New York: CEU Press.

Makarkin, Alexei. 2016. "Alexei Makarkin: Murov's Resignation Is a Serious Political Success for Viktor Zolotov, Who at One Time Was His Ally." *Politcom.ru.* May 26, 2016.

Mathews, Owen. 2007. "Russia: Was Stalin So Bad? By Pushing a Patriotic View of History and the Humanities, the Kremlin Is Reshaping the Russian Mind." *Newsweek International.* 2007. https://alt.religion.christian.east-orthodox.narkive.com/hNBGeQYp/newsweek-back-to-the-u-s-s-r.

Michlin-Shapir, Vera. 2021. "Is Moscow Playing a Double Game in Iran?" *Institute of Modern Russia.* May 5, 2021. www.imrussia.org/en/analysis/3281-is-moscow-playing-a-double-game-in-iran.

Nikolskiy, Aleksei, Yelena Mukhametshina, and Petr Kozlov. 2016. "The National Guard Will Become a Powerful Security Agency." *Vedomosti.* April 6, 2016. www.vedomosti.ru/politics/articles/2016/04/06/636601-natsionalnaya-gvardiya.

Odom, William E. 2000. *The Collapse of the Soviet Military.* New Haven: Yale University Press.

Orlova, Karina. 2016. "Russia's Plot to Smear Magnitsky." *The American Interest.* June 16, 2016. www.the-american-interest.com/2016/06/16/russias-plot-to-smear-magnitsky/.

Orttung, Robert. 2015. "The Tension Is Going to Build Up in Russia Until You Have a Revolution." *Institute of Modern Russia.* November 18, 2015. http://imrussia.org/en/opinions/2478-robert-orttung-%E2%80%98the-tension-is-going-to-build-up-in-russia-until-you-have-a-revolution%E2%80%99.

Ostrovsky. 2016. *The Invention of Russia: From Gorbachev's Freedom to Putin's War.* New York: Viking.

Pastukhov, Vladimir. 2018. "Three Presidential Cards." *Novaya Gazeta.* March 24, 2018. www.novayagazeta.ru/articles/2018/03/24/75929-tri-prezidentskie-karty.

———. 2021. "Heavenly Praskoveyevka." *Novaya Gazeta.* March 19, 2021.

"Patriarch Kirill: Russia Has Special Civilization Path." 2015. *OrthoChristian.Com.* November 12, 2015. https://orthochristian.com/87635.html.

Pavlovsky, Gleb. 2015. "There Is No Logic to Russia's Political System." *Rzeczpospolita.* January 24, 2015. https://archiwum.rp.pl/artykul/1266226-W-rosyjskim-systemie-brak-logiki.html.

Petrovskaya, Irina. 2016. "The Russian Media are the Most Truthful in the World. You Yourselves are the Camels." *Novaya Gazeta.* April 8, 2016. https://issuu.com/novayagazeta/docs/novgaz-pdf__2016-037n/24.

Pomerantsev, Peter. 2015. *Nothing is True and Everything Is Possible: The Surreal Heart of the New Russia*. New York: PublicAffairs.

Pozdnyakova, Yelena. 2016. "Flight from Diversity: How Russians Consume Information." *Politcom.ru*. April 6, 2016. http://politcom.ru/20957.html.

Putin, Vladimir. 2007. "Annual Address to the Federal Assembly." *President of Russia*. April 26, 2007. http://en.kremlin.ru/events/president/transcripts/24203.

Rakela, M. 2018. "Milosevic's Ghost Haunts Putin." *Vijesti*. July 28, 2018.

Robinson, Neil. 2017. "Russian Neo-Patrimonialism and Putin's Cultural Turn." *Europe-Asia Studies* 69 (2): 348–366.

Roldugin, Oleg. 2016. "2015 is the Year of the Family. The Rotenberg Families." *Sobesednik Online*. January 6, 2016. https://sobesednik.ru/rassledovanie/20160106-2015-y-god-semi-semi-rotenbergov.

Romanova, Anna, and Boris Korbal. 2017. "The End of Sechin's Special Forces." *New Times Online*. December 4, 2017. https://newtimes.ru/articles/detail/132259.

Sakwa, Richard. 2010. "The Dual State in Russia." *Post-Soviet Affairs* 26 (3): 185–206. https://doi.org/10.2747/1060-586X.26.3.185.

———. 2021. "Heterarchy: Russian Politics between Chaos and Control." *Post-Soviet Affairs* 37 (3): 222–241. https://doi.org/10.1080/1060586X.2020.1871269.

Schreck, Carl. 2016. "Kremlin Insiders Cashing in on Government Contracts." *Radio Free Europe/RadioLiberty*. www.rferl.org/a/putin-insiders-state-contracts-forbes-ranking/27576535.html.

Slabykh, Igor. 2021. "How the Russian Government Uses Anti-Extremism Laws to Fight Opponents." Institute of Modern Russia. June 4, 2021. https://imrussia.org/en/analysis/3291-how-the-russian-government-uses-anti-extremism-laws-to-fight-opponents

Sharafutdinova, Glunaz. 2021. "Do Digital Technologies Serve People or Autocrats?" *Riddle*. June 25, 2021. www.ridl.io/en/do-digital-technologies-serve-people-or-autocrats/.

Shevtsova, Liliya. "Kremlin is Using all Means to Undermine Ukraine." *Ukrayinska Pravda*. February 24, 2015.

Shulman, Yekaterina. 2017. "Flexible Like a Caterpillar, Hybrid Russia." *Rosbalt*. January 2, 2017. www.rosbalt.ru/russia/2017/01/02/1579820.html.

Stanovaya, Tatyana. 2017. "For or Against Putin. How Sanctions Pressure Will Change Businesses' Attitude Toward the Regime." *Republic*. December 6, 2017. https://republic.ru/posts/88173.

Starobin, Paul. 2005. "The Accidental Autocrat." *The Atlantic*. March 2005. www.theatlantic.com/magazine/archive/2005/03/the-accidental-autocrat/303725/.

Sukhov, Ivan. 2015. "Putin's Russia Is Not Back in the USSR." *The Moscow Times*. June 10, 2015. www.themoscowtimes.com/2015/06/10/putins-russia-is-not-back-in-the-ussr-op-ed-a47299.

Surkov, Vladislav. 2008. "Russian Political Culture: The View from Utopia." *Russian Social Science Review* 49 (6): 81–97.

———. 2019. "Putin's Lasting State." Translated by Bill Bowler. *Nezavisimaya Gazeta*. February 1, 2019. www.bewilderingstories.com/issue810/putins_state.html.

Szakonyi, David. 2018. "Governing Business: The State and Business in Russia." *Foreign Policy Research Institute*. January 22, 2018. www.fpri.org/article/2018/01/governing-business-state-business-russia/.

Torop, Anastasiya. 2017. "The Eternal President." *The New Times*. June 26, 2017. https://newtimes.ru/articles/detail/115812/.

"Treasury Releases CAATSA Reports, Including on Senior Foreign Political Figures and Oligarchs in the Russian Federation." *U.S. Department of the Treasury*. January 29, 2018. https://home.treasury.gov/news/press-releases/sm0271.

Trudolyubov, Maxim. 2021. "You Decide Is Putin Running an Illiberal Democracy or a Mafia State?" *Meduza*. July 7, 2021. https://meduza.io/en/feature/2021/07/07/you-decide.

Umland, Andreas. 2017. "Kyiv's Leadership Is on Its Way to Reinvent Ukraine's Patronalistic Regime." *OpenDemocracy*. July 11, 2017. www.opendemocracy.net/en/odr/kyiv-s-leadership-is-on-its-way-to-reinvent-ukraine-s-patronalistic-regime/.

"Under Siege: The Kremlin Has Isolated Russia's Economy." 2021. *The Economist* 439 (9242): 18–19.

Vinokutov, Andrei, Elizabeta Mayetnaya, Natalya Galimova, and Vladimir Dergachev. 2015. "Pioneers Returning." *Gazeta.Ru*. October 29, 2015.

Walker, Shaun. 2016. "Russia's 'Valiant Hero' in Ukraine Turns His Fire on Vladimir Putin." *The Guardian*. June 5, 2016. www.theguardian.com/world/2016/jun/05/russias-valiant-hero-in-ukraine-turns-his-fire-on-vladimir-putin.

Wilson, Andrew. 2015. "Four Types of Russian Propaganda." *Aspen Review*. April 2015. www.aspen.review/article/2017/four-types-of-russian-propaganda/.

Yerofeyev, Oleg. 2016. "Aleksey Venediktov: Kremlin's View Towards Baltic States Determined by Three Narratives." *Delfi*. January 4, 2016.

Yevstifeyev, Dmitriy, and German Petelin. 2016. "National Guard for Putin's Bodyguard – Why Putin Needs National Guard." *Gazeta.Ru*. April 5, 2016.

Zevelev, Igor. 2016. "Russian National Identity and Foreign Policy." *Center for Strategic and International Studies*. December 12, 2016. www.csis.org/analysis/russian-national-identity-and-foreign-policy.

6

PUTIN'S OPERATIONAL CODE

Inferences and implications for regime stability

Introduction

Attempts to characterize Soviet decision-making use the metaphor of "black box" to illustrate the complexity of the process and the lack of knowledge of those not present "in the room" where decisions are made (Adomeit, 1982). In the Cold War adversaries were presented with a Soviet decision. They could identify some of the factors that might have been taken into account in forming the decision, but the decision-making process itself is an enigma, wrapped in Churchill's mystery and inside a riddle. In an attempt to address the riddle, Nathan Leites, in his seminal *The Operational Code of the Politburo*, argued that decision-making and negotiating behavior within the 14-men Soviet Politburo was guided by a Bolshevik 'operational code'. This meso-code outlined the rules, causal relationships and fundamental assumptions which were believed to be necessary for effective political action and which guided Bolshevik interactions with the outside world (Leites and Rand Corporation, 1951/2007; Leites, 1953).

Thus, Leites identified a set of enforceable principles developed by Lenin then Stalin and meant for core ideological supporters – Communist Party members. Such beliefs are usually internally consistent and logically coherent. Leites noted that the Bolsheviks believed in the inevitability of class struggle and its ultimate triumph; they were intellectually prepared for retreats and advances and could therefore act unpredictably. They placed an emphasis on the primacy of leadership, were suspicious of enemies and advocated violence and propaganda as means to necessary ends. Leites identified Soviet diagnostic and prescriptive beliefs such as "politics is war", "push to the limit", "there are no neutrals", "avoid adventures", "resist from the start", "retreat before superior force" and "war by negotiation." Leites explained such beliefs through three motivational images: first, the question of *kto-kovo?* ("Who beats or destroys whom?"); second, the fear of annihilation and, third, the principle of the pursuit of power (Walker, 1983, 180). Contemporary commentators have also noted black-and-white Manichean binary thinking as a feature of post-Soviet politics, from the 1990s through to assertions that the choice of president is Putin or Navalny. Boris Vishnevsky captures this reality well, noting: "Whoever is not for Gaydar's reforms is for a return to communism", "whoever is not for the dispersal of the Supreme Soviet is for the Red-Browns",

DOI: 10.4324/9780429261985-6

"whoever is not for Yeltsin for president is for Zyuganov", "whoever is not for Putin is for the terrorists", "whoever is not for Navalny for mayor is for the Kremlin and Sobyanin." In short, the classic zero-sum Bolshevik proposition prevails: "whoever is not with us is against us!" (Vishnevsky, 2017).

An "operational code" identifies how decision-makers perceive the world, process information, develop options, make choices and react (Haas, 2020; Herd, 2019). Rather than looking at meso-codes, most analysts attempt to identify individual or elite subgroup codes of foreign policy decision-makers. The focus would be on Putin rather than the code of Putinism. A core assumption is that the individual or elite subgroup acts rationally, is/are well informed, open-minded and consistent and goal orientated. In reality, most decision-makers are shaped by their beliefs, and rigid views can distort the information processing. The beliefs in any given decision-maker's 'operational code' act as a filter that structures and orders their reality and helps them "sort the signals from the noise."

Building on the work of Leites – operationalizing it so to speak – George understood the operational code in terms of a "prism that influences the actor's perceptions and diagnoses of the flow of political events . . . that [in turn] influence the actor's choice of strategy and tactics, his structuring and weighing of alternative courses of action." George identified two sets of beliefs – philosophical and instrumental. Philosophical beliefs relate to how fundamentally hostile or benign a given actor views the world and how much control a given actor perceives themselves to have over their environment. Instrumental beliefs indicate the cooperative or conflictual means an actor adopts to achieve desired ends – these beliefs therefore concern the "norms, standards, and guidelines that influence the actor's choice of strategy and tactics, his structuring and weighing alternative courses of action" (George, 1969, 191). A clear understanding of President Putin's operational code allows the crafting of policy responses that contain a combination of sticks and carrots and incentives and punishments that can achieve preferred Western policy outcomes.

Can we discern a relationship between what Putin says and what Putin does, between his thoughts and words that refer to himself and others and highlight the philosophical beliefs, actions and deeds, which can be cooperative or conflictual and highlight instrumental beliefs? Dyson and Parent take a big data content analysis approach, using a computer algorithm to analyze "every word President Putin has ever said on the major issues of foreign policy" (Dyson and Parent, 2018). These findings were derived from computer-enabled content analysis of 13 foreign policy topics from May 2000 through to December 2016, using "a complete and verbatim record of Putin's public speaking engagements," including set piece speeches and interviews, categorizing Putin's statements

> as hostile (punishments, threats, or words of opposition) or cooperative (appeals, promises, or rewards). By aggregating a large number of these statements, the approach produces a read-out of how the leader expresses their beliefs about international relations. Public speech is taken to reveal, at least to some extent, the world as it exists in the mind of the speaker.

Dyson and Parent conclude that Putin's beliefs are issue specific, and that this suggests that a western "policy of decoupling is plausible. A mix of rivalry on some issues and partnership on others is consistent with his varied operational code." They stress the importance of Putin's formative political experience of Dresden, noting "the disintegration of order and threats to his own power are red-lines for Putin" (Dyson and Parent, 2017, 12).

As participant observation is not possible, quantitative and qualitative content analysis (i.e. an analysis of the evolution of publically spoken and written statements or principles by leaders over time) represents one approach to identifying an operational code. However, this approach has three weaknesses. First, the presidential website does not reflect "a complete and verbatim record." On 9 May 2021 in a Victory Day Parade speech to commemorate the Soviet defeat of Nazi Germany, the official transcript of the speech in Russian and English on the Kremlin website has President Putin stating:

> We shall always remember that this noble feat was committed precisely by the Soviet people. At the most difficult time of war, in decisive battles which determined the outcome of the battle against Fascism, our people was alone – alone in the laborious, heroic and sacrificial path towards victory.

However, an earlier official Kremlin transcript contains the word "united" ("yedin") rather than the word "alone" ("odin") ("One letter", 2021). Changing the record is especially prevalent in give-and-take press conferences. In the Kremlin's transcript of a briefing by German President Frank-Walter Steinmeier on Crimea in October 2017, Steinmeier noted that ties between Russia and Germany were "far from normal" – "There are still open wounds and unresolved issues, first and foremost when it comes to the annexation of Crimea and the conflict in eastern Ukraine, which are a burden and remain a burden on our relationship." A transcript of the briefing on the Kremlin's website and a live translation on the Kremlin-funded RT television network's Ruptly service substituted the word "annexation" for "reunification" and had the German President saying: "Crimea becoming part of Russia" (Kremlin Blanks, 2017).

Second, this approach appears to ignore policy, practice and procedures on the ground and to confuse Russian foreign policy as articulated by President Putin, Foreign Minister Lavrov and Russian ambassadors, with the reality of Russian external relations. Dave Johnson argues that Russia's state policy on nuclear deterrence presents a selective and distorted picture of Russia's nuclear strategy: "Russian statements and guidance documents on nuclear policy and strategy should continuously be held up to the mirror of actual capabilities, force structure and posture, related exercises and operations, and, more broadly, Russia's evident revanchism" (Johnson, 2021). Tatyana Stanovaya notes that President Putin expresses himself in terms of "rhetorical camouflage" and "ornamental proprieties" and so

> If we totally exclude the political context of what is happening – that is, disregard the events that are actually happening in Russia and the current

conservative trends – and simply read the main points from Vladimir Putin's speeches, then his value system taken out of context is no different from the value system of the majority of leaders of developed democratic countries.

By contrast,

> there exists a completely different world, the "real" world in which Vladimir Putin lives and makes decisions. This is the harsh geopolitical reality that it has always been awkward and improper to talk about. The conspiracy ethos that this world so resembles has always been something for losers. But for Putin this is only an apparent similarity, and only a select few can understand the difference. Within the framework of this logic Russia lies at the center of hostile aspirations on the part of the outside world, an object of close interest from intelligence services, and the target of biological, genetic, nuclear, and chemical weapons. In Putin's real world there is no equality between states, international norms are exploited within the logic of double standards on the principle that "might is right," and human rights activity is merely a cover for interference in sovereign states' affairs.
>
> *(Stanovaya, 2017)*

Key statements by Russian decision-makers are therefore best validated by observable strategic behavior on the ground. Empirical evidence clearly indicates that Putin's statements are not a good indicator of Russia's actions.

Third, President Putin's 'operational code' is driven by his personality (a function of his education, training, life experiences and psychology-emotional state). A leader's upbringing shapes his goal seeking once in office. Putin's analogical reasoning – his understanding of history and use of historical analogy as a shortcut to the present reality – is a product of socialization. For Putin, the Great Patriotic War and the Yalta–Potsdam conferences and total strategic political-military victory, not the October Revolution and the Russian Civil War, constitute a core frame of reference. When occupying the role of leader, the context of world politics also shapes his operational codes. Other variables, including a *status quo* political system predicated on the continuity of the current elite in power and stresses on legitimacy in the context of a deteriorating economy and declining popularity of the president, would apply to Putin specifically. These dynamics are not necessarily reflected in speeches, written by a roster of presidential speech writers.

An alternative but complementary approach is to synthesize the observations of analysts who look to the timing and the manner in which decisions are announced, check rhetoric against the reality and on this basis draw informed inferences as to the nature of decision-making. In terms of philosophical beliefs – how Russia sees the world – strategic calculation is based on poor threat analysis and understanding of the strategic environment, with the notion of Russia as a besieged fortress having canonical status. Decisions made appear to have more to do with affirmation, validation, acknowledgment and the need for respect, particularly from the United States, than achieving the stated aim. Rule-breaking does not prohibit action. According to this understanding, to break rules without being punished is the hallmark of a great power. The Russian foreign minister argues that Russia upholds the UN Charter while the West does not: "Make no mistake: there is nothing wrong with the rules per se. On the contrary, the UN Charter is a set of rules, but these rules were approved by all countries of the world, rather than by a closed group at a cosy get-together" (Lavrov, 2021). In terms of instrumental beliefs – how Russia should address the world – Putin's understanding of risk, perception of costs/benefits and tipping points determine when decisions are made and define the intent of the decisions (see Table 6.1). Let us examine first two of Putin's philosophical and then three of his instrumental beliefs.

TABLE 6.1 Putin's Operational Code: Inferred Explanations and Implications for Regime Stability

Beliefs	Decision-Making Black Box: Inferred Explanations	Implications of Decision-Making: Regime Stability and Political System Evolution?
Threat Perception	1) **Strategic culture:** Putin as Nevsky, Suvourov, Zhukov, as heroic 'Sword and Shield' main stabilizer, focus of symbolic reunion; 2) **Competitive intelligence:** *Razvedchiki* – no information critique or feedback loops; gatekeepers reward worst-case scenarios; 3) **Group think:** national security elite zero-sum paranoid worldview (encirclement, breakout, victories)	1) **'Broken lens':** conspiratorial belief in aggressive West, partial political-strategic assessments; vision fuzzy, flexible tactics and improvisation; 2) **Cumulative losses:** trading short-term geo-political grandeur for long-term geo-economic failure (state economy; semi-international isolation – no allies; global shift from commodity-based economy; 3) **Risk calculus:** as window of competitive advantage closes, takes greater risks; promote worldview (identity) over material interests; gradual decline, disruptive spoiler role and risky brinkmanship
The United States as Strategic Benchmark	1) **Behavior:** belief that the United States breaks rules and lies so Russia has right and duty to lie; to follow rules is to be marginal irrelevant player; 2) **Reciprocity:** belief that the U.S. destabilizes Russia and that Russian "active measures" are "psychological revenge"; 3) **Outcome:** belief of new sphere of influence and rules-based Global Concert of Great Powers	1) **Strategic schizophrenia:** belief that the U.S. in decline, but is a dangerous enemy and top priority as it ignores Russia and seeks to harm its interests; 2) **Forced dialogue and coercive mediation:** use destabilization compellence to gain conditional détente not reconciliation – pragmatic *realpolitik* legitimate interest-based relations; 3) **Inferiority complex:** "grandiose" and "vulnerable" narcissism: needs external validation, fear/enmity, but not indifference/ignored

(Continued)

TABLE 6.1 (Continued)

Beliefs	Decision-Making Black Box: Inferred Explanations	Implications of Decision-Making: Regime Stability and Political System Evolution?
Defensive Reactive Motivation	1) **Rational deterrence theory**: Russia persuades West that its strategic capabilities are tactical; Russia's tactical capabilities are strategic; 2) **Prospect Theory**: take greater risk to hold onto what 'has' (Ukraine/Belarus); 3) **Escalation**: push to the limit as default position – 'threshold warfare'; military key component of Russia self-identification	1) **'Imperial subaltern' syndrome**: great power restoration as return to *status quo ante* not revisionism; 2) **Chekistocratic counter-intelligence state**: *silovye struktury* ("force structures") rivalry; 'neo-KGB state' – KGB is the state, not state within a state; 3) **Good governance as existential danger:** delegitimize regime; de-modernization, de-globalization, 'adhocracy', 'downshift'; *Zakharovshchina* (criminal slang) of public discourse
Manual Control	1) **"Palace politics"**: information monopoly, last-minute decisions; keep inner-circle off-balance; maintain loyalty, suppress dissent, avoids entrapment by "loyalists"; 2) **Strategicsurprise**: short decision-cycle, hybrid 'asymmetric response' as 'equalizer' with West; 3) **Profession**: counter-intelligence case officer – secret operations' preference, fuse micro-history of Putin family (loss of brother, parents experiencing near death in WWII) and Russia's macro-history	1) **Stagecraft and vision trumps statecraft/strategy**: expediency, vendetta and self-preservation; preservation of predatory authoritarian kleptocracy as primary goal results in short-term tactical gains, long-term strategic losses; immunity from political shock as blame enemies; 2) **Vse Putem ("All is well/Putin")**: personalist regime, no succession or contingency planning possible; popularity declines as strategic vulnerability (triggers succession war); brittle regime; 3) **Eternal spoiler role**: Russia has higher pain threshold which allows negative-sum games; cannot make Russia stronger so make West weaker (power is relative)
Ambiguity	1) **'Kuratory system'**: plausible deniability; draw line around what NOT to do – maintain options; flexibility to reinterpret 'victory' or evade blame for losses (move goal posts); Palmyra or *pol mira*?; 2) **Asymmetric deterrence rational choice**: manage confrontation via nonlinear exploitation; great power game without great power resources; "fail fast; fail cheap" – "no lose" scenarios; 3) **Putin Doctrine**: "redlines," intimidation/fear; hooligan ('throw first punch')	1) **Managed chaos/conflicts as business'**: use of Transnational Organized Crime groups and Private Military Corporations for disruption; "profit is patriotic"; Putin's friends control assets, Putin's managers carry out orders; 2) **Russia as hybrid state**: no ideological constraints, no checks and balances, divide and rule, blurring of boundaries; networks of informal clans and connections, not robust institutions; merge national and imperial to blur borders; from "power of authority" to "authority of power"; historical exceptionalism provides mandate for wide-ranging action; 3) **'Neo-modernism'**: nationalism, transactionalism, holism, historicism – indicates path dependency patrimonial pattern, *status quo* based "order and stability" trumps reform agenda

Beseiged fortress belief

Russian strategic calculation is based on poor threat analysis and understanding of the strategic environment. Internally, events are closely monitored. The Russian Federal Protection Service (FSO) conducts 500 surveys and opinion polls every year, as well as studies of the content of social networks and the blogosphere, to examine Putin's popularity; protest potential, national and regional political actor standings and provide forecasts of election results, and expert and business community opinions and social expectations, as well as reactions to federal government initiatives. This enables the presidential administration to identify potential problems, threats, red lines and emerging negative trends (Ivanko, 2020). However, despite access to such sources, the notion of "Trojan Horses", "Fifth Columnists", "Color Revolutions" and a Russian opposition which allegedly operates under "orders from the West," politics as special operations are the logically predestined outcomes of such thinking: "The fight against the imaginary 'anti-Russia' has become the meaning of his life" (Eggert, 2021). As a result, Russia overinterprets the role, power and influence of the West and often misunderstands thinking and identity and how it can evolve, as well as the right of elites and society in its neighborhood to agency.

President Putin channels a "traditional and instinctive Russian sense of insecurity," convinced as he is that Western intelligence agencies and economic sanctions combine to actively destabilize Russia, as the West's main geopolitical rival ("Department of State", 1946). Referencing the "Russian bear," President Putin himself stated that "someone will always try to chain him up . . . they will tear out his teeth and claws . . . he will be stuffed" ("Meeting of the Valdai," 2015). On another occasion, he stated:

> so-called ruling circles, elites – political and economic – of these counties, they love us when we are impoverished, poor, and when we come hat in hand. As soon as we start declaring some interests of our own, they feel that there is some element of geopolitical rivalry.

The President's press secretary echoed this fear: "The West loves Russia only when it is weak." Vladimir Frolov, an independent Russian foreign policy analyst, commenting on the *Zapad-17* exercise, observed:

> Russia is acting on a faulty threat assessment and seeks to fashion a military response to largely imaginary threats and challenges that are not military in nature. It's all about strategic messaging of coercion and compellence directed at the U.S. and NATO, to prevent things the West has no intention of doing or the capability to accomplish.
>
> *(Birnbaum and Filipov, 2017).*

What are we to make of the January 2016 statement by Nikolai Patrushev, secretary of the security council, regarding regime change in Russia? Patrushev advances the argument that:

> The US leadership has identified for itself the goal of dominating the world. In this connection it does not need a strong Russia. On the contrary, it needs to weaken our country as much as possible. The attainment of this goal through the disintegration of the Russian Federation is not ruled out either. That will open up access for the United States to the very rich resources which in its opinion Russia does not deserve to own.
>
> *(Rostovskiy, 2016)*

Why would the United States seek the disintegration the Russian Federation to gain Russia's "very rich resources" when Russia sells hydrocarbons freely, in record post-Soviet volumes, at low prices, and the United States is energy independent and, and the same time, raises the risk of several thousand nuclear weapons falling into the hands of non-state actors or becoming weapons in an intra-elite struggle for power or used against the United States itself? The belief that external states seek Russia resources highlights two core sensitive realities: first, Russia's economy is largely based on the sale of natural resources; second, Russia's political elite is also its economic elite: those that run Russia own Russia. Vygaudas Usackas, head of the EU Delegation in Moscow, in a farewell interview, noted that: "The Russian authorities, with the help of a media campaign, have convinced themselves and people living in the country that what happened on Maydan was a CIA operation under the EU flag" (Usackas, 2017). Andrew Wood notes that through the Putin years one constant marks official Russia's attitudes toward Russians themselves as well as neighbors:

> Nothing is ever Russia's fault. Moscow is always sinned against. Putin's historic mission is to restore his country's status as a great power, with the right to establish and protect its hegemony over its neighbors. Those neighbors have no right to object, let alone to look to outside powers to support their independence. Putin and his colleagues have public support in Russia for such a stance, as did their tsarist predecessors in analogous circumstances.
>
> *(Wood, 2019)*

Explanations for such a poor threat assessment capability are multiple. According to Russia's dominant national security narratives, Russia is encircled, besieged and threatened by enemies within and without:

> During his career in the KGB, Vladimir Putin learnt to see the result of someone's machinations in everything and to divide the world only into friends and enemies (which is actually wrong: the overwhelming majority of the people on the planet, and even of politicians, simply could not care less about

him and his country). So, he cannot assess the real degree of threat – both to Russia and his own regime – and his "strength" virtually always represents no more than an overreaction. That is why a significant amount of what occurs is considered in the context of "conspiracy theories" and virtually everyone is suspected of some form of villainy or "opposition to the regime."

(Inozemtsev, 2017)

Such zero-sum thinking generates certain imperatives regarding the nature of a leader. Only a strong leader of a great power – a Prince Alexander Yaroslavich Nevsky, General Alexander Vasiliyevich Suvorov and Minister of Defence Georgy Konstantinovich Zhukov – can act as a heroic 'sword and shield of the state', fulfil the function of main stabilizer, indispensable leader and act as the population's focus of symbolic reunion and solidarity. For Putin to take his place in this proud pantheon and fulfil the same symbolic functions, Russia has to be under threat, and the threat must be existential following the logic: the greater the threat; the more indispensable the leader.

Every threat is evaluated in terms of its potential to trigger regime change in Russia with encirclements, 'everything for the front,' breakout and victory providing a triumphant narrative arc. Worst-case scenarios predicated on the certainty of malign intent dominate any strategic analysis. Decisions reached reflect a paranoid and zero-sum worldview dominated by 'group think' – where national security decision-makers look for the most consensual and harmonious decision and evidence-based 'objective analysis' understood to be a process in which President Putin fixes the objective and the analysts find evidence to support it. Gleb Pavlovsky, though, offers caution – the decision-making process is not necessarily utterly cynical, given: "Moscow views world affairs as a system of special operations, and very sincerely believes that it itself is an object of Western special operations" (MacFarquar, 2016).

A competitive operational culture determines information flow and its analysis.

> The efficiency of the manual control (*ruchnaya control*) of the Russian president has been subject to much speculation. Putin is said to not to be using the internet but to be presented with three thick leather-bound folders every morning: one compiled by the FSB, another by the SVR and a third by the FSO.

(Judah, 2014)

Igor Ivanov, before his departure from the presidential administration in 2016, and Nikolai Patrushev act as information gate-keepers and set the tone of the types of analysis President Putin receives. The presidential administration has an agenda setting function: All of [the Kremlin's] decisions on serious issues are collegial and coordinated. The final decision is up to the president, but the agreed upon point of view goes to him for approval." A system of competitive intelligence exists between the GRU, FSB and SVR. To gain Putin's attention – and so receive resources, promotion and demonstrate loyalty – results in worse case scenarios marinated in extreme language being passed on to the President by the gatekeepers, with little information critique or feedback loops apparent. As Mark Galeotti notes:

> In broad terms, the strength of the agencies contributes to several key policy tendencies: a combination of strategic caution and tactical risk-taking, multitrack approaches driven by individual and institutional initiative, and an essentially isolated and covert decision-making mechanism that makes it difficult for alternative views to be considered.
>
> *(Galeotti, 2019)*

Contradictory or dissonant information or evidence is filtered out, discredited, minimized or ignored, and in this respect the decision-making process is deficient (Galeotti, 2016; Wallander, 2015). This indicates the prevalence of propaganda and a belief in the illusion of strength:

> A network of false stories in which reptilians are prowling around the Kremlin has been imposed on top of reality. There are real threats, but you cannot see them because you are told they have found fascists from the Moon in 'Memorial' [human rights organization]. I am convinced that the memoranda on Putin's desk are reports of attacks by reptilians and of UFOs shot down over the week.
>
> *(Vinokutov et al., 2015)*

An overestimation of President Putin's ability to assess negotiating partners is in evidence. Following the financial crisis, President Putin believes solidarity and shared responsibility in Europe are diminished. He believes that Western states prefer to act according to their own immediate interests and priorities, prioritizing them above the longer-term economic interests of the preservation of peace in the international system – whether it be Russian gas (Germany), arms sales (France), or banking and investments (UK). The perceived need of the United States to use Moscow's leverage in global strategic hotspots, to act with it in concert to contain the fallout in Syria, manage the Iran nuclear dossier or the six-party talks on North Korea's nuclear program would, Putin calculates, limit a potential Western backlash against Russia. President Putin has underestimated the decision-making capacity of western institutions and overestimated the power of his own personal diplomacy.

The United States as Russia's strategic benchmark

A second philosophical belief is that:

> Putin's regime defines its place in the world through rejection of the U.S. global leadership and, simultaneously, through mimicking what it believes to

be American behaviour in the international arena. Russia's own subversive, yet often erratic, behaviour on the global stage can, to some degree, be seen as a continuous attention-grabbing stunt aimed at compelling Washington to ask Moscow for cooperation.

(Shekhovtsov, 2021)

Igor Ivanov, Russia's foreign minister from 1998 to 2004, unconsciously highlights this dependency in attempting to characterize the importance of the 16 June 2021 Biden–Putin Geneva Summit:

> the upcoming meeting between the presidents of the United States and Russia is incontestably a huge international event. No matter what people say about the balance of power and influence projections in the 21st century, or the emergence of a multipolar/polycentric world order for that matter, Washington and Moscow continue to play a unique role in international affairs, while shaping the direction of global events to a large extent.
>
> *(Ivanov, 2021)*

The "spiritless" United States is the constitutive other for a "spiritual" Russia (Kurilla, 2021). As such, Russian strategic decisions appear to have as much, if not more to do with affirmation, validation, acknowledgment and the need for respect from the United States, as in achieving the stated aim. Russian Security Council Secretary Patrushev recounted his meeting his opposite number, U.S. National Security Advisor, ahead of the Putin–Biden Summit:

> After the negotiations with Jacob Sullivan, we recalled a significant event in the two countries' shared history. Namely 1863, when at the height of the American Civil War, the Russian Empire decisively supported Washington in its struggle for the unity of the country, sending two squadrons of cruisers to New York and San Francisco. Their crews were enthusiastically welcomed by the Americans. American newspapers described this event as a moment of unity between the two nations. To a large extent, amid the expedition of our fleet, the British Empire abandoned its plans to intervene in the war on the side of the separatists.
>
> *(Interview, 2021)*

In this telling, Russian support swung the Civil War in the Republic's favor and prevented Britain from supporting the Confederacy.

Putin uses both Russia's historical past as well as what other great powers, especially the United States, are now perceived to be gaining to gauge Russia's losses. Cooperation with the United States in Syria through the creation of a risk management mechanism, for example, would ideally from a Russian perspective become the precursor for a Yalta–Potsdam-II type "grand bargain" with the United States. As part of a formally codified restoration of parity, the two would negotiate a new balance of power, agree to new spheres of influence and construct anew a rules-based, predictable, stable international system. With regard to the United States, two principles operate: "you cannot ignore and isolate us or change our country" and *par in parem non habet imperium* ("an equal has no authority over an equal"). Russia has equality with the United States, as, like the United States, Russia is sovereign and strategically autonomous, as underscored by Russia's Syrian intervention. When we examine strategic decisions in Putin's Russia and the explanations offered to account for them, decisions made are always framed as much in terms of gaining U.S. recognition (respect and validation), demonstrating Russia has parity and equality with the United States or in terms of castigation of the United States (blame) and then 'victory' over the United States, as securing the stated aim.

At the same time, Russia seeks to outsmart the United States and achieve victory at United States' expense. Following a "very constructive" phone call between President Trump and President Putin to discuss Russia's plans to send a plane with medical equipment to the United States to help counter COVID-19, state-run channel *Rossiya 1* reported: "today, in the U.S. they are awaiting the arrival of a Russian aircraft with humanitarian aid. The special flight will deliver medical appliances, equipment, and protective gear for the fight against coronavirus." Putin's press spokesman Dmitry Peskov noted that "in offering his American colleagues help, Putin was acting on the basis that when medical producers in the USA gain momentum, in case of need they will be able to respond reciprocally" and stressed the need for "mutual help and partnership" (Herd, 2020). The aid was billed as free, with the expectation that the United States would reciprocate if need be. Then, when the U.S. officials corrected the record to note that .the United States had purchased the aid, Russian media outlets reported the costs had been equally split.

Thus, a successful Russian policy would be one that is supported by the majority of states and opposed by a diplomatically isolated United States, whatever its intrinsic merits as a policy be. Nuclear signaling highlights the fact that Russia has a nuclear triad (three quarters of Russia's military budget is spent on nuclear weapons), and in this dimension parity with the United States. Putin believes Russia has the right to break international rules and, indeed, that to break rules without being punished is the hallmark of a great power. To put it simply: Russia believes the United States breaks rules and lies so Russia has the right and duty to follow suit: rule breaking does not prohibit action, rather it encourages it; rule breaking allows Russia to exploit the predictability of interlocutors in the international system.

At a 22 January 2016 meeting of Russia's National Security Council, it appears that a decision was made to use "all possible force" in support of the Trump candidacy as his presidency would promote two Russian strategic objectives: "the destabilisation of the US's sociopolitical system" and weaken Washington's international standing and negotiating position (Harding et al., 2021). This election interference may have been justified as self-defense and a form of strategic *sderzhivanie* − "Russia could be acting to coerce the United States into ending what Moscow sees as an aggressive policy and to force Washington to be restrained" (Charap, 2020). Sir Andrew Wood, the UK's former ambassador in Moscow, commented:

> The report is fully in line with the sort of thing I would expect in 2016, and even more so now. There is a good deal of paranoia. They believe the US is responsible for everything. This view is deeply dug into the soul of Russia's leaders.
>
> *(Harding et al., 2021)*

Russia believes the United States seeks to destabilize Russia through color-revolution-type technology and so would understand its hybrid war against the West as its reciprocal great power response – a form of reciprocal psychological revenge that restores parity – as president Putin remarked: "each action has a counter reaction."

Putin appears to almost fetishize his ability to take decisions without constraints, and this may be a reflection of his relationship with George W. Bush, and what Putin viewed as Bush's ability to launch an invasion of Iraq without any particular constraints. It follows that the corollary to this is that to follow the rules as set by the West is to be a marginal and irrelevant player – a "Greater Kazakhstan with nuclear weapons" (to reprise the Soviet-era "Republic of Upper Volta with rockets" epithet). President Biden's conditional offer of "stable and predictable" relations should Russia refrain from malign activity is problematic for Russia: to be both stable and predictable is to be strategically irrelevant. Russia seeks to be stable but unpredictable to maintain its strategic relevance.

Defensive–reactive motivation

Turning to instrumental beliefs, President Putin portrays his own motivation as "defensive reactive," restoring the *status quo ante* rather than being revisionist. Russia is under siege; therefore, any action taken to counter or deter the siege can only be understood as being defensive and reactive, an attempt to uphold the *status quo*. Putin acts to demonstrate a capacity to act and a willingness to escalate but understands escalation as preventative, as in "preventative occupation" and "preventative annexation." According to this logic, if Russia does use "offensive tactical-operational means," it is only to achieve "defensive strategic ends." Under this reading, Putin's decisions and actions appear taken more to stop something happening than to make something happen.

According to this perspective, the Crimean annexation of 2014 can be viewed as revenge and payback for perceived insults from the West. Taken to its logical conclusion, "Ukraine's president [Zelenskiy] should cool down. If he constantly talks about joining Nato, Russia cannot help but attack!" Clearly, though, as President Putin noted in his 21 April 2021 "red line" speech, Russia chose to respond or not to perceived insults and infringements on its interests (Tüür, 2021). Vladislav

Surkov revealingly exemplifies this generally held defensive–reactive mind-set when he characterizes his role in Russian policy toward Ukraine: "I am proud that I was part of the reconquest. This was the first open geopolitical counter-attack by Russia [against the West] and such a decisive one. That was an honor for me" (Foy, 2021).

Putin makes decisions either when the benefits outweigh the costs or when the costs become acceptable, with order and stability counterpoised to paralysis, chaos and disintegration (Dyson and Parent, 2017, 9–10). As a result, Putin's costs/benefits risk calculus is critical to understanding when and why strategic decisions are made. This characteristic can be amply evidenced: the decisions to use coercive force in South Ossetia and Abkhazia in 2008, as well as Russia's recognition of these break-away republics as independent states; the "preventative annexation" of Crimea in February 2014; nuclear signaling and the notion that tactical nuclear weapons can "prevent a wider conflict"; subversion in Donbas and, the Syrian intervention (Winkler et al., 2017). Rostislav Ishchenko, the head of the Center for Systematic Analysis and Forecasting, a Russian think tank close to the Kremlin, published a report in April 2015 titled 'On the Necessity of the Preventative Occupation of the Baltic Region,' detailing how and why Russia and Belarus might be obliged to occupy Estonia, Latvia and Lithuania (Weiss, 2016). "Preventative occupation" and "preventative annexation" perfectly capture the notion of the "defensive reactive" in Russian strategic thinking. Russian defense correspondent Pavel Felgengauer provides another example, when he notes that: "If the Kremlin comes to realize that Ukraine is slipping away or that it is not going to fall apart, then its resorting to a military option will be quite likely" (Fedyk, 2016). In the face of pushback, we see another aspect of decision-making: "The system is effective, destructive and very simple. It works only by simplifying complicated issues. When it hits a strategic impasse, the Kremlin just raises the stakes and escalates the conflict, while also increasing the risks involved" (Pavlovskiy, 2015). The corollary of this is that President Putin would avoid a solution as long as he benefited from a crisis. Putin appears to operate under the 'shadow of the future' – the expectation based on past experience of possible future developments and how they might impact on the present. For President Putin, regime change is the greatest fear and avoiding this prospect the prime motivating factor explaining his analysis, intent and commitment to any given decision.

Critics of rational deterrence theory argue that psychological factors, misperceptions and biases prevent states from learning the requirements of deterrence: emotions precede choices; calculations differ; we learn differently from history; we have difficulty in accepting new information that contradicts existing beliefs and, credible threats can be distorted by motivated and unmotivated factors. Following this reasoning, the best guide to understanding Putin's policy choices is not ideology or conceptual frameworks but that he reacts to unacceptable provocations – a personal dimension to an insult is especially provocative for Putin, given his impunity in Russia, where he is above the law and free to act without restraint. In such circumstances, Putin understands himself to react defensively. Putin acts to demonstrate a capacity to act and a willingness to escalate but understands escalation as being preventative. As President Putin noted: "Fifty years ago the streets of Leningrad taught me a lesson: if a fight is inevitable, throw the first punch" ("Meeting of the Valdai," 2015).

'Prospect theory' suggests that individuals are more cautious when they feel they have an advantageous position and winning hand in any given situation, but they exhibit riskier behavior when they think they are in the weaker position and hold the losing hand. Russia's rhetoric reflects the former in that Russia portrays itself as being a rising power on the right side of history. In reality, President Putin understands U.S. actions after 1991 as having destroyed a stable Cold War regulatory structure and that Russia needs to restore the lost ground and be willing to take risks to that end. Putin appears much more prepared to accept risks and is prepared to suffer greater losses than opponents to prevent what he perceives to be a negative outcome than to secure a positive gain. Putin exhibits a higher tolerance for escalation and brinkmanship to mitigate the risk of perceived loss. It is also likely that over time Putin's nominal escalation ceiling is raised as his tolerance for risk increases.

Russia perceives itself as a *status quo* power, as opposed to the collective West which Russia argues attempts to revise the existing order and overturn the current accepted *status quo* out of a desire to dominate the world politically and economically, reflected in the Russian case as a fear of Russian greatness, greed for Russian hydrocarbon wealth and jealousy of Russia's moral dignity. Thus, Russia's strategic orientation is "defensive," and Russia preserves the *status quo* through its unique status in its self-declared "zone of privileged interest." The rhetoric is also a strategic communication influence operation masking cross-domain coercion and compellence. Russian leaders' risk calculus is predicated on the fundamental tents of prospect theory, displaying more caution when they feel Russia is in an advantageous position and has a winning hand but exhibiting riskier behavior when in a weaker position/having a losing hand. Through their behavior, Russian leaders have repeatedly shown that they are willing to take greater risks to prevent anticipated defeats than they would to pursue potential opportunities.

For Putin, the annexation of Crimea represents a reaction to a more or less genuine sense of encirclement, Western expansionism and Russian resistance. The cases of the Russo-Georgian War of 2008, Crimea and the Russian intervention in Syria show that Moscow evaluates prospects largely from losses' frame. In these cases, Russian leaders sought, respectively, to prevent the expansion of a hostile alliance (NATO) to Russia's borders, to avoid the loss of control in a buffer state that they saw as essential to Russia's security and to save a critically important client regime facing imminent military defeat. These practical considerations are intertwined with strategic implications about political loss in both the international and domestic arenas: loss of regional power, loss of great power status and internal costs in domestic politics (Gorenburg et al., 2017, 6). This explains why Russia exhibits escalation and brinkmanship with regard to non–institutionalized Ukraine, but not the EU and NATO Baltic states (Gorenburg, 2019).

For Vyacheslav Morozov, the weight of history provides another useful avenue of investigation and gives us a purchase on contemporary reality. Colonial theory offers a sound explanatory framework to understand decision-making motivation (Morozov, 2013, 2015). According to Morozov, Russia suffers from an "imperial subaltern syndrome" in that it is at the same time part of the global imperial core (i.e. Europe) and finds itself at the periphery of the political West. A feature of Russian historical development has been that a Europeanized Russian elite sitting at the heart of empire in Moscow or St. Petersburg colonized its imperial periphery. It did so on behalf of a Westernization and Europeanization narrative, even as Russia itself was dependent in economic and normative terms on a Europe, a Europe of which Russia constituted a semi-integrated periphery. Putin's neo-traditionalist regime celebrates so-called "genuine Russian values" but frames the arrival of a post-Western democratic multipolar world order in terms of Western democratic discourse, justifying interventions which either undercut Western influence.

Manual control (*ruchnoe upravlenie*) – opportunistic and tactical

The belief in and practice of "manual control" are also evident. Strategic decision-making takes place in small groups operating outside of formal structures, checks and balances and can be best understood as opportunistic, informal, tactical and improvised responses to changing circumstances. Putin uses the Security Council to listen not make decisions. This allows for opportunistic, informal, tactical and improvised responses to changing circumstances.

Soviet security agencies were largely autonomous, a tradition that continued and increased as successor KGB security services were not reformed in the post-Soviet period, and restructuring and relabeling rather than lustration was the dominant approach. As Walther Ulf notes:

> The KGB/FSB has proven for almost the entire period that, in a predetermined, deficient legal and regulatory framework, it is able to not only provide information, but also to exert influence. Its conspiratorial and therefore non-transparent approach has increased the effect of penetration and prevented the basic conditions necessary for a democratic limitation of the accumulation of power by the secret service.
>
> *(Walther, 2014)*

The First Chief Directorate of the KGB, which subsequently became the Foreign Intelligence Service (SVR), received the top 25 percent of graduates and was considered the most prestigious service. However, the Second Chief Directorate, today's FSB, was the most powerful, perhaps influenced by its ability to gather *kompromat* on sitting presidents and key members of the elite, not least in the case of Putin, the Prosecutor General of the Russian Federation (Marten, 2017;

Waller, 1994, 13–15). Security service officers infiltrated the banking, media, heavy industry sectors and Russia's defense industrial complex. This gives current security services an agenda-setting ability when it comes to domestic and foreign policy. The *siloviki's* cohesion and unity has been questioned, with some analysts highlighting a mafia clan-type entity, in which unity is illusionary – a "mixed pattern of bureaucratic infighting and personal rivalry" within and between the services predominates (Galeotti, 2016; Bateman, 2014). The weakness of institutional power in Russia is well illustrated by the gap between the formal role of the State *Duma* Committee on Defense and Committee on Security (theoretical oversight over Russia's military budget) and the reality: "The so-called representative branch has completely abandoned all attempts to control the *siloviki* through the state budget" (Golts, 2017).

As with each identifiable characteristic, a number of explanations can be advanced, not least the requirements of palace politics. President Putin's information monopoly and last-minute decision-making maintain his decision-making autonomy and space, keep his own elite (the "Kremlin Towers") off-balance, maintain their loyalty and act to prevent and so suppress dissent. Former Kremlin adviser Sergei Pugachev notes that Putin's decision-making is hostage to the will of his inner circle, such as Nikolai Patrushev and Igor Sechin and other former associates from St Petersburg. This was evident in summer 2007 when "Sergei Ivanov, Putin's first deputy prime minister and the youngest ever general in Russia's foreign intelligence service, was widely considered the frontrunner to become president the following year, ahead of another Putin ally, Dmitry Medvedev." However, some in Putin's inner circle briefed against Ivanov, fearful that if Ivanov became president, he would monopolize power. According to Pugachev, "They began telling Putin that Ivanov is very dangerous. He is very aggressive. He will take power and then you will never be able to get rid of him. They were collecting all kinds of *kompromat* on Ivanov. Almost everyone was against him" (Belton, 2020). Putin's decision-making in this case was heavily influenced by others with their own agendas.

The sudden announcement by President Putin that Russia would create a new 350,000–400,000 law enforcement body, the Federal Service of the National Guard Troops – "a new federal executive power body" – whose remit is to tackle terrorism, organized crime and 'illegal protests', came as a surprise. Col-Gen Victor Zolotov, former deputy director of the Russian Federal Protection Service (FSO), was appointed deputy commander-in-chief of the Russian Interior Ministry troops (September 2013), then first deputy interior ministry before becoming "commander-in-chief of the troops of the Russian Federation National Guard" with federal minister rank. The decision occurred with no prior public discussion, and the secrecy suggests both that President Putin does not trust Russia's other institutions and that he needs to signal to his own elite that he is the boss and *the* autonomous strategic decision-maker in Russia, perhaps to preempt or prevent bureaucratic pushback. In the case of Zolotov, although the presidential edict stated he would have a permanent seat in the Security Council, the Security

Council website then reported that Zolotov was in fact only a member of the "expanded" Security Council (which meets the president once every 3 months) (Kozlov, 2016).

In August 2016, Putin announced that he had accepted the resignation of Sergei Ivanov, the head of his presidential administration. Why and what does this resignation tell us about how power is being reformatted in Russia? Psychological explanations centered on lack of trust or tiredness accumulated over time aside; for some the reshuffle indicated Putin had embarked on an intra-*siloviki* rebalancing (Meakins, 2018). Ivanov and Putin share the same worldview. But disagreements could have arisen over how to renovate Russia to best address its strategic challenges. Alternatively, Putin may have acted in order to prevent further consolidation of an increasingly autonomous power alliance between an FSB-based clan run by Igor Sechin and Sergei Ivanov. This grouping appears to have sought to monopolize control of policing the financial services and the economic sphere, as well as the Investigations Committee (three deputies arrested) and Federal Customs Service (the home and offices of Federal Customs Service head Andrei Belyaninov were searched on 26 July 2016, and he was arrested). With such an instrument, the Sechin–Ivanov group would be well positioned to discipline the elite, including Putin's family, then Putin. The replacement of Ivanov by his deputy (Anton Vaino, former head of protocol), a bureau-technocrat, reduces FSB pretentions, as does the promotion of FSO officers in other appointments (Aptekar, 2016). Restructuring and staff rotation continued with Vyacheslav Volodin, first deputy head of the presidential administration, moving to Speaker of the *Duma* – Sergei Kiriyenko, former Rosatom head and a technocratic compromise candidate on first name terms with Putin replaces Volodin – with Sergei Naryshkin, the old speaker, becoming head of the SVR (Rostovsky, 2016; Kozlov and Mukhametshina, 2016).

Last-minute announcements prevent lobbying to modify or even derail the decision itself. From Putin's perspective, unpredictability in the making and announcement of his decisions may also act to preempt potential entrapment of the president by formally loyal subordinates. The fact that Putin is so clearly making the decision also signals or messages his inner circle and the wider elite that the answer to the classic question – *kto khozyain?* (Who is the boss?) – is Putin. To that end, Putin can adopt the typical '*ZeK*' behavioral traits of Soviet/Russian prisoner-recidivists, emphasizing his status, hierarchy and punishment. Putin is at pains to emphasize that he and he alone is the decision-maker, the final arbiter, albeit one increasingly hostile to questioning. In terms of personality-based explanations, narcissism and personal drama are said to characterize the desired end-result of decisions, if not the decision-making process itself. Joseph Burgo argues that while Putin's decisions and actions can be explained in terms of a rational approach to foreign and domestic policy and strategy, he may also be a 'bullying narcissist' and that he therefore must constantly demonstrate that he has the power and autonomy to make decisions and that these decisions lead to 'victory,' as in the Crimea annexation (Burgo, 2014).

Personal preferences mesh with profession experience, training and learning. As a counter-intelligence case officer working in Dresden in the last 1980s, rather than for example a former military commander used to working in hierarchical structures and commanding troops, Putin has a penchant for secret and hybrid operations that can have powerful asymmetric effects. As he noted in *First Person*, "the role of one man can be that of an army" (Putin et al., 2000). The preference for covert and undetected action over diplomacy is clear. Secrecy denotes a mode of operation hardwired into the behavior of President Putin and his national security team, which, for the first time in Russian history, is dominated by secret policemen:

> The group is opaque: secrecy is its stock in trade – and it's good at its trade. Putin and this *komanda* (team), in power since late in 1999, may well remain in power for another decade at least . . . As Soviet intelligence services were militarized – with ranks, uniforms and a martial ethos – they all have a military background and are trained in the use of weapons.
>
> *(Wilson, 2015)*

Opportunism and improvisation are the hallmarks, suggesting a tactical rather than strategic mind-set. As Sergey Aleksashenko, a former deputy finance minister and first deputy chairman of the Russian Central Bank, has observed:

> Putin is extremely good at tactical moves, but fails in strategy. His favorite sport is judo. Here, all you need is a general vision in mind – victory – but you can hardly build any strategy and instead, you hope tactical decisions will lead you to your goal. Putin's lack of strategy has meant it is impossible to predict moves and actions. The continuing economic slide will force Putin to dedicate more time and efforts to the economy in the coming years. At the same time, we can expect his decisions to be chaotic and they will hardly allow the economy to recover.
>
> *(Aleksashenko, 2016)*

Manual control lends itself to secrecy and improvisation and allows for quick decisions, and this constitutes an 'equalizer' when compared to western adversaries as it facilitates 'strategic surprise.' Galeotti argues that while there is no single command and control center, the presidential administration, with its key departments (particularly, first deputy chief of staff Alexei Gromov, who coordinates foreign affairs) and Presidential Councils and over 2000 staff, acts as the command and control hub for active measure operations (Galeotti, 2017). Although the Russian Security Council is tasked with coordinating all security-related issues, relative to the presidential administration it is a much smaller entity with only 200 plus staff, and in reality exercises a more limited secretariat-type function (providing threat assessments and other reports). Within this framework, Galeotti (2017, 11–13) identifies two occasions in which Putin becomes more directly involved in the implementation of active measure operations: first, when cross agency coordination is required, as none of the ministries has the power to tell others what to do and, second, when the scale and risk of operation carry strategic level implications should the operation backfire.

Manual control is the logical extension of equating the state of Russia and Russian national interests with that of Putin the person and hence regime security. The conflation of the two suggests that there is also a blurring of interests as reflected in strategic "red lines." Russian 'red lines' can be characterized as four inter-enabling "must nots," as acceptance of any one would signal a diminution of Russia's great power status: Russia "must not" accept interference and interventions in its domestic affairs; Russia "must not" allow its influence and strategic importance to be rejected, ignored or marginalized by external actors; Russia "must not" accept restrictions on its freedom to act and, Russia "must not" lose the right or ability to influence strategic decisions and set conditions.

Ambiguity

A "style of indirect interpretation," ambiguity and opportunism characterizes the communication of decisions. Control is maintained through "a technique of uncertainty." Orders are "issued in the form of an indirect hint or, as they say, a 'signal,' and that launches a new series of deals." Gleb Pavlovsky, in his book *The Russian Federation System. Sources of Russian Strategic Behavior*, characterizes Putin's 2012–2015 style of management model as "the style of indirect interpretation" in which his entourage has "an incomplete idea about what has been decided and trying to remember the words Putin uttered." Pavlovsky observes that President Putin "builds relations in such a way that he can always say: I did not know that and I did not promise that" and he has "constructed above the regime an unreachable floor where he alone resides. And although he still has contact with his entourage, he does not want to bear responsibility for decisions" (Vinokutov et al., 2015). The most recent example of this characteristic relates to the Kremlin's non-response ("that is not the Kremlin's prerogative") and 'meaningful silence' in the face of protests that first erupted on July 17 over the disqualification of opposition candidates ahead of an election to Moscow's City *Duma* on 8 September 2019. Mark Galeotti argues that Putin is not an originator or initiator of specific operations but rather identifies "broad objectives and aspirations", "sets the tone" and then "arbitrates between rival approaches, picks from a menu of options, or gives people enough rope to hang or lift themselves" (Galeotti, 2017, 8–10). Michael Kofman concurs, noting:

> Moscow knows its desired ends and available means, but retains flexibility. In many cases, Moscow eschews a deliberate strategy because it might prove to be confining and difficult to adjust. This is confusing to follow when Russia's goals are set, and yet operational objectives change as they run through cycles

of adaptation. It is also a method whereby success begets success and failure is indecisive, simply spawning a new approach.

(Kofman, 2017)

The broad objectives are to destabilize West in order to uphold Russia's center of gravity – the belief of population in military patriotic mobilization in support of a strong leader to defend a besieged fortress under attack by external adversaries who fear Russian greatness.

Ambiguity clearly has a utility when conducting *maskirovaka* operations and destabilizing neighbors with a combination of conventional and sub-conventional actors as it evades responsibility and attribution and compounds the distraction, destruction and dismay of Russia's adversaries. Its application is thus purposeful and strategic. However, less prosaic explanations can also be advanced. First, such ambiguity suggests that Putin does not fully trust his own wider elite, just the inner core group that exactly shares and reinforces his own worldview. Conflicting and contradictory messages to subordinates can be the result. Second, ambiguous direction may also be a result of Putin telling subordinates and so drawing a line precisely around what subordinates cannot do to achieve a goal, rather than what they can. Third, the instruction "do as you think best" also allows for plausible deniability – at least from the president – and maintains his ability to evade blame for losses by moving goal posts after the fact. Ambiguity also allows for flexibility in interpretation to redefine success and failure, to attribute responsibility for either accordingly and allows for a gap between Putin's words and actions to exist. Fourth, it may also reflect the notion that foreign policy under President Putin is as much about symbolic acts that assert Russia's international presence and boost patriotism at home and thereby 'simulate sovereignty as achieving stated goals.' As military expert Viktor Murakhovsky noted, signalling through hints a useful tool:

> The supreme commander-in-chief has a right sometimes to reveal some things from these documents. And if not to fully voice them, then, at least, relying on state interests, to hint about them. And this was a serious hint from the supreme commander-in-chief. He made it clear to the United States: it will not be possible to organize and conduct a limited nuclear war only in Europe that does not affect the territory of the United States itself.
>
> *(Bozhyeva, 2021)*

At the end, President Putin may have a line-of-sight on where he wants to take Russia – 'the vision thing' – but he is increasingly unable to effectively communicate it, let alone provide a clear understanding of the ways and means to get there. He has 'vision' and tactics but not strategy, and as a result a corrosive sense of drift fills the vacuum. A deficit of strategy and statecraft may also reflect his need to compensate through the surfeit of stagecraft and theatricality that accompanies each decision.

Ambiguity can be constructive in the sense that it allows President Putin to play a great power game without great power resources. President Putin can "fail fast; fail cheap" and use ambiguity to construct "no lose" scenarios. The advance of what can be termed "creeping annexation", "borderization" or "salami-slicing" of Georgian territory by Russian-controlled South Ossetian army and militias is underway. In early July 2017, South Ossetian border posts were moved by 500 m and are now by 400 m from main east-west transport highway. This constitutes a "no lose" or "win-win" proposition for Russia. If the Georgian military uses kinetic force to reestablish the line-of-control, then Russia will declare this as a provocation and respond with overwhelming kinetic force to formally seize more territory in a defensive reactive manner. If the only response is a barely noticed diplomatic protest note – as was the case – then the expectation is that by winter, a further undeclared border advance will incorporate the highway into South Ossetia, dealing a death blow to Georgia as a viable sovereign state. In this case, Georgian 'Plan B' options are stark: start to build a new highway to the South; resist with force and face the consequences. Ambiguity has a central role in the Putin doctrine.

Conclusions

The key and disproportionate determinant on Putin's operational code remains Russia's security services. They can and do leverage their "soft power" and privileged institutional position to provide information, analysis and policy prescriptions directly to the Kremlin, reinforcing Putin's threat perception and so philosophical beliefs (world view) and Putin's fixation with the status quo: "Their very Manichean and confrontational view of the world inclines them to believe that serous reversals abroad would be exploited ruthlessly and disastrously by Russia's enemies" (Galeotti, 2019). We can also conclude that in identifying the operational code of President Putin, actions speak louder than words. Russia's deployment of force in Georgia, Ukraine, Syria as well as attempted destabilization in Europe and the United States through coercive diplomacy and the combination of conventional and subconventional tools (as outlined in Chapter 2) are better pointers to Russian strategic behavior than Putin's speeches. We should also keep in mind that Putin may have different operational codes for different decision issue areas and make a distinction between his fundamental beliefs and situational or context-specific strategic thinking. Putin's operational codes will likely have greatest influence on his decision-making when there is a "lack of clarity in power relations, institutional constraints and shared norms" (Haas, 2020). Indeed, on occasions where Putin himself has no fixed policy preference, the operational code may act as a default setting.

At the end, Putin's operational code can change over time. Vladimir Pastukhov questions the extent to which manual control is a feature of late Putinism:

> The decisions in their ultimate form are made and executed by others, some-times collectively and sometimes in isolation. Putin intervenes only when

needed, he does not tell them what to do but can step in when he feels that they are not doing what they should. For example, as a hypothesis: they might have themselves poisoned Navalny but for him to be let out to Germany, active consent from Putin was required.

(Pastukhov, 2021)

This suggests, particularly if Putin maintains the presidency to 2036, that a study of the agenda-setting power of the bureaucracy and the FSB, the role of the Security Council, presidential administration and regional elites – a factor COVID-19 responses have emphasized – as well as the nature of rival competitive goals of other key institutional actors (given Putin's decision can represent a compromise arbitration between them) are critical. These factors are at least as relevant as Putin's operational code. Indeed,

> A fixation on Putin leads to at least three problems: 1) an obsession with Putin's thinking at the expense of attention to other factors; 2) a narrative of Putin's almost unique power, which suits the Kremlin; and 3) a difficulty in combining complexity with critique.
>
> *(Noble and Schulmann, 2021)*

As Pastukhov notes,

> This "politics bot," consisting of a faceless bunch of administrative and financial chains and primitive ideological programming, has long posed a greater threat to Russia's future than any decisions of the president. Not only that, but it is a self-teaching system that is gradually accumulating the skills to live without Putin.
>
> *(Pastukhov, 2021)*

Selected bibliography

Adomeit, Hannes. 1982. *Soviet Risk Taking and Crisis Behavior: A Theoretical and Empirical Analysis*. Studies of the Russian Institute, Columbia University. London: Allen and Unwin.

Aleksashenko, Sergey. 2016. "Storm Clouds Ahead: Putin Lacks Strategy to Save Russia's Economy." *The Moscow Times*. August 11, 2016. www.themoscowtimes.com/2016/08/11/storm-clouds-ahead-putin-lacks-strategy-to-save-russias-economy-a54956.

Aptekar, Pavel. 2016. "Russian Investigations Committee Held Captive by FSB; How Arrest of Three High-Ranking Investigators Alters the Special Services' Disposition of Forces." *Vedomosti*. July 21, 2016.

Bateman, Aaron. 2014. "The Political Influence of the Russian Security Services." *The Journal of Slavic Military Studies* 27 (3): 380–403.

Belton, Catherine. 2020. "Exclusive: Former Kremlin Insider Recounts Putin's Moves to Retain Power." July 29. www.reuters.com/article/us-russia-putin-succession-exclusive-idUSKCN24U1O2.

Birnbaum, Michael, and David Filipov. 2017. "Russia Held a Big Military Exercise This Week. Here's Why the U.S. Is Paying Attention." *The Washington Post*. September 23, 2017.

www.washingtonpost.com/world/europe/russia-held-a-big-military-exercise-this-week-heres-why-the-us-is-paying-attention/2017/09/23/3a0d37ea-9a36-11e7-af6a-6555caaeb8dc_story.html.

Bozhyeva, Olga. 2021. "Murakhovsky Told How the New Russian Military Doctrine Can Surprise." *Moskovsky Komsomolets*. April 3, 2021. www.mk.ru/politics/2021/04/03/murakhovskiy-rasskazal-chem-mozhet-udivit-novaya-rossiyskaya-voennaya-doktrina.html.

Burgo, Joseph. 2014. "Vladimir Putin, Narcissist?" *The Atlantic*. April 15, 2014. www.theatlantic.com/health/archive/2014/04/vladimir-putin-narcissist/360544/.

Charap, Samuel. 2021. "Strategic Sderzhivanie: Understanding Contemporary Russian Approaches to "Deterrence." *MC Security Insight*. No. 62, September 2020. www.marshallcenter.org/en/publications/security-insights/strategic-sderzhivanie-understanding-contemporary-russian-approaches-deterrence-0.

Department of State. 1946. "Telegram, George Kennan to George Marshall ['Long Telegram'], February 22, 1946. Harry S. Truman Administration File, Elsey Papers." *Department of State*. https://upload.wikimedia.org/wikipedia/commons/6/68/The_Long_Telegram.pdf.

Dyson, Stephen Benedict, and Matthew J. Parent. 2018. "The Operational Code Approach to Profiling Political Leaders: Understanding Vladimir Putin." *Intelligence and National Security* 33 (1): 84–100.

Eggert, Konstantin. 2021. "Putin Wrote His Own History of Ukraine." *DW*. July 17, 2021. www.dw.com/en/opinion-putin-wrote-his-own-history-of-ukraine/a-58288225.

Fedyk, Ihor. 2016. "On Russia's Tremendous Patience with Developments in Ukraine." *Defense-Express*. March 11, 2016.

Foy, Henry. 2021. "Vladislav Surkov: 'An Overdose of Freedom is Lethal to a State.'" *Financial Times*. June 18, 2021. https://on.ft.com/3iSRzqn.

Galeotti, Mark. 2016. "Putin's Hydra: Inside Russia's Intelligence Services." *European Council on Foreign Relations*. May 11, 2016. https://ecfr.eu/publication/putins_hydra_inside_russias_intelligence_services/.

———. 2017. "Controlling Chaos: How Russia Manages Its Political War In Europe." *European Council of Foreign Relations (ECFR)*. September 1, 2017. https://ecfr.eu/publication/controlling_chaos_how_russia_manages_its_political_war_in_europe/.

———. 2019. "The Intelligence and Security Services and Strategic Decision-Making." *MC Security Insights*. No. 30, May 2019. www.marshallcenter.org/en/publications/security-insights/intelligence-and-security-services-and-strategic-decision-making-0.

George, Alexander L. 1969. "The Operational Code: A Neglected Approach to the Study of Political Leaders and Decision-Making." *International Studies Quarterly* 13 (2): 190–222.

Golts, Aleksandr. 2017. "How to Tell Jokes in a Madhouse." *The New Times Online*. October 10, 2017.

Gorenburg, Dmitry. 2019. "Russian Strategic Culture in a Baltic Crisis." *MC Security Insights*. No. 025. www.marshallcenter.org/en/publications/security-insights/russian-strategic-culture-baltic-crisis-0.

Gorenburg, Dmitry, Michael Kofman, Paul Schwartz, and Samuel Bendett. 2017. "Analytic Framework for Emulating Russian Decision-Making." *CNA Research Memorandum*. Arlington, VA: CNA. www.cna.org/CNA_files/centers/cna/sppp/rsp/Emulating-Russian-Decision-Making.pdf.

Haas, Michael. 2020. "Operational Codes in Foreign Policy: A Deconstruction." In *Oxford Research Encyclopedia of International Studies*. Oxford: Oxford University Press.

Harding, Luke, Julian Borger, and Dan Sabbagh. 2021. "Kremlin Papers Appear to Show Putin's Plot to Put Trump in White House." *The Guardian.* July 15, 2021. www.theguardian.com/world/2021/jul/15/kremlin-papers-appear-to-show-putins-plot-to-put-trump-in-white-house.

Herd, Graeme. 2019. "Putin's Operational Code and Strategic Decision Making in Russia." In *Routledge Handbook of Russian Security*, edited by Roger E. Kanet, 17–29. London: Routledge.

———. 2020. "COVID-19, Russian Responses, and President Putin's Operational Code." *MC Security Insight.* No. 50, April 2020. www.marshallcenter.org/de/node/1427.

Inozemtsev, Vladislav. 2017. "Strength and Weakness of Vladimir Putin." *Snob Online.* August 31, 2017. https://snob.ru/entry/150896/.

Interview with Nikolai Patrushev, Secretary of the Russian Security Council. 2021. "Without Fear and Reproach." *Rossiyskaya Gazeta Website.* May 31, 2021. https://rg.ru/2021/05/31/patrushev-raskryl-neizvestnye-podrobnosti-zhenevskoj-vstrechi-s-sallivanom.html.

Ivanko, Igor. 2020. "Powerful, But Not Omnipotent Special Correspondent Andrey Pertsev Answers All of Your Questions about Russia's Presidential Executive Office." *Meduza.* November 3, 2020. https://meduza.io/en/feature/2020/11/03/powerful-but-not-omnipotent.

———. 2021. "Geneva Meeting: A World in Waiting." *The Moscow Times.* June 9, 2021. www.themoscowtimes.com/2021/06/09/geneva-meeting-a-world-in-waiting-a74162.

Johnson, Dave. 2021. "Russia's Deceptive Nuclear Policy." *Survival* 63 (3): 123–142. https://doi.org/10.1080/00396338.2021.1930410.

Judah, Ben. 2014. "Behind the Scenes in Putin's Court: The Private Habits of a Latter-Day Dictator." *Newsweek.* July 23, 2014. www.newsweek.com/2014/08/01/behind-scenes-putins-court-private-habits-latter-day-dictator-260640.html.

Kofman, Michael. 2017. "A Comparative Guide to Russia's Use of Force: Measure Twice, Invade Once." *War on the Rocks.* February 16, 2017. https://warontherocks.com/2017/02/a-comparative-guide-to-russias-use-of-force-measure-twice-invade-once/.

Kozlov, Petr. 2016. "Reshuffle in Security Council May Continue. Departure of Boris Gryzlov and Reduction in Status of Viktor Zolotov are Interrelated, Experts Believe'." *Vedomosti.* April 13, 2016.

Kozlov, Petr, and Elena Mukhametshina. 2016. "Sergei Kyrienko's Arrival in the Kremlin May Change Russia's Domestic Politics, But It Is up to Vladimir Putin What Exact Nature of the Change Will Be." *Vedomosti.* October 6, 2016. www.vedomosti.ru/politics/articles/2016/10/06/659823-naznachenie-kirienko.

Kurilla, Ivan. 2021. "Russia and the U.S. Have Defined Themselves Through Opposing Each Other for Almost a Hundred Years." *Institute of Modern Russia.* June 8, 2021. https://imrussia.org/en/opinions/3296-ivan-kurilla-"russia-and-the-u-s-have-defined-them-selves-through-opposing-each-other-for-almost-a-hundred-years."

Lavrov, Sergei. 2021. "The Law, the Rights and the Rules." *Ministry of Foreign Affairs Website,* Moscow. June 27, 2021.

Leites, Nathan. 1953. *The Study of Bolshevism.* Chicago: The Free Press.

Leites, Nathan, and Rand Corporation. 2007. *The Operational Code of the Politburo.* Santa Monica, CA: RAND. http://bibpurl.oclc.org/web/63735; www.rand.org/pubs/commercial_books/CB104-1/; www.rand.org/pubs/commercial_books/CB104-1/.

MacFarquar, Neil. 2016. "A Powerful Russian Weapon: The Spread of False Stories." *The New York Times.* August 28, 2016. www.nytimes.com/2016/08/29/world/europe/russia-sweden-disinformation.html.

Marten, Kimberly. 2017. "The 'KGB State' and Russian Political and Foreign Policy Culture." *The Journal of Slavic Military Studies* 30 (2): 131–151.

Meakins, Joss I. 2018. "Squabbling Siloviki: Factionalism Within Russia's Security Services." *International Journal of Intelligence and Counter Intelligence* 31 (2): 235–270.

"Meeting of the Valdai Club." 2015. "Vladimir Putin Meets with Members of the Valdai Discussion Club. Transcript of the Final Plenary Session of the 12th Annual Meeting." *Valdai Club.* October 22, 2015. https://valdaiclub.com/events/posts/articles/vladimir-putin-meets-with-members-of-the-valdai-discussion-club-transcript-of-the-final-plenary-sess/.

Morozov, Viatcheslav. 2013. "Subaltern Empire?" *Problems of Post-Communism* 60 (6): 16–28.

———. 2015. *Russia's Post-Colonial Identity: A Subaltern Empire in a Eurocentric World.* Central and Eastern European Perspectives on International Relations. London: Palgrave Macmillan.

Noble, Ben, and Ekaterina Schulmann. 2021. "It's All about Putin – Russia Is a Manually Run, Centralized Autocracy." In *Myths and Misconceptions in the Debate on Russia: How They Affect Western Policy, and What Can Be Done.* London: Chatham House.

"One Letter Change Alters Putin's Victory Day Speech." 2021. *BBC Monitoring.* May 9, 2021.

Pastukhov, Vladimir. 2021. "Heavenly Praskoveyevka." *Novaya Gazeta.* March 19, 2021.

Pavlovskiy, Gleb, 2015a. "The Kremlin Is Living Without Sensing the Country Beneath It." *Gazeta.Ru.* December 26, 2015. www.gazeta.ru/politics/2015/12/25_a_7991945.shtml.

Pavlovskiy, Gleb. 2015b. "Russia's System of Managed Chaos." *The Moscow Times.* October 22, 2015. www.themoscowtimes.com/2015/10/22/russias-system-of-managed-chaos-op-ed-a50433.

Putin, Vladimir, Nataliya Gevorkyan, Natalya Timakova, and Andrei Kolesnikov. 2000. *First Person: An Astonishingly Frank Self-Portrait by Russia's President Vladimir Putin.* New York: PublicAffairs.

Rostovsky, Mikhail. 2016. "Where Bastrykin is Wrong; and What Does His Fellow Student at the Leningrad Law Faculty Vladimir Putin Think of His Former Group Monitor's Calls?" *Moskovsky Komsomolets.* October 5, 2016.

Rostovskiy, Vladimir. 2016. "Nikola Patrushev: The International Community Should Thank Us for Crimea: Russian Federation Security Council Secretary Says Why Russia Will Not Disintegrate Like the Soviet Union." *Moskovsky Komsomolets.* January 26, 2016. www.mk.ru/politics/2016/01/26/nikolay-patrushev-mirovoe-soobshhestvo-dolzhno-skazat-nam-spasibo-za-krym.html.

Shekhovtsov, Anton. 2021. "The Self-Unfulfilling Prophecy of a 'Dialogue with Russia'." *The Moscow Times.* June 10, 2021. www.themoscowtimes.com/2021/06/10/the-self-unfulfilling-prophecy-of-a-dialogue-with-russia-2-a74177.

Stanovaya, Tatyana. 2017. "Sovereign and Liberal, or How Vladimir Putin's Secret World Becomes Revealed." *Republic.* November 1, 2017. https://republic.ru/posts/87384.

Tüür, Karmo. 2021. "Karmo Tüür: Russia Is Just Forced?" *Arvamus.* April 19, 2021. https://arvamus.postimees.ee/7227827/karmo-tuur-venemaa-on-lihtsalt-sunnitud.

Usackas, Vygaudas. 2017. "Russia's Road to Europe Goes Through Kyiv." *Kommersant.* September 27, 2017.

Vinokutov, Andrei, Elizabeta Mayetnaya, Natalya Galimova, and Vladimir Dergachev. 2015. "Pinoneers Returning." *Gazeta.Ru.* October 29, 2015.

Vishnevsky, Boris. 2017. "Same Old Songs about the Real Thing. If Navalny Aspires to Power He Must Get Used to Criticism. Boris Vishnevsky's Response to Yulia Latynina." *Novaya Gazeta.* July 18, 2017. https://monitoring.bbc.co.uk/product/c1dk5xra.

Walker, Stephen G. 1983. "The Motivational Foundations of Political Belief Systems: A Re-Analysis of the Operational Code Construct." *International Studies Quarterly* 27 (2): 179–202.

Wallander, Celeste. 2015. "Putin's Tactics May Be Brilliant." *Meduza.* November 12, 2015. https://meduza.io/en/feature/2015/11/12/putin-s-tactics-may-be-brilliant.

Waller, Michael J. 1994. *Secret Empire: The KGB in Russia Today.* Boulder: Westview Press.

Walther, Ulf. 2014. "Russia's Failed Transformation: The Power of the KGB/FSB from Gorbachev to Putin." *International Journal of Intelligence and Counter Intelligence* 27 (4): 666–686.

Weiss, Michael. 2017. "The Baltic Elves Taking on Pro-Russian Trolls." *The Daily Beast.* March 20, 2017. www.thedailybeast.com/articles/2016/03/20/the-baltic-elves-taking-on-pro-russian-trolls.

Wilson, Kyle. 2015. "Putin the Chekist: A Sacred Calling." *The Strategist.* November 4, 2015. www.aspistrategist.org.au/putin-the-chekist-a-sacred-calling/.

Winkler, Thomas, Luke Harding, and Julian Borger. 2017. "The Threat from Russia: Realities and Reactions." *The Guardian.* October 24, 2017. www.theguardian.com/world/2016/oct/24/cold-war-20-how-russia-and-the-west-reheated-a-historic-struggle.

Wood, Andrew. 2019. "Putinist Rule Minus Putin?" *The American Interest.* July 29, 2019. www.the-american-interest.com/2019/07/29/putinist-rule-minus-putin/.

7

RUSSIA'S GLOBAL REACH

Reality and rhetoric

Introduction

In 1992, Russian Foreign Minister Andrei Kozyrev predicted:

> No doubt Russia will not cease to be a great power. But it will be a normal
> great power. Its national interests will be a priority. But these will be interests
> understandable to democratic countries, and Russia will be defending them
> through interaction with partners, not through confrontation. In economic
> matters, too, once on its own feet and later, after acquiring a weight com-
> mensurate with its potential in world trade, Russia will be a serious economic
> competitor to many but, at the same time, an honest partner complying with
> the established rules of the game in world markets.
>
> *(Kozyrev, 1992)*

This vision of a post-imperial "normal great power" has not emerged.

Russia's global activism legitimizes the current political order in Russia by
boosting Russia's status, both in the international community and also in the
minds of the Russian population: "Most Russians wish to believe that Russia is a
great power, a global player which has now risen from its knees, straightened itself
up and is actively participating in global politics" (Ventsel, 2021). Russia engages
regions differently, with different objectives, approaches and roles, each with its
own strengths and weaknesses. Given Russia's official foreign policy narratives justifying foreign policy decisions to both domestic and foreign audiences, we should
be careful to distinguish between what Russia says and what Russia does, between
words and deeds, rhetoric and reality. Studying and understanding these differences provide opportunities to engage with Russia more effectively in each region.
Russia's global activism is often characterized as opportunistic, transactional and
reflective of Russia as a state in structural decline. Russia has global ambitions and
aspirations but lacks the resources to institutionalize gains and attain goals. Reality
is somewhat different.

The foreign policy elite in Moscow has reached a consensus and articulated
a strategic doctrine that consists of a set of strategic goals with global scope and

DOI: 10.4324/9780429261985-7

ambition. Russia's 2 July 2021 NSS signals that the Russia views itself as an independent stakeholder (and strategically autonomous actor) able to 'go it alone' in the international system (National Security Strategy, 2021; Buchanan, 2021). Russia aims to be a sovereign great power with global reach. According to Alexander Golts, Putin's own worldview is critical to how this role is exercised:

> The world is ruled by the strong; the weak are pushed and shoved. The world belongs to the brave. If Russia has nuclear weapons, then the country's leader can do whatever he wants. And no-one will dare to object to him, even when he tells obvious lies. Why should he not tell lies, if the population under his control likes them? After all, there's no such thing as democracy; it is just that hypocritical Westerners deceive their people more skilfully. That said, we're doing rather well in this field also these days.
>
> *(Golts, 2021)*

This aspiration has systemic consequences. Russia seeks to promote a global system compatible with its interests and in opposition to the "totalitarian West" which Russia claims promotes one set of values and norms and one power – "one master, one sovereign," as President Putin asserted in 2007 – the United States. Thus, Russia's conception of world order is fundamentally incompatible with and in opposition to the interests of the United States, its friends and allies. Russia is caught in a geopolitical Catch-22 situation. In order to be strategically relevant, Russia must reach out to and engage with a range of strategically important powers – such as, Japan, India, Germany and Vietnam – but in order to oppose the United States, Moscow must form a functional if not friendly anti-western alignment or axis with China.

Russia also seeks through linkage to leverage its global activism to both break strategic isolation after the annexation of Crimea in February 2014: "Russia is now in a state of strategic isolation and is trying to establish contact with anyone it can in an attempt to show that is not, in fact, isolated" (Golts, 2015). But, in addition, Moscow uses these contacts to increase support for Moscow's assertion of primacy and the strengthening of its own strategic depth in its neighborhood. For Russia,

> The conquest of Central Asia in the nineteenth century was an important element of Russia's competition with the British Empire. The Crimean War of 1853–1856 was waged against Russia by a coalition that included the Ottoman and British Empires and France.
>
> *(Rumer and Sokolsky, 2020)*

In other words, if historically Russia has sought to assert hegemony in its neighborhood to further competition with European great power, today Russia's global reach can also reinforce Russia's influence in its neighborhood. After the annexation of Crimea, Prime Minister Medvedev attempted to use Russia's global reach to solicit states to recognize the annexation. A similar process occurred after 2008 conflict with Georgia, when external legitimation of the self-declared statehood of Abkhazia and South Ossetia was sought.

This appreciation of Russian aspiration and ambition is not shared. In 2014, for example President Barack Obama described Russia as a "regional power in structural decline." Senator John McClain characterized Russia as "a gas station masquerading as a state." As an unevenly developed great power, thus far incapable of structural economic reform, Russia aspires to attain more influence internationally than the size its economy suggests is merited. Assessments of Russia's global reach at the start of the Biden administration highlight Russia's global activism and chart its efforts to resist a U.S.-led international order. Assessments of Russian relative strength and traditional measures of power projection also take into account its capacity to build new relations and instruments that damage and dilute the ability of the United States to lead a disrupted global order (Stoner, 2021). Russian global activism allows Russia to pose as an alternative partner to the United States and balance western influence; it raises the costs of U.S. leadership. Russia adopts transactional, flexible, adaptable, non-ideological, and asymmetric approaches to great power competition: "Moscow boasts an agile and skilled diplomatic establishment and lacks ethical constraints in pursuit of its objectives" (Stronski, 2019). In the context of a great power competition, Russia presents a credibility trap: given Russia's combined strengths and fragility, what is the optimum policy balance that upholds the interests and values of the United States and its friends and allies and also constructively shapes Russian strategic behavior, while avoiding the risk of miscalculation and escalation?

In Chapter 2, we introduced the notion of geo-spatial imaginaries, noting that Russia constructs and engages with five "spatial imaginaries": first, Belarus and Ukraine as part of an East Slavic Orthodox foundational core; second, the wider hinterland of former Soviet space, over which Russia should have an ordered producing and managerial role; third, Europe's function in Russian strategic identity is to validate Russia's exceptional civilizational identity as a besieged fortress and alternative model and, fourth, the United States, which serves as a marker of Russia's great power status, serving as it does as Russia's strategic benchmark. What then of the fifth imaginary: the wider global imaginary? Russia's global activism reshapes and expands Russian perceptions about its own borders. In an address to the permanent members of the Russian Security Council, President Putin noted that the escalation of hostilities in the Middle East was taking place in proximity to Russia:

> I would like to ask our colleagues to speak about the situation in the Middle East, namely, about the aggravation of the Palestinian-Israeli conflict, which is taking place in close proximity to our borders and directly concerns our security interests.
>
> *(Belenkaya, 2021)*

Five core ways and means

How does Russia align its ways and means with its strategic goals? What are the principal ways and means? Russia maintains its great power strategic relevance through global hotspot engagement. When anticipated costs are low or Russia has strategic interests at stake, Russia can opportunistically insert itself into a crisis and exploit power vacuums. Russia cultivates the role of neutral mediator and honest power broker, one able to provide a constructive stabilizing presence. Increasingly, Russia uses engagement in one conflict to project power and influence into the next. It projects itself as alternative partner to the West, the upholder of principles of respect for international law, equality, and noninterference in the internal affairs of states, the peaceful settlement of disputes and a commitment to multilateral actions. It is a sovereignty and security provider. Russia advances its economic interests to secure political influence.

Russia maintains its great power strategic relevance through the exercise of its veto power and spoiler role in global hotspots, leveraging its United Nations Security Council Permanent Five (UNSC P5) status, and on issues of "strategic stability" (nuclear issues) and outer space. Russian interventions project power over choke points in the eastern Mediterranean and Suez (through its new naval base in Sudan), and in Libya and Syria, Russia has the ability to control migration, trafficking and energy flows. Though Russia is less able to dictate outcomes, it can complicate and threaten the security interests of the United States and its friends and allies. Russia demonstrates that direct military intervention to resolve strategic challenges can be swift, effective and can garner international support, not isolation. Russia can leverage ties with Soviet era allies ("traditional relations") such as Vietnam, Cuba and Syria. In the Middle East and North Africa,

> Russia is now a prominent factor in Syria and Libya, a partner of Iran, a partner with ambitions in Egypt, and an interlocutor with the Gulf states (especially the United Arab Emirates and Saudi Arabia), Israel, the Afghan government, the Taliban, and the Palestinians, among many other political entities.
>
> *("Russia in the Middle East", 2021)*

Indeed, Foreign Minister Lavrov intends to develop a ministerial-level meeting of the Middle East Quartet (Russia, the United States, the European Union and the United Nations) "to facilitate direct dialogue between the Palestinians and Israelis in order to resolve all fundamental final-status issues" ("Associated Press", 2021).

Although security politics is the ability to manipulate antagonisms, Russia cultivates a perception of itself as a neutral mediator, an honest power broker and having a constructive stabilizing presence. For Russia, the greater the number of players or actors in a given conflict, the more violent and chaotic that conflict becomes, and so the greater the need for mediation. In such cases, Russia can leverage its outsider arbitrator status to become the largest external player and so hold the balance of power and use mediation to build a new *status quo*. Within conflict states, Russia is able to speak to all sides (incumbents and opposition or "equidistance" policy) and is unhampered by colonial legacies. In reality, "Russia plays multiple sides against each other within countries experiencing internal conflict, using these conflicts as a wedge to deepen its regional influence" ("Russia in the Middle East", 2021).

In Yemen, Moscow works with a Saana-based alliance led by Houthis and a UAE-backed separatist Southern Transitional Council (STC) Aden-based group. In the Central African Republic (CAR), Russia has ties with the Bangui-based Touadéra government and the Séléka CPSK-CPJP-UFDR alliance rebels militia group (almost entirely Muslim) in the north of the country. Russia is the only power that speaks to all actors in the Middle East, even those regarded as adversaries: Turkey and the Kurds, Hezbollah and Israel, Saudi Arabia and Qatar, as well as Palestine, Egypt, Iran, Jordan and the United States. Sergei Lavrov, for example, promotes a diplomatic initiative designed to institutionalize a security and cooperation organization in the Persian Gulf (PGSCO), which, "even if it fails to materialize, is a way to emphasize its neutrality in the region and that its approach to regional security differs from Tehran's." In addition,

> Showcasing an "inclusive" and "comprehensive" diplomatic initiative in the region is meant to ensure that Russia gains a seat at negotiation tables regardless of its limited material resources, hence preserving an aura of great power through the framing of regional debates.
>
> *(Czerny, 2021)*

In practice, Russia's effective use of coercive mediation in the Middle East and North Africa has a constructive impact on Russian–Chinese relations, helping to rebalance it. Russia seeks to establish itself as the Middle East's conflict manager by promoting itself as the "kingmaker in partnership with U.S. allies and adversaries – a result unfortunately facilitated by the US itself" (Lobel, 2021). Russia uses instability to expand its influence. We can also identify instances where the lack of a mediated agreement with external actors, such as Japan and the Kurile Islands/Northern Territories, can be used to consolidate domestic support, enhance regime security and signal globally Russia's great power status; great powers do not trade their own territory to the strategic ally of its main adversary, in this case, the United States. Russia views U.S. security assistance and cooperation in zero sum terms.

Russia finds new geopolitical partners through its positioning as a predictable hedge and balancing alternative to the United States outside of the Asia-Pacific. Within the Asia-Pacific, Russia poses as an alternative to China for Japan, Vietnam, India and ASEAN states. While Russia lacks economic weight in South Asia, it is politically influential, able to leverage: "China's rise, the Sino-Indian border conflict, and the convergence of Pakistani and Russian interests in having the Taliban at the helm in Kabul" (Singh, 2021). For India, "Challenges of deficient strategic assessment, continental-centrism, and Russian dependence – though structural and path-dependent but not determinative – have posed significant obstacles to a tighter U.S.-Indian alignment to balance China" (Lalwani, 2020). More generally, Russia argues that the world needs a strong, strategically relevant Russia as multi-polarity diffuses bipolar U.S.–China tensions. Russia seeks to translate resultant influence into United Nations General Assembly (UNGA) votes. Russia is able to develop narratives that appeal to societies and elites and tarnish the idea of democracy and the notion of a U.S.-led liberal international order. President Putin, for example, contrasts Russia's approach to cooperation with Africa to the West's desire to "pressure, frighten and blackmail" African leaders in order to "reap super-profits" (Text, 2019).

Russia is an urbanized, educated and technologically advanced country, but its quality of governance, based on rent-seeking and corruption, is akin to underdeveloped states in Africa and Latin America. Shared and compatible "bad governance" norms enable Russia to interact flexibly with a range of partners and interlocutors in the international system. "Bad governance" is not a hindrance to forging transactional interest-based relations: it provides an ideal operating environment for the promotion of malign influence and activities. China and Russia share antagonism with the United States, viewing Responsibility to Protect (R2P) as a challenge to sovereignty and mask for regime change. Both provide each other mutual support (Chen and Yin, 2020). Russian Constitutional changes of 2020 amended Articles 79 and 125(5)(b) of the 1993 Constitution and highlighted the issue of Russian legal sovereignty. These changes brought into question "whether the Russian Federation is committed to the international legal order as it so often contends" (Fisher, 2021). As President Putin can under Article 83 remove Constitutional Court judges for committing an act discrediting the honor and dignity of their office, the executive can bring pressure to bear on the Constitutional Court. If there are conflicts or misalignments between international norms and Kremlin preferences and interests, then the Kremlin and "autocratic legalism" will prevail.

That "There can be no security without Russia" is a Lavrovian theme, if not meme. Russia posits itself as a sovereignty and security provider, as a reliable "bulwark against revolutions" and "champion of counter-revolution," ready to share mutual lessons learned on authoritarian controls and anti-protest measures. "Color revolutions" are considered the core threat to regime stability. Russia is able to provide outsourcing of risk to non-state or quasi-state actors and local partners who are eager to avoid costly military and economic commitments. Russian–Pakistani support for the Taliban in Afghanistan has a direct impact on U.S. interests, as the "Taliban bounties'" active measure attests. These proxy forces can create footholds for Russian enterprises (e.g. *Rosoboronexport, Rosatom, Rostec*), which can follow through and capitalize on any successes.

David Lewis has outlined several principles of Russian conflict management that promote an illiberal or authoritarian peace, arguing that Russia practices coercive diplomacy which is always context-specific and predicated on a careful study of the correlation of forces and takes into account local and regional power dynamics. For Russia, the goal is to stop the fighting and achieve a minimum political order compatible with Russian geopolitical interests. Russia believes a stronger state is the precondition for peace, and powerful regional states are more effective peace talk mediators than weak, neutral states. Russia understands that military activities and peace talks are closely interrelated, as in effect peace talks accompanied by coercive pressure, covert actions, information war and control and the instrumentalization of humanitarian or development aid as means to Russian ends reflect the view of peace talks as war by other means. At the end, for Russia, the West is part of problem, not part of solution. Russia believes that U.S. foreign policy is underpinned by a strategy of "managed chaos" (*upravlyaemyi khaos*), involving "color revolutions," military interventions, covert support for anti-government rebellions (Lewis, 2021).

The Sino-Russian functional axis has a strong military component, based on joint exercises and arms sales. From 2015, joint Sino-Russian naval exercises have taken place in the Mediterranean, Black and Baltic Seas and in the Yellow, East China and South China Seas and the Seas of Japan and Okhotsk. The Peoples Liberation Army has participated in the Russian-led *Kavkaz*, *Tsentr* and *Vostok* exercises and may develop joint defensive cyber exercises, though given the roles of their respective intelligence services and the fact that both states hack each other, coordinated or shared offensive operations and capabilities appear unlikely. In 2019, Russia and China initiated a joint long-range bomber aircraft patrols over the Pacific Ocean and announced that they would create an early warning missile defense system. SIPRI reports that from 2016 to 2020, 77 percent of Chinese arms imports were bought from Russia (Singh, 2021). In addition, China, Iran and Russia have conducted naval drills in the Indian Ocean and Gulf of Oman (Joscelyn, 2020). Michael Kofman predicts that

> Military-to-military exchanges, exercises, and training programs will ultimately permit Russia and China to be able to execute three potential contingencies: a joint intervention in Central Asia, dividing the region into separate operational level theaters, a joint expeditionary operation in Africa or the Middle East, and a coordinated deployment of forces along separated operational fronts in the event of a military crisis in the Asia-Pacific region. This is a probabilistic though not an exhaustive list of contingencies.
>
> *(Kofman, 2020)*

Russian and Chinese officials describe the relationship between the two states in terms of a multifaceted strategic cooperation and comprehensive partnership. China and Russia share some common goals, both supporting, for example, the DPRK, Venezuela, Syria and Iran and have some converging, overlapping and symbiotic energy and security interests. Over the last two decades, Russia and China have created a moderate degree of institutionalization, which creates the foundations needed for an alliance. An alliance entails integrated military command, joint troop placement and/or military base exchange and a common defense policy to counter the United States (Korolev, 2019). Such deep institutionalization is yet to occur. Thus, rather than a traditional alliance, Russo-Chinese strategic relations resemble an entente, that is flexible and reassuring relations between strategically autonomous major powers who both reject U.S. hegemony and promote a multipolar international order (Kofman, 2020). It is more akin to a functional non-aggression pact allowing strategic deconfliction and for both states to leverage complimentary capabilities and needs, leading to technological advancements. Both states "contest the United States, in a way that is "together, but separate," forcing the United States to compete on both fronts at the same time." Thus, alignment avoids the possibility of "second front competition with China," while inceasingly China's power draws "U.S. resources further into a contest in the Asia-Pacific region and away from vital Russian interests in Europe" (Kofman, 2020). The net effect of this entente and axis is that both Russia and China help each other to individually project more power, eroding U.S. military advantage in the Indo-Pacific and more generally complicating U.S. defense plans and capacity in different global regions.

In return for providing security, Russia gains influence and access to resources, from diamond and gold deposits in the case of CAR and infrastructure and energy in the case of Libya. Russia also promotes security cooperation: Russia has, for example, military and technical cooperation agreements with over 30 countries in Africa. In 2019, Russia signed an agreement to create a material-technical support facility in Port Sudan, whose geographical centrality "gives the Russian navy and potentially the Russian Air Space Force the capacity to control several choke points and focal areas," not least the Bab el-Mandeb Strait (Muraviev, 2020). This follows the Soviet naval tradition of logistics support centers in South Yemen (with a forward operating base on Sokotra Island), Ethiopia, the Seychelles and Somalia. Russia has renewed its presence in unstable countries and is the largest arms supplier to Africa (35 percent of the total) (Hedenskog, 2018), organizing counter-terrorism training with Botswana, Burkina Faso, Burundi, Cameroon, the Central African Republic, Chad, Ethiopia, Gambia, Ghana, Guinea, Guinea-Bissau, Mozambique, Niger and Rwanda. Russia perceives security provision as a means of mirroring what it understands to be U.S. power behavior and a means to balance: Venezuela plays the same function of Ukraine in the respective backyards. U.S.-Russian nuclear weapons' developments and arms control measures do have implications for Chinese, Indian and Pakistani approaches to these issues.

Russia exploits weapons' markets which the United States has vacated, both to secure foreign currency and to optimize geopolitical influence. Kostas Grivas, professor of weapons systems at the Hellenic Military Academy, notes that "Weapons exports are critical for the Russian economy, unlike the U.S. which is such a huge market on its own that it doesn't really care about exports" (Psaropoulos, 2021). Both Egypt and Turkey, for example, have purchased Sukhoi Su-35 advanced multi-role fighter aircraft, after the United States has refused to sell them its fifth-generation F-35 fighter-bomber. Algeria is responsible for half the defense spending in Africa and Russia's largest partner. Iran is also in the market for Russian weaponry, likely to be joined by the UAE after the Biden administration suspended the sale of F-35s to the UAE. Russia is adept at monetizing conflict, able to sell weapons to both sides in the same conflict. In Africa, for instance:

> Russia primarily exports the Soviet Union's heritage: our officials are travelling to Africa for old time's sake, plus Russian weapons are actively coming there. Our weapons are competitive goods on the continent; they are quite cheap and reliable. And these arms deliveries, unlike those from the United States, are not burdened, for example, by human rights requirements.
>
> *(Khachaturov et al., 2019)*

Russia's global reach also seeks to advance Russian economic interests or, more precisely, those in Putin's inner circle who dominate state-owned enterprises where they can privatize profit and pass risk onto the state. Russia is also a key player in the global energy nuclear market, accounting for 7 percent of the world's uranium production, including "20% conversion and 45% enrichment of this element, as well as for the construction of 25% of nuclear power plants in the world" (Glazunova, 2019). The business interests of the core Russian political, economic and military–security elites (e.g. Aleksandr Bortnikov, Sergey Chemezov, Konstantin Malofeev, Nikolay Patrushev, Sergey Naryshkin, Viktor Zolotov, Igor Sechin, Sergey Shoigu and Vyacheslav Volodin) allow for corruption, ensure loyalty and shape Russian interventions and power projections. Russia's foreign economic policy strengthens oligarchic capitalism at home. It delays the need for structural economic reform and the potential threats this poses to Russia's elite and their desire for continuity in power. In addition, Russia is adept at reaching out to other militaries also connected to cronies – for example high-ranking Myanmar junta military delegation sent to Moscow, led by Air force chief General Maung Maung Kyaw and well-known Myanmar tycoon U Tay Za, to discuss over 20 megaprojects including procurement of Russian air defense system and surveillance drones (Myanmar, 2021). Myanmar *coup* leader Senior General Min Aung Hlaing headed to Russia from 22 to 24 June 2021 to attend the Moscow Conference on International Security (MCIS-2021). While overall trade between Russia and Myanmar remains low, Russia is now the number two military exporter to Myanmar behind China.

Russia seeks to sanction-proof itself and, like Venezuela, turns to state-backed cryptocurrencies to evade and bypass financial institutions that can be compelled to help enforce economic sanctions. As part of sanctions resilience, Russia calls for alternative partners in new non-western markets. Russian exports to the Middle East, for example, include arms sales, machinery, oil and gas, as well as petrochemical, metallurgical and agricultural products. The Middle East is also a core destination for Russian grain exports. These exports offset the negative effects of Western-imposed sanctions. Growing digital and artificial intelligence collaboration with China allows for the development of non-Western technology and expertise. Russia's integration into the global financial system through the internationalization of the stock market allows Russian elites to raise capital from foreign investors and legitimize their wealth without improving the local business environment (which would entail a rule of law not rule by law and a reduction of levels of corruption) (Logvinenko, 2019). For oil producers with large sovereign wealth funds, Russia itself becomes an attractive market and investing in Russia enables them to diversify their investment portfolio away from overdependence on Western Europe and the United States.

Assessing Russian statecraft

What is the rationale of Russian actions beyond in a global context? To what extent are the ways and means Russia adopts successfully aligned to achieve its strategic ends? What is the relationship between increased Russian activity and success, between completed actions and outcomes leading to positive impacts that advance Russian national interest? Does increased Russian activity translate into greater influence? Does greater influence enable Russia to achieve its preferred policy outcomes outside the historical perimeter of the 400-year-old Russian empire? Does the external perception of Russian success trump reality or are they aligned? How then might we assess the challenge and threat of contemporary Russian statecraft (Troitskiy, 2019)?

Russia's ways and means could be inter-enabling and self-reinforcing: Moscow demonstrates its strategic relevance by using its mediation and arbitration power to exercise a *de facto* veto on attempts at conflict resolution on terms that do not meet its interest. This would then allow Russia to shape and build a new *status quo* around alternative non-Western or even anti-western governance models and norms. Russia then provides security to uphold the new normal and can advance its economic interests. The consensus is that in practice, Russia "punches above its weight." Through the skillful deployment and coordination of its limited ways and means, Russia is said to "play a weak hand well." The sum of Russia's agile and skilled diplomatic corps' transactional and pragmatic approach to strategic competition is considered to be more than its parts. When we survey the totality of Russian global activism, from regional and cross-regional thematic perspectives, does this consensus hold? What is our assessment of contemporary Russian statecraft?

This chapter has argued that Russia maintains its great power strategic relevance through the exercise of its veto power and spoiler role in global hotspots and through regional interventions. Such activities signal Russia's strategic relevance and great power status. However, with such activism, Russia faces the challenge of prioritizing and maintaining coherence, translating short-term tactical military successes into longer-term strategic engagements, while avoiding costly reputational-sapping entanglements. Syria, Ukraine, Venezuela, Central African Republic (CAR) and Libya are test cases for these propositions. In Latin and South America, for example, Russian support for revisionist states such as Cuba and Venezuela boosts Russia's strategic relevance. At the same time, however, support for Cuba and Venezuela directly undermines the position of Brazil, a member of the far more strategically influential BRICS grouping (Brazil, Russia, India, China and South Africa) as well as Mexico and Argentina, core regional leaders within the G20 grouping. Support for Maduro in Venezuela alienates 11 of 14 states in the Lima Group. In Syria, Russia needs to pacify Idlib (in northwestern Syria) to eliminate threats (drone and rocket attacks) to its base in Hmeimim and to prevent a domestic political crisis and, possibly, regime failure. At the same time, Russia's strategic goal is to maintain its transit through the straits of Bosporus, which entails securing good relations with Turkey. Russia considers the Middle East a secondary priority and will have difficulties maintaining its influence.

Russia cultivates a role as a neutral mediator and an honest power broker, with constructive stabilizing presence. Russia finds it easier to support *status quo* incumbents than opposition leaders and groups proposing regime change, not least given official Russian narratives around which norms are appropriate (i.e. noninterference in domestic affairs). However, there are clear gaps between what Russia says and what it itself does. Putin's words are not reliable indicators of intent, as his own claims of withdrawal of Russian armed forces in Syria clash with the reality of a permanent presence. Russia's attitude to third parties in its "sphere of special interest" (in the former Soviet space) and how it projects power globally mark another gap, pointing to a "do as I say, not as I do" approach. Maintaining "ties with all and corresponding lack of close allies impede its ability to move forward on key issues, most notably Syria" (Czerny, 2021). We find other dichotomies in Russia's core narratives. For example if "incumbents good; regime change bad" is a Russian foreign policy mantra, how can we account for the role of rebels in Russian foreign policy? How can we account for Russia's emphasis on state-based rights and rules and the reality of a political system built on connections, clientelism and the subordination of law to power? Russia positions itself to lead an anti-imperial axis in the global context, yet practices neo-imperial policies toward its near neighbors. It undertakes a war on democratic governance yet advocates the democratization of the international system.

From a Russian perspective, to make the international system more democratic is to make it more pluralist, that is to reduce the role of U.S. leadership in the system. Chinese Belt and Road Initiative (BRI) activity and foreign investment in critical national infrastructure raise its profile in the former Soviet space, particularly Ukraine and through Central Asia in the last decade. Former Soviet states may look up to China as a third party actor to balance Russia either through adopting Russia's mediation role or by bolstering their multi-vector and equidistance-based foreign policies. It is notable that Russia does not offer itself as a mediator between India and China. Andrey Kortunov notes that:

> Russian–Chinese cooperation should have its own foundation, not a common enemy. Besides, an unmitigated U.S.-Chinese confrontation contains multiple military, geopolitical and economic risks for Russia – ranging from a devastating global recession, which would severely damage the fragile Russian

economy, to a large-scale military conflict, which Russia might be dragged into against its will.

(Kortunov, 2020)

In addition, such alignment with China means that Russia cannot act as an 'honest broker' between China and the United States.

Russia finds new geopolitical partners through its positioning as a predictable hedge and balancing alternative to the West, particularly the United States. Russia promotes its role as an alternative partner that states in regional confrontations can turn to as a hedge and balancing partner. In Northeast Asia, for example, Japan, the Republic of Korea (ROK) and Mongolia look up to Russia to balance China and as a hedge against the United States becoming isolationist, as under the previous administration. However, history, current strategic partnerships, public sentiment and a new U.S. administration all combine to limit further alignment between Russia and states in the region, though Mongolia may prove an exception. In other regions, such as Latin America, states like Cuba, Venezuela and Bolivia look up to Russia and China to balance the United States. Russian engagement is based on three core pillars: arms sales, support for multilateralism and grey zone activities. All are designed to establish a presence and counter U.S. influence.

However, Russia's regional approaches are weakly institutionalized, and Russia lacks the capacity and economic influence to ensure that its political and diplomatic initiatives in Africa, Latin America and Asia develop into more lasting influence. Moreover, Russia has to contend with a "rising China" factor, in which Russia is a situational and transactional partner for China, with different approaches to world order and different interests. China projects an image of being a defender of a reformed global economic system; Russia seeks to replace it. While Russia thinks in terms of G3, China is focused on a G2 world, with Russia, EU, Japan and India having second tier status. Outside of the Asia-Pacific, China adopts an economic not military-first approach, which demands a stable operating environment, not disorder. Indeed, while "China is a revisionist power in Asia-Pacific where Russia is a *status quo* power, and the inverse is true in Europe" (Kofman, 2020). China acts as a strong constraint and moderating influence on Russian power-projection in Europe, the militarization of the Arctic being perhaps the best illustration.

Russia's anti-Western foreign policy creates greater dependence on China; this results in a less diversified, comprehensive, rounded and constructive Russian Asia-Pacific policy. Indeed, potential alternative Russian partners, such as ROK) and Japan, are U.S. treaty allies. Russia also faces the danger of being instrumentalized by other states. Turkey's S-400 purchases signal to the West that it has alternatives and so increases its strategic value. Does China use Russia as a stalking horse against U.S. and European interests, while viewing Russia itself as a safe strategic rear and raw materials' base? Does the Central African Republic (CAR) President Faustin-Archange Touadéra use Russian presence as leverage to increase concessions from France?

Russia posits itself as a sovereignty and security provider, as a reliable "bulwark against revolutions" and "champion of counter-revolution." Russia articulates a narrow legal positivist approach to Syria and yet insists on red lines when engaging with Belarus and Ukraine, while in Libya it supports Haftar against the government. Security is provided by both direct Russian conventional military intervention and the deployment of proxy forces. Proxies exemplify a tension between control and deniability; the more they are deniable, the less Russia can exert a measure of control. It is also difficult to send strategic signals via proxies, inter-agency coordination is harder and the monetization agendas of such autonomous actors may limit their utility. Russia provides security to unstable clients that have not first turned to either the United States or China, as Russia lacks the resources to outbid the other two given current power disparities. In Sudan, Wagner Group PMCs aided President Omar al-Bashir's attempt to retain the presidency, as well as combatted Islamic extremists in Mozambique's Cabo Delgado province, and in Madagascar it promoted pro-Russian election candidates (Ramani, 2020). Russian proxies and active measure operations can be poorly coordinated, pursue contradictory goals and, when unmasked, can severely damage diplomatic relations and cause reputational damage. As a result, Russian inroads can be reversible. In 2019, Sudan's former President Omar al-Bashir negotiated a port access agreement for a Russian logistical naval base in Port Sudan 2019 when visiting Moscow, but the draft law was not signed once he fell, though "understandings" with Russia facilitated the arrival of Russian forces ("Report Discusses", 2021). Russia continues to seek military port access in Libya, Egypt, Sudan and Eritrea: it has the intent (if not necessarily the capacity) to become a player in the strategically important eastern/southern Mediterranean and Red Sea.

While China's surveillance model is based on "information management," Russia's low-tech model of digital authoritarianism is more readily adaptable, affordable and enduring as it is easier to replicate. Russian companies, for example, MFI Soft, have been selling System of Operative Search Measures or SORM-related technologies to Belarus, Kyrgyzstan, Kazakhstan and Ukraine, as well as states in Latin America, Africa and the Middle East (Polyakova, 2016). Russia's "strategic partnership" with China, highlighted by growing security cooperation since mid-2014, appears to be an embryonic undeclared military alliance. Russia's growing economic dependency on China and closer conventional military cooperation mean that for Russia to remain strategically autonomous, it must rely more heavily on the one dimension of power in which it has dominance: its strategic nuclear triad. However, short of offering to extend its nuclear umbrella, it is very difficult for Russia to accrue political dividends in terms of extending its authority and influence in the international system.

Russia's global reach seeks to promote Russian economic interests or, more precisely, those of Putin's inner circle that dominate state-owned enterprises where they can privatize profit and pass risk onto the state. One clear tension in Russia's foreign economic policy lies between the desire for geopolitical influence and economic rationality and profit principle that animates Russian state-owned enterprises (SOEs). Igor Sechin, the manager of *Rosneft*, backs Bolivarian regimes, and *Rosneft* appears to advance Russian geopolitical interests at the expense of its shareholders. Russian debt forgiveness ($20 billion) in Africa clears a path for further economic cooperation and is officially characterized as a "pragmatic approach" to managing bilateral relations. Russia advances loans to states that purchase Russian arms, in so doing subsidizing production lines running in its defense industrial complex, replicating the failed Soviet model of relations with Cuba. By contrast, China gives loans to build infrastructure and takes control of infrastructure in lieu of repayment.

Russia embodies a "Sovereign Globalization" approach: it integrates into global markets, transport, logistics, information and supply chains to survive economically but seeks to isolate its population culturally, psychologically and politically within the walls of its besieged fortress, as inoculation against democratization processes. Tensions arise between President Putin's rhetoric about global cooperation and global responsibility and the need for continuous military-patriotic mobilization against external enemies. Russia faces two economic vulnerabilities. First, Russia is economically overdependent on China. China is Russia's most significant trading partner. Since 2015, China has been the largest consumer of Russian oil, and China supplies Russia with essential technological goods. China has also become Ukraine's largest investor and is the largest investor in the Balkans, as well as in Latin America and Africa (in trade), to take some examples. Second, Russia is unable to affect the price oil globally.

When we view Russia's global activism, we find that Russia pivots more to commodity-based economies in the Middle East and North Africa (MENA) through the application of hard conventional and proxy power than it has toward China and the Asia-Pacific wider region, through soft power, trade and enhanced economic relations. However, the Asia-Pacific is central to global order/disorder. We find here the most potent geo-political rivalries, where global governance ideas and norms are contested and where innovation (AI, robotics, quantum computing) occur. Russia's soft power deficit and China alignment are inadequate to meet this challenge. In reality, adopting or emulating the basic characteristics of Putinism entails embracing ineffective authoritarianism, economic stagnation and overly Russian national-conservatism. To be resurgent, Russia must be a constructive autonomous player with a positive agenda beyond "conservatism."

Russia adopts ambitious goals designed to highlight its activism and global reach, but implementation is under-resourced, poorly coordinated and often at cross-purposes. India's shift from strategic autonomy to alignment with a "free and open Indo-Pacific" and deepening its collaboration through participation in joint exercises as part of the U.S.-led Quad (a grouping of four states – India, the United States, Australia and Japan) in an effort to curb China's regional influence is perceived in Moscow as an attempt to undermine Russian–Indian ties. In reality, a combination of Chinese imperiousness, opportunism, reactiveness and even sense of insecurity and vulnerability has resulted in diplomatic missteps and pushback (Small and Jaishankar, 2020). An aggressive and expansionist

Chinese behavior drives interest convergence, enabling democracies to abandon their hedging strategies and in a concerted and coordinated manner balance and counter China (Chellaney, 2020). Russia and Pakistan support the inclusion of the Taliban in Afghanistan's government following U.S. troop withdrawals in September 2021. The ostensible reason for both is to reduce U.S. influence in the region, but Pakistan also views collaboration with Russia in select areas as a means of balancing India, thereby shaping Russo-Indian ties.

After 5 years of low-cost expeditionary coalitional operations in Syria, Russia is the principal external actor, but without an exit strategy, Syria could become a costly reputation-sapping entanglement. Russia is able to control escalation through intervention but not necessarily de-escalation and risks increase over time. If, for example

> Lebanese Hezbollah "resistance forces" and other pro-Iranian Shiite groups decide to open a second front with Israel from Lebanon and Syria, and if Israel responds with massive strikes against these countries, it would cause serious damage to Russia's position, not to mention threaten Russian military and civilian personnel in the region.
>
> *(Belenkaya, 2021)*

To give another example of inherent risk that follows activism, in a leaked interview, Iranian Foreign Minister, Mohammad Javad Zarif, argued that Russia tried to disrupt the Joint Comprehensive Plan of Action (JCPOA) as improved Iranian relations with the West were not in Russia's strategic interest. To that end, Zarif claimed that President Putin, on his initiative and without reference to the Ministry of Foreign Affairs of Iran, met with former Commander of the Iranian Revolutionary Guard Al-Quds Force Qasem Soleimani on 25 July 2015 to agree that Russia would intervene in Syria to save Bashar al-Assad. This meeting occurred only 11 days after the JCPOA had been signed in Vienna by the United States, UK, France, China and Russia – plus Germany (P5+1 format) and, as Zaif stated, "its objective was to destroy the JCPOA" (Michlin-Shapir, 2021). In 2020, it was reported that Russia funneled money to the Taliban for bounties on U.S. troops in Afghanistan. In February 2021, Russia hosted Hamas representatives in Moscow; in April 2021, it was the turn of a Hezbollah delegation. These contacts undercut Russia's projection of itself as "indispensable moderator." The suspicion arises: does Russia play a double game? "While its diplomats engage with Western actors and moderate regional forces in legitimate diplomatic settings ostensibly for further stabilization in the region, behind closed doors Russia collaborates with the most radical forces to do the absolute opposite" (Michlin-Shapir, 2021).

Russia's global activism is characterized by differentiated regional engagement. There is a clear focus of strategic effort in post-Soviet space and the Western Balkans. Elsewhere, Russian behavior is more opportunistic. Russian influence as a security provider is more positive in some states that are less developed and democratic – for example Tajikistan. In the Middle East, "Engagement with Russia allows Israel achievements in degrading Iranian military capabilities and entrench-ment in Syria, with limited Russian disruption of its operations" ("Russia in the Middle East", 2021). In some areas and in some conflicts, Russia refrains from "activism"; this can be seen from the South China Sea to Tibet and from Yemen to Kyrgyzstan. Russia appears ready to share influence with China in Central Asia and in Iran, Vietnam and Pakistan. Russia takes geostrategic gains when it has the opportunity, even at the expense of monetization opportunities (Venezuela), and in cases where there are no real prospects of geo-strategic influence, such as CAR, Russia takes what it can.

Russia adopts a fusion approach, using official conventional and unofficial subconventional hard power to create territorial influence in Africa, creating beachheads through which it can further extend influence over choke points and gain access to resources and maritime ports. Russia's influence in 8 to 10 states in Africa has appreciably increased, through security partnerships, arms sales and the extension of development loans. These states include Libya, Mali, Egypt, Guinea and Central African Republic (Siegle, 2021). Russia is a viable alternative:

> For local African elite the arrival of well-connected Russians offers many benefits. First, it provides an opportunity to diversify economic partners, as one observer notes, many African governments are "slowly waking to the realities of China's murky lending, and long aware of the West's conditional, and ever scarcer loans." Second, Russian military equipment is "relatively cheap." Deals with Moscow are not "held up by human rights concerns," and shipments can occur quickly. Third, and most importantly, new geopoliti-cal rivalries allow local elites to consolidate power domestically and increase their own wealth – a phenomenon scholar Jean-Françoit Bayart labelled *extraversion.*
>
> *(Lechner, 2021)*

The dangers of Russia crossing a threshold of technological and trade depen-dence on China before 2036 are apparent. Before then, China's development of 5G networks in Central Asia and Eastern Europe will bring these regions into China's technological sphere of influence, creating tensions with Moscow (Segal, 2020). In the meantime, if Ukraine can strengthen its democratic institutions, then geopolitical and geo-economic competition between Russia, the West and China may allow it:

> the possibility to combine its pro-Western foreign policy orientation with active economic cooperation with China. It can respect the red lines of its Western partners in relation to China while making the most of the eco-nomic opportunities offered by the Belt and Road Initiative (BRI).

This would reduce its sense of disempowerment and increase its opportunities for autonomous decision-making (Malyarenko et al., 2021).

U.S.-Russian federation relations

Though the administration is only months old, certain approaches are already apparent. The Biden administration promises to be more predictable, professional, pragmatic, experienced and stable than the Trump administration. Atmospherics have certainly changed. The United States under President Biden seeks to emphasize multilateral diplomacy ("diplomacy as a tool of first resort"), using force only when counts and in a sustainable and proportional way. However, there are continuities between the Biden and Trump administrations. Each prioritizes long-term geo-strategic competition with China. Russia, though, is viewed as a major threat, one that seeks to damage U.S. interests and values and that of its friends and allies. Following President Biden's first phone call to Vladimir Putin, the White House readout reported that President Biden warned that the United States would act "firmly in defense of U.S. interests in response to actions by Russia that harm us or our allies" ("Briefing Room", 2021). In President Biden's first foreign policy speech, he promised to defend and advance democratic values and human rights and to impose costs and consequences on Russian malign activity in defense of U.S. vital interests, in collaboration with friends and allies. This sentiment was reinforced with the release by President Biden and Prime Minister Boris Johnson of a revitalized Atlantic Charter on 10 June 2021. Without naming Russia, the United Kingdom and the United States committed to "working closely with all partners who share our democratic values and to countering the efforts of those who seek to undermine our alliances and institutions" and "strengthen the institutions, laws, and norms that sustain international co-operation to adapt them to meet the new challenges of the 21st century, and guard against those that would undermine them" ("The New Atlantic Charter", 2021).

William Burns, at his Senate confirmation hearing, noted:

> Putin's Russia continues to demonstrate that declining powers can be just as disruptive as rising ones and can make use of asymmetrical tools, especially cyber tools, to do that. We can't afford to underestimate them. As long as Vladimir Putin is the leader of Russia, we're going to be operating within a pretty narrow band of possibilities, from the very sharply competitive to the very nastily adversarial.
>
> *("Biden Nominee", 2021)*

The Biden administration has not adopted a new reset with Russia, as since 2012,President Putin embarked on more revisionist and revanchist policies. The United States and Europe can coordinate approaches to "impose real costs" to reduce Russian military and diplomatic efficacy through disruption. Disruption can cause friction, overextend and unbalance Russia and thereby control Russian escalation and deter further malign activity. The tools at the disposal of the United States and its friends and allies that facilitate the imposition of costs are varied and context specific.

These tools can be diplomatic, economic and cyber. Diplomatic tools include "attribution diplomacy" ("name and shame"), diplomatic expulsions and closing diplomatic properties. In public diplomacy terms, the West can restructure the narrative from Putin's preferred besieged fortress Russia encircled by an aggressive, dysfunctional and failed West to one about a Russian elite kleptocracy and oligarchy ("Kremlin blacklist") versus Russian civil society. Economic tools are also varied. The expansion of U.S. anti-money laundering regime beyond traditional banks as well as the Global Magnitsky Human Rights Accountability Act, which imposes visa bans and freezes the assets of individuals anywhere in the world who are responsible for committing human rights violations or acts of significant corruption, is complemented by the European Magnitsky Act, established in December 2020. The Global Fragility Act calls for all parts of the U.S. government to coordinate strategies to prevent violence and extremism and to focus foreign assistance on averting conflict in fragile countries. Sanctions constitute a framework of deterrence, a means of signaling Russia and, with regard to Nord Stream 2, for example, repositioning U.S. relations with friends and allies (Hess, 2021). Tariffs, full embargoes and restrictions on technology sales necessary for hydrocarbon exploration and production could shape Russia's malign strategic behavior.

Cyber tools can be used to reveal or freeze Putin's secret assets and expose corruption, and a policy of "defend forward" or "hack back" can be used. Russia clearly understands this policy to be active. Following cyber-attacks against government institutions in Russia in May 2021, Nikolai Murashov, the deputy director of Russia's National Coordination Centre for Computer Incidents, part of the Federal Security Service (FSB), argued that:

> Based on the complexity of the means and methods used by the attackers, as well as the speed of their work and level of training, we have reasons to believe that this group has the resources available to foreign intelligence services.
>
> *("Russia's Lavrov", 2021)*

The promotion of democratic security building, a major theme in the 1990s, needs revival. As well as countering Russia directly, the West needs to invest in narratives that point to the advantages that liberal and democratic practices can offer and the connections between rule of law, transparency and accountability with development, progress, peace and stability, as well as help countries build their capacity and strengthen their statehood (sovereignty and territorial integrity).

A 'theory of change' underpins personal sanctions against the Russian oligarchic business elite close to Putin. Sanctions are designed not to crash the Russian economy or force regime change but rather to impose a cost on those sanctioned, and thereby change Russian strategic behavior from destabilizer to constructive international relations' actor. Sanctions against named individuals can prevent their travel abroad and freeze or seize their foreign assets and bank accounts. This, the logic assumes, undercuts their mobility, causes them to withdraw political support and loyalty from Putin and then insist on normalizing relations with the

West. Given their desire to pass on status and wealth to their children – an inter-generational transfer of power – they push for the rule of law, respect for property rights, clear rules of the game and the functioning of official institutions. Sanctions against the energy, defense and finance sectors can inhibit external investment and reduce the elite to a stark choice: receive money from the state budget or attempt to be globally competitive and opt for international cooperation.

In reality, however, U.S. policy responses cannot avoid generating unintended consequences in Russia, such as a rally around the flag effect. While this coercion-plus-dialogue statecraft approach to Russia may better manage conflicts and disputes at lower risk and is supported by U.S. allies (Charap, 2021), a trade-off exists between widening negotiations to create leverage between issues areas and increasing the legitimacy of the Putin regime through high level dialogues and summits (Petrov, 2021). Moreover, President Biden's conditional offer of stable and predictable relations should Russia refrain from malign activity is problematic for Russia: "The problem for the Kremlin with this invitation to refrain from military threats, cyberattacks and other international security transgressions is that Russia's role in European affairs would then shrink to irrelevance, instead of desired dominance over its recognized domain" (Baev, 2021). To be strategically relevant, Russia must be stable and unpredictable or, to put it another way, predictable only in its unpredictability.

The impact of sanctions varies according to regime type of the targeted country. Authoritarian leaders are more insulated from macro-economic pressures and less accountable to dissatisfaction among the electorate. Putin can profit from sanctions by redistributing resource rents to strengthen the existing system and elite cohesion (Connolly, 2016). Businesses personally attached to Putin will accept more political responsibilities, weaker businesses will ally with stronger ones and ideological accommodation will increase, even as the economy becomes more statist and Russians more psychologically and institutionally isolated and closed. Sanctions provide an alibi for economic downturn (in reality attributed to a hydrocarbon dependence, crony capitalism and corruption) and bolster the belief that import substitution will allow for strategic autarky. Sanctions also encourage sanctions-proofing: the de-dollarization of Russia's Sovereign Wealth Fund (SWF) planned for the end of June 2021 and use of a digital rouble and other alternatives to SWIFT are all in the works. In addition, Russia can impose counter-sanctions to generate a lever of influence over some of its nearest neighbors. In the event of a Green Party-CDU/CSU coalition government in Germany in September 2021, and the suspension of cancellation of the Nord Stream 2 project, Russian narratives will point to: "US sanctions and pressure. In the ultimate version of this logic, the thesis sounds like this: Nord Stream is the price that Russia has to pay for Crimea" (Barabanov, 2021).

Attribution diplomacy can be ineffective when *siloviki* in Russia have *de facto* immunity from prosecution. Adverse publicity can intimidate opponents and instruct and educate society into submission and be worn as a badge of loyalty. In late April, Russia announced that an official list of unfriendly states has been developed. Foreign Minister Sergei Lavrov noted that the list was still being elaborated. Such a list sends a signal to domestic audiences that Russia will no longer be the passive object of external sanctions and will respond with new sanctions, perhaps targeting economic cooperation, tourism and academic exchanges, in addition to preexisting food import restrictions (Ventsel, 2021). Information secrecy in Russia is justified as is greater KGB-SVR cooperation "to counter Western destabilization." The "theory of change" that animates Western policy appears unproven.

Conclusions

Russia's construction of a global imaginary is work in progress, and "tactical globalism" allows for incremental gains at low cost. Russia's global reach and activism are shaped by the breakdown of relations with the political West, the need to diversify and exploit new markets, to mitigate the risks associated with sanctions and signal its great power status. However, it appears that: "as a means of placating sanctioned elites and providing jobs to ordinary citizens, Russia's return to Africa is a sign of Moscow's political isolation and economic weakness, not a sign of strength" (Lechner, 2021). Russia's critique of a Western "rules based order" is powerful, but Russia does not offer a positive attractive alternative conception of world order. In addition, while Russia may leverage its global reach to assert primacy in its neighborhood, it is not yet able to harness these linkages to create a modernization agenda. At the end, while the consensus appears to be that Russia has played a weak hand well globally, has Russia played a weak hand poorly in its neighborhood, and especially with regard to the Central Front – Europe?

Russia has yet to face a fundamental rethink of the logic of its current strategic posture which by 2036 will become a stark choice: accept the necessity of rapprochement with the West or accept unequal inferior junior status with China, which, when facing a food–water–energy scarcity nexus, will become an even more dominant economic player in Russia. For now, Putin's opposition to the United States appears to be its guiding principle. As noted in Chapter 6, Putin suffers from a broken lens syndrome:

> because for already 20 years he has watched the world through four lenses – FSB, SVR, GRU and FSO. Hence during the talks there should be fewer political philosophical arguments and more U.S. intelligence data. As an experienced judoka, Putin takes advantage of both enemy's strong and weak points in defence. He does not rush, he waits, eyes an opportunity for a successful attack. And the USA has offered such opportunities for him during the last few years (Georgia, Crimea, Ukraine, Syria, 2016 presidential elections).
>
> *(Jushkin, 2020)*

The tragedy of Putinism is, then, that its management system cannot ultimately achieve genuine regime legitimacy (as measured by popularity and longevity) but can sustain itself for another 10 years before collapse and reset. Macro-economic stability and 1.5–2.0 percent economic growth allow for a state of stable order in Russia, but limited resources mean less ability to institutionalize foreign policy gains.

How might current processes of de-globalization and deinstitutionalization in the context of long-term economic decline drive the next phase of Russia's global activism? "Late Putinism" will be characterized by increased factionalism and inter-institutional competition, a culture of overreach and overstretch, and a growing preparedness to accept tactical while avoiding strategic risk. As the Russian elite fragments, does it turn in on and cannibalize itself in a battle for self-preservation (*in lieu* of other 'internal enemies') and control over national security decision-making in Russia? Intra-*siloviki* conflict, confrontation and mutual recrimination benefit the Kremlin in that the warring security services can only form situational coalitions and are unable to create stable and influential clans able to challenge Putin. Given that Russian strategic decision-makers own Russia, it is likely that Russia's global activism will become increasingly driven by economic as much as geopolitical aims, as well as less coherent and less effective.

The United States, its friends, and allies have little direct leverage over Russian strategic behavior; Russian cooperation will be conditional and transactional. Beyond START III, Russia views indications of cooperation as "concessions," that is signs of weaknesses. While Russia backs Assad in Syria, military deconfliction is possible but not cooperation. In Ukraine, where the United States is not part of the multilateral framework and where the discord is antagonistic, cooperative potential is very limited. Thus, offering concessions to Russia or compromising on human rights in the name of pragmatic and flexible cooperation will not alleviate Russia's narrative of western encroachment, encirclement and containment. The West does not have to confirm Russia's claim to great power status as it defines it. Russia's placing of its own interests above the sovereignty of neighboring states is neither aligned with Western national interest nor with its democratic norms and values.

Selected bibliography

Associated Press. 2021. "Russia Says It's Ready to Promote Direct Israeli-Palestinian Contacts | The Times of Israel." *The Times of Israel.* May 5, 2021. www.timesofisrael.com/russia-says-its-ready-to-promote-direct-israeli-palestinian-contacts/.

Baev, Pavel K. 2021. "Russia Recoils From Possibility of Stable Relationship With US." *The Jamestown Foundation.* May 10, 2021. https://jamestown.org/program/russia-recoils-from-possibility-of-stable-relationship-with-us/.

Barabanov, Oleg. 2021. "Why is Nord Stream 2 in Such Plight." *Vedomosti.* May 7, 2021.

Belenkaya, Marianna. 2021. "Russia's Timid Approach to the Israeli-Palestinian Conflict." *The Moscow Times.* May 18, 2021. www.themoscowtimes.com/2021/05/18/russias-timid-approach-to-the-israeli-palestinian-conflict-a73930.

"Biden Nominee to Head CIA Sees Russia as a Potential Threat." 2021. *RadioFreeEurope/ RadioLiberty.* February 25, 2021. www.rferl.org/a/biden-nominee-to-head-cia-sees-russia-as-potent-threat/31120852.html.

"Briefing Room." 2021. "Readout of President Joseph R. Biden, Jr., Call with President Vladimir Putin of Russia." January 26, 2021. www.whitehouse.gov/briefing-room/statements-releases/2021/01/26/readout-of-president-joseph-r-biden-jr-call-with-president-vladimir-putin-of-russia/.

Buchanan, Elizabeth. 2021. "Russia's 2021 National Security Strategy: Cool Change Forecasted for the Polar Regions." *RUSI Commentary.* July 14, 2021. https://rusi. org/explore-our-research/publications/commentary/russias-2021-national-security-strategy-cool-change-forecasted-polar-regions.

Charap, Samuel. 2021. "Expanding the Scope for Statecraft in U.S. Russia Policy." *War on the Rocks.* May 14, 2021. https://warontherocks.com/2021/05/expanding-the-scope-for-statecraft-in-u-s-russia-policy/.

Chellaney, Brahma. 2020. "China Alone." *Project Syndicate.* August 21, 2020. www.project-syndicate.org/commentary/indo-pacific-security-quad-chinese-expansionism-by-brahma-chellaney-2020-08.

Chen, Zheng, and Hang Yin. 2020. "China and Russia in R2P Debates at the UN Security Council." *International Affairs* 96 (3): 787–805.

Connolly, Richard. 2016. "The Empire Strikes Back: Economic Statecraft and the Securitisation of Political Economy in Russia." *Europe-Asia Studies* 68 (4): 750–773.

Czerny, Milan. 2021. "Russia's Security Mirage in the Gulf." *Riddle.* April 4, 2021. www.ridl. io/en/russia-s-security-mirage-in-the-gulf/.

Fisher, Paul. 2021. "Russia's Constitutional Amendments and International Law: Cause for Concern?" *Riddle.* May 7, 2021. www.ridl.io/en/russia-s-constitutional-amendments-and-international-law-cause-for-concern/.

Glazunova, Lyubov. 2019. "Russia's Nuclear Chain Reaction in Africa." *Riddle.* October 21, 2019. https://www.ridl.io/en/russia-s-nuclear-chain-reaction-in-africa/.

Golts, Alexander. 2015. "Russia's Military Lacks Direction." *The Moscow Times.* April 20, 2015. www.themoscowtimes.com/2015/04/20/russias-military-lacks-direction-a45918.

———. 2021. "Forcible Deportation into the World of Vladimir Putin." *Yezhednevny Zhurnal Website.* June 7, 2021. http://ww2.ej.ru/?a=note&id=36189.

Hedenskog, Jakob. 2018. "Russia is Stepping Up its Military Cooperation in Africa." FOI Memo 6604. December 2018.

Hess, Maximilian. 2021. "Biden's Russia Policy after 100 Days." *Riddle.* May 5, 2021. www. ridl.io/en/biden-s-russia-policy-after-100-days/.

Joscelyn, Thomas. 2020. "The World's Most Dangerous Alliance." *The Dispatch.* July 16, 2020. https://vitalinterests.thedispatch.com/p/the-worlds-most-dangerous-alliance.

Jushkin, Vladimir. 2020. "Putin's June Thesis." *Postimees.* July 8, 2020.

Khachaturov, Arnold, Anastasia Torop, and Maria Yefimova. 2019. "They end up in tropics: Russia returns to Africa with pomp to repeat past mistakes," *Novaya Gazeta,* Moscow, in Russian, October 28, 2019.

Kofman, Michael. 2020. "The Emperors' League: Understanding Sino-Russian Defense Cooperation." *War on the Rocks.* August 6, 2020. http://warontherocks.com/2020/08/the-emperors-league-understanding-sino-russian-defense-cooperation/.

Korolev, Alexander. 2019. "On the Verge of an Alliance: Contemporary China-Russia Military Cooperation." *Asian Security* 15 (3): 233–252.

Kortunov, Andrey. 2020. "Does China-US confrontation meet Russia's interests?" *Global Times.* July 17, 2020. https://www.globaltimes.cn/content/1194832.shtml.

Kozyrev, Andrey. 1992. "Russia: A Chance for Survival." *Foreign Affairs* 71 (2), Spring. www. foreignaffairs.com/articles/russia-fsu/1992-03-01/russia-chance-survival.

Lalwani, Sameer. 2020. "Revelations and Opportunities: What the United States Can Learn from the Sino-Indian Crisis." *War on the Rocks.* July 10, 2020. https://warontherocks. com/2020/07/revelations-and-opportunities-what-the-united-states-can-learn-from-the-sino-indian-crisis/.

Lechner, John. 2021. "To Counter Russia In Africa, America Should Rethink Its Own Role." *War on the Rocks.* May 20, 2021. https://warontherocks.com/2021/05/to-counter-russia-in-africa-america-should-rethink-its-own-role/.

Lewis, David. 2021. "Russian Diplomacy and Conflict Management." In *Russia's Global Reach: A Security and Statecraft Assessment,* edited by Graeme Herd. Garmisch-Partenkirchen: George C. Marshall European Center for Security Studies. www.marshallcenter.org/en/ publications/marshall-center-books/russias-global-reach-security-and-statecraft-assessment/chapter-13-russian-diplomacy-and-conflict-management.

Lobel, Oved. 2021. "Russia Is Astutely Playing the Players in Yemen." *The Strategist.* April 29, 2021. www.aspistrategist.org.au/russia-is-astutely-playing-the-players-in-yemen/.

Logvinenko, Igor. 2019. "Local Control and Worldwide Access: How Russian Elites Have Comer to Use the Global Financial System to Defend their Wealth." New Voices on Russia, Video Presentation, YouTube, April 17, 2019. https://www.youtube.com/watch? v=FVFyxHy8vzA&list=PLnYhtecpqY0hV3gP0l3itQieQLZhkCj4e&index=11.

Malyarenko, Tetyana, Stefan Wolff, and Tetyana Malyarenko. 2021. "Pawns, Partners, and Smart Leadership: Ukraine's Opportunities in the China-Russia-West Triangle." *PONARS Eurasia.* May 25, 2021. www.ponarseurasia.org/pawns-partners-and-smart-leadership-ukraines-opportunities-in-the-china-russia-west-triangle/.

Michlin-Shapir, Vera. 2021. "Is Moscow Playing a Double Game in Iran?" *Institute of Modern Russia.* May 5, 2021. www.imrussia.org/en/analysis/3281-is-moscow-playing-a-double-game-in-iran.

Muraviev, Alexey. 2020. "Russia's Red Star in the Red Sea." *The Interpreter.* November 30, 2020. https://www.lowyinstitute.org/the-interpreter/russia-s-red-star-red-sea.

National Security Strategy. 2021. "National Security Strategy of the Russian Federation." *President of the Russian Federation Website.* July 2, 2021. http://publication.pravo.gov.ru/ Document/View/0001202107030001?index=0&rangeSize=1.

"The New Atlantic Charter." 2021. *The White House.* June 10, 2021. www.whitehouse.gov/ briefing-room/statements-releases/2021/06/10/the-new-atlantic-charter/.

Petrov, Nikolai. 2021. "What Comes after Putin Must Be Better than Putin." In *Myths and Misconceptions in the Debate on Russia*, 96–100. London: Chatham House.

Polyakova, Alina. 2016. "Putinism and the European Far Right." *Institute of Modern Russia.* January 19, 2016. https://imrussia.org/en/analysis/world/2500-putinism-and-the-european-far-right.

Psaropoulos, John. 2021. 'In arms race for air superiority, Russia challenges US hegemony', *Al Jazeera,* May 3, 2021. https://www.aljazeera.com/news/2021/5/3/hold-russia-drives-power-competition-in-the-mena-with-arms-sales

Ramani, Samuel. 2020. "Engaged Opportunism: Russia's Role in the Horn of Africa." *Foreign Policy Research Institute.* July 2, 2020. www.fpri.org/article/2020/07/engaged-opportunism-russias-role-in-the-horn-of-africa/.

"Report Discusses Russian Naval Presence in Sudan." 2021. *BBC Monitoring.* April 26, 2021. https://monitoring.bbc.co.uk/product/c202j0ot.

Rumer, Eugene, and Richard Sokolsky. 2020. "Etched in Stone: Russian Strategic Culture and the Future of Transatlantic Security." *Carnegie Endowment for International Peace.*

September 8, 2020. https://carnegieendowment.org/2020/09/08/etched-in-stone-russian-strategic-culture-and-future-of-transatlantic-security-pub-82657.

"Russia in the Middle East: National Security Challenges for the United States and Israel in the Biden Era." 2021. Washington, DC: Wilson Center: Kennan Institute and Institute for Policy and Strategy. www.wilsoncenter.org/publication/report-russia-middle-east-national-security-challenges-united-states-and-israel-biden.

"Russia's Lavrov Rejects Western 'Rules-based World Order'." *RIA Novosti*, Moscow, in Russian. May 7, 2021.

Segal, Adam. 2020. "Peering into the Future of Sino-Russian Cyber Security Cooperation." *War on the Rocks*. August 10, 2020. https://warontherocks.com/2020/08/peering-into-the-future-of-sino-russian-cyber-security-cooperation/.

Siegle, Joseph. 2021. "Russia and Africa: Expanding Influence and Instability." In *Russia's Global Reach: A Security and Statecraft Assessment*, edited by Graeme Herd, 80–90. Garmisch-Partenkirchen: George C. Marshall European Center for Security Studies.

Singh, Anita I. 2021. "Russia's Asia Diplomacy." *The Interpreter*. April 16, 2021. www.lowy institute.org/the-interpreter/russia-s-asia-diplomacy.

Small, Andrew, and Dhruva Jaishankar. 2020. "For Our Enemies, We Have Shotguns": Explaining China's New Assertiveness." *War on the Rocks*. July 20, 2020. https://waron therocks.com/2020/07/for-our-enemies-we-have-shotguns-explaining-chinas-new-assertiveness/.

Stoner, Kathryn. 2021. "How Much Should We Worry About a Resurrected Russia? More Than You Might Think." *PONARS Eurasia*. January 14, 2021. www.ponarseurasia.org/how-much-should-we-worry-about-a-resurrected-russia-more-than-you-might-think/.

Stronski, Paul. 2019. "Late to the Party: Russia's Return to Africa." *Carnegie Endowment for International Peace*, October 16, 2019. https://carnegieendowment.org/2019/10/16/late-to-party-russia-s-return-to-africa-pub-80056.

"Text of the Official English Translation of President Vladimir Putin's Interview with State-Owned TASS News Agency on the Upcoming Russia-Africa Summit to Be Held in Sochi on 23–34 October." 2019. *Kremlin.Ru*. October 20. http://en.kremlin.ru/events/president/news/61858.

Troitskiy, Mikhail. 2019. "Statecraft Overachievement: Sources of Scares in U.S.-Russian Relations." *PONARS Eurasia*. October 21, 2019. www.ponarseurasia.org/statecraft-overachievement-sources-of-scares-in-u-s-russian-relations/.

Ventsel, Aimarimar. 2021. "Moscow May in the Future Bully Unfriendly States More Seriously." *Eesti Paevaleht*. May 3, 2021.

8

PUTIN, THE COLLECTIVE PUTIN AND ALTERNATIVE POWER TRANSITION SCENARIOS

Introduction

At his "direct-line" phone-in with the nation on 30 June 2021, President Putin was asked "if there is a man in your team" who Putin would hand over power, and Putin replied: "Time will come, of course, when I hope I will be able to say that this person or that person is in my opinion worthy of leading a wonderful country such as our motherland, Russia" (BBC Monitoring, 2021). Prior to January 2020 and the resetting or zeroing of the presidential term clock, discussions of presidential succession in 2024 involve rumors, speculation, phobias and conspiracies. The prospect of succession and power transition refers not to an evolution from authoritarian to democratic political system, but to transition within an enclosed elite. As a result, it dominates the minds of Putin's entourage:

> state policy is already somehow being constructed in the context of this transit, economic agents are already thinking about this, commentators explain everything by this transit. Transit in a closed society by definition generates conspiracy theories, and these conspiracy theories become an independent sphere of activity.
>
> *(Sinitsyn, 2019; Pavlovsky, 2019)*

In such an atmosphere, observers interpreted domestic and foreign policy initiatives through the prism of the succession process and speculated as to how the weight of different carriers of Russian strategic culture would be affected by alternative power transfer processes and outcomes.

A study of succession and possible power transitions in Russia in 2024 or 2030 can neither promise to be comprehensive nor claim to be predictive: there are too many variable factors to take into account, not least contingency and accident and even the changing personality of an aging Putin. Alternative scenarios do, however, stress-test our assumptions about power in Russia. Who would be an acceptable successor, to whom and why? To that end, this chapter first notes that President Putin had reset the presidential clock in January 2020 and was therefore likely to run for the "first" time in 2024. The chapter then examines

DOI: 10.4324/9780429261985-8

other alternative scenarios, related them to Russian and Soviet historical experience. It highlights their core characteristics and identifies the assumptions that would underpin their coming to pass. The second scenario is titled 'Putinism with Paramount Putin': *Densyaopinizatisitskya* Scenario or a 'Kazakh way forward'. The third is branded 'Putinism with Partial Putin' or as an 'Enhanced Brezhnev' Collective Leadership Scenario. The fourth looks to '"Putinism without Putin" or a post-Stalin 1953–56 Scenario'. The fifth, examines 'Neither Putin nor Putinism' or a 'Liberal Dictatorship' Scenario. The sixth and final envisages a 'Neither Putin nor Putinism' or 'Populist People Power 2011–12' Scenario (Herd and Lewis, 2019).

Such a study highlights the possibility of counter-intuitive outcomes, where current weakness might become a future strength. With regards to former Prime Minister Medvedev, his current political weakness increases his dependency on Putin, which serves as a guarantee of his loyalty to Putin and so, in turn, increases his chances of becoming a successor (a factor that enabled him to move ahead of Ivanov in 2007):

> Medvedev, it would appear, is once again really counting on a key role in the course of the transition of power. The lack of elite support here could be a plus since it weakens the positions of a possible successor in advance and increases his dependence on his predecessor.
>
> *(Makarkin, 2019; Krasheninnikov, 2019)*

On the other hand, the less stable the internal domestic political environment, the more Putin is able to present himself as the only possible and indispensable savior, according to the logic *après moi le deluge*. In addition, elite phobias based on a U.S. 'Trojan horse' strategy and CIA-Soros post-modern "color revolution" *coup d'état* scenarios suggest that a broken lens threat perception could lead to miscalculation, overreaction, escalation and destabilization.

Russian power transition scenarios: governing assumptions

The first round of the 2024 Russian presidential election will be held on Sunday, 10 March 2024, and, if necessary, the second round on 7 April 2024. The winner will be inaugurated on 7 May 2024. In principle, in an emergency scenario where Putin is incapacitated, Medvedev as Prime Minister is a key player and becomes acting President, with a shortened 90-day election cycle, before fresh presidential elections (this scenario unfolded in the Yeltsin–Putin transition in 2000). In practice, Article 81 of the Russian Constitution is clear that presidents can only serve two consecutive terms. Although the good health of Putin and his retinue would make a third term (2024–2030) viable, Putin cannot constitutionally take part in the 2024 presidential election. The succession race will become a real focus of political life in Russia after the September State *Duma* 2021 elections, but thinking about the succession does force us to identify and make explicit core assumptions we hold that shape our understandings of Russia before testing them. Let us make three such general assumptions explicit.

First, in seeking to identify potential candidates, we can assume that individuals who have publically expressed interest in running are least likely to actually achieve the presidency, while those undeclared potential candidates with federal experience, personal relationships to Putin, resources, assets and supporters are the real contenders. The most credible is Maxim Oreshkin, Minister of Economic Development, who was promptly publically humiliated by the speaker of the State *Duma*, a signal for others not to break ranks. All the usual suspects have also been declared, including systemic opposition party leaders and former presidential candidates: Pavel Grudinin, CEO of the Lenin State Farm, 2018 presidential candidate; Maxim Suraykin, Deputy of the Legislative Assembly of Ulyanovsk Region, leader of the Communists of Russia, 2018 presidential candidate; Grigory Yavlinsky, former Deputy of the State *Duma* presidential candidate in 1996, 2000 and 2018; Vladimir Zhirinovsky, Deputy of the State *Duma*, leader of the Liberal Democratic Party, presidential candidate in 1991, 1996, 2000, 2008, 2012 and 2018 and, Ksenia Sobchak, TV anchor, opposition activist and journalist, Civic Initiative's presidential nominee in 2018. Regional representatives and businessmen include Lev Schlosberg, Deputy of the Pskov Region Council of Deputies; Vladimir Mikhailov, Deputy of the Kostroma Region *Duma*, entrepreneur and inventor; Dmitri Nossov, sportsman, judoka and former Deputy of the State *Duma*; Sergei Polonsky, businessman and Boris Yakemenko, public activist and founder of the *Nashi* movement. Ramzan Kadyrov has publically stated that he will not run, while Navalny has been barred from running through imprisonment in 2021. It is likely that many of these candidates will run, but none will win, and most have no intention of mounting a serious campaign but will maintain profiles and enhance their standing in the post-Putin period.

Putin himself had addressed the succession issue, speaking on his annual televised Direct Line with the Russian people:

> I'm certainly always thinking about this. "There isn't a successor in the classical meaning of the word. He will be designated by the Russian people, by the voters of the Russian Federation. Of course, I'm thinking that a new, young generation of administrators has to be brought up – responsible people who will be in a position to take responsibility for Russia."
>
> *("Putin says", 2018)*

The first would be Dmitry Medvedev, Prime Minister of Russia and former President of Russia. Three regional governors are notable: Alexey Dyumin (born 1972), Governor of Tula Region, former commander of the Special Operations Forces and Deputy Minister of Defense; Dmitry Mironov, Governor of Yaroslavl Region and, Andrey Vorobyov (born in 1970), Governor of the Moscow Region. Those with executive experience include Sergey Naryshkin, Director of the Foreign Intelligence Service; Sergey Shoygu, Minister of Defense; Yevgeny Zinichev, Minister of

Emergency Situations and former acting governor of Kaliningrad Region; Sergey Sobyanin, Mayor of Moscow and Sergey Kiriyenko (born in 1962), the presidential administration's First Deputy Chief of Staff and former Prime Minister of Russia. Those with legislative experience include Andrey Turchak, Senator from Pskov Region and Deputy Chairman of the Federation Council, and Vyacheslav Volodin, Deputy and Chairman of the State *Duma*. Absent from this list are the super elite kingmakers from the SOEs, such as Igor Sechin of Rosneft or Sergey Chezemov from Rostec, and the oligarchs around Putin, the Kovalchuks, Rotenbergs and Timoshenko. These individuals will not run, but we could assume that the SOE heads will promote their own protégés from within this list, while seeking to undermine other candidates, while the oligarchs in Putin's personal entourage will place their resources at the disposal of Putin's preferred candidate in the hope that their wealth and property will be protected. We can also assume that the succession process itself will reshape selectorate calculus, current situational alliances, elite preferences and psychology and understandings of consensus and cohesion.

Second, Putin's management role will be central to the succession process outcome. We can surmise that the more powerful, the more able Putin is to secure his preferred succession outcomes; the less powerful, the weaker and more symbolic his position after 2024. As Kirill Rogov notes of Putin:

> His ambition, the degree of personal risk he takes, his awareness of threats suggests that, unlike his predecessor Boris Yeltsin who at the time was only two years older than Putin is today, the current president is unlikely to retire any time soon or leave office on his own accord.
>
> *(Rogov, 2019, 26)*

Maintenance of the *status quo* is critical to Putin's survival; Putin's survival in turn is critical to the current *status quo* regime survival: "the lack of separation of power and property automatically turns any real handover of power into, at the very least, a new economic redistribution" (Vinokurov, 2017). Thus, succession is a critical test of both the formal political system and process in Russia and the informal *Sistema*, and it provides the supreme test of system's ability to self-reproduce and so sustain itself. Legitimation of power transition in authoritarian systems is not straightforward. Succession poses greatest threat to personalistic regime as historical-charismatic legitimacy cannot be passed onto a successor. Such regimes have a pathological incentive structure as successful leaders eliminate able, charismatic competitors so consolidating their power but imperiling the transfer to a successor. If the political authority of the successor cannot be charismatic-historical, then it must be legal–rational, but there is no post-Soviet authoritarian precedent for peaceful democratic power transfer. If Putin changes the Constitution to uphold the current order, he demonstrates the irrelevance of the Constitution to the current order.

We can surmise that Putin will want as free a hand for as long as possible to make decision as late as possible to maintain arbitration and mediation role. By checking and balancing elite factions and avoiding the reality of lame duck status,

Putin is able to manage as stable a succession as possible. While a successful transition demonstrates the invulnerability of the regime, the pathway should also be as unique and nonderivative as possible, both in terms of Putin's own history (Putin's "castling move" with Medvedev in 2008 and the "emergency scenario" of 2000 that brought him into the presidency) and that of 'vassals' or adversaries in post-Soviet space, as well as China. Originality would highlight the role of Putin as a leader not follower and preempt counter moves to weaken too obvious a 'crown prince':

> He perceives himself as an exceptional demiurge and unconventional decision-maker. He will think of a plan to leave while remaining that will be different from Nazarbayev's; it will have to be a uniquely Russian model – both sophisticated and cynical – just like his 2011 castling move with Dmitry Medvedev.
>
> *(Dubnov, 2019)*

The pathway needs to be visibly different from other pathways, but secures Putin in permanent position of power. Constitutional changes to term limits or institutional relevance are possible, for example by making the advisory State Council (senior legislators, regional governors, party leaders) more powerful.

In the post-succession period, in the absence of a strong rule of law, protected rights and functioning democratic institutions, Putin's successor needs to be strong enough to protect Putin but not so strong as to turn on him, which suggests some dependence on Putin. Putin's own experience of the Medvedev presidency was instructive in this regard:

> The new head of state, despite his indisputable loyalty to his "political father", proven through decades of irreproachable faithful service, was, like a fragile vase, surrounded on all sides by the foam rubber of Putin's personnel, not even allowed to form the Presidential Staff at his own discretion. At the same time, Putin himself was breathing down his successor's neck, controlling his every move from posts as head of the government and leader of the ruling party.
>
> *(Kamakin, 2017)*

If Putin fails to find the right equilibrium, then imprisonment, exile or death could follow. For these reasons, the prevailing assumption is that Putin will select a successor from the group around him.

Third, President Putin's supporters (Putinists) may display their Putinism more eagerly than Putin himself. This raises the question: can Putinism exist without Putin? Putinists exist in the elite and also in the society. In the elite, actors who support Putin owe everything to Putin. These elite individuals owe their position to Putin and benefit through privileged monopoly control over Russia's business corporations, bureaucracy, defense and security sectors and government. These wider elite have deep-rooted shared interests in the *status quo*:

> To begin to change it would require not just the constant and long term endeavor of a committed new set of political leaders able to force the *siloviki* to submit to their will, but also a major and, again, long term effort to reconstruct Russia's court and penitential systems, together with the laws that are supposed to govern their conduct. Nothing of that nature is in prospect, nor is any apparent thought being given to the wider but daunting possibility of improving and cleansing the operations of Russia's bureaucracy as a whole.
>
> *(Wood, 2018)*

As their interests are configured with Putin's and a new reconfiguration will occur under Putin's successor, an interdependent symbiosis can exist. Given Putin's preference is to handle elite conflicts behind the scene, secrecy can become a vulnerability if the *siloviki* present the president with a *fait accompli*. In such circumstances, Putin must make visible changes to reverse the situation, thus highlighting his weakness.

Beneficiaries of current authoritarian system exist outside of the elite. Russia has a population of 144 million, 82 million of whom are of working age. These include two million state and municipal employees, 5.8 million state employees (public and social policy-related), one million military personnel, 1 million civilian employees of the armed forces, 1 million police officers (MVD) and 1 million employees of other special services. To this 11–12 million, we can add 12 million workers from 'corporate Russia', those employed by parastatal or state-owned companies and enterprises (e.g. Gazprom, Rostec, Rosneft, Roskosmos, Russian Post, Rostelekom and Russian Railways), as well as formally private but in fact state-controlled entities (e.g. AFK Sistema, Lukoil, Metalloinvest, NLMK, Norilsk Nickel, Sibur, Surgutneftegas, Transmashholding and UMMC) or so, taking the total to 24 million or 30 percent of employed workers in Russia (Luzin, 2019). Putin avoids creating a rational bureaucratic management system, ensuring that there is a weak state but strong, agile, innovative, complex, flexible system, where networks can "grab, snatch and reconquer" in pursuit of their interests and so circumvent the state (Sennikov, 2019). Traditional Russian political, business and civic elites lack both the motive and the means in the shape of independent political capital or structures (e.g. the Russian Army) and institutes to advance and implement independent agendas or policies to counter Putin (Rogov, 2019, 23–37).

Fourth, under the stress of the succession process, alliances that look solid can turn out to be situational. Andrew Wood acknowledges that:

> It is hard for any authoritarian leader definitively to leave with an easy confidence in his future. Those closest to Putin are beholden to him for their wealth and power. They are also of advancing age and therefore have their

own succession problems to think about. Russia's real governing system is based on "understandings" upheld by shared corruption and predation. None of those at the top can know what would happen to them personally if Putin were to be replaced.

(Wood, 2019)

Transition psychology and changing dynamics generated by the succession process itself reshape individual and institutional transactional calculus. In a patrimonial system, the struggle between influence groups can manifest itself in attacks by one patron on the clients of another ahead of the succession in order to weaken the other. Such attacks can involve the weaponization of non-systemic opposition elite figures. This power paradigm is predicated on an anti-fragile regime-building strategy: the regime thrives on ordered disorder and controlled chaos but is vulnerable to tranquility. Both 'Putin's Collective' (network) and the 'Collective Putin' (clans/corporations) are resilient in the face of external pressure, but they are susceptible to internal infighting. Without purges the *siloviki* become ungovernable, with purges the risks of a palace *coup* increase.

COVID-19 and constitutional reform?

Just before COVID-19 threat became apparent to the wider Russian population, President Putin surprised the world by announcing at his annual Presidential Address to the Federal Assembly on 16 January 2020, inexplicitly, proposals to amend the 1993 Constitution of the Russian Federation. On 20 January 2020, these amendments were submitted as a draft bill to the State *Duma*. After a 2-hour reading on 23 January 2020, the 22 presidential constitutional "proposals" were unanimously (432–0) approved. Subsequently, a further 800 amendments were submitted by the public. The second reading occurred on 10 March 2020 and a vote for the number of presidential terms (currently "two consecutive terms") to be reset to zero if planned constitutional reforms were passed in a nationwide vote (the "Tereshkova amendment") was accepted 380–0, with 44 abstentions. Putin then addressed the State *Duma*:

> [This] proposal effectively means removing the restriction for any person, any citizen, including the current president, and allowing them to take part in elections in the future, naturally, in open and competitive elections – and naturally if the citizens support such a proposal and amendment and say "Yes" at the All Russian vote on 22 April of this year.
>
> *(Putin, 2020)*

However, as the impact of COVID-19 in Russia became more apparent. President Putin was forced to postpone the 22 April 2020 "All Russian vote" on constitutional amendments.

Three hours after Putin's Annual Address, the Medvedev government resigned. President Putin appointed Mikhail Mishustin, former head of the Federal Tax Police, to serve as prime minister. Dmitry Medvedev was appointed deputy head of the Security Council 4 hours before the legal act establishing this new office was introduced into the State *Duma*. The speed of these changes and general surprise suggest advanced secretive preparation and planning, though as Putin subsequently admitted, Medvedev at least "knew what was going on." President Putin approved the new 31-member executive cabinet proposed by Mishustin on 21 January 2020. Approximately, 50 percent of posts were reshuffled, making the government more technocratic, younger (average age 50 rather than 53) and more professional, with new members having made careers during the Putin era running large-scale projects in the public sector. Change in leadership personnel in the "problem portfolios" – economic development, health, culture, and education – was taken to signal that these respective policy areas will receive greater attention. Putin did not indicate what his role would be within this new constitutional order, except to state that he would not stand for president in 2024 and that the amendments were not designed "to extend my term" (Herd, 2020).

The most popular proposals were those that seek to improve socioeconomic conditions and uphold traditional values. These have societal support. In addition, a number of more arcane and less relevant amendments from a societal perspective do address governance and have foreign and security policy implications. A key proposal reemphasizes Russia's commitment to state sovereignty by privileging domestic over international law. As protections for foreign investors are formally abolished, foreign direct investment will likely decrease. The reduction of such external dependencies increases the instrumental power of state-owned enterprises (SOEs) through personalized lobbying by informal networks, so consolidating the Putinite regime. Limits placed on citizens' ability to seek human rights protection through recourse to international courts and agreements suggest that improved relations with the West are not a priority. By implication, manipulations of Russian elections by the presidential administration, as in the State *Duma* elections in 2011, will continue, if not intensify.

Another proposal addresses Putin's long-standing goal of "nationalizing the elites" by limiting who can stand for office by tightening residency and citizenship regulations. Putin stated:

> Presidential candidates must have had permanent residence in Russia for at least twenty-five years [ten years in the 1993 Constitution] and no foreign citizenship or residence permit and not only during the election campaign but at any time before it too.
>
> *(Putin, 2020)*

Thus, one needs to be 35 years older and should have lived in Russia for 25 years consecutively. This effectively means that future presidential candidates who have studied abroad would be 55 years or older. This restriction impacts disproportionately on the wealthy educated expatriate and émigré Russian community (10.5 million, 7 percent of the total) who may be less loyal to and dependent on the state. This also disciplines the current elite. It makes any ambitious politician wary of spending any time in the West, while promoting the upward mobility of loyal dependent indigenous home-grown Putin protégés. The older generation with foreign connections and passports are eased out, making way for new statist corporatists (*gosudarstvenniki*) from 40 to 50 years old, keen to embrace new technologies and administrative reform, but not political liberalization.

The rest of the amendments adjusted the existing governance structures and positions Putin might occupy after 2024. Most attention has been on the State Council, a body that has existed since 2000 (and functioned in czarist times as an advisory body), but has never had any real power. This body currently meets once or twice a year and is composed of the speakers of the State *Duma* and Federation Council, heads of political parties, ministers, heads of corporations and banks, all regional governors, and some former governors appointed by the president. Under the proposed bill, the president will form the State Council (*Gossovet*) for the purposes of "coordinated functioning and interaction" of state bodies, and setting out "the main directions" of domestic and foreign policy. The details are unclear. One possibility is for the body to be a powerful inter-institutional policy arbitration platform able to discuss key strategic issues, a collective presidency or Central Committee of the Communist Party of the Soviet Union equivalent to the Security Council's Politburo 2.0. Or will it have a more limited weight in the system as a kind of informal chamber of the Russian regional and federal elites? All of Putin's counterparts will be present in the State Council, so it may become the key arena for backroom horse-trading and informal power games.

Why were these proposals announced on 15 January 2020, 20 years into the Putin era and 4 years before 2024? Why after the announcement were the proposed amendments rammed through the State *Duma* at such speed? Speculation over the reset and reconfiguration suggested a number of alternative directions of travel. Putin is an institutionalist and seeks to transform the regime that he created into an institutionalized state, involving increased checks and balances and limited pluralism to embed Putinism. This can as an unintended side effect liberalize and even democratize Russia's political system. This understanding, it turned out, was overly reliant on President Putin's words and stated intent, rather than actual actions and deeds.

The timing of the proposals could be indicative of Putin's predictive thinking. By 15 January 2020, Putin knew something the general public in Russia and internationally did not. His proposals to reform the constitution were, in hindsight, indicative that Putin's predictive thinking understood that things are going to get worse. Given that the COVID-19 outbreak occurred in 2019, and that first U.S. intelligence reports even in November 2019 were warning of the coming virus, it is more than likely that Russian intelligence services were reporting the same to President Putin. The coming disruption would be multifaceted: economic and societal depression; growth of protest potential; and a resultant decline in Putin's popularity, triggering elite infighting might all have been considerations. Putin may have realized that Russia economic cushion ($570 billion in the Bank of Russia and $124 billion in the National Welfare Fund) could not quell the political effects of COVID-19. Associated uncertainty raised the threat that his president-for-life project option would be derailed, hence the need for speed.

For authoritarian regimes, the absence of intra-elite political conflict is the greatest indicator of regime stability. Putin's constitutional changes represent a deep state "Fourth Way" approach to avoiding this pitfall. Putin seeks to avoid Stalin's first-way example in the early 1950s of no succession plan, resulting in a power struggle. The second way, nonfunctional stagnation and gerontocratization ("coffin carriage race") in the late 1970s and early 1980s are leapfrogged. Best of all from a Putin perspective, the third way offered by Gorbachev scenario (a projected Putin-led *perestroika* II) of uncontrolled liberalization and political breakdown in the late 1980s is sidestepped. The "Fourth Way" approach sees Putin redistribute leverage in his administration to avoid intra-elite conflict. He reformats the structure of his agency by reshuffling the government, changing the balance between branches of power and between formal and informal processes using administrative and legal mechanisms. He creates a power-transfer infrastructure that can manage the transfer of power from older elites made up of loyal personal friends from his generation (1970s), who find safe spots in the Federation Council or State Council, to younger elites represented by loyal professionals who came of age in the first decade of his rule (2000s) – the successor generation – who can take over the day-to-day running of the country (Herd, 2020).

It is clear in retrospect that the constitutional changes only consolidated an unambiguously authoritarian regime. President Putin enacted a constitutional *coup d'état* from above (a "state coup"), with more powers transferred to himself. Putin weakened further regional and municipal self-government and the independence of the judiciary. In 2021, Alexander Golts summarized the content of speeches Putin gave in St. Petersburg, noting that two connecting key messages are conveyed by all texts:

> First, every nation should live with the dictator who managed to seize power in that specific country. After all, any protest is definitely inspired by enemy secret services. And therefore, "It doesn't matter, no matter how it is, whoever says that some regime is suppressing something there, changes in any society will take place in accordance with the objective circumstances associated with the development of that society anyway. One should never interfere in this." Briefly then, let's allow authoritarian rulers to rule peacefully until the end of their days. That is, let's agree on general rules for those who, in fact, legally deny people's right to assemblies and marches (and punish those who risk peaceful protest), and those who consider this right to be unshakable.
>
> (Golts, 2021)

Alternative transfer for power pathways and scenarios

Russian Constitutional changes allow Putin to run again in 2024 until 2036. If we assume that Putin's control of the 'Putin Collective' is uncontested and institutions that form the 'Collective Putin' are very much subordinated to Putin's inner circle, Putin will safely manage re-election in 2024. Putin's will, capacity and interests are indeed strong enough to withstand reputational damage when he reset term limits, even though:

> if there is no Constitution, there is no Constitutional Court ['*na nyet, kak govoritsya, konstitutsionnogo suda nyet'*, a play on the saying '*na nyet i suda nyet'*] (what cannot be had must be done without.] If the old law becomes invalid, then the restrictions it imposed also become invalid. In the new state, the old Russian President will begin political life with a clean constitutional slate.
>
> *(Pastukhov, 2019)*

Second, it assumes that continuity reflects an alignment of the interests of Putin around the existential issue of his own personal security and elites through the combination practicality and emotion: deferred modernization, which enables dynasticism, and fear of losing control of a reform process. This suggests a more volatile and unpredictable foreign policy, marked by overt anti-Westernism. Legitimation of Putin's political authority is based on increased and controlled confrontation with the West. It assumes both a strengthened power position and implies that continuity in office is Putin's personal preference and not a default choice made out of fear of prosecution or influence of his entourage or even the 'Collective Putin.' Alternatively, and in principle, Putin could serve 2024–2030, change place with his prime minister (as he did with Medvedev in 2008) and return to the presidency for his new second presidential term between 2036 and 2042, or, indeed, his prime minister could be president for 2024–2036, with Putin beginning his new "first" term 2036–2042 and his "second" to 2048.

We can, though, identify a number of alternative scenarios to resetting the presidential clock and acting on it, as well as the assumptions that underpin them. This exercise allows us to better understand the distribution and practice of power in contemporary Russia today. We can posit a second key scenario: 'Putinism with Paramount Putin': *Densyaopinizatisitskya* Scenario (Pastukhov, 2019) or a 'Kazakh way forward.' Putin is prepared to exercise power from a position other than the president and prepares the ground through a smooth, slow, gradual transition. There are successful and unsuccessful precedents to act as a guide. Deng Xiaoping was paramount leader of the People's Republic of China (PRC) from 1978 until 1989, influencing third and fourth generations of CCP leaderships, though holding no official position. After his resignation in 1990, Lee Kuan Yew held the permanent Cabinet post of "First Minister" and then "Minister Mentor" until his death in 2015. More recently, Nursultan Nazarbayev's management of power transition and succession is characterized by him voluntarily giving up power mid-term (March 2019) in a carefully choreographed manner marked more by continuity in control of multiple levers of power than change. Nazarbayev remains Chair of the Security Council, leads the *Nur Otan* party, has the title of "First president of the Republic of Kazakhstan – Yelbasy" and receives immunity from prosecution, with his assets and family fully constitutionally protected (Solovyev et al., 2019; Golosov, 2019; Rogov, 2019, 23–26). However, Leonid Kuchma (Ukraine), Mikheil Saakashvilli (Georgia) and Sergz Sargysan (Armenia) all failed to retain power when attempting to create a new post-president position of power.

In the Russian context, the dynastic or hereditary option is not possible. The nearest to family Putin has is the FSB. Putin ensures that only he has control over the FSB and that there is no contender from within the FSB that could potentially lead Russia after Putin. This could suggest that a new combination of institutional interests will come to the fore and be dominant after Putin is no longer president and/or that Putin uses the FSB in his post-presidency as a bulwark and means to secure his own interests: immunity from prosecution, continued mobility (foreign travel), continued consumption habits (of family) and deployed in defense of or even against, if necessary, his selected successor.

On 14 February 2008, Putin stated: "During all these eight years, I have worked like a galley slave, from morning to night, and I have done this sparing no effort" (Kamakin, 2017). According to this scenario, by 2024, Putin relinquishes "galley slave" status. In effect, Putin solves the "2024 problem" through domestic policy changes. This scenario is based on three assumptions. The first is that Putin seeks to utilize constitutional change to rebalance power between the President and Prime Minister and boost the power of alternative nonelective collegial bodies such as the State Council and/or Security Council. The second assumption is that, given this, these bodies represent a good enough open-ended (no term limits) platform to dominate Russian foreign and security policy and strategic decision-making inside Russia. Medvedev as deputy chair of the Security Council can ensure some enhanced control over the security services. Third, we must assume that to effectively exercise veto power, Putin must maintain directing control of FSB, National Guard, prosecution bodies, Gazprom and the state budget and *obshchak*, a reserve shadow fund or black cash notebook that details who keeps what assets where and on behalf of whom.

The limitation of this 'Paramount Putin' scenario – and likely factors in Putin's calculus to advance the Constitutional changes in 2020 – is the creation of two different decision-making centers of power: the weak formal Putin-anointed successor and the strong Putin-centric informal institution. This raises the dual key problem of secondary control and the successor's dilemma, in that successors "rarely live up to the "patrons's expectations, and even more rarely to the expectations of the "close circle" and that this "creates the risks of a split within the executive coalition" (Rogov, 2019, 33, 38). Former Kremlin adviser Sergei

Pugachev addresses this problem, which resulted in confusion among the elite between 2008 and 2012:

> First people ran to Medvedev, and then they ran to Putin. People didn't understand. If you did something Putin gave you the go ahead to do, the next day Medvedev could reproach you. For people it's unacceptable when there are two presidents, or one and a half. It's very important for them to understand who the Tsar is.
>
> *(Belton, 2020)*

Thus, we can assume that it could only be managed by Putin from a position of absolute strength, with full control of the FSB and National Guard and prosecution bodies able to enforce decisions and so remain final arbiter. Putin also maintains the ability even outside the presidency to control the system of funding, which includes state budget allocations, reserve shadow funds ("Putin's *obshchak*" i.e. "the records as to who has kept assets under Putin's control, where, and what those assets are") and the obligations of "men of property" (Morozov, 2019). This masked or façade transition would also need to be acceptable to the elite and society. Given the State *Duma* is empowered, the ruling party would need to be popular and have legitimacy. We can also assume Putin has the will, capacity and interest in maintaining shadow control and is open to the possibility that being 78-year-old in 2030 he can come back as president, which in itself suggests that there is no single alternative person the inner circle recognizes as leader.

If this pathway can be managed, it provides Putin with the benefits of office without all the responsibilities and risks of blame. For this scenario to unfold, it would assume that Putin's charismatic-historical legitimacy has grown stronger, allowing him to stand above the 'Collective Putin' and even his own Collective and appeal directly to the people, over the heads of technocratic-managerial elites (Kolesnikov, 2019). Putin leaves the presidency with a caretaker rather than commander-in-chief as president. A variant of this option was exercised by Putin during the Medvedev presidency, 2008–2012, when 'Medvedism' was either unable or unwilling to be articulated as a governing philosophy or "Medvedev doctrine."

A third alternative power transition scenario can be marketed as 'Putinism with Partial Putin' or as an 'Enhanced Brezhnev' Collective Leadership Scenario. This scenario provides a second alternative that we can characterize as "impotent omnipotence." This is an inertia, drift and neo-stagnation scenario. Maduro-like, Putin is the hostage of the 'Collective Putin,' unable to stand down or maintain strategic autonomy from wider institutions, possibly combining with defectors from a weakened inner circle. Putin loses ground in domestic policy and is reduced to stranded figure, a weak symbolic president, with lukewarm popular support. Power slips from his network to state institutions. The 'Collective Putin' – the military-political apparatus of the long state – can emasculate Putin but chose to retain him as they cannot agree on the successor. They can lobby the Kremlin to promote their interests and control information streams Putin receives. Putin has the power to stop almost anything but not to implement and execute decisions. He is 'captive in the Kremlin,' a handmaiden/dependent puppet to/of powerful elite interests. As Gleb Pavlovskiy notes:

> Russia is in him. He is the symbol of Russia, he knows his own rating, he has his own internal yardstick for his greatness. But he cannot change anything – a symbol does not have the right to change. Vladimir Ilich Lenin did not leave the Mausoleum to build Communism. What can Putin do? Almost nothing. On the other hand, he can stop almost anything in the country. That is the final iteration of his power: He can bring everything to a standstill. But launching a process which will then develop spontaneously without him means handing power to someone.
>
> *(Davydov, 2018)*

Putin becomes an emblem, icon and brand of the system, a historical charismatic figure and the founder of the post-Soviet Russian state. He created the operating system but is now just a user. Putin's arbiter role is a function of his ability to guarantee decisions.

This scenario assumes that the logic of autocracy is harsh:

> The owner of one-man-rule resource sooner or later becomes hostage to his own "power vertical." He becomes hostage to those who are protecting him. To those who provide him with information. To those who prepare decisions for him. To those who transmit his thoughts. And lastly to those who feed him.
>
> *(Shevtsova, 2019a)*

This enhanced Brezhnev scenario resonating with the public. As economist Yevgeniy Gontmakher noted:

> Our public associates reforms with Putin. People are unhappy with living standards and corruption but believe that only he can address these issues. There is a fairly high level of confidence in the President as the person who embodies the public's concept of what kind of country this should be: It must be reckoned with in the international arena but at the same time its people must live well. People want an enhanced Brezhnev scenario.
>
> *(Mukhametshina and Bocharova, 2018)*

This scenario also assumes that Putin is partly politically incapacitated, having lost control of the state budget and *obshchak*, with increased overt and covert competition and conflicts between clans and factions over resources, particularly over the regulation of trade and investments with China. Control of regional cash-generating enterprises is transferred from the FSB/*siloviki* to inter-agency criminal groups backed by armed militias (Sokolov, 2019). Society is apathetic and believes that under this scenario things will at least not get worse. The divided 'Collective Putin' cannot agree with a successor and believe a successor's war would be too destabilizing. The 'Collective Putin' still needs Putin the man to personify power as President, and his icon role continues to be legitimizing. Moreover, in certain selected areas, Putin's personalized relationships are indispensable to the 'Collective Putin': Putin's *krysha* function for Kadyrov maintaining stability in the North Caucasus is a case in point. Thus, Putin can be weakened but not be discarded, while the inner circle becomes even more dependent on Putin for protection, banking on a combination of societal apathy, an acceptance that stagnation will not get worse.

A fourth scenario can be identified as "Putinism without Putin" or a "post-Stalin 1953–56" Scenario. In this scenario, Putin is a much weakened figure, akin to Yeltsin post-1996. He is no longer able even symbolically to occupy the post of president. His continuation in office has no utility for the 'Collective Putin' and the inner entourage, with everything to lose, unable to prevent the change. A new 'Collective Putin' leadership rules in the name of Putinism, allowing a stable transfer of power in absence of functioning independent institutions. A soft neo-Stalinist regime rules under Putin's portrait. It completely monopolizes the interpretation of Putin's legacy to the extent that Putin is forbidden from explaining or commenting on his own policy (this was the fate of the Yeltsin legacy and Yeltsin under Putin, though not Gorbachev under either). This behavior is understandable: "How else can it rule the country under the conditions of the confrontation with the West and the growing popular discontent? It has no other option but to exert pressure – on the rampant elite, among others." The new leader purges Putin's entourage, as Putin purged Yeltsin's, but Putin's immunity from prosecution is guaranteed in return for his compliance in the process. The collective departure of 'Putin's Collective' "will be the legitimization of the new regime which will draw the people's support from the overthrow of the old rulers" (Shevtsova, 2019b).

This scenario assumes that the stakeholders/inner circle and chiefs inside the system negotiate and bargain and can agree and find a consensus over the successor team or 'transition alliance'. This suggests that evenly balanced factional interests are a feature and that the military-political apparatus of the 'long state' is resilient and coherent enough to agree and strong enough to reach a consensus and impose a chosen collective leadership successors on the system. It also assumes that direct or collateral damage from anti-corruption campaigns eliminates Putin's network but strengthens 'Putinism.' Putinist benchmarks, particularly the restoration of Great Power status through confrontation with the West, though, form an enduring legacy that cannot be discarded along with Putin, just as Chiang Kai-shek's nationalist 'nine dash line' sets a benchmark of attainment for the five generations of CCP leadership in the PRC after 1949 with regard to territorial claims in the South China Sea. Thus, 'Putinism' is not Putin dependent, and a stable transfer of power can occur in the absence of functioning, independent institutions. In policy terms, we would likely see soft neo-Stalinist societal repression, rhetorically confrontational foreign policy but domestic public opinion and a weak economy limit aggressive action.

A fifth possible scenario appears and can be characterized as: "Neither Putin nor Putinism" or a "Liberal Dictatorship" Scenario. In this scenario, Putin is no longer president and Putinism delegitimized as governing philosophy following intra-elite catastrophic breakdown (akin to August 1991 and October 1993), characterized by missteps and a loss of control. An isolationist Russia determined to compete in a league of its own emerges. It is liberal in so far as it adopts pro-Western foreign policy to guarantee stable international relations environment. This context enables a strong prime minister to push ahead with structural economic and other fundamental reform in a variant of "modernization from above" under conditions of domestic repression.

This scenario is predicated on a sudden crisis that acts as a trigger for drastic change, such as Putin's physical incapacitation and an emergency scenario; an increasingly unpopular Putin but no elite consensus over successor and a 'war of protégés' and loss of control over 'anti-corruption' (i.e. fight for sphere of influences) arrests and prosecutions resulting in an intra-*siloviki* 'war of all against all' – an "intra-species struggle for survival" in which "Either you survive (jail your rival or leave the country in time and do not come back – delete as applicable), or they outlive (dismiss, jail, ruin) you" (Novoprudskiy, 2019). Anti-corruption efforts are understood by society as a clan fight to redistribute spheres of influence (Mukhametshina, 2019). The FSB remains the last bastion defending Putin (as with Beria in 1953) but is devoid of hard power in Moscow when push comes to shove. A broader and wider coalition of different power groups emerges and is consolidated enough through rejection of the *status quo* to unite and act effectively. The Putinite 'winner takes all system' is ultimately revealed to be a brittle construct.

Potential drivers of authoritarian top-down reform efforts could include a realization within the regime that the absence of reforms creates more instability than stability. Given the *siloviki* are rich, cynical and pragmatic and determined to hold onto power, if reform and change are the means to that end, then reform and change they will. In addition, fear of trade and technological dependence on China and the resultant loss of strategic autonomy could also provide an impetus. Russian pride, prestige, concern for status and power is a key motivating factor. Reform is a means to preserve Putinism and resist Xi-ism. Reform impulses might also be the byproduct of intra-elite struggles as the competitive goals of key factions clash: reforms enable a redivision of property and so become a means to enrichment and power. The generational dimension within the *siloviki*, too, is a potential driver of change. The current seniors have very different horizons than the 50-something-year-old colonels, who do the heavy lifting in the system, but still have up to twenty years in service and another decade or two in retirement to have to consider. These younger mid-level managerial strata are all members of the Russian middle class with stable incomes and predictable career trajectories. At the end, reform might be in response to the frictional pressure of gradual loss of active support in population. Reform provides a safety valve and new political narrative that can bind Putin's passive majority to the regime and encourage conformism. The performative politics involved in anti-corruption show trials, for example, and can be the answer to the perennial demand that "something must be done."

At the end, let us consider a sixth "Neither Putin nor Putinism" or "Populist People Power 2011–12" Scenario. As the specter of Bolotnaya and ghosts of August 1991 and October 1993 haunt elite nightmares, all efforts are made to preempt such an outcome. As retired Colonel Igor Korotchenko, editor in chief of the military magazine *Natsionalnaya Oborona* [National Defense] and member of the Ministry of Defense's Public Council, has argued that: "If a new Gorbachev comes along, then all of us are doomed" (Sargib, 2019). Anti-Maidan National Guard forces are strengthened, structural reform is deferred and entrenchment and stagnation and its attendant political stability are manageable, even if inefficient:

> In the eyes of the Kremlin, the opposition is a fifth column, opposition politics, including the exposure of cases of corruption, the fight for freedom of speech on the internet, is the continuation of war by other means, military action with the help of Trojan horses, the role of which can be played by the internet, among other things.
>
> *(Trudolyubov, 2019)*

In this scenario, the post-system change reconstituted decentralized state with weak president and strong parliament capable of undertaking structural economic reform. A rank nonsystemic charismatic populist outsider comes to power on a wave of popular demand for anti-corruption, anti-establishment sentiment, distrust of and opposition to old elites and for human rights, dignity and justice. Examples of nonsystem liberal populists, capable of appealing to youth and making a moral case for power can be found: Volodomyr Zelensky ('Servant of the People' TV Show) in Ukraine won the first round presidential election on 31 March 2019 and anti-corruption campaigner Zuzana Čaputová (Progressive Slovakia) who was elected president on 30 March 2019. The challenger's outsider status/ lack of past makes him/her invulnerable and is supported by internal constitutional centrists, and left-liberal Russian "opposition from a distance" is a useful resource. Navalny is the obvious candidate for a "Russian Zelenskyy" (Makarkin, 2019), and precedent featuring Zhirinovskiy's trickster/jester archetype role as a systemic opposition figure in the 1990s is there: "But in our politics all the clowns are usually vicious" (Sennikov, 2019).

This scenario assumes that the 'Collective Putin' power vertical is brittle and 'Putin's Collective' a situational alliance (akin to Poroshenko's network in Ukraine). It also assumes that a deteriorating economy and anti-corruption campaign lead society to see all establishment power as corrupt. The regime criminalized not only political, but also civic activity. As a result, civil society is politicized, with Navalny a symbol of moral resistance to the regime. A broken social contract and high levels of corruption drive the opposition and animate civil society protest. Society is ready for a radical democratic breakthrough (Åslund and Gozman, 2021).

However, as Russians are habituated to the circumstances and rules of an authoritarian political regime, street-protest-led democratic breakthrough is highly unlikely. Rational conformism results in the Putin majority voting for Putin-approved candidates. The managers of the authoritarian system, including or above all the *siloviki*, do not fear a radical democratic breakthrough resulting from mass protest but worry about the accumulated friction and costs imposed on them in their role as managers of stability. They feel embattled and defensive and so embrace entrenchment. Managers want to hold on to power and money (not just to control but to continue *own* "resources") at all costs.

The role of the mid-level bureaucracy could prove decisive. In the late Stalinist period of 1950–53, repression and terror enabled upward mobility. In the late Brezhnev era, instead of a 3-year wait before becoming secretary of a district committee or secretary of the party committee at a large factory, the waiting period was 18–21 years. Thus, the bureaucracy supported *perestroika* when Gorbachev championed it. However, as soon as Gorbachev effectively purged the gerontocracy, and upward mobility was restored, support among the bureaucracy for wider reform "evaporated," undercutting the legitimacy of the new government (Khvostunova, 2021). As Nikolai Petrov notes when considering the potential for democratic breakthrough in Russia:

> This begs the question of how realistic it is to expect the emergence of advanced democratic institutions after Putin leaves office, when there are currently no foundations to speak of . . . in order for this 'beautiful Russia of the future' to emerge, the country will need a new professional cadre of elite bureaucrats and policymakers, along with the resources for their rapid mobilization. The conditions needed to achieve this are not present in today's Russia, and it will therefore take a long time to develop and establish new elites from scratch. This is a far cry from the Russia of the *perestroika* era under Mikhail Gorbachev, when new elites clamouring for change were emerging from within the old system.
>
> *(Petrov, 2021)*

In short, Putin has completed the nationalization of elites, technocrats are beholden to him and are his hostages. As a result, an elite conspiracy in the shape of a 'palace coup' against Putin is not possible. Indeed, as the breakup of the FSB would be one of the first reforms in a democratic breakthrough scenario, Bortnikov, Ivanov and Patrushchev (current and former FSB directors) will resist any regime change until the end.

Conclusions: scenario insights

This chapter first noted President Putin had reset the presidential clock in January 2020, and this demonstrated his strength and ability to dictate. The chapter then examined other alternative scenarios, related them to Russian and Soviet historical experience, highlighted their core characteristics and identified the assumptions that would underpin their coming to pass: second, 'Putinism with Paramount Putin': *Densyaopinizatisitskya* Scenario or a 'Kazakh way forward'; third, 'Putinism with Partial Putin' or as an 'Enhanced Brezhnev' Collective Leadership Scenario; fourth, 'Putinism without Putin" or a post-Stalin 1953–56 Scenario'; fifth, 'Neither Putin nor Putinism', or a 'Liberal Dictatorship' Scenario; sixth, 'neither Putin nor Putinism' or 'Populist People Power 2011–12' Scenario.

The first (reset Constitutional clock) and second ('Paramount Putin') scenarios are clearly Putin-dictated, and their coming to pass would suggest continuities in strategic culture, operational code, including strategic behavior. Given the third ('Partial Putin') and fourth ('Putinism without Putin') alternative scenarios are 'Collective Putin' ('chiefs inside-the-system', regional heads, Federal Assembly) or selectorate-led scenarios. If Russia's power transition operated by this logic, then this would suggest strategic culture continuity but operational code changes, with elites in scenario four being paralyzed and divided, and in five united and decisive. The radical rupture from the past scenarios five ('Liberal Dictatorship') and six ('Populist People Power') suggest that both strategic culture and operational code change, along with the current regime and political system.

In terms of possible direct observable and indirect proxy indicators and how they related to the alternative scenarios, some indicators can fit multiple scenarios, some are scenario-specific and some appear in all but with different effects. Energy prices are "central to the Russian economy and political regime" ("Energy Dependence", 2019). Gazprom profits service the elites closest to Putin, while the price of oil is critical to system stability: the government cannot maintain domestic order if the price is at $25–30 per barrel (pb), fitting radical change scenarios. The 'Collective Putin' remains more dominant with prices around $30-$50 pb, in line with elite-managed transitions. Putin remains the central lynchpin of the system in control with oil at $50 plus pb, as suggested by the first scenarios outlined. Decentralization elements characterize most scenarios. Disruptive unknowns include regional debt defaults, technological breakthroughs that can undercut Russia's commodities export business model and political blunders (such as the Navalny Novichok-botched assassination attempt).

Putin or selectorate-controlled scenarios appear more likely than uncontrolled ones, as control represents a steady state or inertia model, an extrapolation of present practice onto the future. Putin views the preservation of the balance he has created as the key to long-term stability. This logic promotes

> a form of leadership that relies on a consensus among the key stakeholders rather than having a single individual directing policy. Doing this effectively

though requires not just changing the law but also changing political culture and thus needs a certain foundation of stability, rather than a system built around one man's connections and charisma. This has meant a counterintuitive extension of Putin's time in office to facilitate transition and reform towards a post-Putin era.

(Hawn and Tack, 2021)

As the Constitutional amendments passed, compliant elites will bake in the notion that Putin continues in power and make this factor a fixed feature of future planning and calculus. Continuity of Putin in power suggests continuity in foreign policy. The scenarios in which Putin and "Putin's Collective" is paramount in foreign affairs and controls the strategic agenda and the "Collective Putin" has a more enhanced role in running domestic affairs would appear best to replicate current practice. 'Putin' and 'Putinism' discourse masks an underlying competition between power exercised through networks ("Putin's Collective") and institutions (the "Collective Putin").

Putin came to power in 2000 aged 48 and will be 83 years old by 2036. By extending his time in power, Putin has extended the transition to the future post-Putin period:

In private conversations in the Kremlin they say that Putin is not going to be a lifelong president and is only waiting for a moment when the transit of supreme power will not threaten the country's stability . . . Will such a perfect moment really come?

(Rostovsky, 2021)

Putin has, in effect, postponed the future. The challenge for Putin in the forever-present will be to maintain domestic balances between the normative state, para-statal entries and oligarchic groupings. As the link between internal and external is blurred and as Russia's global reach provides a safety valve to reduced domestic infighting over resources, the role of Russia's global reach will increasingly not simply shore up Russian influence over its neighborhood, but also become a battlefield between different competing internal actors. 'Putin' and 'Putinism' in different combinations, either by the presence or the absence of these terms, will dominate discussions on succession. No other individual, governing philosophy and ideological construct or doctrine, is on offer as an alternative. Indeed, alternatives are criminalized.

Selected bibliography

Åslund, Anders, and Leonid Gozman. 2021. "Russia after Putin: How to Rebuild the State." *The Atlantic Council.* February 24, 2021. www.atlanticcouncil.org/in-depth-research-reports/report/russia-after-putin-report/.

BBC Monitoring, 2021. *Rossiya 1 TV*, Moscow, in Russian. June 30, 2021.

Belton, Catherine. 2020. "Exclusive: Former Kremlin Insider Recounts Putin's Moves to Retain Power." July 29. www.reuters.com/article/us-russia-putin-succession-exclusive-idUSKCN24U1O2.

Davydov, Ivan. 2018. "Ivan Davydov Interview with Gleb Pavlovskiy. Everything Happening in The World Is Seen as a Special Operation by an Enemy." *The New Times.* May 3, 2018.

Dubnov, Arkady. 2019. "Kazakhstan: What Is Nazarbayev's Transition Plan About?" *Al Jazeera Online.* March 31, 2019.

"Energy Dependence." 2019. In *Russia Scenarios 2030,* 9–21. Washington, DC: Free Russia Foundation.

Golosov, Grigoriy. 2019. "How to Prepare To Leave in Order To Remain." *Vedomosti.* March 21, 2019.

Golts, Alexander. 2021. "Forcible Deportation into the World of Vladimir Putin." *Yezhednevny Zhurnal Website.* June 7, 2021. http://ww2.ej.ru/?a=note&id=36189.

Hawn, Jeff, and Sim Tack. 2021. "Time to Think About a World Without Putin: The Russian Leader is Contemplating His Mortality – As Are His Backers." *Foreign Policy.* February 10, 2021. https://foreignpolicy.com/2021/02/10/world-without-putin-russia-what-is-next/.

Herd, Graeme. 2020. "COVID-19, Russian Power Transition Scenarios, and President Putin's Operational Code." *051. Security Insights.* Garmisch-Partenkirchen: George C. Marshall European Center for Security Studies. www.marshallcenter.org/en/publications/security-insights/covid-19-russian-power-transition-scenarios-and-president-putins-operational-code.

Herd, Graeme, and David Lewis. 2019. "Collective Putin or Putin's Collective and Transition Pathways: Assumptions and Implications for Russian Strategic Behavior. George C. Marshall European Center for Security Studies Discussion Paper." George C. Marshall European Center for Security Studies: Garmisch-Partenkirchen.

Kamakin, Andrey. 2017. "Putin in 2018: Who Might Replace the President." *Moskovsky Komsomolets.* May 29, 2017. www.mk.ru/politics/2017/05/28/putin-v-2018-godu-kto-mozhet-zamenit-prezidenta.html.

Khvostunova, Olga. 2021. "Lev Gudkov: 'The Unity of the Empire in Russia Is Maintained by Three Institutions: The School, the Army, and the Police'." *Institute of Modern Russia.* May 3, 2021. https://imrussia.org/en/opinions/3278-lev-gudkov-.

Kolesnikov, Andrei. 2019. "Putin's Art of the Purge." *Moscow Carnegie Center.* April 15, 2019. https://carnegie.ru/2019/04/15/putin-s-art-of-purge-pub-78893.

Krasheninnikov, Dmitriy. 2019. "Why Dmitriy Medvedev Is Not Nervous Before Going to the State Duma: Premier's Distrust Rating Rose to Record High, But His Weakness Is His Strength." *Vedomosti.* April 17, 2019.

Luzin, Pavel. 2019. "Why Corporations Are the Kremlin's Best Friends." *The Moscow Times.* September 2, 2019. www.themoscowtimes.com/author/pavel-luzin.

Makarkin, Aleksey. 2019. "Phenomenon Z: Could Russians Vote for Unexpected Candidate." *RBK.* April 8, 2019.

Morozov, Alexander. 2019. "Succession after Putin's Unexpected Death." In *Russia Scenarios 2030,* 165–170. Washington, DC: Free Russia Foundation.

Mukhametshina, Yelena. 2019. "One-Third of Russians Are Satisfied with High-Ranking Officials Arrests, But Only a Quarter of Respondents Consider Them a Manifestation of a Real Fight Against Corruption." *Vedomosti.* May 7, 2019.

Mukhametshina, Yelena, and Svetlana Bocharova. 2019. "Half of Russians Wish to See Putin as President Beyond 2024." *Vedomosti*. June 18, 2019. www.vedomosti.ru/politics/articles/2018/06/19/773128-putina-prezidentom.

Novoprudskiy, Semen. 2019. "Spektr Press: You Jail Them or They Will Jail You. Why Former Minister Abyzov Came Back, and How His Arrest Exposes Russia's Domestic Policy." *Ekho Moskvy*. March 27, 2019.

Pastukhov, Vladimir. 2019. "The Year of Constitutional Fantasies: How Can What Does Not Exist Be Changed?" *Ekho Moskvy*. January 8, 2019. https://mbk-news.appspot.com/sences/god-konstitucionnyx-fantazij/.

Pavlovsky, Gleb. 2019. "Twenty Years of Vladimir Putin: Leader's Transformation. Danger of Counting on Leadership." *Vedomosti*. August 20, 2019.

Petrov, Nikolai. 2021. "What Comes after Putin Must Be Better than Putin'in." In *Myths and Misconceptions in the Debate on Russia*, 96–100. London: Chatham House.

"Putin Says Russian People to Determine His Successor." 2018. *BBC Monitoring*. June 7, 2018. https://monitoring.bbc.co.uk/product/c1dpbq1w.

Putin, Vladimir. 2020. "Presidential Address to the Federal Assembly." *President of Russia*. March 10, 2020. http://en.kremlin.ru/events/president/news/65418.

Rogov, Kirill. 2019. *A New Prince: Non-Democratic Transfer of Power in the Post-Soviet Space*. Washington, DC: Free Russia. www.4freerussia.org/wp-content/uploads/sites/3/2019/06/NON-DEM_web_eng.pdf.

Rostovsky, Mikhail. 2021. "Temptation by Volodin: will Putin Fall into a Political Trap?" *MK*. July 6, 2021. www.mk.ru/politics/2021/07/06/iskushenie-volodinym-popadet-li-putin-v-politicheskiy-kapkan.html.

Sargib, Aleksandr. 2019. "The Most Important Thing Is That After Putin, There Is No New Gorbachev!" *Argumenty Nedeli*. February 13, 2019.

Sennikov, Yegor. 2019. "The Transfer of Power To a Successor Is Impossible." *Republic*. April 10, 2019. https://republic.ru/posts/93481.

Shevtsova, Liliya. 2019a. "They Are Stuck." *Ekho Moskvy*. January 9, 2019.

———. 2019b. "The Collective Putin." *Ekho Moskvy Online*. January 9, 2019.

Sinitsyn, Andrey. 2019. "Spring Planting Plan: Why Does the Abyzov Case Seem Political?" *Republic*. March 28, 2019.

Sokolov, Denis. 2019. "Russia as a Proxy Superpower for China." In *Russia Scenarios 2030*, 53–61. Washington, DC: Free Russia Foundation.

Solovyev, Vladimir, Aleksandr Konstantinov, and Kirill Krivosheyev. 2019. "First of All Those Alive. Nursultan Nazarbayev Takes Up Post of Lifelong Leader of Kazakhstan." *Kommersant Online*. March 20, 2019.

Trudolyubov, Maksim. 2019. "War by Other Means – Russia's Chances Were of at Least Partially Filling the Political and Strategic Voids Now Being Left by the United States." *Vedomosti*. March 20, 2019.

Vinokurov, Andrey. 2017. "Democracy May Become a Phenomenon of the Past." *Gazeta. Ru*. October 29, 2017. www.gazeta.ru/politics/2017/10/29_a_10962296.shtml.

Wood, Andrew. 2018. "Dilemmas Old and New: Change in Post-Putin Russia?" *The American Interest*. November 28, 2018. www.the-american-interest.com/2018/11/28/change-in-post-putin-russia/.

———. 2019. "Putinist Rule Minus Putin?" *The American Interest*. July 29, 2019. www.the-american-interest.com/2019/07/29/putinist-rule-minus-putin/.

9

CONCLUSIONS

Putin's paradoxes, institutional subcultures
and world order

Introduction

This book began by asking: do we have a Putin problem or a Russia problem? Is
Putin an anomaly or is he a characteristically Russian leader, a product of its history? To answer this question, we introduced and applied the concepts of political
and strategic culture; operational code with their micro-foundational, meso and
macro dimensions and competitive goals of contemporary institutional actors.
Although these concepts do not seamlessly map one onto the other, they do provide us with an analytical filter and lens through which to better appreciate and
characterize the complexity of factors that account for Russian strategic behavior.
Chapter 1 began with Winston Churchill's challenge: on the eve of the Second
World War, Churchill argued that the master key to understanding Russia action
was Russian national interest. This book argues that by conflating personalistic
regime survival with national security, Putin ensures that contemporary Russian
national interest as expressed in Russian action, that is its strategic behavior, is the
synthesis of its long-standing imperial strategic and Putin's own particular operational code.

As we reflect on the analysis of the previous eight chapters, it is clear that
President Putin focuses on "historical Russia" as a foundational legitimation of
his own political authority (charismatic and historical legitimation). Putin clearly
identifies and then champions an official historical narrative that promotes ethnonationalism within a civilizational triune state concept. The need to promote
continuity, consistency and order and avoid the "ontological insecurity" and
"ontological anxiety" associated with dislocation, trauma and tragedy are central
drivers of Putinism. Unfortunately, this study demonstrates that a poor understanding of history leads to poor policy prescriptions. Putin identifies two "time
bombs" planted by Lenin and Stalin in the Soviet period – Constitutional pro-
visions and the over-dependence on the state of only one unifying source (the
Communist Party) – which exploded in 1991, triggering "the greatest geopolitical tragedy of the 20th century." However, and following Putin's logic, has he
himself, as a system-forming figure and founder of the post-Soviet Russian state,
unwittingly planted ticking "time bombs" within his Putinist project?

DOI: 10.4324/9780429261985-9

To answer this question, let us first look to the nature of Putin-centric leadership: the results of this governance as expressed in Russian foreign and security policymaking and implementation and the implications of this for the policy responses of Russia's adversaries. We can unpick these contradictions and highlight the paradoxes embedded in the fabric of Putinism, with the understanding that 'Putinism' can only be considered sustainable if Putin's regime can manage the destabilizing gaps and contradictions that it itself generates. Second, we can use this context to more fully assess their effects on the competitive goals of sub-institutional actors in Russia and how situationally or ideologically they are wedded to the current status quo. At the end, which world order paradigm best reflects the realities of Russian strategic behavior – that is the sum of Putin's operational code and Russia's imperial strategic culture?

The prince and pauper: power, crises and Putin's paradoxes

Putin instrumentalizes history to suggest that Putinism provides an integrative and unifying field theory of Russian past, present and future. In reality, and as Lilia Shevtsova argues, Putin's Russia survives by paradox as Putin is able to convert "weakness into strength, tactics into strategy, exceptions into rules, defeats into victory and a civilizational enemy into a resource for survival" (Goble, 2017). When President Putin was asked the film he would recommend to somebody trying to understand Russia among *Doctor Zhivago* or the *The Godfather,* he responded:

> "I do not know. You see, we have a famous poem, which goes: "You will not grasp her with your mind or cover with a common label, for Russia is one of a kind – believe in her, if you are able." But the Russian culture is multifaceted and diverse. That is why if you want to understand, to feel Russia, you should certainly read books – Tolstoy, Chekhov, Gogol, Turgenev – listen to Tchaikovsky's music and watch our classical ballet.
>
> *("Russia," 2016)*

The more the regime and political system bases its legitimation of political authority to its adherence to traditional orthodox beliefs, norms and values, whether religious or based on Russian governance, the more the paradoxes are generated that undercut the central narrative. Acceding to this logic, feeling is believing, and seeing is illusion.

Indeed, in Putin's narrative "affiliation to Russia is not the result of deliberate choice but the result of a struggle or achievement of a dream," thus Putin "can create any nation" to his liking "because a genuine Russian nation does not exist" (Kashin, 2016). President Putin

> embodies the hopes of all groups and strata, he is the chief liberal, and imperialist, and nationalist, and socialist – turns Putin in the eyes of many people

into the chief reformer as well. The impression created is that this would be the most desirable and convenient of the scenarios for everyone: changing everything without changing anything, without sacrificing anything, and without risking anything, and without making any effort. The regime will change itself! The problem is just that there is no way that all of this will happen.

(Volkov and Kolesnikov, 2017)

Presidential advisor Vladislav Surkov suggests that Russia is not a third civilization between Asia and Europe, but:

Rather, a double and dual one. One that incorporates both East and West. Both European and Asiatic at the same time, and therefore neither entirely Asiatic nor entirely European. Our cultural and geopolitical affiliation is reminiscent of the shifting identity of someone born in a mixed marriage. He has relatives everywhere, but nowhere is he a native. At home among aliens, and an alien among his own people. Understanding everyone, but understood by no one. A half-caste, a metis, some sort of freak. Russia is a West-East half-caste country. With its two-headed statehood, hybrid mentality, intercontinental territory, and bipolar history, it is – as befits a half-caste – charismatic, talented, beautiful, and lonely.

(Surkov, 2018)

This characterization echoes President Putin's 7 May 2021 Victory Day speech in which he claimed that Russia "alone" defeated Nazi Germany and ended the Great Patriotic War.

The words orthodox and paradox share the same Greek root – *Doxia* – that is common belief or popular opinion. Orthodox beliefs are those that are self-evident and generally accepted, while adherence to paradox is belief in apparently self-contradictory or logically unacceptable conclusions. One type of paradox, the Liars Paradox, for example, highlights the differences between word and deed, and its essence captured in these two generic examples: "Impossibility is not a word in my vocabulary" or "This statement is false." The power of paradox is not unlimited and should not be overstated. As a corrective, we can acknowledge the Bonini Paradox: when we model a complex system, the more complete the model becomes, the less we understand it. Similarly, no conceptual analysis can be both fully correct and fully informing: the paradox of "less is more" holds, and the Socratic Paradox of "All I know is that I know nothing" comes into play.

Paradoxes are not unique to Russia, but we can surmise that the peculiar nature of Russia's paradoxes is particular to Russia. After all, Russian paradoxes are generated by Russian elite–society and center–periphery relations, the interplay of structure and agency, the need for a discursive 'Other', how Putin exercises power and how Putinism is understood and accounts for Russian strategic behavior. Because Russian paradoxes are the sum of Russian strategic and political culture, they highlight underlying truths or the inner logic and functioning of the Putin system, which we may not otherwise realize. To identify a Russian paradox is to declare what we consider as contradictory. This in and of itself can help us identify our core assumptions and cognitive biases and so promote critical thinking. For example Michael McFaul argued that Putin promoted positive economic agendas but a negative political agenda (McFaul, 2004). This is a paradox only if we assume Russia is seeking to consolidate a market-democratic political order but entirely logical and rational if we understand Putin to be developing an oligarchic capitalist authoritarian system, albeit under the banner of liberal reforms. Richard Sakwa rightly points to the "democracy paradox" of the 1990s that is now at the heart of Putinite governance: "The self-proclaimed guardians of democracy become its executioners" (Sakwa, 2020, 4, 2021). Another actual paradox: the Kremlin is the most censored territory in the Russian Federation (Davydov, 2014). The presidential administration certainly creates discourse and narratives in state media, which become very powerful filters that then control the flow of the type of information that reaches the Kremlin.

In terms of leadership, is President Putin an amalgam of absolutist *Tsar* and autocratic General Secretary? Or, after 21 years, does President Putin become the function of every other Russian leader – a symbol, an emblem and icon, a historic figure who created the operating political system, but is now just a user? Is he a leader lacking strategic autonomy, a defenseless captive in the Kremlin, hostage to his entourage and nominal subordinates to implement 'his' agenda? Does his "impotent omnipotence" become the greatest threat to the regime?

Putin can be understood as the embodiment of both conditions, if we accept that Icarus-like, Putin is a victim of his own success: the more Putin appears to strengthen the power vertical, the more dependent the system of power becomes on Putin's personalism, the weaker the system becomes (Goble, 2018). Putin is a strong ineffective leader, one with formidable near dictatorial formal powers and undisputed political preeminence as decisive decision-maker. However, if we examine what Putin chooses to do with these powers, Putin performs badly even when compared to the 14 other former Soviet republics in terms of government effectiveness, rule of law, corruption and inequality. This suggests "an absence or failure of leadership rather than strong leadership," and, as a result, Putin appears an "average leader at best" (Wilson, 2021, 93; Frye, 2021). More broadly, and as noted in Chapter 8, Putin and "Putin's Collective" operating through networks appear paramount in foreign affairs and in control of the strategic agenda, but the effects since 2014 of "strategic action" and "distraction" are narrowing his options and constraining his strategic autonomy, just as stakes are being raised. The institutionalized "Collective Putin" has a more enhanced role in running domestic affairs, with Putin more as Chairman of the Board, striving to avoid a vote of no confidence, not least in the September 2021 *Duma* election.

A Potemkin-like facade exists in which the gap between the rhetoric of an imagined ideal structure projected in state propaganda which is communicated to the population daily and the reality of an increasingly dysfunctional hollowed out system is apparent. The elite pretend to give meaningful orders, bureaucracy pretends to implement them and society pretends that policies achieve goals. As Glunaz Sharafutdinova notes, modern autocrats "are modern because they modernize . . . the tools of political communication and persuasion" (Sharafutdinova, 2021). In terms of societal support, the 'Crimean Majority' consolidated around military-patriotic mobilization ("Making Russia Great Again") and ultraconservatism is buoyed by the belief that "Putin can fix things" and security-service and state media supported passive conformism. Indeed, as Svetlana Alexievich, a Belarusian Literature Nobel Laureate, highlights a psychological dimension, noting that "there is a collective Putin, consisting of some millions of people who do not want to be humiliated by the West. There is a little piece of Putin in everyone" (Donadio, 2016). Indeed, and remarkably, Russians under 25 years old – 'Generation P', millennial and post-millennial youngsters or 'Puteens' – whose outlook and beliefs are most shaped by Putin's rule appear to be the most conservative and reactionary pro-Putin group. Vladislav Surkov notes that: "An overdose of freedom is lethal to a state. Anything that is medicine can be poison. It is all about the dosage" (Foy, 2021). This Orwellian construct ("Freedom is Slavery"), perhaps unintentionally, implies that the Russian people are the addicts and users of the system and Putin their drug supplier, dealer and systems operator, able to course correct and adjust the dosage to boost collective belonging, pride and self-esteem.

After 2018 when Putin's popularity began to decline, already mechanisms were in place to ensure that no political alternative (*bezalternativnost*) could exist in Russia: real electoral competition, institutional channels and mechanisms to articulate popular interests were barren shells and moribund. The imitation of a democratic order occurs through utilizing administrative measures and bureaucratic censorship to control who stands in self-declared "democratic" elections, who monitors them and so the outcome. "Systemic" or imitative and controlled loyal opposition was a central and deliberate design feature, as the ubiquitous Surkov notes: "When I started my work in 2000, I suggested a very simple system to bring law and order. We split the opposition into systemic and non-systemic. And what is systemic opposition? That is one that obeys the rules, laws and customs" (Foy, 2021). Through 2020–21, the criminalization of 'non-systemic opposition' (banned political parties and movements) in Russia continued, with tendencies to terrorism as an additional charge. Thus, we see that as Putin's popularity declines, the more Putin's conformist majority and the elite fear instability and a succession crisis, and so the more they cleave to Putin. While Russia's state-controlled media projects Putin as the *sine qua non* of stability, in line with the autocratic and absolutist logic of "No Putin, no Russia," Putin exercises leadership through the weaponization of uncertainty and ambiguity. To that end he leverages deinstitutionalization and de-globalization processes, the selective application of the rule of law and fermentation of administrative battles to prevent intra-elite cohesion and the potential consolidation of actors against him. The weaker he appears, the longer he survives and maintains his player status. But as David Lewis notes, "the rule through the exception – a willingness to break the rules – challenged the very order that the authorities sought to achieve" (Lewis, 2020, x).

'Putinomics' is characterized by a pathological relationship between notions of development and stability. In 2017, Finance Minister Anton Siluanov expressed his opposition to the buildup of defense and security expenditure that constitutes more than 30 percent of the budget: "We produce a tank, but then you will not be using it for plowing and for bringing in marginal product. It will not bring in any additional GDP. The obsession with military expenditure in 1987–1989, to which was added the fall in oil prices, led to the state's collapse" (Khachaturov, 2017). Yevgeniy Gontmakher noted that it shapes Russian modernization and development choices and pathways:

> There is development on European lines – evolutionary and by means of reform. The second option is development of the mobilization type. It is being declared that we are in a hostile encirclement, surrounded by all sorts of foes that want to tear off a piece of our land. And all spheres of life, including the economy, are switching to a military track. This is not war, but a besieged camp.
> *(Polovinko, 2017)*

Russia once again experiences its imperial paradox of a "bloated state of emaciated people" (Kozeyrev, 1992).

However, the greater the militarization the more difficult it is to maintain combat potential without increases to the military budget, and so the greater the risk of social explosion. A vicious and self-defeating logic is at work: Putin and his elite desire security from external intervention and stability; stability is guaranteed by a loyal elite running and owning Russia's strategic assets. Thus, while structural reform would destabilize the elite and so Russia; a lack of structural reform creates long-term economic decline and so instability. The elite's autonomy is compromised by personal assets and falsified income declarations, but the informal elite social contract of 'loyalty in return for pillage' is under strain as opportunities for pillage are reduced. Society can endure, barter and adopt self-help survivalist strategies, but the social contract based on rising living standards in exchange for the unaccountability of corrupt elites has been replaced by socioeconomic decline in return for geo-strategic grandeur.

Might authoritarian enthusiasm pose a greater danger to the regime than open opposition? After all,

> authoritarianism, which has neither development, nor powerful patrons, nor its own eschatology, will face difficult times. Resilience is undermined not so much by the rebels from below, as by their own functionaries, tired of taking risks and eager to finally exchange their loyalty for peace and safety. It was, for example, this fatigue of the *nomenklatura* from political "voluntarism" that cost Nikita Khrushchev his power.
> *(Sakhnin, 2021)*

This scenario extrapolates from the present, suggesting that conditions deteriorate, but Russia is resilient in the face of gradual system erosion. Stability plateaus are followed by mini-crises (e.g. Navalny protests), and short-term responses to manage them accelerate the process.

Since 2007, Putin's Russia has actively looked to destabilize neighboring states in order to stabilize itself, to gain Crimea only to lose an alienated Ukraine (and Poland) and undermine the notion of pan-Slavism as an alternative to Western-ism. Not only is Russia's self-description, self-understanding and national narrative not possible without Ukraine, but also without Ukraine Russia's integrative projects in post-Soviet space lack critical mass (Teslya, 2018). Continued negotiations between Russia and Belarus over integration only make more visible and public the obstacles to union. In an era of confrontation between Russia and the West, the more isolated Russia becomes, the greater the military-strategic alliance and psychological significance of Minsk as a stable and predictable ally for Moscow, the more Russia provides economic and politico-security support to maintain the *status quo* (Melyantsou, 2021). Russian trade embargoes against Georgia, Ukraine and Moldova, which are intended to dissuade them from joining the EU Association Agreement, decrease their trade dependence on Russia and so reduce Moscow's leverage over them.

Russia conceives of itself as a great power, with Moscow as the controlling civilizational center within a geopolitical bloc, a sphere of influence that encapsulates historical Russia. As such, Russia has the historical duty to acts as the "sword and the shield" within this space. Russia determines who is friend and who is enemy, the extent to which third-party activity (no foreign military bases) can occur and the strategic orientation of lesser-controlled states within the sphere, including pro-western economic union (EU) or military alliances (NATO). Russia justifies its assertion of regional hegemony with three core arguments. First, hegemony aligns with its historical role, self-identity and ontological security. Second, spheres of influence rather than cooperation and interdependence create balance, predictability and stability in international relations. Third, and paradoxically, hegemony at regional level is necessary to counter U.S. hegemony at a global level. Thus, Russia assets its own absolute sovereignty within its sphere of influence while simultaneously both enforcing a doctrine of limited sovereignty for lesser states and positing itself as the champion of the Westphalian ideal on global stage (Deyermond, 2016; Lewis, 2020).

Russia is caught in a confrontation syndrome in which an aggressive Russian foreign policy is an expression of weakness not strength. Its manufactured conflict with the West and manufactured consent at home give the regime legitimacy and allow the Kremlin to position Russia as "the only real European country, the protector of old European values and traditions, rejecting the notion of multiculturalism" (Shlapentokh, 2021). Forceful disruption abroad enables stabilization at home. Russia projects itself as a militarily able and strategically relevant, autonomous and exceptional great power not a *pariah* or rogue state. As such, Russia is a state deserving respect, acknowledgment and recognition at a new

Yalta-type great power conference in which a Russian sphere of influence would be formally recognized, functioning as a buffer zone to minimize direct borders with the West. Paradoxically, though, "the assertion of exceptionality as the basis of sovereignty – and therefore of political order – has the effect of undermining order in the normal sphere, in everyday judicial processes, business transactions and security operations" (Lewis, 2020, 219). When the exception becomes the norm, the world is turned upside down.

However, the ways in which Russia instrumentalizes supposed threats (liberalism, democracy, rules-based order) and cultivates traditionalism generate insecurities and vulnerabilities within Russia, which undermine the regime. Russian elite anti-Americanism is not a temporary phenomenon but critical to Russia's center of gravity defense narrative of "Besieged Fortress." Indeed, "Putin and his anti-Western rhetoric remain popular in Russia precisely because he expresses a view widely held domestically (and reinforced by ceaseless anti-Western propaganda)" (Petrov, 2021). Putin has proved to be a master at exploiting the dominant phobias, expectations, myths and emotions of *Homo sovieticus* (Gretskiy, 2021), mainly because he himself shared them and so could ride "the wave of the public disorientation, frustration, resentment, and diffused aggression" (Khvostunova, 2021). Putin legitimizes contemporary centralized political order and power in Russia and scapegoats' pluralism and diversity through an

> ideology of state paternalism and patriotism that appeals to and draws legitimation from the past . . . There is no need for representative or legal institutions. Civil society is perceived first as an opponent, then as an enemy of sovereign power.
>
> *(Khvostunova, 2021)*

Andrei Kolesnikov astutely observes: "In Russia, there can be no modernization without de-Stalinization" (Kolesnikov, 2021).

Poor relations with the West are not based on misperceptions: Russia has a very clear headed and fixed view of the United States as an adversary. Indeed, "Every step in bolstering solidarity among Western democracies and in upholding democratic values constitutes a threat to the existence of this corrupt autocracy, and no détente or a "reset" can possibly mitigate that threat in the Kremlin's eyes" (Baev, 2021). Russia celebrates the *status quo* and stability in Russia but supports anti-*status quo* actors abroad: Russia acts as both fireman and arsonist, and fear is Russia's most successful export commodity, not hydrocarbon energy. Russia is not afraid that neighbors are afraid of Russia, but rather Russia fears that its neighbors do not fear Russia's abstract collective military might. The greater the number of destabilizing challenges, the less the ability of the state to address them, and the more the tendency to blame the West and internal traitors/terrorists (the opposition) for the deteriorating dynamic. And so it goes. In reality, Russia is too weak for the United States to recognize as an equal and too strong to be willing and able to accept unequal tactical allay status (Menkiszak, 2017).

Institutional strategic subcultures and crisis

As noted in Chapter 6, operational codes of decision-makers are influenced by two sets of beliefs: philosophical and instrumental. Philosophical beliefs can be evidenced by strategic policy, as outlined in official public pronouncements and written strategies, doctrines and guidelines. The instrumental beliefs of decision-makers center on their understanding of how and what combination of tools should be deployed to engage the world, and as such these beliefs are particularly elite-cohort-dependent. In other words, instrumental beliefs are best inferred through a study of Russian strategic behavior, the results of short-term strategic decision-making. In the case of contemporary Russia, they reflect the 'code of Putinism', the Putin-specific set of beliefs, emotions, and habits which are shared by other members of Putin's national security team and the subcultures and personalities of the institutions they lead. The "cognitive traits" displayed in the national security team's philosophical beliefs are based more on holistic–dialectic deductive field-dependent reasoning (shared more broadly by society as a whole), while their instrumental beliefs are driven by logical–analytical inductive reasoning. Instrumental beliefs in operational codes can change as decision-makers evaluate and assess the effectiveness of particular policies and operations. The instrumental beliefs of specific elites – such as Putin, coming from a counter-intelligence milieu with its subculture and particular set of beliefs – are not necessarily shared by each generation of decision-makers.

Fourth-generation strategic culture theorists understand that in a permissive environment, services and departments inside the services compete over cultural interpretations as to who is friend and who is foe and given this, how to preserve the *status quo* (Anand, 2020; Libel, 2016; Bloomfield, 2012). In preceding chapters, we have attempted to identify and understand the historically conditioned competitive goals – maintain status, increase budgets and quality of recruited personnel, define missions and control narratives (Zimmerman et al., 2019) – of the carriers of these subcultures, as set against the overall evolution of Russian strategic culture in *Tsarist*, Soviet and contemporary times, especially taking into account the influences of the last 20 years. The ability to define threats and enemies that need to be addressed is key, as from this budget, personnel and narratives follow. Chapter 2 highlighted the importance of identifying the key institutional carriers of strategic culture and exploring how existing subcultures influence strategic decision-making, shape strategic agendas and implement policy. Chapter 8 highlighted how power transition psychology and the dynamics generated by the succession process itself can reshape individual and institutional transactional calculus. In a patrimonial system, the struggle between influence groups can manifest itself in attacks by one patron on the clients of another ahead of the succession in order to weaken the other, and such attacks can involve the weaponization of nonsystemic opposition elite figures.

When addressing the various strategic culture carrier categories, what are the relevant subgroups/subpopulations that should be mapped and analyzed? Do some subgroups greatly impact the dynamics and positions of other categories of strategic culture carrier? Do some subgroups within the same category have differing motivations and goals? Do the tensions between these carrier groups serve to define the carrier groups' culture? For example might infighting spur constant innovation and/or deep opacity in processes? In terms of ethos and guiding ideals: What principles motivate and coalesce strategic culture carrier members? In terms of core competencies: why does this group exist, and why does it matter to the overall power structure? In terms of competitive goals: What is the ideal outcome for this group? What does winning mean to this group? In terms of arenas of competition (or arenas of influence): What broadly defined arenas does this group prefer to participate in? How do different actors compete and vie for influence? Are these the right questions to ask?

Let us identify the relevant subgroups/subpopulations that should be mapped and analyzed (see Table 9.5). We can have narrower or broader understandings of what constitutes a "carrier" or "keeper" of a strategic culture, what we understand to constitute "strategic" when it comes to the use of coercive force and even what we understand by "coercive force" itself. The broadest or most expansive approach would be to include the carriers that make the strategic decisions around the use of coercive force (Putin, the National Security Council and "inner circle"), carriers that develop the tools/weapons that enable force to be used (the Defense Industrial Complex), carriers that implement the use of force (the Russian military, special forces and National Guard), carriers that ratify the use of force (State *Duma* and Federation Council, Investigations Committee and Prosecutor General), carriers that provide norms to justify the use of force (Constitutional Court and increasingly the Russian Orthodox Church), carriers that inform the use of force through strategic threat assessments, or link state to society, explaining, justifying and assessing the results of the use of force to society (community of strategic experts/opinion formers in state–sponsored media) and, at the end, society itself which supports the use of force through military-patriotic mobilization.

A narrower definition of "carrier" or "keeper" of strategic culture might focus just on decision-makers and the military-security actors that implement the use of force (Galeotti, 2020a). The primary focus would be on the military-security elites and their decision-making function, rather than their role as core implementers of the decisions. Brian Taylor defines the power or force structures (*silovyye struktury*) – special services, power ministries and their troops or units – as the Ministry of Interior (MVD), the Ministry for Civil Defense (MChS), the Dinistry of Defense (MO), the Federal Security Service (FSB), the Foreign Intelligence Service (SVR), the Federal Guard Service (FSO), the Federal Border Service (FPS), the Federal Customs Service (FTS), the Federal Custom Service (FSKN) and the procuracy (Taylor, 2011). In the contemporary Russian context, not all potential decision-makers are formally military or intelligence and security services. When we look to permanent members of Russia's Security Council as of May 2018, we can see that Sergei Lavrov, Valentina Matvienko, Dmitrii Medvedev, Anton Vaino and Vyacheslav Volodin are civilians (Bacon, 2019). We can make assumptions about their relative influence, but it would be bold indeed to declare that because of their civilian status all of them are out of the strategic decision-making loop on every occasion when decisions to use force are made.

Institutions and organizations that constitute the regime have competing preferences. Though they are strategically aligned in support of Putin, they are tactically divided, with some adopting more statist and some more ideological stances. In the late Soviet period, the KGB and Party competed as did the KGB with the

TABLE 9.1 Russia's Sub-Institutional Actors: Competitive Goals and Relationship to Use of Force

Actors	Competitive Goals	Current Relationship to Use of Force
Putin: Family and Putin-dependent entourage	**Personal and regime security**: Putin creates "Great Game" ("geopolitical heroism") conflicts only he can manage – defers problems of transformations; balance development and defense blocs; power to "stop almost anything in the county"; notions of collective Putin/Putin's collective	**Function**: Decision-maker; arbiter; resource distributor; savior of the nation; "re-gatherer of lost Russian land"; inner circle informal consultative body **Threats**: to personal property (freeze foreign assets), mobility, familial consumption habits; oligarchs need access to financial markets and new technologies
Pres. Admin. (2000 staff) **and Security Council** (30 members, 200 staff)	**Regime and state security**: media control shapes threat perception; provides integrated politico-military strategic level guidance; bureaucracy and elite demand certainty; confrontation with West strengthens Security Council	**Function**: decision-making forum; COA's threat assessments; inter-agency coordination; bureaucratic–technocratic culture **Threats**: to regime legitimacy; protect Russia from interdependence pressure; West humiliation/betrayal
Intelligence and Security Services – FSB, GRU, SVR, FSO, SBP, MVP, FSNG	**State, corporate and regime security**: strategically unified/loyal; tactically divided, overlapping competencies generate infighting; compete for Putin's approval; business corruption; Ministry of State Security (MGB: SVR-FSB-FSO merger) to counterbalance FSNG?; security providers for private companies	**Function**: inform decisions; NG focus on popular revolt; FSB's SEB Dept K discipline elite; internet regulation media space control; conflict enhances prestige; force multiplier; **Threats**: internal and external enemies and conspirators; oppose mass protest, socio-political destabilization; "controlled Maydan" scenario/US Trojan Horse strategy

TABLE 9.1 (Continued)

Actors	Competitive Goals	Current Relationship to Use of Force
Min. Def (MO), Gen. Staff and Emergency Ministry (MChS RF)	**State security**: super Ministry – MO and MChS RF (ops, crisis management) – VPK subordination to MoD?; land, naval, aerospace, strategic missile, airborne troops; GPV-2027 focus on continental military domination; politicization – Main Military-Political Directorate; youth army	**Function**: war fighting, military-patriotic mobilization; 'active defense'; sufficiency of force, 'limited action operations'; A2AD; provide feasibility assessments and shape threat perceptions **Threats**: conventional and nuclear; 'enslavement'; bureaucracy tensions (war fighting vs. parade)
Defense Industrial Complex (VPK) –*Rostec*, (Sergei Chemezov)	**Parastatal corporate security**: State Armament Program 2018–27 (GPV-2027); imports substitution, diversifies production, evades embargoes, dual-purpose; increases civilian products' share in VPK factories to 30 percent (2025) and 50 percent (2030); merges Industry and Trade and Energy Ministries?	**Function**: *Rosoboronexport* reports $13 billion arms exports in 2020, *Rostec* reports $53.8 billion future orders – employs 2 million people, political-military needs drive choice of conflict (arms test and sales), incentive to monetize conflict; **Threats**: to geopolitical and industrial interests (embargoes); strengthen protectionism and special conditions for defense companies
SOEs – Russia Inc. (e.g. Rosneft, Gazprom, Rosatom, Transeft)	**Parastatal corporate and regime security**: Gazprom "powerful political and economic lever of influence"; Rosneft as "pseudo-corporate shadow MFA"; foreigners barred from investments in 40+ industries "critical for national security"	**Function**: generate 70% GDP, 33% jobs, ineffective, corrupt but guarantee social stability **Threats**: 'bureaucratic prosecutions' by state officials, LEAs, business competitors; to Russian strategic autonomy; to SOE corporate global economic linkages/levers
'Economic Bloc': Central Bank, Ministry of Finance, of Economy – in-system liberals	**State security**: Support structural economic reform options; promote competitiveness and engagement as being essential for Russia's own long-term prosperity; "our entire foreign policy should be subordinated to the task of technological development" (Kudrin); symbolic reconciliation with West	**Function**: Provide macro-economic stability – balanced budget, technocratic, professional approach **Threats**: to macro-economic stability and balanced budget; sanctions (capital and technology); poor quality of implementing bureaucracy and resistance by rent seekers; "weaponization of the budget"

(Continued)

TABLE 9.1 (Continued)

Actors	Competitive Goals	Current Relationship to Use of Force
Ministry of Foreign Affairs	**State security**: defensive-reactive rhetoric and compellence and coercive diplomacy reality; IL mediation and arbitration role increased in G-Zero world order; brigandage, criminalization delegitimize; external confrontation strengthens relevance	**Function**: Provides legal and moral norms to justify use of force; defends policy decision internationally; narrative generation function. **Threats**: hegemony of Liberal West (the United States); revision of *status quo*; to traditional moral values, heritage, moral dignity, classical, state-centric vision
Russian Orthodox Church (ROC)	**Spiritual/state security:** influence on conflict duration, escalation dynamics and deterrence effectiveness; develop orthodox jurisprudence ("just war" theory), nuclear orthodoxy	**Function**: role in draft/mobilization; Political-Directorate; para-diplomacy **Threats**: to conservative religious values, moral dignity, heritage, exceptional civilizational space
Russian Constitutional Court (RCC)	**State Security/ Constitutional Order:** reduced from 19 to 11 judges, ratified 2020 constitutional changes: unconditional regime support	**Function**: legitimizes use of force; state of emergency legislation **Threats**: to constitutional order; stability; extreme politicization
Duma, Political Parties, Federation Council and State Council	**State security – center–periphery relations:** neocorporatist model – parties granted representational monopoly in return for state control; United Russia can amend Constitution alone if qualified majority (301 seats)	**Function:** ritualized politics; maintained obedient political culture; broad responsibility for adopting laws on foreign policy **Threats:** between branches (1993); to public order if protest triggered by stolen election and falling living standards
Strategic Studies Expert Community	**State security:** state, parastatal and oligarchy funded; provides "master narratives"; demonstrates loyalist status and avoids 'foreign agents' list – seeks domestic legitimacy/credibility; growing independent critical analysis	**Function**: thought entrepreneurs mediate between state and society; explains defense and security decisions; knows leadership objectives – provides supporting analysis; **Threats**: as defined by sponsors; to academic, think tank, technocratic-scientific norms
Society – 'Public Mood' – State-Sponsored Civil Society	**State regional, local and personal security:** internal détente and passive conformism eroded: spontaneous local non-ideological protest reflects perception that government humiliates the people; civil self-organized protest activism, politicization of local issues' risk increases.	**Function**: "Security/strong leader" not "social progress"; accepts norms and narratives via Presidential Admin. and Ostankino pressure; nostalgia **Threats**: disruption to collective memory, ontological insecurity and anxiety; threats to *byudzhetntiki*; belief in enemy image of West and internal dissent (5th columnists) nexus

Ministry of Interior. Thirty years later, we see such dualities in FSB–Kadyrov relations, as well as those between the MoD and private military corporations (contributing to the Wagner Group debacle in Syria, February 2018) and the Central Bank with its focus on macro-economic stability versus the interests of those that wish "to utilize cryptocurrencies – either by supporting independent ones or by creating its own – to try and weaken the United States' financial clout in order to hasten its broader decline in international politics" (Smith, 2019). Fluid alignments and institutional factional rivalries exist, for example, between the Interior Ministry and police who resent OMON and National Guard (NG). Temporary alliances exist, for example, between NG and FSB, who together are in the vanguard of repression, but even these have their limits: the FSB vetoes the NG's attempts to create its own investigation committee, as this encroaches on the power of the FSB. One possible division within the law enforcement and security bloc may be between "Technocrats" and "Securocrats." – technocrats in the shape of, for example, Interior Minister Kolokoltsev and General Prosecutor Krasnov, who are "professional rather than political in their primary orientation" and "situationally rather than ideologically committed to the current official line," with the 1990s constituting their formative years in government service. "Securocrats," in the shape of the heads of the National Guard Zolotov and Investigations Committee Bastrykin, are "less concerned with legality in its own right and more with the security aspect of their mission," have a vested interest in justifying the domestic political threat and are older representative of the Putin generation, entering government service in the Soviet period. A generational fault line runs through this elite (Galeotti, 2020b).

Risk tolerance differs, with the presidential administration more risk averse than the intelligence services. In addition, the Ministry of Foreign Affairs is much less influential than its formal function suggests: Putin's

> friends in business may also drive foreign policy in some areas more directly than the Ministry of Foreign Affairs does; after all, Moscow's stance on Venezuela owes more to the concerns of Igor Sechin's Rosneft corporation than to anything else. Putin's defense minister and former political impresario – Sergei Shoigu and Vladislav Surkov, respectively – have shaped policy toward Syria and the Donbas.
>
> *(Galeotti, 2020b)*

As Chapter 5 noted and further complicating the picture are hybrid entities that intersect with and operate within the power network. These include 'polygarchic' groups that interweave politicians with oligarchs; 'silovarchic' entities that join *siloviki* with oligarchs; 'burness', where bureaucracy meets business and, stoligarchs, the state-sponsored oligarchs who control as fifth of the Russian economy (Aris, 2016). Thus, a focus on institutional carriers of strategic culture may miss the reality of clans that exist across institutions and operate according to network principles.

This indicative chart raises a key question, relevant to late Putinism: how do these carriers of strategic culture align in different crisis situations? We can ask, under what conditions, in what type of crisis, does or could a splintering or mis-alignment between the different carriers of the culture occur? How do we account for the splits? Are the splits related to access to resources, competitive goals, values and identity, norms regarding justifying the use of coercive force? Do different carriers have different red lines and risk calculus? Might previously compatible norms and "red-" and bottom-lines clash, resulting in a new synthesis or ordering of norms? This would then contribute to a reshaping and evolution of Russian strategic culture.

Nikolai Petrov had highlighted five inter-enabling elements that could culmi-nate in a crisis in Russia, force adaptation or result in collapse (Petrov, 2016). He noted the overconcentration of power, military mobilization, shortening horizons, elites in conflict and the necessity of manual control. He predicted that a crisis could be triggered by the result and dissatisfaction of an election coupled with unexpected events such as a terrorist attacks that damage credibility of security service, an egregious corruption scandal or an ultra-loyalists *siloviki* squabble that goes public. Internal crisis response is particularly illuminating. Decision-makers failed to use decisive Tiananmen-type force against protesters in August 1991. The presidential administration struggled to have the former KGB's Alpha Brigade supported by Russian military tanks storm the White House in October 1993. In this context, the institution of the National Guard, as a regime defense mechanism against foreign-inspired internal dissent ('Trojan Horse strategy') is the natural product of both the maturing of Russia's current strategic culture and the Russian elite's contemporary risk assessment. It also underscores the notion that in Russia "foreign policy is driven by domestic political concerns, and this also extends to a hyper-consciousness wandering into the paranoia at the extent to which unrest (such as Euromaidan or Bolotnaya) actually reflect external influence" (Galeotti, 2019a). Crisis illuminates in that previously compatible norms can clash, and potentially new syntheses or ordering of norms can occur.

For at least 21 years, President Putin has been the core strategic decision-maker in Russia. If he continues in this role until 2036, the accumulation of stresses, vul-nerabilities and complexities that he currently faces will be exacerbated. Despite pockets of military innovation, inherent conservatism permeates Russian domestic policy, evidenced by *status quo* elite that continue to defer modernization. Russia currently resembles what Mark Galeotti has termed an "adhocracy" of competing, semi-autonomous actors, who are able to work toward the state's broad objectives, generating their own plans to those ends (Galeotti, 2019b, 16–21). It is a hard truth, but global reach and activism and foreign policy successes may reinforce domestic elite legitimacy and they cannot compensate for the lack of structural economic reform. At heart, the fundamental obstacle to reform and renewal is Russia's *status quo* dynastic elite, particularly Putin's inner circle that has most to lose and least to gain from change. These elites are driven by twin opposing fears: on the one hand, they fear that they will lose control of a failed reform process, as Gorbachev did, as this results in chaos, then regime and political system change; on the other, they fear reform will succeed, with the same end result but perhaps without the chaos.

The fourth-generation strategic culture approach encourages us to focus on and disaggregate the specific strategic subcultures from the whole. To that end, it is helpful to apply the concept of institutional competitive goals to these groupings. In doing so, we see that there are important differences in threat focus, for example, between internal and external originated threat and between kinetic and non-kinetic responses to these threats. Internal protest-type threats generate greatest dissonance between the actors, creating a zero-sum context where the institutional relevance of some is clearly advanced while others sit on the sidelines. The National Guard, FSB and prosecution services demonstrate their utility and relevance by tackling the symptoms of protest, rather than fundamental reform, thereby ensuring future relevance.

We can also discern that most institutions have greater relevance – that is potentially benefit in terms of resources, defining missions, attracting the best personnel and controlling narratives – in strategic contexts that are characterized by greater confrontation and much fewer in contexts that require a 'reduction of costs' and a policy of de-escalation, if not outright cooperation with the 'political West'. With regard to external threats, institutional incentives promote a drift to greater confrontation, but confrontation of a certain type – one that feeds fear and justifies greater state resource allocation to the core institutional actors, but one that also generates least risk to the institutional actors themselves. Intriguingly, Vladislav Surkov hints at future drama and unpredictability: "Some exciting things are ahead of us. There will be many new dramatic transformations. Yes, I would like to understand when it will happen. If I live long enough, when it happens, then I will have a job" (Foy, 2021). Which strategic context might best align with the internal dynamics we have outlined in the first two sections of this book's conclusions?

Russia and world-order paradigms

Russia's preferred "official" future, in keeping with its great power status and historical experience and the objective reality of an emerging multipolar and poly-centric ('democratic multipolarity') world, is one within which a global concert of great powers dominates. This is the world order Russia projects through its critique of the current liberal international order.

> If we analyze both Russian declarations and set these against its strategic behavior on the ground, including resources allocation, it is clear that the narrative arc structuring Russian grand strategy is the belief that a strong and sovereign great power, bolstered by "our own spiritual values, our historical tradition and the culture of our multiethnic nation" can defend and advance its core interests in being a Eurasian hegemon and exercising global reach. Russia believes a dysfunctional West-centric global order under U.S. leader-ship gives way to a more stable and prosperous order punctuated by many

power centers. However, getting there is problematic: geopolitical instability and greater risks of conflict are the result of Western resistance. As Putin bluntly noted: "Western domination of international affairs, which began several centuries ago and, for a short period, was almost absolute in the late 20th century, is giving way to a much more diverse system.

('Text of Report', 2021).

In this world-order paradigm, Russia, alongside the United States, China, India and Japan, who collectively represent 70 percent of global GDP, would exercise an influential leadership role on the world stage. Through transactional strategic dialogue and informal negotiation, Russia would direct and manage the global strategic agenda, while still able to take unilateral action in its sphere of privileged interest (Haass and Kupchan, 2021). This global concert world order would be a contemporary expression of the 1815 Concert of Europe – Vladimir Putin proposing a "Yalta-2" conference of the U.N. Security Council permanent members (P-5), including China, the United States, the United Kingdom, and France, to agree on new rules of the road for global security. Analysts have listed other issues of mutual interest including COVID-19 and climate change cooperation, discussing the Iranian nuclear program, the situation in Afghanistan, countering terrorism, to give some examples.

The 16 June 2021 Putin–Biden Geneva Summit provides just such a legitimizing spectacle, one that underscores Russia's great power status. The "strategic stability" discussions that emerge look likely to be large, complex and lengthy, providing greater opportunities for Russia to define the parameters. The talks become an end in and of themselves: they signal that Russia has parity with the United States: political theatre and stagecraft trumps statecraft. However, three factors hinder the realization of this historically grounded vision. Relative to other great powers, Russia is relatively one-dimensional – military-nuclear. If collectively Russia, China, India and Japan constitute 70 percent of global GDP, Russia's share is less than 2 percent. Although before annexation of Crimea in 2014, President Putin had pledged that Russia would have the world's fifth largest GDP, and, in 2011, the Center for Economic and Business Research predicted Russia would be the fourth largest, the IMF October 2020 World Economic Outlook projected Russia's 2011 GDP ranking as eleventh. In addition, while Russia is relevant in the existential field of "strategic stability" (nuclear weapons and arms control), and it is undoubtedly an Arctic great power and has spoiler potential in regional crises, other great powers do not acknowledge and recognize this status. The emotional neuralgias of a mature autocracy and the phobias of Putin's generation, in particular, prohibit trust: grievance and resentment that the "empire was taken from us" animate Putin's inner circle (Galeotti, 2021a). Russia's nineteenth-century worldview is not shared by other states and in fact would be resisted by middle powers, the friends and allies of the United States.

Indeed, rather than Concert, confrontation is the norm. The United States, Russia and China appear to be locked into a pattern of escalation, unable to step back. Are we therefore reaching a "Cold War 2.0" inflection point, as relations between the United States, its friends and allies on the one hand, and Russia and China on the other, rapidly deteriorate? In a presentation to a Federal Security Service Board meeting on 24 February 2021, President Putin addressed what he termed the United States' "so-called containment policy towards Russia." Attaining these goals – whether in reality or whether "mission accomplished" is a state-controlled media mantra – legitimizes Russian elite political authority and so justifies their continuity in power. President Putin stated:

> This is not competition as a natural part of international relations, but a consistent and highly aggressive policy aimed at disrupting our development, at slowing it down and creating problems along our external perimeter and contour, provoking internal instability, undermining the values that unite Russian society, and ultimately, at weakening Russia and forcing it to accept external management, just as this is happening in some post-Soviet states.
>
> *("Russia," 2021)*

On 18 May 2021 at a Russian–German Potsdam Meetings Forum, Russian Foreign Minister Sergei Lavrov has accused Germany, via video link, of stepping up its containment policy toward Moscow: "Russian-German relations are also going through a difficult period. We have to admit that Berlin has only intensified its policy of systemic containment of Russia" ("Moscow says", 2021). As noted in Chapter 1, at the UNSC May 2021 online meeting, Lavrov had already stated that Moscow views as unacceptable attempts by the United States and the EU to impose totalitarianism and insrumentalize the notion of a "rules-based order" to prevent the process of the formation of a polycentric world (Lavrov, 2021).

However, national interest places limits on the inevitability of a slide into "Cold War 2.0." Although President Putin accuses the Biden administration of having embraced a comprehensive neo-containment policy, this is not the case. The United States' competitive advantage in strategic competition is its network of friends and allies, who are prepared to support targeted "pushback" against specific malign activity, especially "active measures" and to build resilience in defense of shared core democratic values and practices but not adopt a comprehensive neo-containment strategy. First, unlike the late 1940s, the world is globalized and increasingly multipolar. In this context, Cold War style "containment" is not possible. Second, in the current strategic context of great power competition "short of war," the United States prioritizes countering China over Russia. From a U.S. perspective, countering China is enabled by the support of coalition partners, not least Japan, South Korea and Germany. Thus, transatlantic unity is at a premium. To that end, the Biden administration dropped sanctions against Nord Stream 2. In December 2020, toward the end of the German presidency of the EU, the EU Council adopted a comprehensive agreement with China on the promotion of mutual investment, though it had yet to be ratified by the European Parliament. Following the U.S. announcement that sanctions against Nord Stream 2 would be dropped, the European Parliament ("whose largest faction is controlled by Merkel") refused to ratify the agreement with China and instead froze it (Bielecki, 2021). The European Parliament was also motivated by objections to China's sanctions against individual Members of the European Parliament and heads of European institutions. This apparent *quid pro quo* had two outcomes: first, China could be prioritized with the EU support; second, Russia's advantage became China's disadvantage. Third, the Biden administration seeks to maintain some Euro-Atlantic cooperation with Russian civil society and parts of its private sector, necessary for restored relations in a post-Putin context. This approach suggests targeted 'Containment 2.0' in that the political West seeks to contain (or constrain) Russian aggressive and malign strategic behavior within "stable and predictable" lines.

Moreover, a Russian alliance with China would expose Moscow's asymmetric dependencies on Beijing and render Russia a junior partner within a Sino-centric technology-trade bloc (*Pax Sinica*), with little or no strategic autonomy. "Shared goals yet constrained cooperation" is not just as characteristic of the digital sphere (Gabuev and Kovachich, 2021). At the Geneva Putin–Biden Summit of June 2021, it was notable that Russia did not highlight its partnership with China in official statements before or during the summit. It did not want to suggest that Russia is strategically relevant only in so far as it has forged a relationship with China, the only "near peer" competitor to the United States. Latent tensions are already emerging in the relationship. Russia's *Tsarist* Empire was perceived in Beijing as acting like an active Western empire during the "century of humiliation," forcing China to cede territories to Russia through "unequal treaties," namely the Treaty of Aigun (1858) and the Treaty of Beijing (1860) (Sharifulin, 2021). Over the longer term, Chinese advances in technology and move to Green GDP undercut Russia's commodity export model.

The strategic context which best aligns with Putinism, the hybrid nature of the Russian state, the presidents operational code is a G-Zero world order. Within such an order, no group of states, such as the G3, G7, nascent G11 or G20, exerts leadership and management of the global strategic agenda, for example, over WMD proliferation, climate change, regional crises and terrorism (Bremmer, 2016). A G-Zero world order favors states that thrive in ambiguity, unpredictability, contestation, where transactionalism is the order of the day. States with well-developed alliance systems are disadvantaged, while states without (not least, Russia, China, and DPRK) are freer to maneuver. Russia can participate in great-power asymmetric competition through leveraging its secret, active and transgressive abilities in great-power subversion: "the practice of trying to gain an advantage by directly influencing a foreign country's domestic politics against its wishes" (Kastner and Wohlforth, 2021).

A G-Zero world order best secures and protects Russia in power decline relative to China. Russia cannot achieve G3 status and can hardly accept unipolarity or even bipolarity if it cannot be one of the poles. Russia's order-producing and managerial role in its shared neighborhood is increasingly compromised by third parties, not least the EU, Turkey and China. In a leaderless world, states that have a spoiler role ability and a higher tolerance for risk-taking thrive and flourish. Russia asserts that as a strategically autonomous great power with a strong sovereign leader (Putin) who is able to declare the exception to the rule. Putin does this by declaring "red lines," that is the declaration of the norm or the law that should not be breached. Dmitri Trenin notes:

> But attempts to expose Russian "red line" deterrence as hollow – whether on the ground, in the air, or at sea – would push Moscow to defend what it cannot give up without losing its self-respect. This would almost inevitably lead to clashes and casualties, which would carry the risk of further escalation.
>
> *(Trenin, 2021)*

However, in seeking to avoid commitment traps and maintain decision-making autonomy, Russia's approach appears to lack clarity on *either* the circumstances *or* the consequences of breaching its "red lines." President Biden's conditional offer of "stable and predictable" relations should Russia refrain from malign activity is problematic for Russia, as to be both stable and predictable is to be strategically irrelevant. In most policy areas, excepting perhaps the Arctic, Russia seeks to be stable but unpredictable to maintain its strategic relevance.

In effect, a G–Zero world order reflects the agenda of the hardliners in Moscow in the 1990s, who argued that should NATO enlarge, Russia's response would be to develop partnerships with anti-Western rogue states, such as Libya, Syria, Iran and North Korea (DPRK); resort to military-patriotic mobilization of its population and modernize its military; adopt autarky; weaponize organized crime and corruption and pivot to China. According to this scenario, soft Stalinist modernization at home would be buttressed by a DPRK-type function in the international system, characterized by 'military first' policies and nuclear signaling intended to demonstrate the political utility of these expensive systems; increased rhetoric promoting strategic autarchy and the less deniable use of organized crime groups to evade sanctions. Russia would also leverage its 'force multipliers' much more than at present. Since 2011–12, Russia has adopted each predicted characteristic, with the apparent exception of closer relations with DPRK. In terms of a further deterioration with relations to the West, Russia's only additional escalatory option may be to resort more openly to nuclear blackmail, accepting greater strategic risk and leveraging such risk tolerance as a competitive advantage. Such a move would be in keeping with a continuum of steady deterioration in relations and escalation. In November 2014, at the height of Russian support for subversion in Ukraine, former Lithuanian President Dalia Grybauskaite noted that Putin's Russia is openly acting as a terrorist state. MH17, explosions at Czech munitions depots, Novichok attacks in 2018 in the UK and against Navalny in 2020 all are empirical evidence of "Russian state terrorism." This raises the question: "how is it possible to talk to an openly hostile state that uses terrorist methods?" (Gritenas, 2021). The cybersecurity debate is a metaphor for a wider problem for Moscow and the West, which undercuts grounds for cooperation. The Kremlin has nominated the FSB as the sole gatekeeper to cybercrime cooperation, but, in effect, "all the doors to cooperation, both government and private, remain shut and sealed, except the door of the FSB – the very agency which is accused of carrying out repressions, poisonings, and cyber-attacks?" Thus,

> the Kremlin's eagerness to score short-term victories and its determination to frame its relationship with the West as competitive not only helps empower hawks in the West who say no meaningful cooperation with Moscow is possible or desirable, but rebound to hurt Russia's own interests.
>
> *(Galeotti, 2021b)*

For all the talk of Russia as a "revisionist spoiler," however,

> the country revises and spoils much less than it could. In Ukraine, it has declined to march on Kyiv. In the Middle East, it has continued to allow Israel access to Syrian airspace. And in the United States, it has held back from deploying its full arsenal of cyber-capabilities, which could surely wreak havoc on the U.S. economy.
>
> *(Klimmage, 2021)*

This relative reticence can be explained by elite understandings that public opinion "balks at the cost of confrontation with West" (Sherlock, 2020). Great power competition through subversion has clear benefits. When compared to conventional statecraft, both costs and risks are lower. If, in the words of Putin "you cannot spoil a spoiled relationship," the risks associated with a breakdown of trust or issues around signaling are no longer balancing factors (Kastner and Wohlforth, 2021). In addition, if Russia fully aligns its grievance and resentment narratives and anti-Western discourses and spoiler capabilities with its actual strategic behavior, then Russian elites will justify dysfunctionality and disintegrative processes as the symptoms of a well-crafted "poison pill" strategy. Ungovernable Russia will be rationalized as the ultimate deterrent and guarantor against the ever-present and pernicious threat of U.S. colonization and forced regime change.

This G–Zero world order, the book concludes, is the default and most likely outcome of current confrontation and systemic rivalry between great powers. International instability stabilizes an anti-fragile Russia: it provides an external arena within which sub-strategic actors can pursue their competitive goals and buttresses the besieged fortress legitimizing narrative (and hence the absence of a broad development and modernization agenda). Most importantly, and as this study has attempted to demonstrate, an inherently unpredictable G–Zero environment best aligns with the drivers of Russia's strategic behavior: a strategic culture rooted as it is in the pre-Westphalian past; the operational code of a counter-intelligence decision-making elite and the realities of Russia as a hybrid state.

Selected bibliography

Anand, V. 2020. "Revisiting the Discourse on Strategic Culture: An Assessment of the Conceptual Debates." *Strategic Analysis* 44 (3): 193–207.

Aris, Ben. 2016. "Meet the Stoligarchs, Putin's Pals Who Control a Fifth of the Russian Economy." *BNE Intellinews.* July 11, 2016. www.intellinews.com/meet-the-stoligarchs-putin-s-pals-who-control-a-fifth-of-the-russian-economy-99918/.

Bacon, Edwin. 2019. "The Security Council and Security Decision-Making." In *The Routledge Handbook of Russian Security,* edited by Roger E. Kanet, 119–30. London: Routledge.

Baev, Pavel K. 2021. "Russia Recoils from Possibility of Stable Relations with US." *The Jamestown Foundation.* May 10, 2021. https://jamestown.org/program/russia-recoils-from-possibility-of-stable-relationship-with-us/.

Bielecki, Jędrzej. 2021. "Opinion: Nord Stream 2 Is a Double Warning for Poland." *Remix.* May 25, 2021. https://rmx.news/article/commentary/opinion-nord-stream-2-is-a-double-warning-for-poland.

Bloomfield, Alan. 2012. "Time to Move on: Reconceptualizing the Strategic Culture Debate." *Contemporary Security Policy* 33 (3): 437–461.

Bremmer, Ian. 2016. "After the G-Zero: Overcoming Fragmentation." *Eurasia Group.* 2016. www.eurasiagroup.net/siteFiles/Issues/After_The_G_Zero_.pdf.

Davydov, Ivan. 2014. "Putin Is Waging War With the Future in Any Scenario." *Slon.* December 25, 2014.

Deyermond, Ruth. 2016. "The Uses of Sovereignty in Twenty-first Century Russian Foreign Policy." *Europe-Asia Studies* 68 (6): 957–984.

Donadio, Rachel. 2016. "Svetlana Alexievich, Nobel Laureate of Russian Misery, Has an English-Language Milestone." *The New York Times.* May 20, 2016. www.nytimes.com/2016/05/21/books/svetlana-alexievich-a-nobel-laureate-of-russian-misery-has-her-english-debut.html.

Foy, Henry. 2021. "Vladislav Surkov: 'An Overdose of Freedom is Lethal to a State.'" *Financial Times.* June 18, 2021. https://on.ft.com/3iSRzqn.

Frye, Timothy. 2021. *Weak Strongman: The Limits of Putin's Power in Russia.* Princeton: Princeton University Press.

Gabuev, Alexander, and Leonid Kovachich. 2021. "Comrades in Tweets? The Contours and Limits of China-Russia Cooperation on Digital Propaganda." *The Moscow Times.* June 3, 2021. www.themoscowtimes.com/2021/06/03/comrades-in-tweets-the-contours-and-limits-of-china-russia-cooperation-on-digital-propaganda-a74099.

Galeotti, Mark. 2019a. "The Intelligence and Security Services and Strategic Decision-Making." *MC Security Insight.* No. 30, May 2019. www.marshallcenter.org/en/publications/security-insights/intelligence-and-security-services-and-strategic-decision-making-0.

———. 2019b. *We Need to Talk About Putin.* London: Ebury Press.

———. 2020a. "The Presidential Administration: The Command and Control Nexus of Putin's Russia." *MC Security Insight.* No 44, February 2020. www.marshallcenter.org/en/publications/security-insights/presidential-administration-command-and-control-nexus-putins-russia-0.

———. 2020b. "The Law Enforcement Agencies: Russian Domestic Security and International Implications." *MC Security Insight.* No. 45, February 2020. www.marshallcenter.org/en/publications/security-insights/law-enforcement-agencies-russian-domestic-security-and-international-implications-0.

———. 2021a. "Emotions Central to the Putin-Biden Summit." *The Moscow Times.* June 14, 2021. www.themoscowtimes.com/2021/06/14/emotions-central-to-the-putin-biden-summit-a74202.

————. 2021b. "Hacking Controversy Highlights Kremlin's Self-Destructive Approach." *The Moscow Times.* May 19, 2021. www.themoscowtimes.com/2021/05/19/hacking-controversy-highlights-kremlins-self-destructive-approach-a73943.

Goble, Paul A. 2017. "Putin's Russia Pursuing Survival by Paradox, Shevtsova Says." *Euromaidan Press.* February 27, 2017. http://euromaidanpress.com/2017/02/27/putins-russia-pursuing-survival-by-paradox-shevtsova-says-euromaidan-press/.

————. 2018. "Window on Eurasia – New Series: The Putin Paradox: The More He Strengthens the Vertical, the Weaker It Becomes, Sociologist Says." *Window on Eurasia.* May 21, 2018. http://windowoneurasia2.blogspot.com/2018/05/the-putin-paradox-more-he-strengthens.html.

Gretskiy, Igor. 2021. "Could the West Have Saved Russia from Itself?" *Riddle.* May 5, 2021. www.ridl.io/en/could-the-west-have-saved-russia-from-itself/.

Gritenas, Paulius. 2021. "Grybauskaite Was Right – Putin's Russia is a 'Terrorist State'." *Delfi* website, in Lithuanian. April 23, 2021.

Haass, Richard N., and Charles A. Kupchan. 2021. "A Concert of Powers for a Global Era." *Project Syndicate.* March 25, 2021. www.project-syndicate.org/commentary/concert-of-powers-for-global-era-by-richard-haass-and-charles-a-kupchan-2021-03.

Kashin, Oleg. 2016. "It Will Be Fun and Scary. What to Expect From New Russian Nation." *Slon.* November 1, 2016.

Kastner, Jill, and William C. Wohlforth. 2021. "A Measure Short of War: The Return of Great-Power Subversion." *Foreign Affairs* 100 (4): 118–131. www.foreignaffairs.com/articles/world/2021-06-22/measure-short-war.

Khachaturov, Arnold. 2017. "GDP Fears Tanks. Finance Minister Siluanov Sharply Criticizes Growth of Budget's Military Expenditure." *Novaya Gazeta Online.* October 11, 2017.

Khvostunova, Olga. 2021. "Lev Gudkov: 'The Unity of the Empire in Russia Is Maintained by Three Institutions: The School, the Army, and the Police'." *Institute of Modern Russia.* May 3, 2021. https://imrussia.org/en/opinions/3278-lev-gudkov-.

Klimmage, Michael. 2021. "When Biden Meets Putin." *Foreign Affairs.* June 9. www.foreignaffairs.com/articles/russia-fsu/2021-06-09/when-biden-meets-putin.

Kolesnikov, Andrei. 2021. "Russia's History Wars: Why is Stalin's Popularity on the Rise?" *Carnegie Moscow Center.* July 19, 2021. https://carnegie.ru/commentary/84991.

Kotkin, Stephen. 2016. "Russia's Perpetual Geopolitics: Putin Returns to the Historical Pattern." *Foreign Affairs* 95 (3): 2–9.

Kozeyrev, Andrey. 1992. "Russia: A Chance for Survival." *Foreign Affairs* 71 (2): 1–16.

"Lavrov Pointed to Attempts to Implant Totalitarianism by the US and the EU." 2021. *Izvestia.* May 7, 2021. https://iz.ru/1161247/2021-05-07/lavrov-ukazal-na-popytki-nasazhdeniia-totalitarizma-so-storony-ssha-i-es.

Lewis, David. 2020. *Russia's New Authoritarianism: Putin and the Politics of Order.* Edinburgh: Edinburgh University Press.

Libel, Tamir. 2016. "Explaining the Security Paradigm Shift: Strategic Culture, Epistemic Communities, and Israel's Changing National Security Policy." *Defence Studies* 16 (2): 137–156.

McFaul, Michael. 2004. "The Putin Paradox." *Center for American Progress.* June 24, 2004. www.americanprogress.org/issues/security/news/2004/06/24/839/the-putin-paradox/.

Melyantsou, Dzianis. 2021. "Why Fears of a Russia-Belarus Merger Never Come True." *Carnegie Moscow Center.* May 12, 2021. https://carnegie.ru/commentary/84512.

Menkiszak, Marek. 2017. "Russia's Best Enemy. Russian Policy towards the United States in Putin's Era." *OSW Centre for Eastern Studies.* February 15, 2017. www.osw.waw.pl/en/publikacje/point-view/2017-02-15/russias-best-enemy-russian-policy-towards-united-states-putins-era.

"Moscow Says Germany Stepping up Russia Containment Policy." *TASS News Agency*, Moscow, in Russian, May 18, 2021.

Petrov, Nikolay. 2016. "Putin's Downfall: The Coming Crisis of the Russian Regime – European Council on Foreign Relations." *ECFR* (blog). April 19, 2016.

———. 2021. "What Comes after Putin Must Be Better than Putin." In *Myths and Misconceptions in the Debate on Russia*, 96–100. London: Chatham House.

Polovinko, Viacheslav. 2017. "If You Want Elections, Prepare for War. What Switching Enterprises to Military Track Means." *Novaya Gazeta Online*. October 11, 2017. https://novayagazeta.ru/articles/2017/11/24/74670-hochesh-vybory-gotovsya-k-voyne.

Russia, Team of the Official Website of the President of. 2021. "Federal Security Service Board Meeting." *President of Russia*. February 24, 2021. http://en.kremlin.ru/events/president/news/65068.

Sakhnin, Alexei. 2021. "Nomenklatura's Fatigue More Important than Opposition Activity." *Vedomosti*. May 4, 2021.

Sakwa, Richard. 2020. *The Putin Paradox*. London: I.B. Tauris-Bloomsbury Publishing.

———. 2021. "Heterarchy: Russian Politics between Chaos and Control." *Post-Soviet Affairs* 37 (3): 222–241. https://doi.org/10.1080/1060586X.2020.1871269.

Sharafutdinova, Glunaz. 2021. "Do Digital Technologies Serve People or Autocrats?" *Riddle*. June 25, 2021. www.ridl.io/en/do-digital-technologies-serve-people-or-autocrats/.

Sharifulin, Valery. 2021. "Pivoting to the East Maxim Trudolyubov on Why Russia Considers China Its Ally in a New Cold War with the West – and Why the Feelings Aren't Mutual." *Meduza*. May 21, 2021. https://meduza.io/en/feature/2021/05/21/pivoting-to-the-east.

Sherlock, Thomas. 2020. "Rusian Society and Foreign Policy: Mass and Elite Orientations After Crimea." *Problems of Post-Communism* 64 (1): 1–23.

Shlapentokh, Dmitry. 2021. "Putin's Dangerous Flirting with Nationalism." *Institute of Modern Russia*. April 16, 2021. https://imrussia.org/en/analysis/3265-putin%E2%80%99s-dangerous-flirting-with-nationalism.

Smith, Nicholas Ross. 2019. "Could Russia Utilize Cryptocurrencies in Its Foreign Policy Grand Strategizing?" *Russia in Global Affairs* (blog). July 30, 2019. https://eng.globalaffairs.ru/articles/could-russia-utilize-cryptocurrencies-in-its-foreign-policy-grand-strategizing/.

Surkov, Vladislav. 2018. "Vladislav Surkov. The Loneliness of the Half-Caste." *Russia in Global Affairs*. April 10, 2018. https://eng.globalaffairs.ru/articles/the-loneliness-of-the-half-breed/.

Taylor, Brian D. 2011. *State Building in Putin's Russia: Policing and Coercion after Communism*. Cambridge: Cambridge University Press.

Teslya, Andrey A. 2018. "Transformation of the Big Narrative." *Russia in Global Affairs*. June 15, 2018. https://eng.globalaffairs.ru/articles/transformation-of-the-big-narrative/.

'Text of report "Valdai Discussion Club meeting"', President of the Russian Federation website, October 25, 2021.

Trenin, Dmitri. 2021. "Sailing Into Troubled Waters. Russia Counters Britain in the Black Sea." *Carnegie Moscow Center*. June 25, 2021. https://carnegie.ru/commentary/84850.

Volkov, Denis, and Andrey Kolesnikov. 2017. "Do We Want Changes?" *Vedomosti*. December 27, 2017.

Wilson, Kenneth. 2021. "Is Vladimir Putin a Strong Leader?" *Post-Soviet Affairs* 37 (1): 80–97. https://doi.org/10.1080/1060586X.2020.1808395.

Zimmerman, S. Rebecca, Kimberly Jackson, Natasha Lander, Colin Roberts, Dan Madden, and Rebeca Orrie. 2019. *Movement and Maneuver: Culture and the Competition for Influence Among the U.S. Military Services*. Santa Monica: National Defense Research Institute (U.S.), and RAND Corporation.

INDEX

Note: Page numbers in **bold** indicate a table on the corresponding page.